BRAIN MATURATION
AND COGNITIVE DEVELOPMENT
Comparative and Cross-Cultural Perspectives

BRAIN MATURATION
AND COGNITIVE DEVELOPMENT
Comparative and Cross-Cultural Perspectives

Edited by

Kathleen R. Gibson and Anne C. Petersen

Sponsored by the
Social Science Research Council

ALDINE DE GRUYTER
New York

ABOUT THE EDITORS

Kathleen R. Gibson is Professor of Anatomical Sciences at the University of Texas Health Science Center Houston, Dental Branch and Graduate School of Biomedical Sciences. She is an Adjunct Faculty member, Department of Anthropology, Rice University.

   Anne C. Petersen is Professor of Health and Human Development and Women's Studies, and Dean, College of Health and Human Development at the Pennsylvania State University.

ALDINE DE GRUYTER
A division of Walter de Gruyter, Inc.
200 Saw Mill River Road
Hawthorne, New York 10532

The paper used in this publication meets the minimum requirements of American National Standard for Information Sciences—Permanence of Paper for Printed Library Materials, ANSI Z39.48-1984.

∞

Library of Congress Cataloging-in-Publication Data

Brain maturation and cognitive development : comparative and cross
 –cultural perspectives / edited by Kathleen R. Gibson and Anne C.
 Petersen ; sponsored by the Social Science Research Council.
     p.   cm.—(Foundations of human behavior)
   Includes bibliographical references.
   Includes index.
   ISBN 0-202-01187-9 (cloth)
   1. Cognition in children.   2. Brain—Growth.   3. Pediatric
 neuropsychology.   I. Gibson, Kathleen Rita.   II. Petersen, Anne C.
 III. Social Science Research Council (U.S.)   IV. Series.
   [DNLM: 1. Brain—growth & development.   2. Cognition—in infancy &
 childhood.   WS 105.5.C7 B8136]
 BF723.C5B62   1991
 155.4'13—dc20
 DNLM/DLC
 for Library of Congress   90-3965
                                                                          CIP

Manufactured in the United States of America

10 9 8 7 6 5 4 3 2 1

CONTENTS

III. PRIMATE AND HUMAN BEHAVIORAL DEVELOPMENT FROM A BIOSOCIAL PERSPECTIVE

IV. BIOSOCIAL SCIENCES AND THE NEUROLOGY OF LANGUAGE

LIST OF CONTRIBUTORS

Adele Diamond	University of Pennsylvania
Marian C. Diamond	University of California at Berkeley
Kathleen R. Gibson	University of Texas Health Science Center at Houston and Rice University
Susan Goldin-Meadow	University of Chicago
Julia Graber	Pennsylvania State University
Hsiu-zu Ho	University of California at Santa Barbara
Jeannette L. Johnson	National Institute of Drug Abuse Baltimore
Melvin Konner	Emory University
Carolyn Mylander	University of Chicago
Brian Morgan	University of Miami Medical School
Helen Neville	The Salk Institute, San Diego
Anne C. Petersen	Pennsylvania State University
Robert Plomin	Pennsylvania State University
James Rebetta	Memorial Sloan Kettering Cancer Center
Jon E. Rolf	The Johns Hopkins University
Arnold Scheibel	University of California at Los Angeles
Charles Super	Pennsylvania State University

ACKNOWLEDGMENTS

The editors of this volume wish to thank the Social Research Council for sponsoring the Committee on Biosocial Perspectives on Parent Behavior and Offspring Development. This volume is a direct outgrowth of a conference organized and sponsored by that committee. We also express appreciation to the Sloan Foundation which provided the financial support for the conference and to the National Institute of Child Health and Human Development for sponsoring earlier workshops which led to the formation of the current committee. The staff of the Social Science Research Council were instrumental in organizing the conference and in handling telephone calls and mailings to contributors. We especially wish to thank Lonnie Sherrod for his aid in this regard. In addition, Melvin Konner and Jane Lancaster helped us with our original conference organization. We also wish to thank the staff of the Smithsonian for their support during the conference. Mary Ellen Thames of the University of Texas provided invaluable secretarial aid during the final manuscript preparations and Edward S. Puente assisted in preparing and relettering the artwork. Finally, the staff of Aldine de Gruyter have been of great assistance throughout the editing of this volume.

PREFACE

This volume is the fourth in a series prepared by the Committee on Biosocial Perspectives on Parent and Offspring Development of the Social Science Research Council. This committee, composed of scientists representing diverse disciplines: anthropology, psychology, history, sociology, and zoology, seeks to elucidate and examine human behavior from an emerging biosocial science perspective. This perspective places humans within evolutionary, ontogenetic and cross-cultural frameworks. The biosocial perspective aids in deciphering the biological roots of human behavior and in elucidating those biological and social interactions most likely to produce optimum human behavioral development. In consequence, it serves to expand scientific inquiry to areas that neither biology nor social science has conceptualized on their own.

The topic of brain-behavioral interactions during development fits nicely within the biosocial science framework. One result of the extensive animal research of the last decades has been the realization that adequate brain development often depends upon species-typical biological and environmental input at particular times in the developmental cycle. Although we must assume that humans resemble animals in this regard, the experimental techniques that have illuminated these developmental processes in animals cannot be used in human research. The biosocial approach is a viable alternative. By examining humans from cross-cultural and cross-species perspectives, it is possible, without extensive experimentation, to delineate those universals of brain and behavioral maturation that are likely to impinge on developing humans in all societies as well as the range of social and biological variation compatible with normal human development. The biosocial approach also avoids and negates the anthropocentrisms inherent in such popular concepts as "animal behavior is instinctive, but humans learn." Finally, it avoids the ethnocentrism that underlies so much American and European social science research.

To explore these biosocial issues as they impinge on human brain and behavioral development, the committee convened a workshop in Elkridge, Maryland in May of 1985. Participants represented a broad range of Biosocial Science: evolutionary biologists, anthropologists, neuroscientists, historians, linguists, sociologists, psychologists and animal behavioralists. This book is an outgrowth of that conference.

FOUNDATIONS OF HUMAN BEHAVIOR

An Aldine de Gruyter Series of Texts and Monographs

SERIES EDITORS

Sara Blaffer Hrdy
University of California, Davis

Richard W. Wrangham
Harvard University

Richard D. Alexander, **The Biology of Moral Systems**

Eric Alden Smith, **Inujjuamiut Foraging Strategies**

Eric Alden Smith and Bruce Winterhalder (Eds.), **Ecology, Evolution, and Human Social Behavior**

Laura L. Betzig, **Despotism and Differential Reproduction: A Darwinian View of History**

Russell L. Ciochon and John G. Fleagle (Eds.), **Primate Evolution and Human Origins**

Martin Daly and Margo Wilson, **Homicide**

Irenäus Eibl-Eibesfeldt, **Human Ethology**

Richard J. Gelles and Jane B. Lancaster (Eds.), **Child Abuse and Neglect: Biosocial Dimensions**

Kathleen R. Gibson and Anne C. Petersen (Eds.), **Brain Maturation and Cognitive Development: Comparative and Cross-Cultural Perspectives**

Warren G. Kinzey (Ed.), **New World Primates: Ecology, Evolution and Behavior**

Frederick E. Grine (Ed.), **Evolutionary History of the "Robust" Australopithecines**

Jane B. Lancaster, Jeanne Altmann, Alice S. Rossi, and Lonnie R. Sherrod (Eds.), **Parenting Across the Life Span: Biosocial Dimensions**

Jane B. Lancaster and Beatrix A. Hamburg (Eds.), **School Age Pregnancy and Parenthood: Biosocial Dimensions**

Richard B. Potts, **Early Hominid Activities at Olduvai**

Wenda R. Trevanthan, **Human Birth: An Evolutionary Perspective**

James W. Wood, **Dynamics of Human Reproduction**

PART I

INTRODUCTION

Chapter 1

Introduction

Kathleen R. Gibson and Anne C. Petersen

Scientists and laymen alike have long debated issues pertaining to the development of the human brain and behavior. Historically, for instance, many Americans have considered that education is best given very early. Thus, the Puritans considered it both possible to teach 2 year olds to read the Bible and essential to do so to ensure the salvation of their souls in the advent of premature death (Vinovskis, 1983). More recently, proponents of early education have argued that young brains are more malleable and more receptive to learning than older brains. Thus, children from economically depressed areas may attend Head Start programs, while the more affluent attend expensive private nursery schools.

Throughout American history, however, the concept of early education has also had its detractors. During the nineteenth century, prominent educators rebelled against the Puritan practice of teaching very young children to read on the grounds that early reading leads to brain damage and insanity (Vinovskis, 1983). More recently, Americans have been warned that early schooling is unnecessary and may lead to frustration and anxiety (Elkind, 1987).

Lying at the core of these arguments is a basic scientific issue—what are the developmental relationships between brain and behavior? Does the 2–7-year-old brain have the cognitive capacity of the adult brain? Can the 2 year old really be taught to read? Older children and adolescents, after all, possess brains of greater histological and chemical maturity than younger ones. Moreover, periods of hormonal maturation such as adolescence may impact rather dramatically on brain function (Wittig and Petersen, 1979). Perhaps, then, some educational experiences are beyond the mental capacity of young children. On the other hand, perhaps critical neurological periods exist. Possibly, certain skills should be taught by 3 or 4 years of age or they will never be learned? Issues of brain–behavior developmental relationships also lie at the heart of other long-standing debates such as which is more important, nature or nuture?

This book consists of a collection of articles that attempt to examine neurological and cognitive maturation from the biosocial science perspective. This perspective suggests that social and physical environments can influence biological development and, in turn, biological development influences behavior. This interactive perspective represents a fundamental change from earlier assumptions that biology is fixed and that only behavior is plastic.

The biosocial approach examines interactions between behavior, evolution, and biological maturation from the multidisciplinary perspectives provided by cultural and biological anthropologists, zoologists, psychologists, sociologists, and neuroscientists. Each discipline has its own unique perspective to bring to bear on these issues. For instance, comparative anatomical data suggest that although mammalian species differ in the timing of their growth cycles and of their neurobehavioral maturation (Gould, 1977), similar neural maturational sequences and events characterize all species (Gibson, this volume; Jacobson, 1978). Thus, although experiments that would help to unravel some of the complexities of behavioral–brain interactions cannot be performed in humans, animal work can provide useful data and theory.

In addition, diverse animal species provide their own natural experiments pertaining to biology and behavior. For instance, biologists once argued vociferously about the relative importance of instinct versus learning in the genesis of animal behavior. Zoologists now claim, however, that in the animal kingdom, instincts are learned (Hailman, 1964) and learning is instinctive (Gould and Marler, 1987). If this is so in animals, should we expect sharp nature versus nuture distinctions in the genesis of human behavior?

Although animal data indicate that instinct and learning interact in all species, they also indicate that individual species possess species-characteristic behavioral and neurological patterns that serve to differentiate them from other taxa. This suggests that in animals critical aspects of neural and behavioral development may be canalized (Waddington, 1956; Fishbein, 1976; Wilson, 1978). That is, species members may share sets of genes programmed to interact with the succession of environments (both internal and external) normally encountered during development in a manner that ensures that structures mature in a normative fashion and in a proper time frame. In other words, in animals, species-characteristic environmental events may channel genetically programmed development in appropriate directions. Thus, developmental regularities displayed by members of a given species reflect not only species-wide similarities in the genome, but also species-wide similarities in environmental experience.

By examining humans from cross-cultural, historical, and cross-species perspectives, it is possible to determine whether some human behaviors are similarly canalized, that is, to determine whether there are universals of human neural and behavioral maturation characteristic of humans growing up in all cultures. Further, comparative perspectives can help provide insights into the types of stimulation that have been the norm for humans throughout their evolutionary history and, thus, are likely to be essential for healthy human development.

Even though all animal species are characterized by species-typical behaviors, individual species members also differ in many behavioral traits. The same, of course, is true for humans. The science of behavioral genetics has helped us to unravel the nature of behavior–genetic interactions in the genesis of individual differences in animals. As delineated by Plomin and Ho, the maturing science of human behavioral genetics is also rapidly developing new methods for analyzing genetic and environmental interactions in the production of behavioral diversity in the human species.

Biosocial science is a young discipline. Its tenets are only beginning to be applied to neural development. Thus, this volume will provide few definitive answers to the provocative questions which plague developmental psychologists and neurologists. It is hoped, however, that it will begin to place human behavior in a new perspective and to encourage others to investigate the two-way interactions which exist between behavior and biology.

Section I. Principles and Regularities of Neural Development

Neural maturation is a long and complex process involving many morphological and physiological parameters. Each region of the brain is initially populated with neurons. Once formed and in place, neurons sprout axons and dendrites. Later, they establish functional synaptic contact with other neurons and develop the chemical and physical properties essential for impulse transmission.

Synaptogenesis is the earliest morphological sign of potential transneuronal impulse transmission. Characteristically, young brains overproduce synapses. As a result, a period of major synaptic pruning follows synaptogenesis (Changeaux, 1985; Huttenlocher, 1979; Huttenlocher, et al., 1982). Presumably, only those synapses that have actually functioned survive. A study of synaptogenesis in five areas of the rhesus monkey brain indicated that synaptic density evidences synchronous changes in all cortical areas and layers (Rakic et al., 1986).

After establishing synaptic function, neurons experience a lengthy period of maturation before gaining full adult functional efficiency and flexibility. During this time, major changes occur in dendritic and axonal morphology. Initially, dendrites are short, tubular, and unbranched. With growth they elongate and develop a tree-like branching structure. These changes enable a neuron to receive impulses from diverse and distant sources. This branching also results in increased versatility and complexity of neuronal function because each dendritic branch represents a "decision point" with respect to the propagation of impulses (Scheibel, this volume). According to Scheibel's work and that of Conel (1937–1969), dendritic arborization patterns exhibit different temporal patterns in different cortical regions.

In parallel with these dendritic changes, many axons acquire a myelin sheath.

When present, this sheath confers major functional advantages. Myelinated fibers fire more rapidly and with greater functional specificity than unmyelinated ones. They have lower thresholds to stimulation and shorter refractory periods. Hence, they can fire more frequently and with less presynaptic stimulation (Bishop and Smith 1964). The cortex exhibits regional differences in time of myelination in both human and rhesus monkey (Conel, 1939–1967; Gibson, 1970, this volume; Flechsig, 1920).

In addition to these neuronal changes, the functional development of the nervous system requires the maturation of neural supporting structures such as glial cells and blood vessels. Hence, although functional potential as illustrated by synaptogenesis may be present quite early, the achievement of mature function involves the development of an entire complex of synapses, dendrites, myelin, glial cells, and blood supply.

Modern theories suggest that the brain functions by means of parallel distributing processing mechanisms. The strength and numbers of cortical connections are the most critical elements underlying the efficiency of such mechanisms (Rumelhart et al., 1987; McClelland et al., 1987). This suggests that myelination and maturing synaptic function play fundamental roles in maturing human memory, intelligence, and language skills.

The first section of the book focuses on brain maturation from these and other perspectives of relevance to the biosocial framework. In the first article, Gibson presents data indicating that the myelination of neural pathways follows a specific sequence that is similar in many species. Thus, the neural developmental sequence appears to be strongly canalized by genetic and environmental interactions that are common to many vertebrates. In both monkeys and humans neural myelination occurs over lengthy periods of time, at least for three and one-half years in the rhesus monkey and at least to adolescence in the human. Thus, at later ages, more pathways are myelinated and functioning effectively, and older children have more neural support for their behavior. These regularities of developmental sequence provide clear support for theories that the developing intelligence of human children is based, in part, on maturing neural function. In contrast, myelination data provide no support for views that the human brain is altricial at birth or neotenous in adulthood.

These cross-species regularities of myelination sequence suggest that some aspects of neural maturation are hierarchical in nature. In rats, rhesus monkeys, and humans, brain stem areas begin to myelinate in advance of cortical areas and, within the neocortex, primary motor and sensory areas begin to myelinate in advance of association areas. Neural maturation is nonhierarchical, however, in that many areas and tracts have protracted periods of myelination. As a result, some brainstem regions, such as the reticular system, myelinate more slowly than some cortical tracts such as the internal capsule. Also, all cortical areas have some myelin before any cortical area is completely myelinated and before certain slowly myelinating regions of the brain stem have completed their myelination.

Thus, neural models must account for developmental overlap and interactions between neural regions. The developmental picture provided by myelination data is similar to that provided by PET scans (Chugani and Phelps, 1986; Chugani et al., 1987), but appears to differ from the synchronous pattern of synaptogenesis (Rakic, et al., 1986). Reasons for these apparent differences are discussed.

Plomin and Ho review findings pertaining to the genetic control of neurophysiological and neurochemical parameters within modern human populations. Although they primarily emphasize behavioral differences among modern humans, rather than behavioral universals, their findings accord with basic tenets of the biosocial approach. Biology, like behavior, is plastic, and shared environment can account for many behavioral and developmental similarities among members of specific populations. Specifically, Plomin and Ho provide data indicating that individual variation in neurochemistry and neurophysiology may be environmentally induced rather than a result of genetic variation. Similarly, not all brain–behavior interactions are under direct genetic control and not all developmental similarity results from shared genes.

In many underdeveloped countries and economically disadvantaged groups, nutritional deprivation is among the most pressing biosocial factors affecting brain and behavioral development. Morgan and Gibson focus on the interactions of nutritional and environmental deprivation on brain development. They point out that the human brain is much more vulnerable to nutritional deficits at young ages when cell division, synaptic proliferation, and myelination are occurring than at older ages. Interestingly, however, environmental stimulation can help mitigate the effects of nutritional deprivation in both animals and humans. Although some catch-up growth is possible when environmental and nutritional rehabilitation is instituted at young ages, it is not known precisely what catch-up growth entails—whether it entails neurogenesis, synaptogenesis, myelination, or glial proliferation. Thus, it is not known whether catch-up growth actually represents growth of the same neural parameters that were initially retarded. Similarly, studies of children nutritionally deprived at young ages indicate that permanently lowered IQ scores may result. Nutritional and environmental rehabilitation if begun at young ages can, however, permit even children severely undernourished during infancy to develop IQ scores within the norm of the American population.

Finally, M. Diamond provides empirical data on various environmental events that may impinge on the development of the rat brain including nutrition, air ions, and cognitive and social inputs. In laboratory rats, variations in many of these environmental factors result in variations in brain size and in the ability to run mazes. The impact of environmental variation is greatest in young animals. Some neural lability, however, continues to very old ages. These data, therefore, support the concept that neural malleability is greater in the young, but they also show that learning is not confined to youth and that "neural exercise" is of value at all ages.

Section II. Primate and Human Behavioral Development
from a Biosocial Perspective

Human adults actively channel environmental inputs to their offspring in various ways such as playing with and offering affection to infants and providing training in social roles and economic tasks for older children. To the extent that neural maturation, the spontaneous activities of children, and the child care activities of adults are genetically canalized processes within the human species, cross-cultural regularities of development are to be expected. To the extent that brain and behavioral maturation are plastic and genes and rearing conditions vary, behavioral maturation will also be expected to vary.

Adele Diamond compares the maturation of the delayed response task in the rhesus monkey to that of the maturation of Piaget's identical A not B task in the human. The two species exhibit a similar sequence of cognitive maturation, but they mature at different rates. In both species, the maturation of these tasks correlates with the maturation of the frontal lobe, a neural region known to mediate cognitive components essential to this task. This chapter illustrates developmental similarities between species and suggests a canalization of cognitive maturational sequence, but not of maturational timing, that extends across species domains. These behavioral data, then, accord with the myelination data.

Given that neural and cognitive maturational sequences are similar in diverse species, but maturational timing varies, human populations might also be expected to strongly resemble each other in maturational sequences but to differ somewhat in rates of maturation. Some investigators actually have suggested that certain human racial groups are precocious in their reflex development. In this volume, however, Konner concludes that these claims are based on poor evidence. Rather, neonatal reflexes, the human smile, bipedalism, and fear of strangers develop at approximately the same times in varied cultures throughout the world. Each of these behaviors also develops in tandem with the myelination of neuroanatomical structures known to play a role in mediating them.

It is sometimes assumed that genes and/or canalized processes primarily affect the growth of behavioral and cognitive systems in early childhood. Indeed, because of difficulties developing "culture fair" tests of cognitive development, it has sometimes been claimed that children in some cultures do not develop all of the cognitive skills of American children. Super discusses this issue and suggests that children in varied cultures develop similar cognitive and motor skills at roughly similar ages, but they may manifest them differently depending on cultural practices. For instance, all cultures recognize that children at about the age of 6 or 7 years exhibit new cognitive abilities that enable them to assume greater responsibility. In the United States, this age marks the entrance into formal schooling. In other cultures it marks a point at which children are given greater economic or child care responsibilities.

Super specifically compares cognitive development in suburban American school children with that of rural Kipsigis children in Kenya. In some ways the cognitive performance of the two groups differs. For instance, Kipsigis children are more likely to classify items on functional grounds (e.g., knife goes with fork) than on taxonomic grounds (e.g., all knives go together). Using various cognitive tests, Super demonstrates that the cognitive skills of the children are, nevertheless, similar in the two cultures. This suggests that certain aspects of cognitive growth in middle childhood are highly canalized in our species. Differences between the functional and taxonomic classification systems can be explained, in part, by a simple cultural phenomena—the number of items possessed by a household. In both American and Kipsigis culture, when people have many items of a similar nature, they are stored and classified together (e.g., all the dinner plates, all the saucers). When only a few are possessed, they are stored in functional groupings (e.g., carving knife and fork).

Adolescence is a particularly critical time in western culture. At this age children begin to evaluate their own physical and mental capacities and to chart their maturing identities as adults. In all cultures, maturing sexuality and maturing identification with adult work and family roles critically impinge on adolescent development. In American society, adolescent development involves increasing sexual dimorphism in several areas, including cognition. Boys begin to exhibit relatively greater interest and accomplishment in math and science, while girls excel in language-related subjects. Graber and Petersen evaluate cognitive maturation at adolescence within the frameworks of other changes for boys and girls and discuss the basic social and biological interactions that impinge on sex differences in academic interest and performance. They present a model through which differential biology and experience could produce differential brain development, as well as differential performance for boys and girls.

Drug abuse is a critical problem affecting contemporary American society. To date, most attempts to curb drug abuse have focused on the legal system. Drug abuse, however, is a biosocial phenomena par excellence. Ultimately, curbing drug abuse will require an understanding of its biosocial origins and sources. Johnson, Rolf, and Rebetta attempt to chart the pathway for a biosocial approach to unraveling the causes of drug addiction by focusing on alcoholism as a particularly apt biosocial problem. Alcoholism produces brain damage, but it may also result from neural or behavioral problems. Many children of alcoholics exhibit impaired cognitive functioning even before they begin to drink. In particular, cognitive defects may characterize male children of alcoholics who later develop problems. The interactions between social environment and the at-risk phenotype are also noted. The importance of an increased focus on developmental data in the assessment and prediction of problems with alcohol is stressed.

Section III. Biosocial Science and the Neurology of Language

Both linguists and biologists have suggested that humans possess innate linguistic predispositions (Chomsky, 1972; Lenneberg, 1967; Gould and Marler,

1987). In Chomsky's view, even grammar is innate. Although it is clear from the many failed attempts to teach apes to speak that genetic differences between apes and humans are fundamental to human linguistic skills, few data exist to rule out shared environment as the critical parameter that results in "universal" grammar.

In this section, Goldin-Meadow and Mylander provide direct confirmation of inborn predispositions to language while at the same time demonstrating the role of environmental input in shaping semantic and syntactic structures. A congenitally deaf child, David, was deprived, by his parents, of training in lip reading and in the American Sign Language of the Deaf. His desires to communicate by language-like means were so strong, however, that he invented a rudimentary signing system of his own. This communication system had both morphemic and syntactic structures, but these structures were less complex than those of formalized signing systems. They were also subject to particular constraints by the quality of objects to which they refer and by the quality and nature of David's interacting system of signs.

Scheibel and Neville each focus on the maturation of the anatomical and physiological bases of language in relationship to hemispheric differences of language function. Scheibel concentrates on the relationship between speech centers and dendritic branching patterns. Speech processing centers in the left hemisphere differ from adjacent cortical regions and from similar regions in the right cortex in the complexity of dendritic branching patterns. These differences relate to developmental timing. During the period of speech development, the left frontal operculum experiences intense branching of second and higher order dendrites; the right operculum experiences less dendritic branching at this point in time. This results in a greater number of higher order branches in the left opercular area as compared to the right. The possible contributions of genetic programming and environmental inputs to these language-related branching patterns are discussed.

Neville discusses event–related potentials (ERP) during language processing in congenitally deaf children who use American Sign Language (ASL) of the Deaf, in hearing children who also use ASL because they were born to deaf parents, and in normal subjects. In deaf subjects, parietal and temporal regions that normally respond to auditory input respond instead to visual input, particularly input from peripheral vision. These results are interpreted in accordance with Changeaux's theory of synaptic proliferation and pruning. In the absence of auditory input, visual fibers grow into neural regions, which ordinarily subserve auditory function. Synapses subserving visual functions are stabilized in these "auditory" regions. Thus, early synaptic proliferation may be genetically determined, but synaptic stabilization may be determined by environmental input. Other data presented in this chapter indicate that left hemisphere specialization primarily pertains to grammatical competence and that areas of the brain mediating syntactic competence are more vulnerable to the effects of early experience than those mediating semantic competence.

Summary

This volume includes chapters by researchers from several disciplines whose work addresses specific aspects of brain–behavioral interactions in development. Examination of development across species and environments advances understanding of essential genetic and environmental conditions and helps clarify how enhancements in either area can advance or limit neural and behavioral development.

The chapters provide evidence, through presentation of data and systematic argument, that the development of both brain and behavior is plastic in response to biological and environmental variations. The possible limits to plasticity are identified, although in many areas these remain to be discovered. Cross-species regularities in development are also charted.

Language is discussed in several chapters. Language provides a useful example of biosocial development because linguistic and brain functions and development can be examined under conditions of both genetic and environmental deprivation. The recent research in this area has produced particularly exciting results pointing to the universality of language capacity among humans and illuminating the processes by which language competence develops.

Taken together, the volume demonstrates the central role of the brain in primate development. Most importantly, the chapters provide evidence that environment is a central factor ensuring that developmental outcome matches genetic potential. This volume also documents the usefulness of a multidisciplinary biosocial perspective on development for elucidating basic developmental processes and pointing to effective intervention.

References

Bishop, G. H., and Smith, J. M. (1964). The size of the nerve fibers supplying the cerebral cortex. *Experimental Neurology*, *9*, 483–501.

Changeaux, J. P. (1985). *Neuronal man.* New York: Pantheon Books.

Chomsky, N. (1972). *Language and mind.* New York: Harcourt, Brace, Jovanovich.

Chugani, H. T., and Phelps, M. E. (1986). Maturational changes in cerebral function in infants determined by [18]FDG positron emission tomography. *Science*, *231*, 840–843.

Chugani, H. T., Phelps, M. E., and Mazziotta, J. C. (1987). Positron emission tomography study of human brain functional development. *Annals of Neurology*, *22*, 487–497.

Conel, J. L. (1939–1967). *The postnatal development of the human cerebral cortex*, Vols. 1–8. Cambridge, MA: Harvard University Press.

Elkind, D. (1987). *Miseducation: Preschoolers at risk.* New York: A. Knopf.

Fishbein, H. D. (1976). *Evolution, development and children's learning.* Pacific Palisades, CA: Goodyear.

Flechsig, P. (1920). *Anatomie des Menschlichen Gehirns and Rückenmarks auf myelogenetischer Grundlage.* Liepzig: George Thomas.

Gibson, K. R. (1970). Sequence of myelinization in the brain of *Macaca mulatta*. Ph.D. Dissertation, University of California, Berkeley.

Gould, J. L., and Marler, P. M. (1987). Learning by instinct. *Scientific American, 256* (1), 74–85.

Gould, S. J. (1977). *Ontogeny and phylogeny*. Cambridge, MA: Harvard University Press.

Hailman, J. (1964). How an instinct is learned. *Scientific American, 221*, 98–108.

Huttenlocher, P. R. (1979). Synaptic density in human frontal cortex—developmental changes and effects on aging. *Brain Research*, 163, 195–205.

Huttenlocher, P. R., Courten, C., Carey, L., and Van der Loos, D. (1982). Synaptogenesis in human visual cortex—evidence for synapse elimination during normal development. *Neuroscience Letters*, *33*, 247–252.

Jacobson, M. (1978). *Developmental neurobiology*. New York: Plenum Press.

Lenneberg, E. (1967). *The biological foundations of human language*. New York: Wiley.

McClelland, J. L., Rumelhart, E. E., and the PDP Research Group. (1987). *Parallel distributed processing*, Vol. 2. Cambridge, MA: MIT Press.

Rakic, P., Bourgeois, J. P., Eckenhoff, M. F., Zecevic, N., and Goldman-Rakic, P. S. (1986). Concurrent overproduction of synapses in diverse regions of the primate cerebral cortex. *Science*, *232*, 232–235.

Rumelhart, D. E., McClelland, J. L., and the PDP Research Group. (1987). *Parallel distributed processing*, Vol. 1. Cambridge, MA: MIT Press.

Vinovskis, M. (1983). Historical perspectives on the development of the family and parental behavior. Paper presented at the Conference on Biosocial Lifespan Approaches to Parental and Offspring Development. Belmont, Maryland, May 1983.

Waddington, C. H. (1956). *Principles of embryology*. New York: Macmillan.

Wilson, R. S. (1978). Synchronies in mental development: An epigenetic perspective. *Science*, *202*, 939–948.

Wittig, M. A., and Petersen, A. (1979). *Sex-related differences in cognitive functioning*. New York: Academic Press.

Chapter 2

Basic Neuroanatomy for the Nonspecialist

Kathleen R. Gibson

This volume attempts to address a diverse audience. As some of our intended audience may lack familiarity with neuroanatomy, this chapter provides a very brief resume of those neuroanatomical terms and functions the reader may encounter in subsequent chapters. This account attempts to serve as an introduction only, not as a "state-of-the-art" treatise on brain function. Thus, those already well versed in neuroanatomy may comfortably by-pass this material.

The Neuron

The basic functional unit of the nervous system is the neuron or nerve cell. In addition to neurons, the brain contains large numbers of supporting cells termed glial cells and a rich vascular supply. Most neurons contain a cell body, a number of dendrites that receive impulses from other neurons, and a single axon that transmits information to other neurons. Cell bodies cluster together into *nuclei* or cortical *layers*. Axons collect together into bundles of nerves or *tracts*. Nerves travel from the spinal cord or brainstem to the skin, muscles, and body viscera. Tracts remain with the spinal cord or brain where they function to connect distant portions of the nervous system. The myelin sheath, which surrounds many but not all axons, confers speed and specificity to nerve transmission.

Junctions between neurons are termed *synapses*. Classically, anatomists considered that all synapses occurred between axons and dendrites. Although we now know that other synaptic types exist, the axodendritic synapse remains the best understood. Neurotransmitters such as serotonin, norepinephrine, dopamine, and acetylcholine mediate the transmission of impulses across synaptic junctions of the classic axon–dendrite variety. These and other neurotransmitters act locally. That is, they influence only those dendrites in the immediate vicinity of their release. In addition to neurotransmitters, other chemicals termed peptides also influence synaptic transmission. Peptides differ from classical neurotransmitters in that they primarily serve a modulator role in neural transmission and may act at a long distance from the point of release.

Brain Stem

The brainstem consists of the *diencephalon*, the *mesencephalon*, the *pons*, and the *medulla oblongata* (Figure 1). The *cerebellum* sits atop the pons.

The diencephalon contains the *thalamus* and the *hypothalamus*. In lower vertebrates, the thalamus serves as a major motor and sensory coordinating center. In mammals the thalamus continues to coordinate motor and sensory information, but it also serves as a major gateway to the neocortex. Thus, practically all impulses traveling to the neocortex from the brainstem or cord first synapse in the thalamus, as do many pathways traveling from the cortex to other subcortical structures. The thalamus contains many nuclei that differ in their appearance, connections, and function. Some critical nuclei mentioned in later chapters are the *lateral geniculate body*, which processes visual stimuli and transmits them to the neocortex, the *medial geniculate body*, which plays a similar role in auditory analysis, the *pulvinar*, which projects to varied neocortical areas and which may be involved in the analysis of higher order multimodal information, the *ventrolateral* and *ventroanterior nuclei*, which function as portions of complex motor circuits, and the *anterior* and *dorsomedial nuclei*, which function as portions of circuits mediating memory and emotion.

The *hypothalamus* is the master regulator of the human autonomic and endocrine systems. Various hypothalamic nuclei regulate hormonal output and physiological states such as temperature, water balance, food intake, and sexual

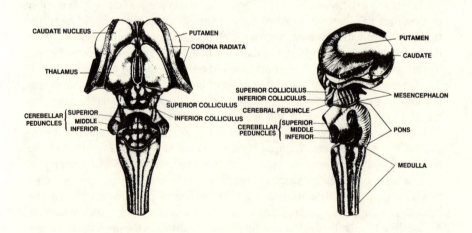

DORSAL VIEW   **LATERAL VIEW**

Figure 1.   Brain stem.

activity. Stimulation of the specific regions of the hypothalamus may also result in overt behaviors such as feeding, drinking, sexual behavior, or rage.

The mesencephalon contains nuclear processing centers regulating the motor output of cranial nerves III and IV, the primary nerves controlling eye movement and pupillary constriction. Also, contained within the mesencephalon are the *substantia nigra* and the *superior* and *inferior colliculi*. The substantia nigra produces dopamine, which is distributed to telencephalic areas such as the cortex and the corpus striatum. Lesions in the substantia nigra result in deficient production of dopamine and in the clinical syndrome of Parkinson's disease. The superior and inferior colliculi are also known as the *optic* and *auditory tectum*, respectively. These structures in the dorsal midbrain are prominent in lower vertebrates such as fish and reptiles where they play critical roles in processing visual and auditory information and in relating visual and auditory space to body maps (Gaither and Stein, 1979). Hence, these areas help provide the spatial constructs essential for reaching for food and other items. In humans, the functions of these regions are less clear, but probably also relate to spatial processing of auditory and visual input.

Nuclei controlling movements of the muscles of mastication and facial expression lie within the *pons*. Pontine nuclei are also critical in the analysis of tactile and proprioceptive sensation from facial areas. Other important nuclei in the pons function as parts of neural circuits interconnecting the cerebellum, thalamus, and neocortex.

The *cerebellum* controls muscle synergy and muscle tone. It also plays other complex roles in mediating smooth muscle actions. Lesions in the cerebellum result in profound disturbances in gait and in an inability to coordinate muscular actions. Patients, for instance, may exhibit very jerky staccato-like motions that result in difficulty in the pronunciation of words, in the fine motor coordination of movements of the extremities, and in the maintenance of balance of the trunk.

The *medulla oblongata* of the brain is sometimes called the "magic inch" because of its vital role in regulating respiration, circulation, and swallowing. It also contains nuclei that control the movements of the tongue, larynx, and body viscera as well as nuclei that function in the perception of taste and of facial pain.

Coursing throughout the spinal cord and brainstem are a number of critical tracts. The *corticospinal tracts* are long, very well-myelinated tracts that originate in the neocortex and travel to the spinal cord. They regulate voluntary movement. If lesioned, paralysis results. These tracts are sometimes called the *pyramidal tracts*. The *spinothalamic tracts*, the *trigeminal lemniscus*, *fasciculus gracilis*, and *fasciculus cuneatus*, and the *medial lemniscus* are also long, well-myelinated tracts. The spinothalamic tracts carry information related to pain, temperature, and tickle sensation to the thalamus. The trigeminal lemniscus carries information related to pain, temperature, and fine touch of the head and neck region to the thalamus. The fasciculus gracilis and cuneatus are located in the *posterior funiculus* of the spinal cord. They carry information related to discriminatory touch and proprioception to the medulla oblongata. The *medial lemniscus*, which originates in the medulla, carries impulses related to discriminatory touch and proprioception to the thalamus. Lesions of the posterior funciculus–medial lemniscus pathway commonly occur in disease states such as multiple sclerosis, tertiary syphillis, or pernicious anemia. They result in ataxias characterized by an inability to maintain proper balance when the eyes are closed and by deficient touch sensation. Patients, for instance, may claim that they feel they are walking on air or on cotton.

Contrasting with these well-myelinated fiber tracts and discrete nuclei of the brain stem is another brainstem system—the *reticular system*. This system contains a number of short, poorly myelinated fibers with interspersed nuclei, and it receives information from diverse sensory modalities. The reticular system functions to regulate state of arousal. Thus, it is important in maintaining consciousness, in alerting and startle reactions, and in regulating sleep and wakefulness. One reticular nucleus, the *locus coerulus*, produces norepinephrine, which is distributed to the neocortex and other higher brain areas. In contrast, the *raphe nuclei* of the reticular system produce serotonin, which is also distributed to higher neural regions. Both of these nuclei and chemicals are important in regulating sleep, wakefulness, and levels of arousal.

The Telencephalon

The *telencephalon* contains the highest coordinating centers in the brain: the *corpus striatum*, the *lumbic lobe* and the *neocortex*.

The *striatum* (otherwise known as the *basal ganglia*) consists of the *caudate nucleus*, the *putamen*, and the *globus pallidus* (Figure 2). The term *neostriatum* refers to the caudate nucleus and the putamen, while the term *paleostriatum* refers to the globus pallidus. The striatum receives numerous fibers from the neocortex and projects to the pallidum in a funnel-like fashion. Fibers from 50,000 to 130,000 striatal cells may synapse with a single pallidal cell (Passingham, 1987a,b; Percheron et al., 1984). The pallidum projects to the thalamus via the *ansa lenticularis* and *thalamic fasciculus* and the *Fields of Forel*. The thalamus, in turn, projects to the motor and premotor cortex. Other connections

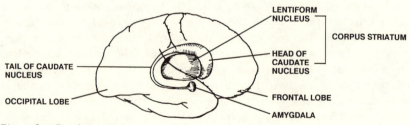

Figure 2.   Basal ganglia.

of the corpus striatum involve reciprocal connections between the pallidum and the subthalamus and between the striatum and the substantia nigra.

Collectively, the nuclei of the corpus striatum and their interconnecting neural regions comprise a complex circuitry involved in the initiation and programming of movements. Although the actual role played in the initiation or regulation of movement by the corpus striatum remains somewhat uncertain, animal research provides important clues. In some species, electrical stimulation of the corpus striatum results in stereotyped species-specific movements such as those used in social and sexual displays (MacLean, 1978, 1985). In addition, pathways through the corpus striatum may be differentially active in movements that require identifying objects and determining the potential utility of objects as food, tools, or other items of interest (Passingham, 1987a,b). Lesions within the corpus striatum result in abnormal movements such as the dyskinesias of Huntington's chorea and/or in paucity and rigidity of movement as occurs in Parkinson's disease.

The *limbic lobe* of the forebrain lies on the medial surface of the cerebral hemispheres where it forms an anatomical border around the brainstem. Three areas comprise the limbic lobe: the *cingulate gyrus*, the *parahippocampal gyrus*, and the *hippocampus* (Figure 3). The limbic lobe interconnects with the neocortex and with the hypothalamus. The limbic lobe and its interconnections constitute the *limbic system* also known as *Papez* circuit. Classically, this circuit involves the hippocampus, the cingulate gyrus, the septum, the *amgydala*, the anterior nucleus of the thalamus, the mammillary body of the hypothalamus, and certain fiber pathways including the *fornix*, the *cingulum*, the *medial forebrain bundle* and the *mammillothalamic tract*.

As a whole, the limbic system plays a central role in the regulation of emotional behaviors. Stimulation of the amygdala, for instance, leads to sexual behavior and aggression, while lesions in the amygdala and adjacent structures lead to inappropriate behaviors such as ingesting inedible items or directing

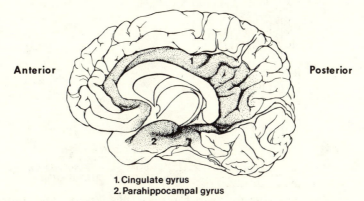

1. Cingulate gyrus
2. Parahippocampal gyrus

Figure 3. Limbic lobe. Medial surface of cerebral hemispheres showing the limbic lobe. (Adapted from Truex and Carpenter, 1964.)

sexual or aggressive acts to inappropriate targets (Klüver-Bucy, 1939). Other regions of the limbic system, such as the hippocampus, aid in the regulation of memory.

The human *neocortex* consists of an outer surface of gray matter containing cell bodies, dendrites, and glial cells and an inner layer of white matter containing axons that enter and leave the cortex. Contained within this subcortical white matter are fibers of the *corona radiata*. These axons enter and leave the various cortical gyri. Many fibers in the corona radiata are directly continuous with those in the great fiber bundle, known as the *internal capsule*. This major fiber bundle contains all of the major tracts passing between the cortex and the thalamus and between the cortex and brainstem and spinal cord. Other fibers known as *arcuate* fibers also lie in the subcortical white matter. These short fibers pass between adjacent cortical gyri.

Other cortical fiber tracts include the *corpus callosum* and the *anterior commissure*, which connect the two cerebral hemispheres and permit hemispheric integration of information, and a variety of long association tracts, which connect diverse regions of the same cerebral hemisphere. These association tracts include the *uncinate fasciculus*, the *occipitofrontal fasciculi*, and the *superior* and *inferior longitudinal fasiculi*.

The gray matter of the neocortex consists of six cortical layers, numbered from I to VI, with the outermost layer being layer I (Figure 4). Cortical layers differ from each other in the types of neuronal cells they contain. In some layers, small cells known as granule cells or stellate cells predominate. These cells have short axons or no axons and possess local processing functions. Other layers contain

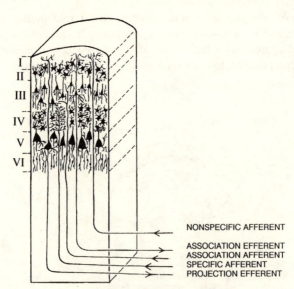

Figure 4. Cross section of the cortex illustrating cortical layers. Note that cells in adjacent layers line up in a vertical fashion. (Adapted from Gibson, 1981.)

mainly pyramidal cells. These cells derive their names and shapes from a single large apical dendrite and two large basilar dendrites, which give the neuron a pyramidal or triangular appearance. Pyramidal cells possess a single long axon and usually project to distant areas.

Layer I, the molecular layer, contains very few neuronal cell bodies. The axons in this layer run horizontally. This layer also contains numerous dendrites derived from cells in lower cortical layers.

Layer II, the external granular layer, contains many granule cells and small pyramidal cells.

Layer III, the external pyramidal layer, contains many small to medium-sized pyramidal cells. Axonal projections from layer III usually extend to other cortical areas.

Layer IV, the internal granular layer, contains small granule cells. This layer varies in thickness in various cortical regions. It reaches its greatest thickness in the visual cortex of primates and is absent from the motor cortex. Layer IV receives the majority of axons that extend to the cortex from the thalamus. Many of its dendrites project into upper cortical areas.

Layer V, the internal pyramidal layer, contains large pyramidal cells. This area reaches its greatest thickness in the motor cortex where it contains giant pyramidal cells, known as Betz cells.

Layer VI, the polymorphic cell layer, contains pyramidal cells as well as many other cell types.

Layers V and VI send their axons to regions outside of the cortex such as the corpus striatum, the thalamus, the spinal cord, and the brainstem, although a small number of neurons project from these layers to other cortical areas. Layer VI primarily projects to the thalamus, while layer V projects to other subcortical areas such as the striatum and spinal cord (Crick and Asanuma, 1987).

In addition to exhibiting a laminar pattern, the cortex is vertically stratified into *columns*. Cortical columns derive from embryonic neuronal migration patterns along vertical pathways determined by glial cells (Rakic, 1988). Cells within a particular vertical column share functional similarities. They respond to the same stimuli and to the same spatial coordinates. Thus, cortical columns may function as local processing areas for discrete packets of information.

The neocortex consists of five *lobes*: *occipital*, *parietal*, *temporal*, *frontal*, and *insula* (Figure 5). Fissures and sulci separate lobes from each other. Among the most important of these are the *lateral fissure* (of Sylvius), which separates the temporal lobe from the frontal and parietal lobes, the *central fissure* (of Rolando), which separates the frontal and parietal lobes, and the *calcarine fissure*, which lies in the occipital lobe and demarcates the main visual area of the cortex.

Each lobe of the neocortex contains a number of cytoarchitectonic areas characterized by specific cellular characteristics. The most widely used cytoarchitectonic system is that devised by Brodmann in the early part of this century

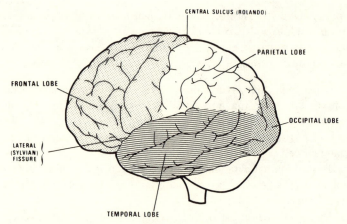

Figure 5.   Major lobes of the neocortex. Insula lies deep to the lateral fissure.

(Figure 6) (Brodmann, 1909). Brodmann's system assigns each cytoarchitectonic area a unique number. Another cytoarchitectonic system, that of von
Economo and Koskinas, uses a lettering system with the first letter of each region
referring to a particular cortical lobe (von Economo and Koskinas, 1925). Thus,
area FA is in the frontal lobe, area PA, in the parietal lobe. For reference
purposes, Table 1 provides the equivalent regions in the differing nomenclatures
of Brodmann and of von Economo and Koskinas.

   Functionally, the left and right halves of the neocortex mirror each other in

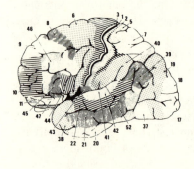

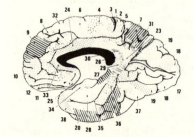

Figure 6.   Brodmann's cytoarchitectural maps
of the cerebral cortex. (After House and
Panksy, 1967.)

Table 1. Equivalent Designates of Cortical Areas between Systems of Von Economo and Brodmann.

1	2	1	2
FA	4	OC	17
FB	6	PB	3
FC	8	PC	1
FD	9	PD	2
FCBm	44	PE	7
FDΓ	45	PEM	5
FDΔ	46	PF	40
FE	10	PG	39
FG	11	TA	22
FL	25	TB	42
IA	14	TC	41
LA	24	TD	52
LC	23, 31	TE	21
OA	19	TE[1]	20
OB	18	TF[2]	36
FF	47	TG	38

certain respects, but differ in major ways. In most people, the left hemisphere mediates the majority of linguistic functions and may play a primary role in sequential analysis of varied stimuli. Certain regions of the left hemisphere are particularly critical for these language processes. These include, among others, Broca's area in the left frontal lobe near the lateral fissure, which is active in the production of speech, and Wernicke's area of the superior temporal gyrus, which is important for the interpretation of the sounds of speech (Figure 7). In contrast, the right hemisphere is more important in the analysis of spatial constructs (Gazzaniga, 1970).

Although usually considered the seat of higher cognition, the neocortex is also a complex sensorimotor processing center. Classically, anatomists have divided the cortex into primary sensory and motor regions, sensory association and

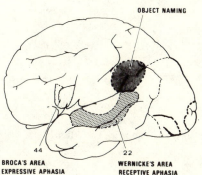

OBJECT NAMING

44
BROCA'S AREA
EXPRESSIVE APHASIA

22
WERNICKE'S AREA
RECEPTIVE APHASIA

Figure 7. Major cortical areas involved in language production.

premotor areas, and association areas. These divisions reflect anatomical projections and functionality (Figure 8).

Primary sensory areas receive fibers directly from sensory processing areas in the thalamus, and they receive and process information pertaining to one modality only, that is, vision, touch, or hearing. Cells within the primary sensory areas respond to discrete aspects of sensory stimuli such as lines or edges, and they possess narrow receptive fields. The primary sensory areas include visual area 17 (OC) in the occipital lobe, auditory area 41 (TC) on Heschl's gyrus deep to the lateral fissure, and somatosensory areas, 1, 2, and 3 (PC, PD, PB) located on the postcentral gyrus of the parietal lobe. These areas apparently detect discrete sensory features such as single edges or discrete pinpricks (Mountcastle, 1978). When lesioned, patients claim blindness, deafness, or lack of tactile sensation, depending on the region of damage.

Similarly, the primary motor area (4, FA) of the precentral gyrus has discrete outputs to subcortical regions and appears to function in the mediation of discrete movements. Lesions in the primary motor area lead to paralysis.

Sensory association areas surround the primary areas. Like the primary areas, sensory association areas function primarily in modality-specific analysis. Cells in the sensory association areas possess larger receptive fields, however, and respond to a broader range of stimuli (Mountcastle, 1978). In the visual association regions, for instance, specific cells may respond to wholistic visual configurations such as hands or faces. Unlike lesions of the primary areas, lesions of the sensory association areas do not produce blindness, deafness, or lack of tactile sensation. Rather sensation remains intact, but patients lose the ability to decipher the meaning of sensory stimuli. Thus, with lesions in visual association areas, patients may lose the ability to identify objects or faces by visual means. With lesions of the secondary somatosensory areas, they may lose the ability to identify objects placed in the hand, and with lesions in the secondary auditory areas, they lose the ability to identify sounds.

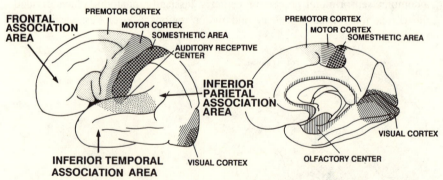

Figure 8. Primary and secondary cortical sensory and motor areas. (After House and Panksy, 1967.)

The premotor area (6, FB) may play a role in the motor system similar to the roles played by secondary association areas in the sensory system. Just as cells in the secondary sensory areas have large receptor fields, so, too, premotor neurons mediate larger fields and less discrete units of motor function than do cells in the motor cortex, proper. Cells within the premotor region may fire in relationship to specific configurations of the hand into precision or power grips. Cells within this region also respond to spatially directed movements. In some cases, a single cell may respond in relation to grasping actions of either the right or the left hand or of the mouth, as long as the spatial position of the object and the intent to grasp remain constant (Rizzolati et al., 1987). In addition to responding to specific hand configurations and spatial positions, the premotor cortex may play a role in the timing of movements, thereby permitting smooth transitions from one movement to the next (Luria, 1966).

Three main association areas mediate higher intellectual functions, the inferior parietal, inferior temporal, and prefrontal areas. Long considered to be multimodal in function, these association areas now appear to be composed of numerous smaller processing units of more discrete sensory or motor functions (Kaas, 1987). To date, however, clinical and behaviorally oriented studies of human brain development continue to lack the capacity to distinguish most of these individual subunits of the association areas. The classical view of the multimodal functioning of these areas remains appropriate for materials such as those covered in this book.

In general, the inferior parietal association cortex mediates functions involving cross-modal integration of sensory stimuli. It plays a particularly important role in spatial analysis and in other behaviors that involve taking a number of separately perceived stimuli and integrating them into new simultaneous wholes (Luria, 1966). Lesions in the inferior parietal association areas result in defects in object naming, in certain aspects of grammatical perception, in distinguishing left from right, in map reading, in recognition of body parts, and in dressing. The actual deficit varies somewhat according to the side and location of the lesion.

With lesions in the left temporal association areas patients exhibit problems in recounting stories in sequential order and in long-term memory. In contrast, lesions in the right temporal region affect visual processes and may result in difficulty in recognizing faces.

Ultimately, the frontal association areas are the master planners of the brain. They organize behavioral acts in proper temporal order to achieve goal-directed actions. Many diverse connections and subfunctions contribute to the frontal lobe roles in the planning of actions. For one, the frontal association areas receive information from body viscera as well as from exteroceptive stimuli. Thus, they can synthesize information from both the inner and outer sensory worlds (Nauta 1971). In addition, the prefrontal cortex aids in the maintenance of working memory and in the anticipation future events. Thus, it can integrate temporally disparate events (Fuster, 1985).

Parallel Distributed Processing Mechanisms

Conceptually, it is easy to speak and think of neural areas as if they were individual, functionally specific processing units mediating distinct behavioral categories such as language, tool use, or sexual behavior. To a certain extent, the preceding account of neural functions mirrors this simplistic view. Modern theory, however, suggests that such views are erroneous. Specific neural inputs reach diverse neural areas, and complex functions are handled by circuitry involving cooperative actions of varied neural regions (Rumelhart et al., 1987; McClelland et al., 1987). For this reason, similar symptoms sometimes result from lesions in diverse areas.

The preceding account of neural functions mentioned two of the brain's major circuits: the limbic system and the circuitry involving the basal ganglia, thalamus, and cortex. Other cortical regions also function as parts of complex circuits. The frontal lobes, for instance, may actually function as a portion of the limbic circuit (Nauta, 1971). Similarly, the motor cortical areas are interrelated with a cerebellar circuit composed of motor and premotor cortex, somatosensory cortex, secondary somatosensory cortex, parietal area 5, putamen, pons, and cerebellum (Passingham, 1987a). Further, at least two separate circuits exist that involve mutual interconnections between the frontal and parietal association areas, the hippocampus and the cingulate gyrus (Goldman-Rakic, 1988). Unfortunately, research into complex neural circuitry and circuit-specific functions remains in its infancy. The more simplistic view presented here should suffice for the generalist reader of this volumes.

References

Brodmann, K. (1909). *Lokalisationslehre der Grosshirnrinde in ihren prinzipien dargestellt auf Grund des Zellenbaues*. Leipzig: Barth.

Crick, F., and Asanuma, C. (1987). Certain aspects of the anatomy and physiology of the cerebral cortex. In J. McClelland and David E. Rumelhart (Eds.), *Parallel distributed processing* (Vol. 2, pp. 333–371). Cambridge, MA: MIT Press.

Fuster, J. M. (1985). The prefrontal cortex, mediator of cross-temporal contingencies. *Human Neurobiology, 4*, 169–179.

Gaither, N. S., and Stein, B. E. (1979). Reptiles and mammals use similar sensory organizations in the midbrain. *Science, 295*, 595–597.

Gazzaniga, M. S. (1970). *The bisected brain*. New York: Appleton Century Crofts.

Gibson, K. R. (1981). Comparative neuroontogeny, its implications for the development of human intelligence. In G. Butterworth (Ed.)., *Infancy and Epistemology* (pp. 52–82). Brighton, England: Harvester Press.

Goldman-Rakic, P. S. (1988). Topography of cognition. Parallel distributed networks in primate association cortex. *Annual Review of Neuroscience, 11*, 137–156.

House, E. L., and Pansky, B. (1967). *A functional approach to neuroanatomy*. New York: McGraw-Hill.

Kaas, J. H. (1987). The organization of the neocortex in mammals: Implications for theories of brain function. *Annual Review of Psychology*, *38*, 129–151.

Klüver, H., and Bucy, P. C. (1939). Preliminary analysis of functions of the temporal lobes in monkeys. *Archives of Neurology and Psychiatry*, *42*, 979.

Luria, A. R. (1966). *Higher cortical functions in man*. New York: Basic Books.

MacLean, P. D. (1978). Effects of lesions of globus pallidus on species-typical display behavior of squirrel monkeys. *Brain Research*, *179*, 175–196.

MacLean, P. D. (1985). Brain evolution relating to family, play and the separation call. *Archives of General Psychiatry*, *42*, 405–417.

McClelland, J. L., Rumelhart, E. E., and the PDP Research Group. (1987). *Parallel distributed processing* (Vol. 2). Cambridge, MA: MIT Press.

Mountcastle, V. (1978). An organizing principle for cerebral function: the unit module and the distributed system. In G. M. Edelmann and V. B. Mountcastle (Eds.), *The mindful brain* (pp. 7–50). Cambridge, MA: MIT Press.

Nauta, W. J. H. (1971). The problem of the frontal lobe: A reinterpretation. *Journal of Psychiatric Research*, *8*, 167–187.

Passingham, R. E. (1987a). From where does the motor cortex get its instructions? In S. P. Wise (Ed.), *Higher brain functions: Recent explorations of the brain's emergent properties* (pp. 67–97). New York: Wiley.

Passingham, R. E. (1987b). Two cortical systems for directing movement. In motor areas of the cerebral cortex. Wiley Chichester. *Ciba Foundation Symposium*, *132*, 151–164.

Percheron, G., Yelnick, J., and Francois, C. (1984). A Golgi analysis of the primate globus pallidus: III. Spatial organization of the striatopallidal complex. *Journal of Comparative Neurology*, *227*, 214–227.

Rakic, P. (1988). Specification of cerebral cortical areas. *Science*, *241*, 170–176.

Rizzolatti, G., Gentilucci, M., Fogassi, L., Matelli, M., and Ponzoni-Maggi, S. (1987). Neurons related to goal-directed motor acts in inferior area 6 of the macaque monkey. *Experimental Brain Research*, *67*, 220–224.

Rumelhart, D. E., McClelland, J. L., and the PDP Research Group. (1987). *Parallel distributed processing* (Vol. 1). Cambridge, MA: MIT Press.

Truex, R. C., and Carpenter, B. A. (1964) *Strong and Elwyn's Human Neuroanatomy* (5th edition) Baltimore.

von Economo, C., and Koskinas, G. N. (1925). *Die Cytoarchitektonik der Hirnrinde des erwachsensen Menschen*. Heidelberg: Julius Springer.

PART II

PRINCIPLES AND REGULARITIES OF NEURAL DEVELOPMENT

Chapter 3

Myelination and Behavioral Development: A Comparative Perspective on Questions of Neoteny, Altriciality and Intelligence

Kathleen R. Gibson

Some scholars consider the newborn human brain to be unusually altricial, that is, immature by comparison to the brains of other newborn mammals. They argue that this neonatal immaturity is a primary determinant of human intellectual and linguistic skills and seek the origins of human altriciality in the fossil record (Fisher, 1982; Gould, 1977, Rader, 1985; Trinkhaus, 1983). Paradoxically, while one segment of the scientific community seeks the temporal origins of human altriciality, others write books with titles such as *The Competent Infant* (Stone et al., 1973) and marvel at the complexity of the behavior of the human neonate (Butterworth, 1981). How can it be that the human neonate is behaviorally competent, but neurologically immature by comparison to other mammalian species?

A similar paradox permeates the literature on the developing child. As children age, they become increasingly competent at intellectual tasks. To many investigators these growing intellectual skills reflect brain maturation and an increasing functional sophistication of neuronal mechanisms (Case, 1985; Gibson, 1977, 1981). Yet, others claim that the human brain never really matures. In their view, the brain is a neotenous or pedomorphic organ that, even in adulthood, resembles the brains of immature animals in important functional respects (Gould, 1977; Lerner, 1984; Rutkowska, 1985). According to this perspective, the immaturity of the adult human brain permits humans to go on learning throughout their lives and accounts for high human intelligence.

These contrasting views serve as testimony to a genuine gap in scientific understanding. Few have actually researched comparative brain and behavioral development. The time has come for a serious examination of comparative brain and behavioral maturation. To this end, this chapter examines comparative data on neural and behavioral maturation of relevance to these complex developmental issues. These data suggest that the extent of neonatal human brain immaturity and human postnatal developmental delay has been exaggerated. Maturational factors, alone, do not appear capable of accounting for the greater intelligence of humans as compared to apes. Rather, some other factor such as brain size or brain organization must account for human skills. As large brain size correlates with prolonged maturational periods in mammals (Sacher and Staffeldt, 1974), whatever correlation does exist between maturation period and intelligence likely reflects the intervening variable of brain size.

This chapter focuses primarily on myelination data as an estimator of neural maturity because more comparative data exist for myelination than for other neural maturational parameters. In particular, most longitudinal studies involving regional maturation of the entire brain have focused on myelination. Myelination patterns are known for salmon (Rogalski, 1933), various urodeles and anurans (Kreht, 1940), opossums (Langworthy, 1928), laboratory rats (Jacobsen, 1963), rabbits (Langworthy, 1926), cats (Langworthy, 1929a, b), dogs (Fox, 1971), starlings and white leghorn hens (Schifferli, 1948), albino mice and Cretan spiny mice (Kretschman, 1967), guinea pigs (Martin, 1962), sheep (Romanes, 1947) rhesus monkeys (Gibson, 1970) and humans (Conel, 1939–1967; Flechsig, 1920; Gilles et al., 1983; Keene and Hewer, 1931, 1933; Langworthy, 1930, 1933; Rabinowicz, 1979; Rorke and Riggs, 1969; Yakovlev and Lecours, 1967).

As axons can propagate impulses prior to myelination, myelination is not an indicator of functional onset (Ulett et al., 1944, 1950). Rather, myelination is a late developmental event and an indicator of functional efficiency and specificity. Myelination data, then, may be considered estimators of those aspects of neural maturation and function related to speed and specificity of nerve transmission. Apparently, the timing of myelination is largely under genetic control (Konner, this volume).

Methods

Myelination Data

Rhesus monkey myelination data derive from 20 rhesus monkey (*Macaca mulatta*) brains of the following ages: birth, two brains; 2 postnatal weeks, two brains; 4 weeks, four brains; 8 weeks, three brains; 13 weeks, one brain; 26 weeks, two brains; 52 weeks, one brain; 56 weeks, one brain; 104 weeks, two brains; 156 weeks, one brain; and 172 weeks, one brain. Sections of these brains were donated to the author by Paul Yakovlev from the William Caveness brain collection at Harvard University. The brains were fixed in 10% formalin, embedded in a solution of 12% celloidin, and cut at 35 μm by technicians at Harvard University. One hundred sections per brain were stained with the Loyez myelin stain (Bertrand, 1930) at the University of California. The Loyez stain is a modification of the Weigert stain, which, like the Weigert, causes myelin sheaths to turn black.

Myelination in fiber tracts and in the white matter of the cortical gyri was rated according to the following criteria: 0—no myelin visible by light microscopic techniques; 1—barely visible myelin under a light microscope; 2—light myelin visible under low power and/or without microscopic aid; 3—myelin stains with medium intensity; 4—myelin is dark; 5—myelin is black.

Many tracts experience a period of rapid myelination to a moderate or dark stain. Subsequently, they continue to myelinate at a slow pace until they reach a black coloration. In this report, the end of the period of rapid myelination is called the "plateau stage."

Within each cortical gyrus, myelination begins in the central region. Until a relatively late maturational date an unmyelinated area lies just below layer VI of the cortical gray matter. The age at which this unmyelinated region becomes myelinated is termed the "gyrus full" stage.

Myelination data for fiber tracts and cortical gyri in the human brain are derived from published studies by Flechsig (1920), Gilles et al. (1983), Langworthy (1930, 1933), Rorke and Riggs (1969), and Yakovlev and Lecours (1967). These studies and the methods used are described in detail in Konner (this volume). Several of these investigators reported only the beginning of myelination. Gilles et al. distinguished three levels of myelination in fiber tracts of the human brain. No investigator of myelination in the human brain has reported as many stages of myelination as were delineated for the rhesus monkey brain (five).

Myelination of the cortical layers of the rhesus brain was recorded in terms of the youngest age in which myelinated fibers could be seen under oil immersion in the light microscope in any brain. Myelination data for the cortical layers of the human brain come from published data by Conel (1939–1967) who studied brains at the following ages: birth, 1 month, 3 months, 6 months, 15 months, 24 months, 4 years, 6 years and 8 years. As with the monkey, the human data report the earliest age in which myelin appears in a cortical layer in any brain. Conel recorded his data using von Economo's nomenclature for cortical areas (von Economo and Koskinos, 1925). To render the monkey and human data as comparable as possible, rhesus monkey cortical areas were also designated according to von Economo's terminology and according to cytoarchitectonic studies of the rhesus brain by von Bonin and Bailey (1947) and Krieg (1963). Homologies, of course, are difficult to determine by cytoarchitectonic methods. Although attempts have been made to report the data in as homologous a fashion as possible, some similarly designated regions may not be strictly homologous.

Chimpanzee Development

For a period of 4 years beginning in September 1981, I visited the home of Jim and June Cook in Texas on a weekly or biweekly basis and observed and interacted with the four chimpanzees that were raised in the Cook home. Two of these chimpanzees were born at the University of Oklahoma primate center directed by William Lemmon. Two were born in the Cook home. Tania, the eldest of the chimpanzees, was the full sibling of Nim (Terrace, 1979).

My own interactions with the Cooks began when two males, Israel, from the Oklahoma colony, and Uriah, offspring of Tania, were 7 and 9 months of age, respectively. At that time, Tania was pregnant with Leah, the youngest of the chimpanzees in the Cook home. For about 6 months when Leah was between 4 and 10 months of age, I took her to my home for one or two evenings a week at the request of June Cook. During these periods of 24 to 48 hours per week, I essentially served as Leah's surrogate mother. During the years I observed them, the young animals remained uncaged. They roamed at will around the Cook home and yard and played with the Cook grandchildren. My observations centered primarily on the animals' object manipulation activities, both as spontaneously exhibited and in response to children's toys that I specifically provided and demonstrated to them. The chimpanzees' activities with objects were recorded on audiotape at the time they occurred and compared to Piagetian analyses of object manipulation in human children.

Myelination Patterns

General Patterns and Sequences of Myelination

Myelination sequences are remarkably similar in fish, amphibians, birds, mammals, and humans (Gibson, 1970). Peripheral and cranial nerves myelinate early as does the medial lemniscus and, where present, the long ascending and descending sensory and motor tracts of the brainstem and cord. Cortical and limbic tracts myelinate later. Among the major neural processing centers, myelination occurs in the following sequence: tectum, thalamus, corpus striatum, limbic cortex and nuclei and neocortex (see Table 1 for myelination of fiber tracts in the rhesus monkey).

Thus, the general pattern is one in which the brainstem myelinates in advance of the telencephalon. In all neural regions, however, structures that are densely myelinated in the adult myelinate earlier than structures that are sparsely myelinated. Thus, densely myelinated peripheral nerves and brainstem tracts myelinate in advance of densely myelinated cortical and limbic tracts. Similarly, slowly myelinating brainstem structures myelinate in advance of slowly myelinating cortical structures. Some temporal overlap does exist, however, between cortical and brainstem myelination. In both the human and the rhesus monkey, rapidly myelinating cortical tracts, such as the internal capsule, complete their myelination in advance of slowly myelinating subcortical regions, such as the reticular system (Gibson, 1970; Yakovlev and Lecours, 1967).

Table 1. Myelination in Fiber Tracts of *Macaca mulatta*[a]
(from Gibson, 1970)

Tract	A	B	C
Internal capsule			
Lenticulostriate	NB	NB	NB
Genu	NB	NB	NB
Medial lemniscus	NB	NB	NB
Tectospinal	NB	NB	NB
Habenulointerpeduncular tract	NB	NB	NB
Posterior commissure	NB	NB	NB
Lateral lemniscus	NB	NB	NB
Medial longitudinal fasciculus	NB	NB	NB
Frontopontine	NB	2	4
Temporopontine	NB	2	8
Subcallosal bundle	NB	8	8
Internal capsule			
Retrolenticular portion	NB	NB	8
Infralenticular	NB	NB	8
Anterior	NB	NB	8
Olfactory stria	NB	NB	8
Septum	NB	4	8
Fields of Forel, H_1 H_2	NB	4	8
Ansa lenticularis	NB	4	8
Brachium pontis	NB	4	8
Brachium conjunctivum	NB	4	8
Restiform body	NB	4	8
Habenular commissure	NB	2	8
Inferior colliculus brachium	NB	2	8
Inferior colliculus commissure	NB	2	8
Mammillary peduncle	NB	4	8
Pyramids	NB	4	8
Lateral olivary fibers	NB	4	8
Medial olivary fibers	NB	2	8
Corpus callosum body	NB	8	13
Corpus callosum splenium	2	8	13
Tapetum	NB	NB	13
Mammillothalamic tract	NB	8	13
Superior colliculus commissure	4	8	13
External sagittal stratum	NB	4	13
Anterior commissure	4	13	26
Internal sagittal stratum	NB	13	52
Cingulum anterior	NB	13	52
Cingulum posterior	NB	8	52
Corpus callosum rostrum	4	13	52
Diagonal band of Broca	NB	8	52
Stria medullaris thalami	NB	4	52
Longitudinal stria	4	13	52
Superior longitudinal fasciculus	NB	13	104
Inferior longitudinal fasciculus	NB	13	104
External capsule (temporofrontal)	2	26	104

Table 1. Continued

Tract	A	B	C
Fornix	NB	8	104
Orbitotemporal	4	104	172
External capsule (occipitofrontal)	4	56	172
Inferior occipitofrontal fasciculus	4	26	172
Uncinate fasciculus	4	26	172
Alveus	NB	8	172
Hippocampal fasciculus	NB	13	172
Stria terminalis	4	8	172
Dentate axons	4	104	172
Hippocampal perforating fibers	2	104	172
Dentate layer I	4	156	172
Fasciola cinera	4	172	172

[a] Numbers in the table refer to age in months.
[a] A, beginning of myelinization; B, plateau stage; C, adult stage. Numbers refer to age in weeks. NB, newborn.

State of Myelination of the Brain at Birth

The decided similarities of sequence in myelination among various species contrast with marked differences in timing. In some species, myelination is almost entirely a postnatal event. For instance, the brains of cats (Langworthy, 1929a, 1929b), laboratory rats (Jacobsen, 1963), albino mice (Kretschman, 1967), opossums (Langworthy, 1928), rabbits (Langworthy, 1926), and starlings (Schifferli, 1948) have little or no myelin at birth or hatching. In contrast, myelination in the brains of other species such as guinea pigs (Martin, 1962) and sheep (Romanes, 1947) is nearly complete at birth.

In both the monkey and the human, myelination begins prior to birth. By the time of birth, the rhesus monkey brain is heavily myelinated (Tables 1, 2, 3, 4). All peripheral and cranial nerves except the olfactory tract are black at birth. All ascending tracts to the level of the thalamus have much myelin, as do the pyramidal tracts, the cerebellar peduncles, and the internal capsule. Many of these tracts already stain with a dark or black coloration. The precentral and postcentral gyri are also heavily stained at birth. Other cortical gyri contain lesser degrees of myelin, but all are partially myelinated at birth except those in the classical frontal and temporal association regions. These are myelinated by 4 postnatal weeks. Some myelin also exists neonatally in various nuclear processing centers, i.e., thalamus, amygdala, medial portion of the globus pallidus, and superior and inferior colliculus. The cortical layers, corpus striatum, cerebellum, and hippocampus are basically unmyelinated at birth with the exception that the lower layers of the motor, premotor, primary, and secondary sensory areas of the neocortex contain a few myelinated fibers. The corpus callosum is

Table 2. Sequence of Myelination of the Cortical Gyri in *Macaca mulatta*[a]

	A	B	C	D
Precentral	NB	NB	4	8
Postcentral	NB	NB	8	26
Superior frontal posterior	NB	8	8	26
Subcentral operculum	NB	8	13	26
Parietal operculum	NB	8	13	26
Insula	NB	8	13	26
Occiptal	NB	8	13	26
Cuneus	NB	8	13	26
Calcarine	NB	8	13	26
Middle frontal	NB	13	26	56
Marginal	NB	13	26	26
Precuneus	NB	13	26	56
Lingual	NB	8	26	52
Frontal operculum	NB	13	26	52
Superior temporal posterior	NB	8	26	56
Entorhinal	NB	8	26	26
Occipitotemporal	NB	13	26	52
Superior parietal	NB	8	26	26
Angular	NB	13	26	52
Fusiform	NB	13	26	26
Inferior frontal posterior	NB	26	26	52
Inferior occipital	NB	13	26	56
Cingulum	NB	8	26	52
Middle temporal posterior	2	13	26	26
Inferior temporal posterior	2	26	26	52
Superior frontal anterior	2	52	104	104
Inferior frontal anterior	2	52	104	104
Superior temporal anterior	4	26	52	104
Frontal pole	4	52	104	104
Temporal pole	4	52	104	104
Middle temporal anterior	4	52	104	104
Inferior temporal anterior	4	52	104	104

(From Gibson, 1970)
[a]A = beginning of myelinization;
B = plateau stage;
C = gyrus full;
D = adult stage.
Numbers designate age of animals in weeks. NB = newborn.

beginning to myelinate at birth, but the anterior commissure and various telencephalic tracts such as the fornix, uncinate bundle, and diagonal band of Broca contain little or no myelin.

At birth, myelination in the human brain is very similar to that of the monkey with the exceptions that most tracts stain with a lighter intensity, no myelin is found in the angular and marginal gyri of the parietal lobe, and no myelin exists

Table 3. Earliest Age in Which Myelin is Found in Each Cortical Layer in *Macaca mulatta.*[a]

Cortical area		Cortical layer					
		I	II	III	IV	V	VI
FA	4f	2	8	4	—	NB	NB
FA	4h	NB	8	4	—	NB	NB
FB	6	8	26	4	4	NB	NB
FC	8	4	56	13	4	NB	NB
FCBm	44	8	56	8	4	NB	NB
FD	9	8	56	8	4	NB	NB
FDΓ	45	52	104	52	26	26	13
FDΔ	46	104	104	52	8	4	NB
FF	47	26	56	52	8	4	NB
FG_1	11b	8	56	4	4	4	NB
FG_2	11d	56	56	8	8	8	4
FDE	10	104	104	52	52	4	2
FL_1	12	104	104	104	104	104	4
FL_2	12	8	104	52	52	52	52
FL_3	12	104	104	52	52	8	52
PB_1	3	8	26	8	NB	NB	2
PB_2	3	4	26	4	NB	NB	NB
PB_3	3	4	13	NB	NB	NB	NB
PB_4	3	4	26	4	NB	NB	NB
PC	1	4	26	4	NB	NB	NB
PD	2	4	26	8	4	NB	NB
PE	5	26	56	8	4	NB	NB
PEM	7	56	56	8	4	NB	NB
PF	40	13	56	26	4	2	NB
PG	39	52	104	52	13	8	4
TA_1	22	52	104	26	8	4	2
TA_2	22	26	56	4	4	NB	NB
TB	42	4	26	4	NB	NB	NB
TC	41	26	26	4	NB	NB	NB
TD	52	26	52	26	13	4	4
TE_1	21	13	104	26	13	4	4
TE_2	20	26	104	26	26	4	4
TF	36	52	104	26	26	4	4
TG	38	26	104	52	26	8	4
OA_1	19	4	52	13	8	4	2
OA_2	19	8	52	13	8	4	4
OB	18	8	26	4	4	2	NB
OC_1	17	52	26	8	4	2	NB
OC_2	17	8	26	8	4	2	NB
OC_3	17	13	26	13	4	2	NB
LA_1	24	8	56	26	13	8	NB
LA_2	24	8	56	8	8	8	2
LC	23	52	56	26	13	4	2
IA		52	56	13	8	8	4
Subiculum		NB	4	2	2	NB	
Entorhinal		4	8	2	2	2	
Hippocampus		NB	8	4			
Dentate gyrus		4	8	52	4	4	4

[a]The letters are the cortical areas, using von Bonin's system. The numbers next to them are Krieg's equivalents. Numbers in the body of the table refer to age of animal in weeks. NB, newborn. (From Gibson, 1970)

Table 4. Age in Which Myelin Reaches Cortical Layers of the Human Brain (Conel, 1939–1967).[a]

Cortical area		*I*	*II*	*III*	*IV*	*Va*	*VB, VIa*	*VIb*
FA	Leg	3	6	15	3	3	3	1
FA	Trunk	3	6	3	3	3	1	1
FA	Hand	3	15	6	3	3	1	1
FA	Head	3	24	24	3	3	3	1
FB	GFS	3	24	24	3	3	3	3
FB	GFM	6	48	24	15	15	6	6
FCBm	GFI	15	48	24	15	15	6	3
FC	GFS	15	48	24	15	15	6	3
FD	GFM	15	48	48	4	6	6	6
FDII	GFI	15	48	48	15	15	3	3
FDm	GFS	15	72	24	15	15	6	3
FDΔ	GFM	15	72	48	15	15	15	15
FDp	GFI	15	96	48	15	15	3	3
FF	G Or	15	48	48	15	15	15	3
FE	p. FR.	15	96	96	4	15	3	3
PB	Leg	6	15	15	3	3	3	3
PB	Trunk	6	24	3	3	1	1	1
PB	Hand	6	24	6	3	3	3	1
PB	Head	15	24	24	15	15	1	1
PC	Trunk	6	48	24	6	3	3	3
PE	S. par lob.	6	48	24	15	15	15	3
PF	Supramarginal	6	48	24	6	6	6	3
PG	Angular	6	48	24	6	6	6	6
PH	Basalis	6	48	24	15	6	6	6
OA	Parastriata	15	48	24	15	6	6	6
OB	Parastriata	15	48	24	15	6	6	6
OC	Striate	6	48	24	1	3	3	3
TA		15	24	24	6	6	6	3
TB		6	24	24	6	6	3	3
TC		6	24	6	6	6	3	3
TE		6	48	48	15	6	6	6
TG		6	72	48	15	6	6	6
IA		6	48	48	15	15	6	6
IB		6	48	24	15	15	6	6
LA		6	48	24	6	6	6	6
LC		6	48	24	6	6	6	6
LD		15	48	24	15	15	6	6
LE		15	48	24	15	15	6	6
MA		1	15	15	15	6	6	6
PC	Hand	15	48	24	6	6	6	3
PC	Leg	6	15	15	3	3	3	3
PC	Head	15	48	24	15	15	3	3
TF		15	48	48	15	15	15	6

[a]Numbers in the table refer to age in months.

in any cortical layer. Thus, while the rhesus monkey brain is heavily myelinated at birth, the human brain is moderately so.

Postnatal Myelination

Among species whose brains myelinate entirely or, in part, postnatally, postnatal myelination may be rapid and complete within weeks after birth as in the rat (Jacobsen, 1963), or slow and complete only after years as in the rhesus monkey and the human.

By 2 to 3 postnatal months in the rhesus monkey and by 8 to 12 months in the human, all of the sensorimotor tracts, including the internal capsule, and subcortical nuclear areas stain with nearly an adult level of intensity suggesting that myelination in these areas is nearly mature. Thus, in both rhesus monkey and human, brainstem myelination is basically a phenomenon of infancy. The exception is the reticular system which continues to myelinate to at least 3.5 years in the monkey and to at least the second decade in the human (Yakovlev and Lecours, 1967).

In contrast to myelination in the brainstem, myelination in cortical and limbic areas is very protracted. The hippocampus, for instance, continues to myelinate well into late childhood in the human (Yakovlev and Lecours, 1967) and to at least 2 years of age in the rhesus monkey.

Detailed reports of cortical myelination exist for the laboratory rat, (Jacobsen, 1963), the rhesus monkey (Gibson, 1970), and the human (Conel, 1939–1967; Flechsig, 1920). Tables 2, 3, and 4 summarize these data for the human and the rhesus. In each species, cortical myelination begins first and proceeds most rapidly in those cortical tracts and layers most directly interconnected with the brainstem and in those cortical areas and gyri that classical anatomists called primary sensory and motor areas. Myelination begins last and proceeds most slowly in those tracts and layers most directly concerned with intracortical connections and intracortical processing functions and in those areas that classical anatomists termed association areas.

Thus, within the parietal, temporal, frontal, and occipital lobes, myelination presents a picture of a slowly spreading wave that begins at one point and gradually spreads to fill the entire lobe. In each lobe, the first areas to myelinate are the classical projection areas that mediate functions in one specific sensory or motor modality: visual area, OC (17), in the occipital lobe; auditory area, TC (41), in the temporal lobe; motor area, FA (4), in the frontal lobe; and somatosensory areas, PB, PC, and PD (1, 2, 3), in the parietal lobe.

In addition to this general pattern there are some regional differences. The motor cortex (area 4, FA) is the first to begin myelinating in the rat, monkey, and human, followed by the premotor area (FB) and the primary sensory (or sensory-specific) regions: somatosensory (PB, PC, and PD), auditory (TC), and visual (OC). The motor and somatosensory areas to the lower limb myelinate in advance of those to the upper limb.

Each cortical area myelinates in a strict pattern. In all areas in each of the three species, myelin first appears in the subcortical white matter. Shortly, thereafter, layers V and VI acquire myelin, followed by layers IV, III, and II in that order. Layer I usually myelinates in conjunction with layer V, but in the monkey, layer I may myelinate as late as layer III. Those regions that begin their myelination first are also the first to acquire myelin in each of the cortical layers.

At birth, some myelin is already present in the lower layers of the neocortex in the rhesus monkey, particularly in the primary sensory and motor regions. The human brain begins to acquire myelin in the neocortical layers by 1 month (Conel, 1939–1967). By 3 months of age, the human brain reaches a level of cortical myelination similar to that exhibited by the newborn rhesus monkey.

Between the ages of 3 and 6 months in the monkey and 1 to 2 years in the human, the corpus striatum and cerebellum achieve an adult state of myelination. By 6 months of age in the monkey and by 15 to 24 months in the human, myelin has reached layer II of primary sensory and motor areas and layer IV of the secondary areas. All cortical areas contain some myelin, at least in the lower layers. Consequently, the ages of 3 to 6 months in the monkey and 1 to 2 years in the human basically mark the end of the infantile stage of brain myelination. During these time periods, all cortical areas contain some myelin, and all brainstem tracts and subcortical processing areas are well myelinated except for the reticular system. It is of interest that one year of age also marks the time of the maturation of heavy glucose utilization in all areas of the human neocortex (Chugani and Phelps, 1986).

Subsequent to 6 months of age in the monkey and 2 years of age in the human, myelination is basically a matter of continuing myelination of the limbic system, reticular system, and neocortex. By 2 years of age in the monkey, all cortical areas and layers have myelin. By age 6 in the human, all layers of most cortical areas have some myelin, although layer II of some prefrontal areas does not evidence myelin until 8 years of age (Conel, 1939–1967). Subsequent to 2 years of age in the monkey and 8 years of age in the human, the cortical layers continue to acquire myelin at a gradual pace at least to 3.5 years in the monkey and at least to adolescence in the human. In the monkey, 3 to 4 years also marks the age of maturing synaptic density (Zecevic et al., 1989). In the human, adolescence is the period of maturing myelination patterns is also the period in which glucose utilization stabilizes at adult levels (Chugani et al., 1987).

The commissural fibers interconnecting the two cerebral hemispheres (the corpus callosum and the anterior commissure) and the association fibers interconnecting cortical areas of the same hemisphere also exhibit protracted myelination. The corpus callosum begins its myelination at birth in the monkey and at a few months of age in the human, but it is not dark until 1 year of age in the monkey and until middle childhood in humans. Long association fibers such as the cingulum, and the superior and inferior longitudinal fasciculi are extremely protracted in their myelination. They are not dark until 3.5 years of age in the

Table 5. Cortical Myelination (Initial Myelination of Cortical Areas)[a]

	Rhesus monkey birth to 2 years (Gibson, 1970)	Human 1 month–8 years (Conel, 1939–1967)
Layer 6		
Motor cortex	Birth	1 month
Premotor, primary sensory, sensory association	Birth	3 months
Association areas	2–4 weeks	6 months
Layer 4		
Primary sensory	Birth	3 months
Premotor, secondary sensory	1 month	6 months
Association	2–6 months	6–15 months
Layer 2		
Motor	2 months	6 months
Premotor, primary sensory	3–6 months	15–24 months
Secondary sensory	6 months–1 year	24 months–4 years
Association	1–2 years	4–8 years

[a]This table states the ages at which myelin first reaches layers VI, IV, and II in the cortical areas in humans and rhesus monkeys.

monkey and until the second decade of life in the human (Yakovlev and Lecours, 1967).

These data suggest that postnatal myelination in the monkey brain is about three to four times faster than in the human brain (Tables 5 and 6). Thus, the state of myelination in the human brain at 3 months resembles that of the rhesus monkey at birth; myelination in the human brain at 8 to 12 months resembles that of the monkey at 3 months; myelination in the human brain at 15 to 24 months resembles that of the monkey brain at 6 months, and myelination in the human brain at 6 to 8 years resembles that in the monkey brain at 2 years.

Table 6. Initial Myelination of Cortical Areas[a]

Rhesus monkey (Gibson, 1970)	Human (Conel, 1939–1967)
birth	3 months
1 month	6 months
6 months	15–24 months
1 year	4 years
2 years	8 years

[a]This table states the ages at which cortical myelination is roughly equivalent in human and rhesus monkey.

Comparisons between Myelination and Other Developmental Indices

Conel's studies of the human neocortex (1937–1967) reported a close corre-spondence between patterns of myelination and several other neural developmental indices including increasing cell size, dendritic maturation and the appearance of dendritic spines, chromaphile substance and unmyelinated axons. Like my-elination, each of the anatomical parameters exhibited a regional pattern of development, maturing first in the primary areas and inner cortical layers and last in the association areas and outer cortical layers.

PET scan data, which provide indices of cerebral glucose utilization, also suggest a regional pattern of maturation during the first year of life (Chugani and Phelps, 1986; Chugani et al., 1987). In human neonates, glucose utilization is high in the sensorimotor cortex, thalamus, brainstem, and vermis of the cere-bellum. It is low in most areas of the neocortex, the striatum, and the cerebellar hemispheres. During the first 3 postnatal months, glucose utilization rises con-siderably in the striatum, the cerebellar hemispheres and the anterior parietal, temporal, and visual cortices. It rises more slowly in the frontal association and visual association areas to approximately 8 to 9 months of age. Subsequent to the first year of life, glucose utilization rises considerably above that of the adult levels and remains high to 9 years of age before declining to reach adult levels in late adolescence.

Although a number of anatomical and physiological parameters suggest re-gional maturation patterns, recent work on the maturation of rhesus monkey brains suggests that synaptogenesis occurs synchronously throughout the entire cortex (Rakic et al., 1986; Zecevic et al., 1989). This contrast between the simultaneous maturation of synapses and the regional maturation of numerous other factors presents an interesting paradox.

These differences may be genuine, but some words of caution are in order. Although regional patterns of myelination have been reported for both rat (Jacobsen, 1963) and monkey, most evidence for regional myelination comes from the human neocortex. In contrast, the primary evidence for synchronic synaptogenesis derives from studies of rhesus monkeys. As monkey brain matu-ration is compressed, synaptogenesis may appear to be more simultaneous in the monkey brain than it would in the human brain. In addition, observers may use different standards of interpretation. In this paper, birth, 2 weeks, 4 weeks, 8 weeks, and 13 weeks are all interpreted as different ages. In contrast, Rakic et al (1986, Figure 1) interpret regions exhibiting peak synaptogenesis periods of 2 and 4 months as maturing synchronously.

Finally, most studies of myelination report beginning of myelination only, whereas studies of synaptogenesis report the entire cycle of synaptogenesis. Many areas and tracts have prolonged myelination cycles. Although some begin to myelinate in advance of others, they may not complete their myelination prior to onset of myelination in other regions. All cortical areas, for instance, have some myelin before any cortical area is completely myelinated and before slowly

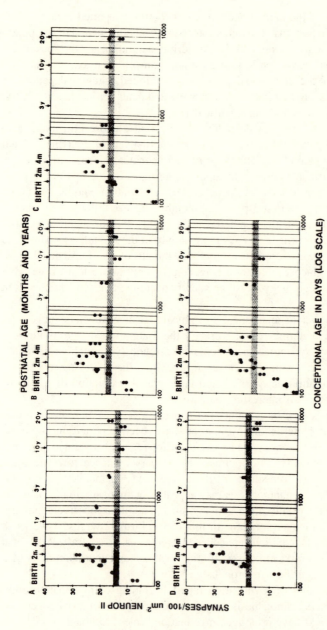

Figure 1. This diagram charts synaptogenesis in the rhesus monkey brain. Note that the density of synapses reaches a peak in motor, somatosensory and prefrontal cortex at 2 months of age and in visual and limbic cortex at 4 months of age, even though synaptogenesis has been described as simultaneous throughout all cortical areas. From P. Ratic, "Concurrent Overproduction of Synapses in Diverse Regions of the Primate Cerebral Cortex." *Science, 232,* 232–35. Copyright © 1986 by AAAS. Reprinted with permission.

myelinating brainstem tracts have completed their myelination. Hence, there is considerable overlap in myelination cycles.

That regional patterns in onset of myelination are genuine rather than reflections of artificial time distinctions is clear, however, when individual brains are examined. Although brains differ from each other in the precise timing of myelination, all brains exhibit similar patterns. In the first months of life, the sensorimotor regions of the monkey cortex are always more darkly myelinated than the frontal and temporal association cortices (see Figure 2). Similar regional variations within individual brains have repeatedly been reported in the human brain (Conel, 1937–1967; Flechsig, 1920; Gilles et al., 1983; Yakovlev and Lecours, 1967).

Reports are lacking for synaptogenesis patterns across individual brains. Rather, reports of synaptogenesis consist of average numbers of synapses over several brains. This is just one of several methodological differences between myelination and synaptogenesis studies. Myelination studies have been qualitative in nature, synaptogenesis studies have been quantitative. Synaptogenesis studies have taken numerous measurements on very few cortical areas. Myelination studies have taken smaller samples over numerous cortical areas. Conel's studies (1937–1967) examined a variety of anatomical variables using techniques more similar to those used in standard myelination studies than to those in the synaptogenesis studies of Rakic's group. This may account for Conel's findings of regional maturation of the human neocortex.

These differences in study technique reflect more than observer preference and, thus, may be difficult to remedy. Myelination and synaptogenesis lend themselves to different modes of study. Myelin is readily observed with the naked eye and with light microscopic techniques, as the presence or absence of myelin can be readily determined by observation of staining intensity. As a consequence, myelination patterns across an entire brain are readily observed. Synaptogenesis, on the other hand, can be studied only through an electron microscope.

Despite these cautions, differences between myelination and synaptogenesis patterns may be genuine. If so, these differences have major implications for the maturation of brain function. Currently, one can only hazard several guesses as to what they might mean based on known properties of myelin and of synapses. Myelination affects speed and specificity of long distance axon impulse transmission. Synaptogenesis reflects the ability for an impulse to be transmitted from one neuron to another. Once myelinated, fibers remain myelinated except in cases of disease. In contrast, many synapses degenerate apparently through functional disuse. One possible interpretation of these differences is that myelination represents established function and functional maturity, whereas synaptogenesis represents functional potential. In addition, as firing patterns and axon transmission are critical for the functional maturation of synapses (Kalil, 1989),

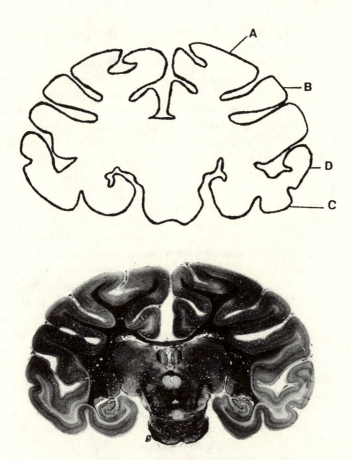

Figure 2. This is a photograph of a cross-section of newborn rhesus monkey brain stained with the Loyez myelin technique. Note that the density of stain varies in differing cortical gyri. Within the superior parietal gyrus (A) and the marginal gyrus (B) the density of stain is already dark at birth. In contrast, the subcortical white matter remains pale in the inferior (C) and middle temporal gyri (D). Note also that in the stained gyri, a narrow, unstained border lies between myelinated fibers and the cortical layers. This narrow region is the last region to myelinate in each cortical gyrus. The age of myelination of this region is termed the gyrus full stage in this manuscript. (From Gibson, 1970).

it is possible that impulse transmission over myelinated fibers plays a critical role in determining which synapses are stimulated and, thus, survive and mature.

Alternatively, as large fibers are more likely to be myelinated than small fibers, regional variations in degree of myelination may reflect regional variations in fiber size, rather than regional variations in functional maturation. Such variations in fiber size would not, however, explain the other regional variations in anatomical maturation described by Conel (1939–1967).

Cross Species Similarities and Differences
in Brain and Behavioral Development

Similarities of Brain and Behavior Developmental Sequence

Cross-species similarities of neural developmental sequence imply cross-species similarities in behavioral development. Behavioral data support this assertion. All mammalian and avian species begin their postnatal life with reflexes and other stereotyped behaviors such as sucking, gaping, pecking, and clinging, which equip them for life in the immediate postnatal environment. In many species, later development involves the inhibition and disappearance of these stereotyped reactions and their replacement by more complex behaviors (Gibson, 1981). Among primates, postnatal development involves the development of complex cognitive abilities. All primates that have been studied exhibit similar cognitive maturational sequences (A. Diamond, this volume; Gibson, 1977, 1981, 1983; Parker, 1977; Parker and Gibson, 1979).

These cognitive developmental similarities seemingly reflect brain–behavioral interactions. Similar cognitive levels mature in both monkeys and humans in synchrony with the myelination of similar neural areas (Gibson, 1977). In most cases, these neural areas plausibly control the behavioral traits in question. In early infancy, for instance, humans exhibit many seemingly complex behaviors such as reaching and grasping, which, when carefully examined, appear to be organized in a manner similar to the behavioral patterns of species with little or no neocortex. These early behaviors are holistic and stereotyped in form. They cannot be broken into component parts or combined with other behaviors to yield more complex behavioral patterns. Thus, many of these behaviors may be primarily controlled by subcortical structures such as the tectum (Gibson, 1981). During this period, the human cortex is, in fact, unmyelinated, but many subcortical processing areas contain considerable myelin. In addition, PET scan data indicate high levels of glucose utilization in the brainstem, but low levels in the neocortex (Chugani et al., 1987).

With the beginning of myelination in the primary motor and sensory areas, many of these early behaviors disappear. Both monkey and human then experience a period in which most of their behaviors involve only one body part or one sensory modality at a time. They may, for instance, follow objects with the eyes, but not attempt to grasp them or grasp, but not look (Parker, 1977; Piaget, 1952). These behaviors may reflect the functioning of the primary cortical areas (Gibson, 1977). These areas are sensory specific and their neuronal receptive fields respond to very discrete stimuli (Hubel and Wiesel, 1968; Mountcastle, 1978).

With the myelination of secondary sensory and premotor areas, infant monkeys and humans begin to coordinate movements of differing body parts and perceptions of differing sensory modalities (e.g., putting fingers in the mouth, handling and viewing objects simultaneously). These behaviors may reflect the functioning of the secondary areas (Gibson, 1977). Neurons in these areas have large receptive fields and tend to respond to complex stimuli (Duffy and Busch-fiel, 1971; Gross et al., 1972). Clinical data also suggest that these areas function to synthesize diverse perceptions into larger wholes (Luria, 1966).

Advanced sensorimotor intelligence, as defined by Piaget (1952), emerges at the same time the neocortical association areas begin to myelinate (Gibson, 1977). These areas are considered to mediate the highest cognitive functions (Luria, 1966).

From the age of 3 to 6 months in the monkey and from the age of 1 to 2 years in the human, all cortical areas and most cortical layers are myelinated to some degree (Conel, 1939–1967; Gibson, 1970). According to PET scan data, all cortical areas in the human neocortex also exhibit high degrees of glucose utilization by 1 year (Chugani et al., 1987). Thus, all cortical areas are probably functional between 1 and 2 years of life in the human and between 3 and 6 months in the monkey. Cortical maturation from that point on involves increasing efficiency or complexity of function of areas that are already functioning at least in rudimentary form by late infancy. All cortical areas continue to gain myelin subsequent to late infancy, but the most dramatic changes in myelination occur in the cortical association areas. The upper layers of the cortical association areas do not begin to myelinate until 4 to 8 years of age and emerge as prime candidates for the mediation of maturing intelligence in childhood.

These points are of interest from the standpoint of the work of Case (1985). According to Case, maturing intelligence in human children from the age of 2 years depends primarily on increases in information processing capacity. Specifically, as children mature they can hold more concepts in mind simultaneously, and they can organize conceptual hierarchies composed of larger numbers of subconcepts. Maturing intelligence becomes, in large part, a matter of increasing capacity to store and synthesize large quantities of information.

Case has proposed that myelination is critical in the development of these conceptual skills because it permits greater speed and efficiency of information transmission. That the cortical areas exhibiting the greatest amount of myelination in later childhood are the association areas is also a critical point. Long ago, Luria (1966) proposed on the basis of clinical data that the cortical association areas focus to synthesize diverse information into new synthetic wholes. Thus, the myelination data and the behavioral data are in accord in terms of the developing abilities of later childhood.

Differences in Brain-Behavior Developmental Rates

Within hours of emerging from the womb, many mammals can swim, walk, or run with their parental group. Included among these precocial species are dolphins, whales, ungulates, elephants, and guinea pigs. Other mammals such as cats, dogs, mice, and rats are altricial. At birth they are so lacking in locomotor skills, they must be cached in nests or dens—sometimes for weeks or months.

Physical distinctions mirror these behavioral divergences. Precocial species are born with body hair, mature temperature regulation, and well–developed visual and motor capacities. Nestlings are usually hairless and rendered functionally blind and deaf by closed eyes and auditory canals. At birth, their behavioral skills may consist of little more than a few protective and suckling reflexes (Portmann, 1967). Life style influences these neonatal distinctions. Mammals born into a migratory herd must keep pace with the social group. Should they lag behind, they succumb to predators. By comparison, the nestling state is a luxury condition afforded only to neonates whose parents occupy a definitive home range and can return repeatedly to a central location (Ewer, 1968).

Most altricial forms fall within the classification of r-selected species. These species have short life spans and minimal brain size and intelligence. In r-selected forms, parents give birth to several immature young at a time. The young grow rapidly after birth and reach adulthood quickly. Hence, little parental investment occurs either prenatally or postnatally, and the young have little time for learning before achieving self-sufficiency. In consequence, prereproductive mortality is high with the opportunistic survival of only a few (Wilson, 1975).

By contrast, most precocial species are K-selected. These species give birth to one or two young at a time, but provide each with intensive pre- and postnatal care. Life span is long, brain size is large, and intelligence is high. Although born relatively mature, the young grow slowly after birth. Much time exists for intensive postnatal learning before achieving self-sufficiency. In consequence, prereproductive mortality is comparatively low. Higher primates including humans have most of the characteristics of K-selected precocial species. They are intelligent, long lived, and large brained. Primate postnatal maturation is protracted, and parental investment is high. Based on these parameters, the human is among the most K-selected of any species. Hence, on theoretical grounds, one would expect primate and human brains to be precocial.

Higher primates including humans, however, lack locomotor skills at birth. Although monkeys and apes compensate for this lack by clinging to maternal fur, human neonates must be cached in nests or carried. Because of this locomotor immaturity, neonatal monkeys and humans are often considered neurologically altricial. Delayed locomotor development, however, may reflect factors other than delayed brain development. In most mammals, limb movements are primarily controlled by brainstem mechanisms. Among higher primates, the neocortex mediates movements of the hands and limbs. Thus, cortical brain damage in humans, but not necessarily in other mammals, results in permanent paralysis. Differential timing of locomotor development could well reflect this differential cortical control of limb movements rather than differential rates of brain development.

Other behavioral data support the view that primates, including humans, are relatively precocial in comparison to other mammals. A host of survival–promoting reflexes equip all primate neonates for life in the extrauterine environment including, among others, sucking, rooting, tactile grasping, startle, micturition, and defecation. Humans are no exception. They are born with many well-functioning reflexes and a motor system that is very mature by comparison to that of most altricial mammals (Portmann, 1967). Human infants are more than mere reflex machines, however. Some infantile reflexes are subject to conditioning and learning from birth, and many other complex behaviors are present neonatally. Within hours or days after birth, the human neonate can discriminate phonetic sounds (Eimas, 1985) and turn his head toward the source of a sound (Butterworth and Castillo, 1976; Wertheimer, 1961). Perhaps more surprisingly, within the first weeks, infants can reach and grasp for objects presented in the visual or auditory mode (Bower et al., 1970; Bower, 1972, 1974; Wishart et al., 1978), imitate simple facial expressions (Meltzoff and Moore, 1977), and raise their hands in a seemingly protective response to a looming object (Ball and Vurpillot, 1981).

Anatomical data support the view that primates are neurologically precocial. Like precocial forms, monkeys, apes, and humans are born with body hair and with open eyes and ears. Comparative studies show that neural altriciality and precociality correlate with state of myelination at birth (Gibson, 1970; Kretschman, 1967; Schifferli, 1948; Table 7). The brains of newborn precocial mammals and birds such as guinea pigs, sheep and white leghorn hens are well myelinated at birth. Those of altricial neonates such as starlings, rats, and albino mice are unmyelinated. Neonatal monkey brains are heavily myelinated, like those of precocial species. Neonatal human brains are intermediate in state of myelination between those of altricial and precocial forms.

In Portmann's scheme, any mammal or bird which has achieved more than 20% of its adult brain size by birth is neurologically precocial (Portmann, 1967; Table 8). By these standards, monkeys and apes are precocious, and the human is semiprecocious or intermediate in its state of development at birth. Most monkeys and apes have achieved 25 to 50% of their final adult brain size by birth. The human has achieved approximately 25% (Sacher and Staffeldt, 1974). The neonatal rhesus monkey which has acquired 68% of its final brain size is among the most precocial of all mammals. Sacher and Staffeldt (1974), for instance, provide tables of brain size at birth for over a hundred species. Only four exceed the rhesus monkey in terms of percent brain size completed at birth.

Histological and physiological measures of neural maturity yield similar results. Cortical synaptogenesis is an entirely postnatal event in altricial rats (Bloom and Aghajanian, 1968), but begins several months prenatally in both rhesus monkey and human (Huttenlocher, 1979; Rakic et al., 1986). Similarly, EEG activity begins prior to birth in the human, but subsequent to birth in altricial forms such as mice, rats, cats, and dogs (Ellingson and Rose, 1970).

Many precocial and altricial animals reach full physical maturity within weeks or months after birth (Gould, 1977). Primates, however, exhibit more prolonged maturation rates. The rhesus monkey brain, for instance, is still myelinating at

Table 7. State of Myelination at Birth[a]

Species	Reference
No Myelin	
Rat	Jacobsen (1963)
Rabbit	Langworthy (1926)
Albino mouse	Kretschman (1967)
Opossum	Langworthy (1928)
Very few myelinated fibers	
Dog	Clark (1968); Fox, (1971)
Cat	Langworthy (1920); Tilney and Casamajor (1924); Windle et al. (1934)
Starling	Schifferli (1948)
Moderate myelin	
Human	Keene and Hewer, (1931, 1933); Yakovlev and Lecours (1967); Flechsig (1920); Langworthy (1933); Rorke and Riggs (1969); Gilles et al. (1982)
Cretan spiny mouse	Kretschman (1967)
Heavy myelin	
Monkey	Gibson (1970)
White leghorn hen	Schifferli (1948)
Virtually adult state of myelination	
Guinea pig	Martin (1962)
Sheep	Romanes (1947)

[a]From Gibson (1970).

3.5 years of age (the oldest age studied from the perspective of myelination, Gibson, 1970). Full physical maturity in adult male rhesus monkeys is achieved several years later (Watts, 1986).

Our closest relatives, the great apes (chimpanzee, gorilla, and orangutan) mature over a much longer period than the rhesus monkey. They nurse for 4 to 6 years. In the wild, chimpanzee females reach menarche at about 11 years of age and give birth to their first infants 2 to 3 years later. Orangutans give birth to their first infants at about 15 years of age. Male chimpanzees do not acquire their full adult size and weight until their late teenage years. Orangutan males do not reach full physical maturity until their early twenties (Galdikas, 1981, 1982, 1985; Goodall, 1973, 1986, Tuttle, 1987). These data suggest that when postnatal neural maturation data are available for the apes, brain development, like other maturational patterns, will prove to be prolonged.

Although, myelination data have not yet been provided for any of the great

Table 8.   Representative Postnatal Brain Size Increases[a]

Precocial		Intermediate	Altricial	
Less than 2 times	2–3 times	3–5 times	5–12 times	12 times
Guinea pig	Noctule bats	Porcupine	Lion (5)	Brown bear (58)
	Long nosed bats		House cat (5.8)	Polar bear (47)
Llama		Wild boar	Tiger (10)	
Zebra	Nutria		Dog (10)	
	Chincilla	Some deer	Red fox (10)	
Fur seal	Beaver			
		Lynx	Tree shrew (6)	
Rhesus monkey	European hare	Gray fox	Hedge hog (11)	
Colobine monkey				
Howler monkey	Elephant	Human	European rabbit (7.6)	
Gibbon				
Gorilla				
	Most deer		Mice (9–10)	
	Antelope		Rats (9–10)	
			Squirrel (10)	
	Dolphin			
	Galago			
	Ring tailed lemur			
	Some macaques			
	Baboons			
	Cebus monkey			
	Chimpanzee			
	Orangutan			

[a]From Portmann (1967) and Sacher and Staffeldt (1974).

apes, Russon has recently summarized cognitive development for rhesus monkeys, apes, and humans (Russon, 1988, 1990). Her comparisons of rhesus and humans are of interest from the standpoint of the myelination data presented in Tables 5 and 6. Just as humans take about three to four times as long as rhesus monkeys to mature in terms of myelination patterns, they also take about three to four times as long to mature on cognitive measures. Thus, behavioral and neurological measures provide very similar estimates of comparative maturation rates in the two species. Russon's comparisons indicate that the developmental time frames for sensorimotor intelligence in the great apes are closer to those of the human than to those of the rhesus monkey. Thus, on cognitive measures, humans at 8 to 12 months resemble chimpanzees at 6 to 10 months; humans at age 12 to 14 months resemble chimpanzees at about 10 months. In other words, great apes, like humans exhibit prolonged postnatal cognitive development.

Qualitative Differences in Human and Ape Behavioral Development

In some respects human behavioral development is qualitatively different from that of the apes (Gibson, 1990 a, b). By six weeks of age, humans exhibit a spontaneous social smile. By four to six months of age, they babble. Apes never exhibit these behaviors. By the end of their first year, humans spontaneously group two or more objects into logical classes and/or use one object to causally manipulate another (Langer, 1980). Apes eventually engage in these behaviors, but they rarely do so in the first year of life.

These distinctive behaviors of the human infant serve as precursors to language, tool use and higher cognitive skills. In other words, they help to canalize human cognitive and linguistic development (Gibson, 1990 a, b). The existence of these infantile behaviors may partially account for one idiosyncratic aspect of ape-human differences in developmental timing. Although apes mature more rapidly than humans, on some cognitive measures ape development is slower and less certain than human development. Specifically, chimpanzees and orangutans raised in human homes and subject to extensive training develop tool using, block building, and other object construction skills at a later age than human children (Gibson, personal observations; Morell, 1985; Mignault, 1985; Miles, 1986; Russon, 1988; 1990); Vauclair and Bard, 1983). Language trained apes acquire signs more slowly than human children (Savage-Rumbaugh and Rumbaugh, 1990).

Human Cognition - Neural Structure versus Neural Maturation

Several competing hypotheses attempt to explain the neurological bases of human intellectual and linguistic capacities. Most authors consider the critical neurological differences between apes and humans to be structural in nature. In their view, human capacities result from the greatly increased human brain size (1200 to 1300 cm^3 as compared to 300 to 400 cm^3 in great apes) (Gibson, 1988; Jerison, 1973; Keith, 1948), or from a structural reorganization of the human brain (Holloway, 1966). More recently, Ragir (1986, 1989) has proposed that human cognition and language result from delayed neural maturation rather than from structural differences between ape and human brains.

Comparative neuroontogenetic data suggest that structural rather than maturational variables are the primary determinants of ape–human cognitive differences. If human language and manipulative skills reflect neural altriciality (Gould, 1977; Rader, 1985), they must reflect the functioning of neural structures which are mature at birth in apes and monkeys but not in humans. Essentially, only the lower layers of the motor and sensory cortices are myelinated in the newborn rhesus monkey, but not in the human newborn. All other cortical areas and layers myelinate postnatally in the monkey, as well as in the human (Tables 2–5; Gibson, 1970). Thus, the areas most concerned with higher intelligence develop postnatally in monkeys just as they do in humans.

Unfortunately, no myelination data exist for our closest phylogenetic kin, the great apes. Data on epiphyseal closure, however, indicate that the chimpanzee is skeletally less mature at birth than the rhesus monkey (Watts, 1986). Chimpanzees are clearly intermediate between rhesus monkeys and humans in terms of the percentage of adult brain size reached by birth. Estimates for rhesus monkey brain maturity at birth range from 48 to 68% of final adult size (Sacher and Staffeldt, 1974). Estimates for humans range from 25 to 29% and those for chimpanzees from 36 to 46% (Table 9). Since state of myelination at birth correlates with percentage of adult brain size acquired, chimpanzees would also be expected to exhibit neonatal myelination states approximately half way between those of rhesus monkeys and humans. If human brains at 3 months of age exhibit myelination states equivalent to those of newborn rhesus brains, then human brains at 1.5 to 2 months would be expected to be as well myelinated as those of newborn chimps.

If this estimate is correct, the difference in neural maturity between the average human newborn and the average chimpanzee newborn may be within the range of variation of neonatal maturity that exists within the human species. Behavioral data support this view. The performance of newborn apes on Brazelton scales of neonatal maturity is somewhat advanced by comparison to that of the *average* human newborn, but within the range of variation exhibited by the human species (Bard et al., 1988, Redshaw, 1989).

If neonatal altriciality plays a critical role in language development, it does so by altering behavioral and developmental conditions in the first few weeks of life, particularly those developmental conditions impinging on the maturation of the primary sensory and motor areas. Although early postnatal linguistic stimulation may be critical for the maturation of auditory feature detectors and/or for the ability to detect language specific phonemes, this seems unlikely (Gibson, 1990 a,b). Humans are born with the ability to differentiate phonetic sounds (Eimas, 1985). Human children reared by deaf parents develop speech despite minimal exposure during infancy, and children readily learn the sounds of foreign languages as late as 10 or 11 years (Lenneberg, 1967).

Actually, most human infants do very little in the first weeks of postnatal life other than sleep and suckle. By 4 to 6 months when humans are actively cooing,

Table 9.   Neonatal Brain Size[a]

Baboon	Macaque	Chimpanzee	Human
40.98	68.56	46	29.33
29.61	48.13	35.56	25.33

[a] Variations in reports of neonatal brain size as a percentage of adult brain size. Data from Sacher and Staffeldt (1979).

babbling, and engaging in other behaviors that clearly facilitate language and tool use, they are already approximately as mature as rhesus newborns in terms of neural myelination. Given the relative inactivity of human newborns, the moderate differences in neonatal neural maturity between monkey and human, and the extreme neonatal altriciality of rats, mice, and dogs, none of whom displays language or unusual intelligence, the evidence that neonatal altriciality is a primary determinate of linguistic and intellectual development appears extremely weak.

Nor do differences in postnatal maturation rates appear to be primary determinants of cognitive differences. Both apes and humans exhibit developmental lability. In human populations, mean age of menarche varies from 12 to 16 years depending on environmental conditions. Normal individuals may experience menarche at 10 years or younger. In chimpanzees, mean age of menarche varies from 8 in captive populations to 11 + in the wild (Goodall, 1986). These population variations in maturational rates have no known cognitive or linguistic consequences. Humans who experience menarche at 10 years have greater linguistic facility than chimps who experience it at 11. Factors other than maturational rates must be active: i.e., brain size and/or brain structure.

Neoteny versus Neural Maturation as Determinants of Human Abilities

Perhaps the most extreme variant of the maturational hypothesis is the neoteny hypothesis which holds that humans are both slow to develop and permanently pedomorphic (infantile) in neural form and function (Gould, 1977). On neurological grounds this hypothesis is clearly false. There is nothing pedomorphic about the adult human brain (Gibson, in press). Initially, the fetal brains of all mammals have smooth cortical surfaces (Goldman-Rakic and Rakic, 1984). Gyri and fissures develop later. Adult humans have the most highly fissurated brains of any primates (LeGros Clark, 1959). Early in development mammalian neocortices have a high ratio of neurons to neuronal connections and glial cells. Later, this condition reverses; the ratio of cellular connections to neurons becomes very high. The adult human neocortex has the highest ratio of connections to neurons of any primate brain (Holloway, 1966). In infantile mammals, the neocortex contains little myelin. Cortical dendrites display a simple morphology (Jacobsen, 1978; Scheibel, this volume). The adult human cortex contains considerable myelin and possesses a complex synaptic morphology.

The neoteny hypothesis derives its major impetus from the views that human learning capacities require neural plasticity and that only young animals possess this plasticity (Gould, 1977; Lerner, 1984). This view is erroneous. Adult monkeys (Merzenich and Kaas, 1982) and very old rats (M. Diamond, this volume) exhibit neural plasticity and learning skills. Not only is there no need to postulate neoteny to account for human learning abilities, it is highly probable that mature primate and human brains exhibit more intellectual capacity than immature brains. Mature brains have fully developed association cortices; they are well myelinated and they possess complex dendritic morphology. Neural function, particularly the function of the association regions, should be more efficient in maturity than in infancy or childhood.

That pedomorphy is not the primary determinant of human learning skills is also evident from a comparison of adult versus infant learning styles. The learning abilities of human and primate adults are qualitatively different from and require much more cognitive capacity than the learning abilities of infants (Case, 1985). In infantile animals, like infantile humans, learning is primarily a matter of conditioning and of the sharpening of innate perceptual and motor skills. The human infant, for instance, can improve its sucking or reaching skills and learn to differentiate faces and voices (Bower, 1974), just as a newly hatched laughing gull can improve its pecking efficiency and learn to differentiate the maternal bill from other objects (Hailman, 1964). Older primates and humans, however, apply more sophisticated cognitive systems to their learning endeavors. They are better able to analyze and synthesize complex information and more capable of abstract thought (Case, 1985; Inhelder and Piaget, 1958, Parker and Gibson, 1979). Thus, they can master complex activities such as hunting, gathering, taking care of infants, drawing, writing, fractions, decimals, or algebra, none of which can be learned by conditioning processes alone.

As no infantile monkey, ape, or human has ever demonstrated such cognitive skills, neoteny or permanent neural immaturity would not seem to account for them. Other factors, such as brain size or brain organization must play critical roles in the differential linguistic, tool-using, and intellectual skills of apes and humans.

Brain Size and Brain Maturation Rates

Although delayed maturation is not the primary determinant of human cognitive skills, a relationship clearly exists between the two: brain size serves as an intervening variable. Among mammals and birds, brain size and body size correlate with maturation rate (Sacher and Staffeldt, 1974). The reasons for this correlation are poorly understood but may relate to metabolic conditions. Large brains are extremely metabolically expensive (Armstrong, 1983; Gibson, 1986; Martin, 1982, Parker, 1990). The adult human brain uses 20% of the oxygen consumed by the human body (Armstrong, 1983). During periods of fetal and postnatal growth, the demands of the brain for fats, proteins, and other nutrients are especially high (Morgan and Gibson, this volume). During the first year of human life, 65% of the total metabolic rate is devoted to the brain in contrast to 9% devoted to muscle tissue (Holliday, 1978). Thus, serious malnutrition delays brain growth and results in reduced brain size. Similarly, body growth and brain growth accelerate in modern well-nourished human societies in comparison to other groups.

This dependence of enlarged brains on ample nutrient supplies may favor extended maturational periods. With prolonged maturation, more nutrients can be obtained during the period of growth and more total neural growth supported. In addition, if brain growth is slow, the rate at which nutrients must be absorbed and metabolized to support brain growth will also be slow. Thus, delayed maturation may increase the probability and ease of obtaining the necessary quantity of nutrients during the period of growth and provide a time-related growth buffer against the potentially damaging effects of temporary food deficits.

Culture and Bipedalism as Determinants of Infantile and Childhood Dependency

Although humans are anatomically and neurologically semiprecocial, they are often considered behaviorally altricial because of their locomotor incapacity and their extreme dependence on maternal care. The paradox of neurological precocity coupled with behavioral altriciality is readily resolved by considering the effects of culture, bipedalism, and hairlessness.

Both ape and human neonates are behaviorally dependent. A newborn chimpanzee weighs less than five pounds and requires round-the-clock contact with the maternal body for months for birth (Goodall, 1986). The human infant appears less capable than the ape. Ape infants cling to maternal fur, but human infants must be carried. This difference reflects bipedalism and hairlessness not state of maturation at birth. The neonatal human nervous system is sufficiently mature that human neonates possess a grasping reflex and can support their body weight with their own hands. Ape infants, however, can cling with two hands and two feet; ape mothers possess long, clingable body hair, and ape neonates can suspend themselves in a gravitationally favorable position beneath the maternal abdomen. Humans have only two grasping appendages. Human mothers have no body hair, and human mothers walk upright rendering it difficult even for ape infants to support their body weight by clinging to human clothes. The easiest way for a human surrogate mother to transport an infant chimpanzee is to carry it in a sling made for human infants (Gibson, personal observations).

The dependency fostering effects of bipedalism are augmented by many cultural practices. In modern industrial societies, cultural conventions have led to many infants being fed prepared formulas from sterilized bottles, weaned on specially prepared baby foods, dressed in clean and well-pressed clothes, placed in cribs with well-laundered blankets, taken to physicians for check-ups and vaccinations, carefully strapped into car seats for long trips, and laboriously trained to use toilets and bathtubs. When these manifestations of modern human mothering are compared to chimpanzee mothering, it is easy to conclude that chimpanzee infants require less care.

Not all human cultures turn child rearing into such a complex endeavor. Some hunting and gathering cultures are content to nurse their infants, to carry them in a sling, and to leave them unclothed (Konner, 1976). Under such circumstances, except for preparing and cleaning the sling, the human infant requires no more care than the chimpanzee infant.

The extent to which culture intervenes to render infant care more complex than actually demanded by the state of infantile neural maturity is obvious from the treatment of chimpanzees raised in human homes. Although no evidence suggests that such chimps are more altricial than chimps born and raised in the wild, home-reared chimps receive at least as much maternal care as human babies. They are diapered, fed formulas from sterilized bottles, taken to pediatricians, strapped in car seats, dressed, blanketed, and toilet-trained. In other words, when raised under similar cultural circumstances, chimpanzee infants are every bit as "altricial" as human infants.

Comparing the care required by human infants in industrial societies with the care required by chimpanzee infants in the wild is not a scientifically valid way to determine maturational rates or levels. The best estimates of maturity at birth are anatomical and physiological. By these measures, the human infant is born in a somewhat less mature state than other primates, but it is still neurologically semiprecocial by comparison to other mammals. The extreme dependency of human infants raised under modern cultural conditions tells us nothing about the neural plasticity or learning capacities of human newborns as compared to ape newborns.

Similarly, humans differ from most apes in requiring years of parental provisioning subsequent to weaning. This also reflects cultural practices. One ape population does provision its young after weaning, that of the Tai Forest, Ivory Coast. This population acquires a major portion of its food through tool use. The young take many years to acquire tool-using skills and must be provisioned until they do so (Boesch and Boesch, 1990). All human societies depend on complex tool-using or economic endeavors. Human young must be supported until they master these tasks. Apes raised in human homes never master them and remain dependent throughout their lives. The period of postnatal dependency, like the degree of neonatal dependency, reflects cultural practices as much as it reflects maturational rates.

Summary

This chapter compares myelination and other neural maturational parameters in humans, rhesus monkeys, and other animals. Sequences of myelination are similar across species and nearly identical in rhesus monkey and human. In contrast, the timing of myelination varies dramatically across species. In comparison with other animals, the newborn rhesus monkey is highly precocial and the newborn human is semiprecocial, both in terms of the percentage of adult brain size achieved by birth and in terms of the state of neural myelination at birth. In terms of the percentage of adult brain size achieved at birth, the chimpanzee is intermediate between the rhesus monkey and the human. Hence, on neural measures the human newborn is not as immature as is sometimes assumed. In fact, by 3 months of age the human newborn is about as mature in terms of myelination patterns as the newborn rhesus monkey.

Postnatal brain myelination proceeds about three to four times as rapidly in the human as in the rhesus monkey. No data exist for myelination in the great apes. On behavioral and physical measures, however, apes mature much more slowly than the rhesus monkey, albeit not as slowly as the human. These and other considerations indicate that the hypothesis that human intelligence derives from neural immaturity at birth and/or from a lingering neural immaturity (neoteny) into adulthood is in error. Increased human intelligence must relate to other factors such as increased brain size or differential neural organization. The increased dependence of human offspring on their parents reflects bipedalism and cultural practices more than it reflects physical maturation rates.

References

Armstrong, E. (1983). Relative brain size in mammals. *Science*, *220*, 1302–1304.

Ball, W., and Vurpillot, E. (1981). Action and the perception of displacement in infancy. In G. Butterworth (Ed.), *Infancy and epistemology* (pp. 115–136). Brighton, England: Harvester Press.

Bard, K., Platzman, K. A., and Suomi, S. J. (1988). "Neurobehavioral responsiveness in neonatal chimpanzees: Orientation to animate and inanimate stimuli." Paper presented at the XIIth Congress of the International Primatological Society, Brasilia, Brasil: July 24–29.

Bertrand, I. (1930). *Techniques histologues de neuropathologie*. Paris: Masson et cie, pp. 131–133.

Bloom, F. E., and Aghajanian, G. K. (1968). Fine structural and cytochemical analysis of the staining of synaptic junctions with phosphotungstic acid. *Journal of Ultrastructural Research*, *22*, 361–375.

Boesch, C., and Boesch, H. (1990). "Transmission aspects of tool use in wild chimpanzees." Paper presented at the Wenner Gren Foundation for Anthropological Research Conference, Tools, language and intelligence: Evolutionary implications, Cascais, Portugal: March, 1990.

Bower, T. G. R. (1972). Object perception in infancy. *Perception*, *1*, 15–30.

Bower, T. G. R. (1974). *Development in infancy*. New York: W. H. Freeman.

Bower, T. G. R., Broughton, J. M., and Moore, M. K. (1970). Demonstration of intention in the reaching behavior of neonate humans. *Nature (London)*, *228*, 679–681.

Butterworth, G. (1981). *Infancy and epistemology*. Brighton, England: The Harvester Press.

Butterworth, G., and Castillo, M. (1976). Coordination of auditory and visual space in new born human infants. *Perception*, *5*, 155–160.

Case, R. (1985). *Intellectual development: Birth to adulthood*. London: Academic Press.

58   Kathleen R. Gibson

Churgani, H. T., and Phelps, M. E. (1986). Maturational changes in cerebral function in
    infants determined by [8]FDG positron emission tomography. *Science*, *231*, 840–
    843.
Churgani, H. T., Phelps, M. E., and Mazziotta, J. C. (1987). Positron emission tomogra-
    phy study of human brain functional development. *Annals of Neurology*, *22*, (4),
    487–497.
Clark, R. (1968). Postnatal myelinization of the central nervous system of the beagle dog.
    Anatomical Record, *160*, 331.
Conel, J. L. (1939–1967). *The postnatal development of the human cerebral cortex*, Vols
    1–8. Cambridge, MA: Harvard University Press.
Duffy, F. H., and Buschfiel, J. L. (1971). Somatosensory system: Organizational hier-
    archy from single units in monkey area 5. *Science*, *172*, 273–275.
Eimas, P. (1985). The perception of speech in early infancy. *Scientific American*, *252*,
    46–53.
Ellingson, R. J., and Rose, G. H. (1970). Ontogenesis of the electroencephalogram. In
    W. A. Himwich (Ed.), *Developmental neurobiology* (pp. 441–474). Springfield,
    MA: Charles Thomas.
Ewer, R. F. (1968). *Ethology of mammals*. London: Elek Science.
Fisher, H. E. (1982). *The sex contract: The evolution of human behavior*. New York:
    Morrow.
Flechsig, P. (1920). *Anatomie des Menschlichen Gehirns und Rückenmarks auf my-
    elogenetishcher Grundlage*. Liepzig: George Thomas.
Fox, M. W. (1971). *Integrative development of brain and behavior in the dog*. Chicago:
    University of Chicago Press.
Galdikas, B. M. F. (1981). Orangutan reproduction in the wild. In C. E. Graham (Ed.),
    Reproductive behavior of the great apes (pp. 281–300). New York: Academic Press.
Galdikas, B. M. F. (1982). Wild orangutan births at Tanjung Puting. *Primates*, *23*, 500–
    510.
Galdikas, B. M. F. (1985). Subadult male orangutan sociality: Reproductive behavior at
    Tanjung Puting. *American Journal of Primatology*, *8*, 87–99.
Gibson, K. R. (1970). Sequence of myelinization in the brain of "*Macaca mulatta*."
    Ph.D. Dissertation, University of California, Berkeley.
Gibson, K. R. (1977). Brain structure and intelligence in macaques and human infants
    from a Piagetian perspective. In S. Chevalier-Skolnikoff and F. Poirer (Eds.),
    Primate biosocial development (pp. 113–157). New York: Garland Press.
Gibson, K. R. (1981). Comparative neuroontogeny; its implications for the development
    of human intelligence. In G. Butterworth (Ed.), *Infancy and epistemology* (pp. 52–
    83). Brighton, England: Harvester Press.
Gibson, K. R. (1983). Comparative neurobehavioral ontogeny and the constructionist
    approach to the evolution of the brain, object manipulation and language. In E. De
    Grolier (Ed.), *Glossogenetics: The origin and evolution of language* (pp. 37–61).
    Paris: Harwood Academic Press.
Gibson, K. R. (1986). Cognition, brain size and the extraction of embedded food
    resources. In J. Else and P. C. Lee (Eds.), *Primate ontogeny, cognition and social
    behavior* (pp. 93–105). England: Cambridge University Press.
Gibson, K. R. (1988). Brain size and the genesis of language. In M. Landsberg (Ed.),
    Language origins (pp. 149–172). The Hague: Mouton Press.

Gibson, K. R. (1990a). New perspectives on instincts and intelligence: Brain size and the emergence of hierarchical mental constructional skills. In S. T. Parker and K. R. Gibson (Eds.), *Language and intelligence in monkeys and apes: Comparative developmental perspectives* (pp. 97–128). Cambridge: Cambridge University Press.

Gibson, K. R. (1990b). "Tool use, language and social behavior - in relationship to information processing capacities." Paper presented at the Wenner Gren Foundation for Anthropological Research conference, Tools, language and intelligence: Evolutionary implications, Cascais Portugal: March, 1990.

Gibson, K. R. (In press). The ontogeny and evolution of the brain, cognition and language. In A. Lock and C. Peters (Eds.), *Handbook of symbolic intelligence*, Oxford: Oxford University Press.

Gilles, F. H., Leviton, A., and Dooling, E. C. (1983). *The developing human brain: Growth and epidemiologic neuropathology*. Boston: John Wright/PSG.

Goldman-Rakic, P. S., and Rakic, P. (1984). Experimental modification of gyral patterns. In N. Geschwind and A. Galaburda (Eds.), *Cerebral dominance* (pp. 179–192). Cambridge, MA: Harvard University Press.

Goodall, J. (1986). *The chimpanzees of Gombe: Patterns of behavior*. Cambridge, MA: Harvard University Press.

Goodall, J., van Lawick (1973). The behavior of chimpanzees in their natural habitat. *American Journal of Psychiatry, 130*, 1–12.

Gould, S. J. (1977). *Ontogeny and phylogeny*. Cambridge, MA: Harvard University Press.

Gross, C. G., Roche-Miranda, C. E., and Bender, D. B. (1972). Visual properties of neurons in the inferotemporal cortex of the macaque. *Journal of Neurophysiology, 35*, 96–111.

Hailman, J. (1964). How an instinct is learned. *Scientific American, 221*, 98–108.

Holliday, M. A. (1978). Body composition and energy needs during growth. In F. Falkner and J. M. Tanner (Eds.), *Human growth* (Vol. 2, pp. 117–139). New York: Plenum Press.

Holloway, R. L. (1966). Cranial capacity, neural reorganization, and hominid evolution: A search for more suitable parameters. *American Anthropologist, 68*, 103–121.

Hubel, D. H., and Wiesel, T. N. (1968). Receptive fields and functional architecture of monkey striate cortex. *Journal of Physiology, 195*, 215–243.

Huttenlocher, P. R. (1978). Synaptic density in human frontal cortex—developmental changes and effects of aging. *Brain Research, 163*, 195–205.

Inhelder, B., and Piaget, J. (1958). *The growth of logical thinking from childhood to adolescence*. New York: Basic Books.

Jacobsen, S. (1963). Sequence of myelinization in the brain of the albino rat: A. cerebral cortex, thalamus and related structures. *Journal of Comparative Neurology, 121*, 5–29.

Jacobson, M. (1978). *Developmental neurobiology*. New York: Plenum Press.

Jerison, H. J. (1973). *Evolution of the brain and intelligence*. New York: Academic Press.

Kalil, R. E. (1989). Synapse formation in the developing brain. *Scientific American, 261* (6), 76–85.

Keene, M. I. L., and Hewer, E. E. (1931). Some observations on myelinization in the human central nervous system. *Journal of Anatomy, 66*, 1–13.

Keene, M. I. L., and Hewer, E. E. (1933). The development and myelinization of the posterior longitudinal bundle in the human. *Journal of Anatomy, 67*, 527–536.

Keith, A. (1948). *A new theory of human evolution*. London: Watts.

Konner, M. (1976). Maternal care, infant behavior and development among the !Kung. In R. B. Lee and I. DeVore (Eds.), *Kalahari hunter-gatherers* (pp. 218–245). Cambridge, MA: Harvard University Press.

Kreht, S. (1940). Die markhaltigen Fasersystem im Gehirn der Anuren und Urodelen und ihre Myelogenie zugleich ein kritischer Beitrag zu den Flechsigschen myelogenetische. *Zeitchronik mikroskopie und Anatomische Forschung, 48*, 108–180.

Kretschman, H. J. (1967). Die Myelinogenese eines Nestflüchters (Acomys cahirnes minous, Bate, 1906) im Vergleich zu der Nesthockers (Albinomaus). *Journal für Hirnforschung, 9*, 373–396.

Krieg, W. J. S. (1963). *Connections of the cerebral cortex*. Evanston, IL: Brain Books.

Lancaster, J. B. (1985). Evolutionary perspectives on sex differences in the higher primates. In A. Rossi, (Ed.), *Gender and the life course* (pp. 3–25). New York: Aldine.

Lancaster, J. B., and Lancaster, C. (1983). Parental investment and the hominid adaptation. In D. Ortner (Ed.), *How humans adapt: A biocultural odyssey* (pp. 33–56). Washington, D.C.: Smithsonian Institution Press.

Langer, J. (1980). *The origins of logic: Six to twelve months*. New York: Academic Press.

Langworthy, O. L. (1926). Relation of onset of decerebrate rigidity to the time of myelinization of tracts in the brain stem and spinal cord of young animals. *Carnegie Institute of Washington Publication 89, Contributions to Embryology, 27*, 125–148.

Langworthy, O. L. (1928). The behavior of pouch young opossums correlated with the myelinization of tracts in the nervous system. *Journal of Comparative Neurology, 46*, 201–240.

Langworthy, O. L. (1929a). A correlated study of the development of reflex activity in fetal and young kittens and the myelinization of tracts in the nervous system. *Carnegie Institute of Washington, Publication 104, Contributions to Embryology, 20*, 127–172.

Langworthy, O. L. (1929b). Histological development of cerebral motor areas in young kittens correlated with their physiological reaction to electrical stimulation. *Carnegie Institute of Washington, Publication 104, Contributions to Embryology, 20*, 179–209.

Langworthy, O. L. (1930). Medullated tracts in the brain stem of the seventh month human fetus. *Carnegie Institute of Washington, Pub. 443, Contributions to Embryology, 27*, 37–52.

Langworthy, O. L. (1933). Development of behavior patterns and myelinization of the nervous system in a human fetus and infant. *Carnegie Institute of Washington, Pub. 443, Contributions to Embryology, 24*, 1–58.

Le Gros Clark, W. (1959). *The antecedents of man*. Edinburgh: Edinburgh University Press.

Lenneberg, E. (1967). *The biological foundations of human language*. New York: Wiley.

Lerner, R. M. (1984). *On the nature of human plasticity*. New York: Cambridge University Press.

Luria, A. (1966). *Higher cortical functions in man*. New York: Basic Books.

Martin, R. P. (1962). Entwicklungszeiten des Zentralnervensystems von Nagern mit Nesthocker and Nestflüchterontogenese (Cavia cobaya Schreb. and Rattus norvegicus Erxleben). *Revue Suisse de Zoologie, 69*, 617–727.

Martin, R. P. (1982). Allometric approaches to the primate nervous system. In E. Armstrong and D. Falk (Eds.), *Primate Brain Evolution* (pp. 39–56). New York: Plenum Press.

Meltzoff, A. N., and Moore, M. K. (1977). Imitation of facial and manual gestures by human infants. *Science, 205*, 217–219.

Merzenich, M. M., and Kaas, J. H. (1982). Reorganization of mammalian somatosensory cortex following peripheral nerve injury. *Trends in Neurosciences, 5*, 434–436.

Mignault, C. (1985). Transition between sensorimotor and symbolic activities in nursery-reared chimpanzees (Pan troglodytes). *Journal of Human Evolution, 14*, 747–758.

Miles, H. L. (1986). Cognitive development in a signing orangutan. *Primate Report, 14*, 179–180.

Morell, V. (1985). Challenging chimpanzees; anthropologists show even humanized apes lack constructive abilities. *Equinox, 22*, 17–18.

Mountcastle, V. (1978). An organizing principle for cerebral function: The unit module and the distributed system. In G. M. Edelmann and V. B. Mountcastle (Eds.), *The mindful brain* (pp. 7–50). Cambridge, MA: MIT Press.

Parker, S. T. (1977). Piaget's sensorimotor period series in an infant macaque: A model for comparing unstereotyped behavior and intelligence in human and nonhuman primates. In S. Chevalier-Skolnikoff and F. E. Poirer (Eds.), *Primate biosocial development* (pp. 43–112). New York: Garland Press.

Parker, S. T., and Gibson, K. R. (1979). A model of the evolution of language and intelligence in early hominids. *The Behavioral and Brain Sciences, 2*, 367–407.

Parker, S. T. (1990). Why big brains are so rare: Energy costs of intelligence and brain size in anthropoid primates. In S. T. Parker and K. R. Gibson (Eds.), *Language and intelligence in monkeys and apes: Comparative developmental perspectives* (pp. 129–156). Cambridge: Cambridge University Press.

Piaget, J. (1952). *The origins of intelligence in children.* New York: Norton.

Portmann, A. (1967). *Zoologie aus vier Jahrzehnten.* Munich: R. Piper and Verlag.

Rabinowicz, T. (1979). The differentiate maturation of the human cerebral cortex. In F. Falkner and J. M. Tanner (Eds.), *Human growth* (Vol. 3, pp. 97–123). New York: Plenum Press.

Rader, N. (1985). Change and variation: on the importance of heterochrony for development. In G. Butterworth, J. Rutkowska, and M. Scaife (Eds.), *Evolution and developmental psychology* (pp. 22–29). Brighton, England: The Harvester Press.

Ragir, S. (1986). Retarded development: The evolutionary mechanism underlying the emergence of the human capacity for language. *The Journal of Mind and Behavior, 6*, 451–468.

Ragir, S. (1989). "Language function and language origins." Paper presented at Language Origins Society Meetings, Austin Texas, August, 1989.

Rakic, P., Bourgeois, J. P., Eckenhoff, M. F., Zecevic, N., and Goldman-Rakic, P. S. (1986). Concurrent overproduction of synapses in diverse regions of the primate cerebral cortex. *Science, 232*, 232–235.

Redshaw, M. E. (1989). A comparison of neonatal behaviour and reflexes in the great apes. *Journal of Human Evolution, 18*, 191–200.

Rogalski, O. T. (1933). Das Ausreifen der Gehirnnerven bei Knochenfischen (Salmo trutta). *Zeitschrift für Anatomie und Entwicklungsgeschichte, 101*, 489–510.

Romanes, G. J. (1947). Prenatal medullation of the sheep's nervous system. *Journal of Anatomy, 81*, 64–81.

Rorke, L. B., and Riggs, H. E. (1969). *Myelination of the brain in the newborn.* Philadelphia: Lippincott.

Russon, A. E. (1988). "Chimpanzee infant peer social development (*Pan troglodytes*): Descriptions and comparative analysis." Paper presented at meeting of the American Primatological Society, New Orleans.

Russon, A. E. (1990). The development of peer social interaction in infant chimpanzees: Comparative social, Piagetian and brain perspectives. In S. T. Parker and K. R. Gibson (Eds.), *Language and intelligence in monkeys and apes: Comparative developmental perspectives* (pp. 379–419). Cambridge: Cambridge University Press.

Rutkowska, J. (1985). Does the phylogeny of conceptual development increase our understanding of concepts or of development?. In G. Butterworth, J. Rutkowska, and M. Scaife (Eds.), *Evolution and developmental psychology* (pp. 115–129). Brighton, England: The Harvester Press.

Sacher, G. A., and Staffeldt, E. F. (1974). Relation of gestation time to brain weight for placental mammals: Implications for the theory of vertebrate growth. *American Naturalist, 108*, 593–615.

Savage-Rumbaugh, E. S., and Rumbaugh, D. (1990). "The invention of syntax." Paper presented at the Wenner Gren Foundation for Anthropological Research conference, Tools, language and intelligence, Cascais Portugal, March, 1990.

Schifferli, A. (1948). Ueber Markscheidenbildung im Gehirn von Hühn and Star. *Revue Suisse de Zoologie, 55*, 117–211.

Stone, I. J., Smith, H. T., and Murphy, L. B. (1973). *The competent infant.* New York: Basic Books.

Terrace, H. S. (1979). *Nim: A chimpanzee who learned sign language.* New York: Knopf.

Tilney, F., and Casamajor, L. (1924). Myelinogeny as applied to the study of behavior. *Archives of Neurology and Psychiatry, 12*, 1–66.

Trinkhaus, E. (1983). *The Shanidar neanderthals.* New York: Academic Press.

Tuttle, R. (1987). *Apes of the world: Their social behavior, communication, mentality and ecology.* Parkridge, NJ: Noyes.

Ulett, G., Dow, R. S., and Larsell, O. (1944). The inception of conductivity in the corpus callosum and the corticoponto-cerebellar pathway of young rabbits with reference to myelination. *Journal of Comparative Neurology, 89*, 1–10.

Ulett, G., Dow, R. S., and Larsell, O. (1950). Hypertrophy of pes pedunculi and pyramid as a result of degeneration of contralateral corticofugal fiber tracts. *Journal of Comparative Neurology, 89*, 1–10.

Vauclair, J., and Bard, K. A. (1983). Development of manipulations with objects in ape and human infants. *Journal of Human Evolution, 12*, 631–645.

von Bonin, G., and Bailey, P. (1947). *The Neocortex of "Macaca Mulatta".* Urbana, IL: University of Illinois Press.

von Economo, C., and Koskinos, G. N. (1925). *Die Cytoarchitektonic der Hirnrinde des Erwachsenen Menschen.* Wien and Berlin: Springer Verlag.

Watts, E. S. (1986). Evolution of the human growth curve. In F. Falkner and J. M. Tanner (Eds.), *Human growth* (pp. 153–166). New York: Plenum Press.

Wertheimer, M. (1961). Psychomotor coordination of auditory and visual space at birth. *Science, 134*, 1692.

Wilson, E. O. (1975). *Sociobiology: The new synthesis.* Cambridge, MA: Harvard University Press.

Windle, W. F., Fish, M. F., and O'Donnell, J. E. (1934). Myelinogeny of the cat as related to development of fiber tracts and prenatal behavior patterns. *Journal of Comparative Neurology, 59*, 139–165.

Wishart, J. G., Bower, T. G. R., and Dunkeld, J. (1978). Reaching in the dark. *Perception, 7*, 507–512.

Yakovlev, P. I., and Lecours, A. R. (1967). The myelinogenetic cycles of regional maturation of the brain. In A. Minkowski (Ed.), *Regional development of the brain in early life* (pp. 3–70). Oxford: Blackwell.

Zecevic, N., Bourgeois, J. P., and Rakic, P. (1989). Changes in synaptic density in motor cortex of rhesus monkey during fetal and postnatal life. *Developmental Brain Research, 50*, 11–32.

Chapter 4

Brain, Behavior, and Developmental Genetics

Robert Plomin and Hsiu-zu Ho

Although the title of this chapter sounds like the brain and behavioral science equivalent of physics' "Theory of Everything," needless to say, this is not the goal of this chapter. However, one of the many ways in which the chapter is not a Theory of Everything is instructive in terms of understanding the state of the science of brain–behavior relationships in development. Physicists know the question they want to answer: What single theory can account for the four major forces such as gravity and electromagnetism? Brain and behavioral scientists do not agree on the questions to be asked and, for that reason, are often uninterested in the answers to the questions that others pose. We are like children in a candy store, pulled this way and that by all of the exciting possibilities. Many researchers want—they think—the whole store: understanding universals of human development. For example, most chapters in this book address evolutionary, comparative, and descriptive aspects of the neural and cognitive development of *Homo sapiens*.

One theme of this chapter is that the quest for universals may not be the most useful focus for understanding the development of brain, behavior, or their relationship. The questions of greatest social relevance concern not universals, but rather the description, prediction, and explanation of individual differences. The chapter begins by comparing these two perspectives and by emphasizing that an individual differences perspective is needed in research on brain–behavior relationships in human development. The rest of the chapter discusses the usefulness of quantitative genetic theory as a framework for exploring and understanding the etiology of individual differences in brain as well as behavioral phenomena and in relationships between brain and behavior: A few fundamentals of quantitative genetic theory are mentioned, followed by a review of quantitative genetic research on brain phenotypes and a discussion of newer concepts such as nonshared environment, genetic correlations among phenotypes within and across ages, and the use of molecular genetic techniques in pursuit of quantitative genetic issues.

The chapter is intentionally provocative—for example, arguing that questions concerning individual differences are more tractable and more important than are normative questions; that, for humans, genetic influence is more apparent for behavioral than for brain phenomena (implying that we need to assess rather than assume genetic influence on the phenomena of neuroscience); that nongenetic factors are of primary importance for brain as well as behavioral phenotypes; that these nongenetic factors operate in a manner quite different from the way that environmental influences have traditionally been assumed to operate; that brain–behavior relationships are not necessarily genetic in origin; that DNA is a source of change as well as continuity in development; and that molecular genetic techniques can be used to detect directly DNA variation as it affects brain and behavioral phenotypes. It is our intention that these arguments be experienced as provocative in the sense of provoking ideas rather that pique.

Individual Differences

The individual differences perspective considers differences among individuals in a population. In contrast, most brain and behavioral science focuses on average differences between groups of individuals within a population, such as gender or age differences, as well as on average differences between populations, such as cultural or species differences—a perspective that could be referred to as universal, normative, or group differences. The distinction between group differences and individual differences is basically the distinction between means and variances. In keeping with the provocative stance of this chapter, we emphasize the importance of an individual differences perspective; however, it is recognized that perspectives can be neither right nor wrong—the issue is their relative utility for specific purposes. Nonetheless, we would argue that the two perspectives differ in important ways that affect our theories and our research and that individual differences merit more attention than they currently receive.

Universal/group approaches dominate developmental psychology. For example, over 78% of the recent edition of the *Handbook of child psychology* (Mussen, 1983) is devoted to this perspective (Plomin, 1986b). Nineteen of the 48 chapters do not include a single page on individual differences—among these are the two chapters on brain development. The individual differences perspective is even less apparent in neuroscience than in psychology, which is surprising in that all biologists recognize that genetic variability is the quintessence of evolution. Among biologists, Ernst Mayr has been most emphatic about the importance of individual differences, which he refers to as population thinking in contrast to what he calls essentialism:

Western thinking for more than two thousand years after Plato was dominated by essentialism. It was not until the nineteenth century that a new and different way of thinking about nature began to spread, so-called population thinking. What is population thinking and how does it differ from essentialism? Population thinkers stress that uniqueness of everything in the organic world. What is important for them is the individual, not the type. They emphasize that every individual in sexually reproducing species is uniquely different from all others, with much individuality even existing in uniparentally reproducing ones. There is no "typical" individual, and mean values are abstractions. (Mayr, 1982, pp. 45–46)

Mayr notes that statistics—the glasses through which we see our scientific worlds—differs for the two approaches. The earliest statistics such as those of Quetelet were essentialistic statistics that attempt, in Mayr's words:

to arrive at true values in order to overcome the confusing effects of variation . . . He hoped by his method to be able to calculate the characteristics of the "average man," that is, to discover the "essence" of man. Variation was nothing but "errors" around the mean values. (p. 47)

In contrast, Mayr emphasizes that "the most interesting parameter in the statistics of natural populations is the actual variation, its amount, and its nature" (p. 47).

This is the most fundamental reason why brain and behavioral sciences need to consider individual differences: Individual differences are real and must be part of any comprehensive theory of biology and behavior. Individual differences are not errors around mean values but the quintessence of evolution. There are at least four other reasons to study individual differences. One particularly provocative argument is that issues of greatest relevance to society are issues of individual differences. For example, although it has been interesting to learn how alcohol affects mammals, society is undoubtedly more concerned about individual differences in human alcohol use and abuse. Equally provocative but more empirical is the argument that differences between groups within a species are usually trivial in magnitude compared to individual differences within groups. For example, it is now generally recognized that average differences between boys and girls are small compared to individual differences among boys and girls (e.g., Jacklin, 1986).

A fourth reason for studying individual differences is that the causes of universals or average group differences are not necessarily—or, in our view, even likely—related to the causes of individual differences. At least implicitly, developmentalists often assume that understanding the causes of universal development will automatically lead to understanding variations on these themes. This assumption is fallacious. For example, understanding why our species has frontal vision is not likely to tell us much about the origins of individual differences in depth perception among members of our species. Understanding why our species uses language will not illuminate answers to the question of why some children are language delayed. Understanding why *Homo sapiens* is a social animal, an aggressive animal, or an altruistic animal will not divulge the reasons why some people are more sociable, aggressive, and altruistic than others.

Finally, we believe that questions concerning the origins of individual differences are more tractable than questions about the etiology of universals or of average group differences. Although average group differences can easily be described, going beyond descriptions to explanations is difficult. Experiments, cross-cultural studies, and other group difference approaches are quite limited in what they can tell us about the causes of average differences between groups (Plomin et al., 1989). In contrast, the theory and methods of quantitative genetics provide a powerful approach to the study of the origins of individual differences, as discussed in the next section.

If individual differences are so important, why do normative perspectives dominate? One reason is historical, as pointed out in the quotation from Mayr—it was not until the nineteenth century that philosophers began to think beyond essentialism. In psychology, William James' (1890) *Principles of psychology* has had a strong influence on psychologists' categories of thought, and James seldom wrote about individual differences.

One reason for the neglect of individual differences that is specific to developmentalists is that differences among children are often thought to be "just" differences in the rate of development and these differences dissolve as time goes by. The most direct counterargument is that individual differences in rate of development could be predictive of differences later in life. Additionally, these individual differences may interact with aspects of the early environment in predicting later differences in cognitive performance (Ho, 1987). However, individual differences need not be predictive to be of interest to developmentalists for two reasons. First, development is as much the study of change as continuity, and this is just as true for the study of individual differences as it is for the normative perspective. Second, differences among children describe their current status and this information can be useful in terms of fostering children's development—maximizing their strengths and minimizing their weaknesses.

Moreover, the significance of developmental rate is most obvious when we emphasize outcome rather than process. For example, a vocabulary test can be thought of simply as a list of words that a child knows or does not know; many words that differentiate children at one age are known by nearly all children at a later age. However, a vocabulary test can also be conceptualized as an index of cognitive processes required to attend to, abstract, categorize, and retain the meaning of new words. Defined in this way, differences among children are not simply differences in rate of development. In addition, there are many areas of development such as temperament for which developmental rate is unimportant because average changes during development are not nearly as impressive as are individual differences among children.

A practical reason for the neglect of individual differences is that the study of individual differences is more demanding in terms of psychometrics and statistics than is the study of group differences. Because group differences can be readily visualized, high-powered statistics are not needed to guide inference; analyses of group differences often mistakenly focus on statistical significance rather than effect size. In contrast, the statistics of individual differences (e.g., correlations and regressions) are more readily translated into the amount of variance explained. Variance explained is often a depressing statistic in the behavioral sciences because it rudely reminds us, for example, that the ubiquitous correlation of 0.30 explains less than 10% of the variance. However, despite its bitter taste, this is important medicine. Developmentalists' preoccupation with statistical significance has left many statistically significant results that are insignificant by any definition of social relevance. The emphasis on variance explained is for this reason a virtue of the individual differences approach. Furthermore, any mean group difference can also be converted to a statement of effect size (Cohen, 1977) and rarely do these effect sizes account for more than 10% of the variance.

A final obstacle to studying individual differences is that individual differences research often appears atheoretical. Without a theory, data gathering can lead to a collection of inconsequential facts. As discussed in the next section, however, quantitative genetics provides a general theory of the etiology of individual differences of scope and power rarely seen in the brain and behavioral sciences.

Quantitative Genetic Theory

Most fundamentally, quantitative genetics organizes a welter of data on individual differences so that they are no longer viewed as imperfections in the species type or as nuisance errors in analyses of variance, but rather as the quintessence of evolution. It begins by partitioning phenotypic variance into genetic and environmental components as a first step toward explaining individual differences. However, the theory goes well beyond the nature—nurture question for which it is primarily known. Novel individual differences concepts flow from the theory: shared and nonshared environmental variance, genetic influence on environmental measures and on relationships between environmental measures and behavioral measures, genotype–environment interaction and correlation, multivariate genetic and environmental influences on covariance among traits, and genetic and environmental sources of change as well as continuity in development. Most of these concepts are discussed below; more detail about them can be found in a recent book (Plomin, 1986a). In this section, a few essential concepts of quantitative genetics will be briefly mentioned; knowledge of basic behavioral genetic methods will be assumed. Several textbooks on behavioral genetic methods can be consulted for greater detail (Dixon and

Johnson, 1980; Ehrman and Parsons, 1981, Fuller and Thompson, 1978, Hay, 1985; Plomin et al., 1990.)

The essential concepts of quantitative genetics are the three P's: population, polygeny, and pleiotropy. Quantitative genetics focuses on the description of individual differences in a population and the extent to which genetic differences among individuals account for these observed differences. It does not address universals, either genetic or environmental. As obvious as this point might seem, it is a frequent source of misunderstanding. One still reads that it makes no sense to attempt to untangle genetic and environmental influences in development because they interact, that is, both genes and environment are prerequisites for development. Although it is certainly true that development will not occur unless there is both an environment and an organism, this truism misses the point that quantitative genetic methods are not applicable to the development of a single individual. Quantitative genetics addresses the genetic and environmental causes of observed differences among individuals in a population.

A corollary of its focus on individual differences in a population is that quantitative genetics describes "what is" in a population rather than "what could be" or "what should be." That is, when quantitative genetic research points to genetic influence, it means only that, given the genetic and environmental influences impinging on that population at that time, genetic differences among individuals account for some of the observed differences. It does not mean that this is the natural order of things: Results will differ if different populations have different genetic and environmental variances; results for a particular sample will differ from the population if the sample is unrepresentative in terms of genetic, environmental, or phenotypic variance. The distinction between "what is" versus "what could be" or "what should be" is that descriptions of the relative magnitude of genetic and environmental influence in a particular population at a particular time has little impact on questions of how the population could be changed, either genetically or environmentally, in the future ("what could be"); most certainly, this descriptive research does not proscribe what should be, which is a question of values (Plomin, 1988).

Another core concept of quantitative genetics is polygeny—genetic influences on development involve the cumulative effects of many genes. Empirically, no single major gene has been demonstrated to account for a significant amount of variance for any complex phenotype. Even though many single-gene mutations have been discovered, these mutations are rare and affect so few individuals that they have a negligible impact on the variance of that trait in the population.

The third concept is pleiotrophy: the effect of genes is indirect and manifold. Genes regulate the production of polypeptides that, in turn, interact with existing anatomical and physiological systems and in this indirect manner affect the complex phenotypes that we observe. There are no genes "for" brains, beauty, or behavior.

In the following section, it is argued that these concepts of quantitative genetics—individual differences within a population, polygeny, and pleiotrophy—are just as relevant to the study of the brain as of behavior.

Quantitative Genetics Research on Neuroscience Phenomena

Individual differences are ubiquitous for the phenotypes of neuroscience. Consider measures of neurotransmitter activity: In mice, 2-fold and 4-fold differences among individuals are usually reported for neurotransmitter processes such as average circulating Dopamine-β-hydroxylase (DBH) level (Stolk et al., 1982), phenylethanolamine N-methyltransferase (PNMT), and tyrosine hydroxylase (TH), and in receptor binding site concentrations in major dopaminergic tracts in the brain (Ciaranello and Boehme, 1982). Twenty-fold differences among humans have been reported for the B variant of monoamine oxidase (MAO; Pintar and Breakefield, 1982). Even though neurotransmitters and neuropeptides are coded directly by DNA and are frequently transcribed, it cannot be assumed that individual differences in their activities or levels are single-gene effects; indeed, it cannot even be assumed that individual differences in these phenotypes are genetic rather than environmental in origin. The evidence reviewed in this section suggests that the story for brain phenotypes is likely to be much the same as for behavioral phenotypes: Genetic effects are polygenic and pleiotropic and nongenetic sources of variance are potent.

These unorthodox positions are reasonable a priori when we consider the complexity of phenotypes such as the activity of a neurotransmitter, that is the product of intricate processes such as synthesis, storage, release, reuptake, and metabolism. It has been estimated that the adult brain contains 100 billion neurons, each with approximately 1500 synapses, and that at each synapse there are a million receptor molecules including over 30 classical neurotransmitters and 200 other neuropeptides (Cowan, 1979; Synder, 1980). Even though neuropeptides are directly coded by DNA, there is little likelihood that the activity of any neuron or group of neurons is significantly determined by a single major gene or that genetic variance alone accounts for individual differences in such phenotypes.

For these reasons, quantitative genetic theory and methods are as important for studying brain phenotypes as behavioral phenotypes. As an antidote to the widespread assumption that variance for brain phenotypes is entirely genetic in origin, we argue that there presently is more evidence for genetic influence for behavioral characteristics than for those biological phenotypes most relevant to neuroscience.

A remarkable amount of variance for complex behavioral phenotypes is genetic in origin. As much as half of the phenotypic variance for major behav-

ioral domains—including personality, psychopathology, and cognitive abilities—is genetic in origin (Plomin, 1986a). Of course, the flip side of this
statement is that as much as half of the variance is nongenetic in origin.
Nonetheless, explaining 50% of the variance of complex behavioral phenotypes
is striking. In contrast, if we put together everything else that we know about
individual differences in these domains of behavior, it would be surprising if
10% of the variance could be explained. Certainly some physical attributes also
show substantial genetic influence such as total ridge count of fingerprints,
height, hair color and texture, and eye and skin color. But when we consider
more dynamic aspects of neurophysiology, it is not clear that such phenotypes
show as much genetic influence as do most behavioral characteristics.

Much less is known about quantitative genetic issues for brain than for
behavioral phenotypes. For example, a review of quantitative genetic research on
neurophysiology (Fuller and Thompson, 1978) found research relevant only to
sensory processes (taste, audition, and vision), EEG, and autonomic responses.
Another review (Claridge and Mangan, 1983), entitled *Genetics of human
nervous system functioning*, also focused on EEG and autonomic responses. As
they stand, these meager data are not at all clear on the importance of genetic
variation on such neurophysiological phenotypes, although a small body of
accumulating research is providing evidence for genetic variance in anatomical
parameters of the brain such as brain weight, neuron number, and neuron
connectivity patterns (Wimer and Wimer, 1985). What follows is a brief review
of quantitative genetic research on background electroencephalogram (EEG)
responses, evoked potential (EP) responses, autonomic activity, hemispheric
lateralization, behavioral pharmacology, neurophysiology, and neuroanatomy.

Background EEG

Most neuroscience research with humans involves EEG. Although twin studies of background EEG tend to yield moderately high identical (MZ) twin
correlations, fraternal (DZ) twin correlations are often nearly zero which violates
the classical twin model.[1] It is possible that EEG, unlike other phenotypes,
involves a great deal of nonadditive genetic variance, which would explain this
odd pattern of results (Lykken, 1982). However, the small sample sizes, the use
of different techniques across studies, and variability in results suggest caution in
accepting this conclusion. For example, one of the largest studies (with only 39
MZ and 43 DZ pairs) included five EEG measures of occipital alpha rhythm
activity (Hume, 1973). Two of the measures—alpha blocking and alpha index
(eyes open)—showed DZ correlations that were actually higher, albeit not
significantly, than the comparable MZ correlation. The only high heritability
estimate occurred for alpha frequency. In a report of the four classic EEG
frequency bands using twins reared together as well as twins reared apart, no
evidence was found for nonadditive genetic variance: MZ correlations were
about .80 and DZ correlations were about .40 (Lykken et al., 1982). In contrast

to the earlier studies, these data are consistent with an hypothesis of heritabilities of about .80.

Evoked Potential

Twin data for evoked potential (EP) also suggest a mixed picture concerning genetic influence. Unlike EEG, EP results tend to yield high correlations for both MZ and DZ twins. For example, one of the largest twin studies with 44 MZ pairs and 46 DZ pairs found MZ and DZ correlations, respectively, of .67 and .48 for visual EP, .83 and .75 for auditory EP, and .50 and .48 for somatosensory EP during the first 88 msec of response (Lewis, et al. 1972). Results were similar for the 90- to 300-msec period of response: .80 and .66 for visual, .74 and .56 for auditory, and .63 and .58 for somatosensory. The average heritability estimate—based on doubling the difference between the identical and fraternal twin correlations—for the various EP measures in this study is only .22. In a recent study of 22 MZ and 21 DZ pairs (Kotchoubei, 1986), evoked potential responses yielded high heritability for the amplitude of the N_1 wave (.75) and the P_2 wave (.86); however, the important P_3 wave amplitude showed low heritability (.27).

Autonomic Activity

Autonomic Activity—electrodermal response, heart rate, blood pressure, and muscle tension—has been the target of twin studies since 1924. A review of 14 modern studies concludes that there is little consistency among them (Fuller and Thompson, 1978). For example, one of the largest studies of blood pressure, with 75 MZ and 84 DZ pairs, reported little genetic influence on pulse rate or diastolic pressure, although the results for systolic pressure suggested genetic influence (Takkunen, 1964). A recent twin study of habituation of skin conductance to loud noises found correlations of .55 for 36 pairs of MZs .08 for 43 pairs of DZs; for 42 pairs of MZ twins reared apart, the average correlation (.53) was similar to that of MZ twins reared together (Lykken et al., 1988). These data suggest substantial nongenetic influence and substantial genetic influence that operates in a nonadditive manner.

Hemispheric Lateralization

Although genetic data concerning handedness and brain lateralization are notoriously complicated, it seems safe to conclude that heritability is modest at most, as indicated, for example, in the conclusion of a review by Fuller and Thompson (1978, p. 287): "the twin and family data, taken at face value, do not seem to offer particularly strong support for genetic determination."

Behavioral Pharmacology

A new neuroscience area at the interface between biology and behavior has grown rapidly relative to more traditional areas of physiology: behavioral pharmacogenetics and genetic influences on drug responses (Broadhurst, 1978;

Horowitz and Dudek, 1983). However, there are few quantitative genetic studies of human drug responses and those that exist are so small that it is difficult to interpret their results. For example, one of the larger twin studies (with only 26 MZ and 26 DZ pairs) found high MZ correlations but low DZ correlations for alcohol effects on EEG (Propping, 1977). A twin study of the behavioral and physiological effects of administration of alcohol reported a complicated picture of genetic influence, although measures were only of modest reliability, especially for physiological measures (Martin et al., 1985). An in-progress study of a similar nature includes adoptee pairs and nontwin siblings as well as MZ and DZ twins; preliminary results indicate little evidence of genetic influence (Wilson and Plomin, 1985). As a final example of human research, Claridge and Ross (1973) studied sedation threshold for intravenous amylobarbitone sodium and concluded that genetic influence is substantial; however, the sample was so small (10 MZ and 11 DZ pairs) that any conclusions are dubious.

Most research in behavioral pharmacogenetics involves mice. These studies have demonstrated significant genetic influence on responses to virtually every class of psychoactive drugs including stimulants, mild tranquilizers, barbiturates, alcohol, anesthetics, nicotine, opiates, and neuroleptics (e.g., Broadhurst, 1978). However, reports of such research often imply that *significant* means substantial. That is, results are usually analyzed merely in terms of mean differences between inbred strains of mice, which provides evidence for significant genetic effects but leaves unanswered the question of effect size.

Neurochemistry

In addition to studies that observe the effects of administered drugs is another new area of neurogenetics that considers genetic influence on transmitter synthesis, metabolism, release, reuptake, and receptor interactions (Breakefield, 1979). Genetic influence has been suggested for many of these processes (Gershon et al., 1981); again, however, researchers seldom assess the magnitude of genetic influence.

Catecholamine synthesis—the metabolic pathway that involves tyrosine, dopamine, norepinephrine, and epinephrine—has received most attention because of its possible role in psychopathology, although few firm conclusions can as yet be drawn. Tyrosine hydroxylase (TH), believed to control the rate-limiting step in catecholamine biosynthesis, shows substantial differences among inbred strains of mice for adrenal TH activity; however, brain TH activity shows less genetic variability (Ciaranello et al., 1972). Because TH and phenylethanolamine *N*-methyltransferase (PNMT), which catalyzes the N-methylation of norepinephrine to epinephrine, do not gain access to the circulatory system, nothing is known about genetic influences for these enzymes in humans.

Dopamine-β-hydroxylase (DBH) converts dopamine to norepinephrine in both the central and peripheral nervous systems; for this reason, DBH can be studied in human blood, although the relationship between DBA circulating activity and brain levels has not been established. A very low level of DBH activity in man appears to be inherited as a single autosomal recessive gene (Weinshilboum et al., 1975); extant data concerning normal levels of serum DBH activity, however, suggest environmental as well as genetic variation. One study of 94 sibling pairs aged 6 to 12 years found a sibling correlation of 0.57 (Weinshilboum et al., 1973) and a small twin study (10 MZ and 28 DZ pairs) reported correlations of .96 for MZ twins and .75 for DZ twins (Ross et al., 1973). Both sets of results are consistent with estimates of moderate heritability (about .50), moderate shared environmental influence (about .25), and moderate nonshared environmental influence (about .25). In rats, studies of circulating DBH levels in inbred strains and their crosses have been interpreted as yielding evidence for a single autosomal dominant gene for males (Stolk et al., 1982); however, a heritability of .50 can be calculated from the data in this study, which suggests that even if a major gene is involved in circulating DBH activity nongenetic influences are also important. Studies comparing inbred strains of mice suggest that brain dopamine receptor concentrations may be one of many factors contributing to genetic variance in the dopaminergic system (Boehme and Ciaranello, 1981).

Catechol-*O*-methyltransferase (COMT) and monoamine oxidase (MAO) are the two major enzymes involved in catecholamine metabolism and, in part, terminate the neuronal response to catecholamines. Both COMT and MAO can be studied in human red blood cells, although the relationship between blood and brain activity is not known. For COMT blood analyses, a study of 56 pairs of siblings 16 to 18 years of age yielded a correlation of .49 (Weinshilboum et al., 1974). Another study of families with primary affective disorders reported a sibling correlation of .53 and a midparent–offspring correlation of .49 (Gershon and Jonas, 1975). Although these correlations are consistent with an hypothesis of substantial genetic variation—and this is the interpretation taken by the authors—the data are just as consistent with an hypothesis of substantial shared environmental variation because siblings and parents and offspring share environment as well as heredity. The midparent–offspring resemblance suggests that nongenetic influences are important because midparent–offspring regressions provide upper-limit estimates of heritability. Twin and adoption studies are needed to demonstrate that familial resemblance is indeed genetic in origin.

A study usually referenced as demonstrating genetic control of MAO activity involved only nine pairs of identical twins (Wyatt et al., 1973). In one small twin study of platelet MAO, an MZ correlation of .76 and a DZ correlation of .39 were reported (Nies et al., 1973). This pattern of twin correlations suggests a heritability of .74, which leaves 26% of the variance as nongenetic. A later study (Pandy et al., 1979) found an even lower estimate of heritability of platelet MAO. A more recent study concludes that platelet MAO in humans shows little genetic influence (Gershon et al., 1980).

Neuroanatomy

Within the past decade, investigations on the normal adult mouse brain have provided evidence for genetically associated variability in brain weight, granule cell number and density, and in the pattern of mossy fiber synapses in the hippocampi (Barber et al., 1974; Gozzo and Ammassari-Teule, 1983; Lipp and Schwegler, 1982; Wimer and Wimer, 1982, 1985). For example, quantitative genetic analyses indicated that the additive genetic component of variance contributed 86% of the total variation in granule cell number (Wimer and Wimer, 1982). Some neuroanatomical variations appear to be substantially associated with learning (e.g., Wimer and Wimer, 1985); whether these brain–behavior associations are genetically mediated, however, is as yet unknown. Furthermore, for obvious reasons, quantitative genetic analyses of neuroanatomical characteristics in humans have not been reported.

Summary

Behavioral scientists are attuned to environmental sources of variability because it seems almost self-evident that individual differences in behavior are greatly influenced by environmental factors. With respect to neurotransmitter activity and other brain phenotypes, it is easy to forget that the environment can contribute to individual differences—from illness and nutritional status to environmentally induced moods and attitudes—even though we all recognize that our neurological makeup has evolved for the purpose of facilitating such responsiveness to environmental factors.

In addition to emphasizing the importance of nongenetic sources of variance, a quantitative genetic perspective stresses the polygenic and pleiotropic nature of complex phenotypes. In contrast, neuroscience research on neurotransmitter processes—in the rare cases when it tests for genetic variation at all—generally searches for single-gene effects, typically using F_1, F_2, and backcross generations in an attempt to verify a single-gene hypothesis. A worthy motive for searching for single-gene effects is the likelihood that the biochemical nature of phenomena will be more readily revealed for single-gene characteristics—as in the case of the single-gene metabolic errors involving amino acids, carbohydrates, the lipids—than for polygenic ones. However, in our view it is unrealistic to expect such simple answers when it comes to the complexities of neurotransmitter production, storage, distribution, and degradation. Polygenic and pleiotropic genetic variation, in combination with environmental variation, is a more reasonable hypothesis.

Thus, contrary to the widespread assumption that variations in brain phenotypes are genetic in origin, this brief review suggests that, for most phenotypes, the case has yet to be made that individual differences show substantial genetic influence. We predict that when the story is told, genetic influences on neuroscience phenomena will be polygenic and pleiotropic and, most importantly, that nongenetic sources of variance will also play a major role.

The Importance of Nonshared Environment

If genetic effects on complex phenotypes are highly polygenic and pleiotropic, it is possible that quantitative genetic analyses will ultimately tell us more about the environment than about heredity. That is, highly polygenic systems are not amenable to new recombinant DNA technologies that sequence, map, and clone single genes. However, on the environmental side, quantitative genetics has already made important advances. For example, research has begun to consider the possibility of genetic influences on measures of environment (Rowe, 1981, 1983), genetic mediation of relationships between environmental measures and developmental outcomes (Plomin et al., 1985), and genotype–environment interaction and correlation (Plomin et al., 1977).

In fact, one of the most important findings in human behavioral genetics involves nurture rather than nature: Nearly all environmental variation relevant to psychological development is nonshared; that is, whatever it is, this environmental variation operates in such a way as to make two children in the same family as different from one another as are pairs of children picked at random from the population (Rowe and Plomin, 1981). A brief background for this important conclusion begins by noting that quantitative genetic analyses can partition environmental variance into two components. One component, referred to as shared environmental variance, is that portion of the environmental variation that makes members of a family similar to one another, which could include family background variables such as socioeconomic status and parenting and schooling factors that are experienced similarly by children in the same family. The rest of the environmental variation is called nonshared environment—it occurs when environmental influences affect a trait but do not make members of a family similar to one another. Methods to partition environmental variance into these two components are discussed elsewhere (Plomin, 1986a). The results of these analyses are dramatic: For personality and psychopathology (Plomin and Daniels, 1987) and for cognitive abilities after adolescence (Plomin, 1988), nearly all environmental variance is of the nonshared variety.

This conclusion is surprising because environmental research typically assumes that the salient features of the environment are shared by members of the same family. The assumption is implicit in the fact that only one child is typically studied per family; this research strategy takes it for granted that other children in the same family experience similar environments. In contrast, the key question in terms of environmental influence is why two children in the same family become so different from one another. The answer to this question will come from studying developmental outcomes of more than one child per family and assessing environments specific to each child.

This brief digression concerning the importance of nonshared environment for behavioral development was included because it is likely to apply to the study of brain phenotypes as well. At the least, as researchers come to think about environmental as well as genetic influences on individual differences in brain phenotypes, it may be helpful to think about research strategies that encompass nonshared environment as well as traditional strategies that are limited to the study of shared environment.

Genetic Correlations

The point of the previous sections is that the variance of brain phenotypes can be due to environmental as well as genetic sources of variance. In the same way, the *covariance* between brain and behavioral phenomena can be induced environmentally as well as genetically. In other words, brain–behavior relationships cannot be assumed to be genetic in origin. Even if a neurophysiological phenotype—platelet MAO, for example—is shown to relate to a behavioral phenotype—schizophrenia, for example—and even if both phenotypes are highly heritable, the relationship between them could be entirely environmentally mediated.

Multivariate quantitative genetic approaches represent an important advance conceptually and methodologically toward understanding the etiology of the covariance between phenotypes, including brain–behavior associates (DeFries and Fulker, 1986). The essential concept is the genetic correlation and its analog, the environmental correlation. Genetic correlations represent the extent to which genes that influence one characteristic also influence another. It is possible that virtually the same set of genes influences two traits or, on the other hand, that the two traits, even though both are highly heritable, are influenced by completely different sets of genes. In an analogous manner, environmental influences that affect one trait might also affect others and give rise to environmental correlations among the traits. Methodologically, the important point is that any quantitative genetic technique that can dissect the variance of a single variable into environmental and genetic components can also be used to decompose the covariance among variables into environmental and genetic components. Description of these methods is beyond the scope of this chapter; for details, readers can consult a monograph edited by DeFries and Fulker (1986). In essence, the methods merely extend the univariate analysis of variance of a single trait to the bivariate analysis of covariance between traits. For example, in the case of the twin method, rather than correlating one twin's score with the twin partner's score on the same variable, one twin's score on one variable is cross-correlated with the co-twin's score on the other variable. In univariate twin analysis, estimates of heritability hinge on the difference between identical and fraternal twin correlations; in bivariate analysis, the difference between identical and fraternal twin cross-correlations estimates the genetic contribution to the phenotypic correlation between the two traits.

Another way to think about genetic correlations is in terms of artificial selection and correlated responses, first discussed by Darwin (1859). That is, selection for one trait produces a correlated response for another trait to the extent that some of the same genes influence both traits. For example, two selection studies successfully selected mice high and low in brain weight and then examined correlated behavioral responses to selection, especially in terms of learning (Fuller and Herman, 1974; Roderick et al., 1976). Only slight correlated responses to selection were found for learning tasks, suggesting that brain weight bears little genetic association with learning.

Another example of a correlated response to selection—involving the other end of the body from the brain—is the longest mammalian selection study in which 30 generations of mice were selected for open-field activity to produce replicated high and low lines (DeFries et al., 1978). A strong correlated response to selection was shown for defecation, implying that genes that affect activity in the open field also affect defecation.

Several studies have selected mice for responses to alcohol (reviewed in a volume edited by McClearn et al., 1981). The most well known study bred selectively for mice differentially sensitive to an hypnotic dose of ethanol (McClearn and Kakihana, 1981); correlated responses to selection have been demonstrated for a wide range of behaviors (Collins, 1981).

As mentioned earlier, any univariate quantitative genetic method can be applied to the analysis of genetic and environmental components of covariance between phenotypes. Twin and adoption studies are beginning to use this multivariate framework in the analysis of human behavioral phenotypes (DeFries and Fulker, 1986; Ho et al., 1987). The techniques are equally applicable to the study of brain phenotypes, although extant examples are primarily limited to nonhuman studies. For example, rates of clearance of bovine DBH and circulating DBH levels have been found to be correlated genetically in studies of inbred strains of rats (Stolk et al., 1982). In the same study, DBH neuronal release and disposal rates were not correlated genetically, suggesting, if heritable, that separate sets of genes influence the two phenotypes. The implication of the latter finding is that the phenotypic association between these two processes is mediated environmentally. In a study of mice, genetic correlations were found among levels of the three major enzymes in the adrenal catecholamine system—TH, DBH, and PNMT—which implies that genetic factors that affect the activity of one enzyme also affect the others (Ciaranello and Boehme, 1982). In one study of evoked potential in twins using a multivariate approach, the amplitude of the P_3 wave appeared to show little genetic relationship to the N_1 and P_2 wave amplitudes, suggesting that different genetic systems might affect components of the evoked potential response (Kotchoubei, 1986). In this way, multivariate techniques could be used to develop genetic models of individual differences in brain processes.

In addition to exploring etiologies of covariance among brain phenotypes and among behavioral phenotypes, application of multivariate techniques to the study of brain–behavior relations represents an exciting new direction for research. Rather than assuming that a particular brain–behavior association is genetic in origin, research that examines the etiology of brain–behavior relations is likely to show substantial genetic correlations for some phenotypic associations and slight genetic correlations for others—the latter implying that the phenotypic relationship is mediated environmentally.

As yet, there appear to be no brain–behavior analyses of this type. However, a study that is relevant conceptually examined the relationship between heart rate and aspects of temperament in a study of 58 twin pairs whose average age was 7 years (Boomsma and Plomin, 1986). A contemporary theory of temperament is based on the finding that emotional children show higher and more stable heart rates in stressful situations than do less emotional children (Kagan et al., 1986). Reductionism tempts us to interpret such a biology–behavior association causally in the direction from biology to behavior. However, it is possible that heart rate differences merely reflect rather than affect behavioral differences. Regardless of the direction of effects, the relationship could be mediated environmentally, despite the usual assumption that biology–behavior relationships are genetic in origin. In the case of heart rate and emotionality, twin analyses indicated that the relationship between them is environmentally mediated, even though both heart rate and emotionality are substantially heritable (Boomsma and Plomin, 1986).

These techniques are especially interesting when applied to analyses that go beyond single bivariate relationships between one brain phenotype and one behavioral phenotype. For example, to what extent does activity of a particular neuropeptide or hormone have pleiotropic genetic effects on a number of behaviors, or on certain types of behaviors rather than on other types? In the end, such research could lead to empirically derived general models of brain–behavior associations at an etiological rather than phenotypic level of analysis.

Age-to-Age Genetic Change in Development

Even more exciting is the application of these multivariate techniques to longitudinal data. Longitudinal analysis involves the same concepts of genetic and environmental correlations as in multivariate analysis (Plomin and DeFries, 1981). However, in longitudinal analysis, these concepts connote age-to-age change and continuity, the core issues of developmental behavioral genetics (Plomin, 1986a). In the case of longitudinal data, the phenotypic correlation refers to phenotypic stability between a trait measured at one age and a trait (not necessarily the same trait) measured at another age in the same individuals. Using the concepts developed in the previous section, phenotypic stability can be decomposed into genetic and environmental components of covariance. In addition, age-to-age genetic correlations can be calculated that indicate the extent to which genetic deviations at one age correlate with those at another age. To the extent that genetic effects at one age do not correlate with genetic effects at another age, age-to-age genetic change is implied. For example, a large-scale twin study of height and weight over 25 years, from young adulthood to middle age, indicated high heritability for both traits at both ages (Plomin, 1986b). As one would expect, the genetic correlation for height over the 25 years is nearly 1.0; however, the genetic correlation for weight is lower, suggesting some genetically mediated changes in weight during adult development.

Application of multivariate genetic–environmental analysis to longitudinal data has much to offer in developmental studies of brain, behavior, and their relationships. Conceptually, this perspective is important because it pries apart the close association that the adjectives "genetic" and "stable" have come to share. Longitudinally stable characteristics are not necessarily hereditary, nor are genetically influenced traits necessarily stable over time. The analysis of age-to-age correlations provides an empirical approach to assessing genetic change as well as continuity during development. For example, developmental transitions could be due to genetic reorganization—if so, age-to-age genetic correlations would be expected to dip during periods of transition.

There are very few longitudinal behavioral genetic studies and none on brain phenotypes or on brain–behavior relationships. The only major longitudinal studies are the classic adoption study of Skodak and Skeels (1949), the longitudinal Louisville Twin Study (Wilson, 1983), and the Colorado Adoption Project (Plomin and DeFries, 1985; Plomin et al., 1988). Skodak and Skeels' study was a parent–offspring adoption design that focused on a single dependent variable, IQ. The Louisville Twin Study, spanning 25 years of research, includes nearly 500 pairs of twins who have participated in a longitudinal study of mental development beginning in infancy and extending to adolescence. The results of this study have been important in pointing to genetic change to two sorts: (1) Heritability of mental development scores increases during childhood, reaching an asymptote by the early school years comparable in magnitude to heritabilities of adult IQ scores; and (2) age-to-age spurts and lags in development are influenced genetically. During the past decade, the Louisville Twin Study has extended its interest to the study of temperament (Wilson and Matheny, 1986).

The Colorado Adoption Project, began in 1975, is a longitudinal, multivariate study of 250 adopted and 250 matched nonadopted children yearly at 1, 2, 3, 4, 7, 9, 10, and 11 years of age. The natural parents of the nonadopted children and the adoptive and biological parents of the adopted children were assessed via a

3-hour battery of behavioral measures. Adoptive and nonadoptive siblings of the probands are studied and will eventually provide samples of adequate size for the analysis of the relatively contemporaneous relationship of siblings. However, analyses to date have involved the parent–offspring design in which there are three types of parents: "Genetic" parents—biological parents who relinquish their children for adoption at birth and thus share only heredity with their children; "environmental" parents—adoptive parents of the adopted-away children; and "genetic plus environmental" parents—natural parents of the non-adopted children. Comparisons among the three types of parents can untangle genetic and environmental sources of resemblance between parents and their offspring.

However, if genetic change occurs during development, parent–offspring analyses of data on adoptees as children are not likely to reveal evidence of genetic influence. Significant resemblance between biological parents and their adopted-away children has three requirements: The characteristic must be heritable in childhood, it must be heritable in adulthood, and the genetic correlation between childhood and adulthood must be positive. In fact, it would be difficult to detect parent–offspring resemblance unless all three factors are substantial because, in effect, they are multiplied to produce the parent–offspring expected correlation (Plomin, 1986b).

This apparent weakness of the parent–offspring design can be a strength from the perspective of developmental behavioral genetics in the sense that the design, from a genetic point of view, is like an "instant" longitudinal study from childhood to adulthood. Developmentalists already know that phenotypic correlations from childhood to adulthood are few and far between; this finding is compatible with the hypothesis of genetic change in development and makes it not surprising that few traits show genetic resemblance between parents and offspring in the Colorado Adoption Project. However, what is surprising is that *some* significant genetic resemblance has been found—especially for mental development, language acquisition, and some aspects of temperament (Plomin and DeFries, 1985). When significant hereditary parent–offspring resemblance is found, we know that the three requirements have been met to some extent. That is, heritabilities in childhood and in adulthood are significant (and likely to be substantial) and, most importantly, the genetic correlation between childhood and adulthood is significant (and probably substantial). Model-fitting analyses of mental development data from the Colorado Adoption Project suggest significant and substantial genetic stability from 2, 3, and 4 years of age to adulthood (DeFries et al., 1987).

Although little is as yet known about the description—let alone the explanation—of age-to-age change and continuity for brain phenotypes, it is reasonable to expect to find change as well as continuity if the necessary longitudinal studies are conducted. Furthermore, I predict that genetics will prove to be an important source of developmental change as well as continuity.

Quantitative Genetics and Molecular Genetics

In closing this chapter, some ongoing research will be mentioned because of its potential significance for the study of brain, behavior, and developmental genetics. At The Pennsylvania State University, research is underway to merge the polygenic perspective of quantitative genetics with the power of molecular genetic techniques to identify DNA fragments that differ among individuals and that relate significantly to behavior. The power of recombinant DNA techniques is undisputed; however, molecular genetic techniques have been employed primarily in pursuit of single genes. As discussed earlier in this chapter, classical single-gene effects that account for substantial portions of variance are unlikely to be found for complex behaviors. The quantitative genetic perspective posits that complex behaviors are influenced by many genes, each with small effects across a population. However, the methods of quantitative genetics are indirect in that they assess components of variation in a population rather than assessing DNA variation directly. The merger of quantitative genetics and molecular genetics can capture the strengths of each and has great potential to advance our understanding of the complex phenotypes of brain and behavior (Plomin, 1990).

Until recently, it has not been possible to assess variation in DNA directly, especially for highly polygenic characteristics. Advances in molecular genetic technology can now be used to screen many DNA segments for their joint contribution to the variance of complex behaviors, even those for which scores of genes may each contribute miniscule portions of variance in the population. The goal of the incipient program of research mentioned above is to identify as many gene fragments as possible, which in concert begin to explain a significant portion of the genetic variation that affects complex behaviors. The approach uses recombinant inbred strains of mice to detect quantitative trait loci associated with complex phenotypes such as behavior, as explained elsewhere (Plomin, McClearn, and Gora-Maslak, 1990). Complex human phenotypes can also be studied in a similar manner using candidate gene probes and large samples to study associations among individuals in a population rather than linkage within a family (Plomin, 1990).

Conclusion

No one needs to be convinced of the importance of the interdiscipline emerging at the borders of brain and behavioral research. The rapid increase in the numbers of psychologists who are members of the Society for Neuroscience is one of many indicators of the growth of this interdiscipline. The theme of this chapter is to promote the potential benefits of a brain–behavior interdiscipline that incorporates a third discipline, quantitative genetics—especially when they are integrated in the context of a fourth discipline, development. The only disadvantage to such interdisciplinary combinations is the string of prefixes necessary to label the field: developmental neuropsychogenetics?

The integration of these disciplines will have synergistic benefits for all four parent fields in terms of asking and answering novel questions about the development of individual differences in brain, behavior, and their relationship. As mentioned at the beginning of the chapter, this is not psychology's equivalent of physics' Theory of Everything. However, it is a Theory of Quite a Lot.

Acknowledgments

Preparation of this paper was supported in part by a grant from the National Science Foundation (BNS-8643938). The Colorado Adoption Project is supported by grants from the National Institute of Child Health and Human Development (HD-10333 and HD-18426) and the Spencer Foundation.

Notes

1. The classical twin method is like a natural experiment in which within-pair similarity is compared for genetically identical monozygotic (MZ) twins and for fraternal or dizygotic (DZ) twins whose genetic relationship is that of first-degree relatives. Coefficients of genetic relationship for MZ and DZ twins are 1.0 and .50, respectively; that is, if genetic effects are additive, for completely heritable traits, MZ correlations will be 1.0 and DZ correlations will be .50. If genetic variance is important for a particular trait that is not completely heritable, MZ twin correlations will be greater than DZ twin correlations. The effect size of genetic influence can also be estimated: Because MZ twins are twice as similar genetically as are DZ twins, heritability (the proportion of phenotypic variance that can be ascribed to genetic variance) is estimated as twice the difference in the MZ and DZ correlations. If genetic effects are not additive, DZ correlations will be less than .50 for a completely heritable trait; if assortative mating (a correlation between spouses) occurs, DZ correlations will be greater than .50 for a completely heritable trait. The MZ correlation will not be affected by nonadditive genetic variance or by assortative mating because MZ twins are genetically identical. Thus, nonadditive genetic variance will inflate heritability estimates based on doubling the difference between MZ and DZ correlations, and assortative mating will lower such estimates. The main assumption of the twin method is that MZ and DZ twins experience equal degrees of environmental similarity. For details, see behavioral genetic textbooks (e.g., Plomin et al., 1990).

REFERENCES

Barber, R. P., Vaughn, J. E., Wimer, R. E., and Wimer, C. C. (1974). Genetically associated variations in the distribution of dentate granule cell synapses upon the pyramidal cell dendrites in mouse hippocampus. *Journal of Comparative Neurology, 156,* 417–434.

Boehme, R. E., and Ciaranello, R. D. (1981). Strain differences in mouse brain dopamine receptors. In E. S. Gershon, S. Matthysse, X. O. Breakefield, and R. D.

Ciaranello (Eds.), *Genetic research strategies for psychobiology and psychiatry*. Pacific Grove, CA: Boxwood Press.

Boomsma D. I., and Plomin, R. (1986). Heart rate and behavior of twins. *Merrill-Palmer Quarterly, 32*, 141–151.

Breakefield, X. O. (1979) (Ed.). *Neurogenetics: Genetic approaches to the nervous system*. New York: Elsevier.

Broadhurst, P. L. (1978). *Drugs and inheritance of behavior*. New York: Plenum.

Ciaranello, R. E., and Boehme, R. E. (1982). Genetic regulation of neurotransmitter enzymes and receptors: Relationship to the inheritance of psychiatric disorders. *Behavior Genetics, 12*, 11–35.

Ciaranello, R. D., Barchas, R., Kessler, S., and Barchas, J. D. (1972). Catecholamines: Strain differences in biosynthetic enzyme activity in mice. *Life Sciences, 11*, 565–572.

Claridge, G. S., and Mangan, G. (1983). Genetics of human nervous system functioning. In J. L. Fuller and E. C. Simmel (Eds.), *Behavior genetics: principles and applications* (pp. 33–87). Hillsdale, NJ: Erlbaum.

Claridge, G. S., and Ross, E. (1973). Sedative drug tolerance in twins. In G. S. Claridge et al. (Eds.), *Personality differences and biological variations: A study of twins* (pp. 115–131). Oxford: Pergammon.

Cohen, J. (1977). *Statistical power analysis for the behavioral sciences*. New York: Halstead Press.

Collins, A. C. (1981). A review of research using the short-sleep and long-sleep mice. In G. E. McClearn, R. A. Deitrich, and V. G. Erwin (Eds.), *The development of animal models as pharmacogenetic tools*. Washington, D.C.: NIAAA Monograph.

Cowan, W. M. (1979). The development of the brain. *Scientific American, 241*, 121–133.

Darwin, C. (1859). *The origin of species by means of natural selection or the preservation of favoured races in the struggle for life*. London: John Murray.

DeFries, J. C., and Fulker, D. W. (1986). Multivariate behavioral genetics and development: An overview. *Behavior Genetics, 16*, 1–10.

DeFries, J. C., Gervais, M. C., and Thomas, E. A. (1978). Responses to 30 generations of selection for open-field activity in laboratory mice. *Behavior Genetics, 8*, 3–13.

DeFries, J. C., Plomin, R., and LaBuda, M. C. (1987). Genetic stability of cognitive development from childhood to adulthood. *Developmental Psychology, 23*, 4–12.

Dixon, L. K., and Johnson, R. C. (1980). *The roots of individuality: A survey of human behavior genetics*. Belmont, CA: Wadsworth.

Ehrman, L., and Parsons, P. A. (1981). *The genetics of behavior*. Sunderland, MA: Sinauer Associates.

Fuller, J. L., and Herman, B. H. (1974). Effect of genotype and practice upon behavioral development in mice. *Developmental Psychobiology, 7*, 21–30.

Fuller, J. L., and Thompson, W. R. (1978). *Foundations of behavior genetics*. St. Louis: Mosby.

Gerhson, E. S., and Jonas, W. Z. (1975). Erythrocyte soluble catechol-O-methyltransferase activity in primary affective disorder. *Archives of General Psychiatry, 32*, 1351–1356.

Gershon, E. S., Goldin, L. R., Lake, C. R., Murphy, D. L., and Guroff, J. J. (1980). Genetics of plasma dopamine-B-hydroxylase, erythrocyte catechol-O-methyltransferase and platelet monoamine oxidase in pedigrees of patients with affective disorders. In E. Usdin, P. Sourkes, and M. B. H. Youdim (Eds.), *Enzymes and neurotransmitters in mental disease* (pp. 281–299). New York: Wiley.

Gershon, E. S., Matthysse, S., Breakefield, X. O., and Ciaranello, R. D. (Eds.) (1981). *Genetic research strategies for psychobiology and psychiatry.* Pacific Grove, CA: Boxwood Press.

Gozzo, S., and Ammassari-Teule, M. (1983). Different mossy fiber patterns in two inbred strains of mice: A functional hypothesis. *Neuroscience Letters, 136,* 111–116.

Hay, D. A. (1985). *Essentials of behaviour genetics.* Oxford: Blackwells.

Ho, H-Z. (1987). Interaction of caregiving environment and infant developmental status. *British Journal of Developmental Psychology, 5,* 183–191.

Ho, H-Z, Baker, L., and Decker, S. N. (1987). Covariation between intelligence and speed-of-cognitive-processing: Genetic and environmental influences. *Behavior Genetics, 18,* 247–261

Horowitz, G. P., and Dudek, B. C. (1983) Behavioral pharmacogenetics. In J. L. Fuller and E. C. Simmel (Eds.), *Behavior genetics: Principles and applications.* Hillsdale, NJ: Lawrence Erlbaum Associates.

Hume, W. I. (1973). Physiological measures in twins. In G. S. Claridge, S. Canter, and W. I. Hume (Eds.), *Personality differences and biological variations: A study of twins* (pp. 87–114). Oxford: Pergamon.

Jacklin, C. N. (1986). What are we explaining? An update. Paper presented at the Annual Meeting of the American Education Research Association, April 17, San Francisco.

James, W. (1890). *Principles of psychology.* New York: Holt, Rinehart, & Winston.

Kagan, J., Reznick, J. S., and Snidman, N. (1986). Temperamental inhibition in early childhood. In R. Plomin and J. Dunn (Eds.), *The study of temperament: Changes, continuities and challenges* (pp. 53–65). Hillsdale, NJ: Erlbaum Associates.

Kotchoubei, B. I. (1986). An analysis of phenotypic correlations of human psychophysiological characters. *Genetica (CCCP), 22,* 2519–2525.

Lader, M. H., and Wing, L. (1966). Physiological measures, sedative drugs and morbid anxiety. *Maudsley Monographs No. 14.* London: Oxford University Press.

Lewis, E. G., Dustman, R. E., and Beck, E. C. (1972). Evoked response similarity in monozgygotic, dizygotic and unrelated individuals: A comparative study. *Electroencephalography and Clinical Neurophysiology, 32,* 309–316.

Lipp, H. P., and Schwegler, H. (1982). Hippocampal mossy fibers and avoidance learning. In I. Lieblich (Ed.), *Genetics of the brain,* (pp. 325–366). New York: Academic Press.

Lykken, D. T. (1982). Research with twins: The concept of emergenesis. *Psychophysiology, 19,* 361–373.

Lykken, D. T., Tellegen, A., and Iacono, W. G. (1982). EEG spectra in twins: Evidence for a neglected mechanism of genetic determination. *Physiological Psychology, 10,* 60–65.

Lykken, D. T., Iacono, W. G., Haroian, K., and Bouchard, T. J., Jr. (1990). *Psychophysiology, 25,* 4–15.

Martin, N. G., Oakeshott, J. G., Gibson, J. B., Starmer, G. A., Perl, J., and Wilks, A. V. (1985). A twin study of psychomotor and physiological responses to an acute dose of alcohol. *Behavior Genetics, 15,* 305–347.

Mayr, E. (1982). *The growth of biological thought.* Cambridge, MA: Harvard University Press.

McClearn, G. E., and Kakihana, R. (1981). Selective breeding for ethanol sensitivity: SS and LS mice. In G. E. McClearn, R. A. Deitrich, and V. G. Erwin (Eds.), *NIAAA monograph: The development of animal models as pharmacogenetic tools.* Washington, DC: U.S. Government Printing Office.

McClearn, G. E., Deitrich, R. A., and Erwin, V. G. (1981)., NIAAA monograph: The development of animal models as pharmacogenetic tools. Washington, DC: U. S. Government Printing Office.

Mussen, P. H. (1983). *Handbook of child psychology,* 4th ed. New York: Wiley.

Nies, A., Robinson, D. S., Lamborn, S. W., and Goldfein, S. (1973). Genetic control of platelet and plasma monoamine oxidase activity. *Archives of General Psychiatry, 28,* 834–838.

Pandy, G. N., Dorus, E., Shaughnessy, R., and Davis, J. M. (1979). Genetic control of platelet monoamine oxidase activity: Studies on normal families. *Life Sciences, 25,* 1173–1178.

Pintar, J. E., and Breakefield, X. O. (1982). Monoamine oxidase (MSO) activity as a determinant in human neurophysiology. *Behavior Genetics, 12,* 53–68.

Plomin, R. (1986a). *Development, genetics, and psychology.* Hillsdale, NJ: Erlbaum Associates.

Plomin, R. (1986b). Multivariate analysis and developmental behavioral genetics: Developmental change as well as continuity. *Behavior Genetics, 16,* 25–43.

Plomin, R. (1988). The nature and nurture of cognitive abilities. In R. Sternberg (Ed.), *Advances in the psychology of human intelligence,* (Vol. 4, pp. 1–33). Hillsdale, NJ: Erlbaum Associates.

Plomin, R. (1990). The role of inheritance in behavior. *Science, 248,* 183–188.

Plomin, R., and Daniels, D. (1987). Why are two children in the same family so different from each other? *Behavioral and Brain Sciences, 10,* 1–16.

Plomin, R., and DeFries (1981). Multivariate behavioral genetics and development: Twin studies. In L. Gedda, P. Parisi, and W. E. Nance (Eds.), *Twin research 3, Part B. Intelligence, personality, and development* (pp. 25–33). New York: Liss.

Plomin, R., and DeFries, J. C. (1985). *Origins of individual differences in infancy: The Colorado Adoption Project.* New York: Academic Press.

Plomin, R., DeFries, J. C., and Fulker, D. W. (1988). *Nature and nurture from infancy to childhood.* New York: Cambridge University Press.

Plomin, R., DeFries, J. C., and Loehlin, J. C. (1977). Genotype-environment interaction and correlation in the analysis of human behavior. *Psychological Bulletin, 84,* 309–322.

Plomin, R., DeFries, J. C., and McClearn, G. E. (1990). *Behavioral genetics: A primer.* 2nd ed. New York: Freeman.

Plomin, R., Loehlin, J. C., and DeFries, J. C. (1985). Genetic and environmental components of "environmental" influences. *Developmental Psychology, 21,* 391–402.

Plomin, R., McClearn, G. E., and Gora-Maslak, G. (1990). Use of recombinant inbred strains to detect quantitative trait loci associated with behavior. Manuscript submitted for publication.

Propping, P. (1977). Genetic control of ethanol action on the central nervous system. *Human Genetics, 35,* 309–334.

Roderick, T. H., Wimer, R. E., and Wimer, C. C. (1976). Genetic manipulation of neuroanatomical traits. In L. Petrinovich and J. L. McGaugh (Eds.), *Knowing, thinking, and believing* (pp. 131–147). New York: Plenum.

Ross, S. B., Wetterberg, L., and Myrhed, M. (1973). Genetic control of plasma dopamine-B-hydroxylase. (should the b be beta?) *Life Sciences, 12,* 529–532.

Rowe, D. C. (1983). A biometrical analysis of perceptions of family environment: A study of twin and singleton sibling kinships. *Child Development, 54,* 416–423.

Rowe, D. C. (1981). Environmental and genetic influences on dimensions of perceived parenting: A twin study. *Developmental Psychology, 17,* 203–208.

Rowe, D. C., and Plomin, R. (1981). The importance of nonshared (E_1) environmental influences in behavioral development. *Developmental Psychology, 17,* 519–525.

Sargent, T. D., and Dawid, I. B. (1983). Differential gene expression in the gastrula of *Xenopus laevis. Science, 222,* 135–139.

Skodak, M., and Skeels, H. M. (1949). A final follow-up of one hundred adopted children. *Journal of Genetic Psychology, 75,* 85–125.

Snyder, S. H. (1980). Brain peptides as neurotransmitters. *Science, 209,* 976–983.

Stolk, J. M., Hurst, J., and Nisula, B. C. (1982). Regulation and inheritance of dopamine-B-Hydroxylase. *Behavior Genetics, 12,* 37–52.

Takkunen, J. (1964). *Anthropometric, electrocardiographic and blood pressure studies on adult male twins.* Annales Academiae Scientiarum Fennicae, Series A., V. Medica 107. Helsinki: Suomalainen Tiedeakatemia.

Weinshilboum, R. M. (1979). Catecholamine biochemical genetics in human populations. In Breakefield, W. O. (Ed.), *Neurogenetics: Genetic approaches to the nervous system* (pp. 257–277). New York: Elsevier.

Weinshilboum, R. M., Rayond, F. A., Elveback, L. R., and Weidman, W. H. (1973). Serum dopamine-B-hydroxylase activity: Sibling-sibling correlation. *Science, 181,* 943–945.

Weinshilboum, R. M., Raymond, F. A., Elveback, L. R., and Weidman, W. H. (1974). Correlation of erythrocyte catechol-O-methyltransferase activity between siblings. *Nature (London), 252,* 490–491.

Weinshilboum, R. M., Schrott, H. G., Raymond, F. A., Weidman, W. H., and Elveback, L. R. (1975). Inheritance of very low serum dopamine-B-hydroxylase activity. *American Journal of Human Genetics, 27,* 573–585.

Wilson, J. R., & Plomin, R. (1985). Individual differences in sensitivity and tolerance to alcohol. *Social Biology. 38,* 162–184.

Wilson, R. S. (1983). The Louisville Twin Study: Developmental synchronies in behavior. *Child Development, 54,* 298–316.

Wilson, R. S., and Matheny, A. P. (1986). Behavior-genetics research in infant temperament: The Louisville Twin Study. In R. Plomin and J. Dunn (Eds.), *The study of temperament: Changes, continuities and challenges* (pp. 81–97). Hillsdale: NJ: Lawrence Erlbaum Associates.

Wimer, R. E., and Wimer, J. S. (1982). A geneticist's map of the mouse brain. In I.

Lieblich (Ed.), *Genetics of the brain* (pp.395–422). Amsterdam: Elsevier Biomedical Press.

Wimer, R. W., and Wimer, J. S. (1985). Animal behavior genetics: A search for the biological foundations of behavior. *Annual Review of Psychology, 36,* 171–218.

Wyatt, R. J., Murphy, D. L., Belmaker, R., Cohen, S., Donnelly, C. H., and Pollin, W. (1973). Reduced monoamine oxidase activity in platelets: A possible genetic marker for vulnerability to schizophrenia. *Science, 173,* 916–918.

Chapter 5

Nutritional and Environmental Interactions in Brain Development

Brian Morgan and Kathleen R. Gibson

Prenatal and infantile nutritional deficiencies are associated with deficient brain growth and with neurological and behavioral anomalies in both humans and animals. The earlier the nutritional deficit occurs, the more severe the brain damage and the less likely it is to be reversed (Dickerson, 1981; Morgan and Winick, 1985; Winick, 1976). Nutrition, however, is not the only variable impinging on brain growth. Environmental stimulation and deprivation also have profound effects (Diamond, 1988, this volume).

Unfortunately, many malnourished infants live in environments that are likely to exacerbate nutrient-influenced brain damage (Cravioto et al., 1966). Although some cases of severe malnourishment result from isolated deficiencies in the maternal placenta or circulatory system, other human prenatal and early infantile nutritional deficiencies are secondary to poverty, child abuse, and neglect, medical ailments that may require frequent hospitalization, or maternal emotional disease and ignorance. Children suffering from malnutrition may also be apathetic and fail to respond to whatever enriching environmental stimulation might be readily available, and they are predisposed to serious infections that may further damage the brain (Chase, 1976; Lloyd-Still, 1976).

For these reasons, it is difficult to determine precise cause and effect in the genesis of nutrition-associated neurological and behavioral problems using human data alone. Animal studies are necessary. This paper summarizes both human and animal data indicating that nutritional deficits can, indeed, be devastating if they occur during certain "critical periods" prenatally or in the first 3 years of life. The nature and severity of the defect depends on the developmental events ongoing at the time of the insult. Environmental stimulation, however, can lessen the detrimental impact of some nutritional insults and enhance the chances of recovery, especially if it is instituted early. In other words, a

91

malnourished child has a better chance of recovery if his rehabilitation includes social and intellectual stimulation as well as enhanced nutrition.

General Aspects of Brain Growth and Maturation

Brain Size

At birth the human brain weighs between 300 and 400 g or approximately 25% of its adult weight. It grows rapidly in the first year of life, reaching a weight of about 1000 g by the first birthday. It then grows much more slowly into adolescence or beyond reaching an average weight of 1230–1275 g in women and 1350–1410 g in men (Aguilar and Williamson, 1968).

In living children, it is impossible to measure brain weight. Thus, brain size is more often estimated by changes in head circumference, which, in most instances, provide a good measure of both cell development and DNA content (Winick and Rosso, 1969). On average, neonatal head circumference is 34 cm. It reaches 46 cm by the end of the first year and then increases about 0.5 cm each year thereafter until reaching an average adult circumference of 52 cm (Yakovlev, 1962).

Brain Anatomy

Brain development consists of series of partially overlapping events (Davison and Dobbing, 1968). Subsequent to the embryological formation of the major divisions of the neural tube, the earliest neurological developmental event is the formation of neurons. Once formed, neurons migrate to their permanent position and experience a number of additional maturational changes prior to achieving mature function (Jacobson, 1978). For one, they enlarge (hypertrophy). For another, they mature anatomically in the sense that they develop axonal and dendritic processes and synaptic junctions. Finally, they mature chemically and physiologically. In addition, neurons do not function in isolation, but require a complement of glia cells and blood vessels.

In humans, neuronal formation is primarily a prenatal event. Most neurogenesis occurs between 10 and 26 weeks of gestation, with a peak period of rapid growth of neuronal numbers at about 18 weeks of gestation (Dobbing and Sands, 1973; Gabriel, 1974). Peak periods of glial cell division are somewhat later than those of neuronal proliferation. Thus, in humans, most glial cells form at about the time of gestation, but the numbers of glial cells continue to increase to at least 2 years of postnatal life (Dobbings and Sands, 1973).

Cellular hypertrophy, synaptogenesis, dendritic arborization, and myelination begin prenatally. Cells continue to increase in size, however, for several years after birth (Conel, 1939–1967). Synaptogenesis continues at a rapid rate until 1 to 2 years of age, followed by a major period of synaptic pruning, which extends to late adolescence (Huttenlocher, 1979). Myelination begins by 7 gestational months and continues at a steady rate to about 4 years of age and then at a very gradual rate to adolescence or beyond (Flechsig, 1920; Langworthy, 1928; Yakovlev and Lecours, 1967). Dendritic arborization is primarily a postnatal event which, like myelination, continues well into childhood, adolescence, or beyond (Conel, 1939–1967; Dobbing and Sands, 1973; Scheibel, this volume).

Although all neurons and all neural regions experience the same developmental events, not all develop at the same rate (see, Gibson, this volume). From a nutritional standpoint, the cerebellum is of particular interest in this regard because its growth spurt begins later than that of the neocortex, but finishes earlier. Thus, it has a shorter period of growth, of vulnerability to nutritional insult, and of potential nutritional rehabilitation (Chase, 1976; Dobbing, 1974).

Brain Chemistry

Each anatomical developmental event is accompanied by biochemical changes. Prior to birth, DNA synthesis is rapid in nature and substantial in quantity. In humans, it exhibits two peaks, one at 18 weeks of age and another at birth, corresponding to peaks of neurogenesis and gliogenesis, respectively. Postnatally, DNA levels increase slowly to about 2 years of age in the cerebellum and to about 6 years of age in the forebrain and brainstem (Winick, 1976; Dobbing and Sands, 1973).

Initially, the ratio of proteins to DNA is low, but it soon begins to rise reaching a peak at about 2 postnatal years and then diminishing (Chase, 1976). The size of the neural pool of free amino acids from which proteins are formed is actually higher in the infantile brain than in the adult brain (Lajtha et al., 1981; Nowak and Munro, 1977; Sokoloff, 1977). In general, in maturing brains, the size of the amino acid pool correlates with rates of protein synthesis (Miller, 1969). Thus, the high levels of free amino acids in young brains reflect the considerable protein synthesis occurring at that time. Eventually, the rates of both protein synthesis and protein degradation slow and ratios of protein to DNA content achieve stable adult levels (Benjamins and McKhann, 1981; Winick, 1976).

Winick (1976) explains these developmental events as follows. Since, with the exception of a few cerebellar cells, all neurons contain equal quantities of DNA (6 pg) (Enesco and Leblond, 1962; Lapham, 1968), periods of rapidly increasing DNA content demarcate rapid cell division and rapid increases in numbers of neurons and glial cells. Once a full complement of cells is achieved, protein synthesis continues for some time causing cellular hypertrophy and permitting the maturation of cellular processes, but resulting in no increase in cell numbers. These hypertrophic events are demarcated by increasing ratios of protein to DNA concentrations. Once the rate of protein synthesis equals the rate of protein degradation, growth stops and neuronal maturity is reached.

Major spurts of myelination and increases in lipid content follow growth spurts of DNA and protein (Benjamins and McKhann, 1981). Lipids are an integral part of cell membranes and of the myelin sheath. Fifty percent of the lipids in adult brains are contained within myelin, which also accounts for 25% of the weight of the mature brain (Chase, 1976). One lipid, cerebroside sulfatide, serves as a good marker for myelination. Another group of lipids, the gangliosides, may serve as measures of dendritic arborization and synaptogenesis (Dickerson, 1981; Ledeen, 1978, Susuki, 1967; Svennerholm, 1974, Yusuf et al., 1977).

In the human brain, lipid concentrations are relatively low to about 7 gestational months and begin to rise at that time. Lipids reach high concentrations in gray matter by 3–6 postnatal months except in the cerebellum, where gangliosides continue to accumulate to 2 years (Brante, 1949; Cummings et al., 1958; Tingey, 1956; Vanier et al., 1971). In white matter, peak lipid accumulations occur between 12 and 24 postnatal months during which time over 50% of the brain concentration of cerebroside-S accumulates (Chase, 1976). Chemically, most lipid deposition in white matter is completed by about 4 postnatal years.

Brain Metabolism

The adult human brain is a metabolically demanding organ. It accounts for about 20% of the total body oxygen consumption and uses energy equivalent to about 20 W/min. This energy use continues during sleep (Sokoloff, 1981). Under normal conditions, the adult brain depends almost entirely on aerobic metabolism of glucose for its energy supply, and decreased supplies of either oxygen or glucose have negative effects on brain function. A loss of oxygen supply for as little as 10 sec may result in loss of consciousness. Diminished levels of blood glucose may cause dizziness, confusion, and, in extreme cases, coma and death (Sokoloff, 1981).

The one exception to this dependence of adult brains on aerobic metabolism of glucose occurs under situations of marked ketosis. Ketones are by-products of fatty acid metabolism that accumulate in the blood under conditions of starvation and diabetes. Under such conditions, the adult brain is capable of using ketones as an alternate energy source. This apparently requires no special metabolic changes. Enzymes capable of metabolizing ketones are normally present in the brain. All that is needed to activate them is the presence of ketones. Despite its ability to derive metabolic energy from ketones, however, the adult brain cannot depend on ketones alone. It always requires at least a minimal level of glucose to function (Sokoloff, 1974, 1981).

In many respects, neural metabolism in growing brains is quite different from that in adult brains. For one, anaerobic metabolism of carbohydrates is greater in the neonate than in the adult. In addition, once infants begin to suckle, their ketone levels rise, apparently as a result of the high fat content of maternal milk. Concomitantly, the levels of enzymes that aid in the metabolism of ketones rise. As a result, both rat and human infants derive much of their neural energy supplies from the anaerobic metabolism of ketones (Sokoloff, 1974, 1981). Infantile brains continue to rely heavily on ketone metabolism until the time of weaning when levels of both ketones and their associated enzymes decline (Klee and Sokoloff, 1967). The timing of the decline in enzymes may be environmentally influenced. For instance, the induction of prolonged ketosis as a result of starvation may delay the decline (Sokoloff, 1974). Conversely, early weaning may accelerate it.

In conjunction with the neonatal brain's reliance on alternate energy sources and metabolic pathways, oxygen consumption is low at birth. Thus, the newborn brain exhibits a greater tolerance to hypoxia than that of the adult. Shortly after birth, however, both blood supply and oxygen consumption begin to rise, along with the levels of enzymes needed to metabolize oxygen. In conjunction with this rise, respiration becomes increasingly important. Neural oxygen consumption reaches its peak in human children at about 6 years of age when the brain uses about 50% of all body oxygen consumed (Kennedy and Sokoloff, 1957; Kennedy et al., 1972; Sokoloff, 1981). Similarly, the glucose uptake of the neocortex reaches its maximum at about 4–6 years (Chugani et al., 1987). Maximal rates of blood flow and oxygen consumption correlate with myelination of white matter and with neuronal maturation (Kennedy et al., 1972; Sokoloff, 1981). In the gray matter, oxygen consumption may correlate with increased dendritic arborization, as dendrites exhibit the greatest ill effects of anoxia (Richter, cited in Aquilar and Williamson, 1968).

Effects of Nutritional Deficiencies on Brain Growth

A variety of events can produce permanent and severe brain damage during prenatal periods including, among others, maternal infection, drug intake, and metabolic disease. Postnatal infantile infections can also take a serious toll on the young brain. Neurological malformations that occur during gestation are considered to be time specific, but stimulus nonspecific (Dobbing, 1972). Thus, a severe insult of any kind during the first prenatal month may result in neural tube defects such as spina bifida, while insults at about 4–6 prenatal months will result in deficient numbers of neurons and a pathologically small brain (microcephaly) (Gabriel, 1974). The time-specific, but stimulus-nonspecific, nature of prenatal neural insults reflects neural maturational events. Those aspects of the brain actively maturing at the time of the insult suffer.

It is reasonable to expect that nutritional deficits occurring early in development will also be time specific in their effects and depend on the phase of anatomical and biochemical maturity at the time of the deficit (Dobbing and Sands, 1971). Thus, nutritional deprivation in the second trimester of pregnancy is likely to result in deficient neuronal numbers. Deprivation in the last trimester and early neonatal life should affect the numbers of glial cells and the maturation of neurons. Deprivation during the first through 4 years of postnatal life will primarily affect myelination and dendritic arborization. The short, circumscribed period of neurogenesis suggests that rehabilitation after birth cannot produce new neuronal numbers (Winick, 1976). On the other hand, the very protracted periods of myelination and dendritic arborization imply that nutritional rehabilitation for postnatal brain damage should be possible at least to 3–5 years of age, and possibly at a later date if continued over a long period of time.

Clinical data suggest that nutritional deficits, even those of specific nutrients, are time specific in their effects. Folic acid deficiency in early pregnancy may lead to irreversible neural tube defects, for instance, but it does not have such effects later in life (Winick, 1989). Similarly, iodine or thyroid hormone deficiency during gestation produces severe brain damage and permanent mental retardation (cretinism) (Kinsbourne, 1974). Similar deficiencies in later childhood or adulthood produce mental slowing but not permanent brain damage or retardation. Deficiencies of amino acids during pregnancy result in deficient brain growth, but deficiencies in adulthood result in transient deficiencies of specific neurotransmitters.

Similarly, studies of rats (Davison and Dobbing, 1966, 1968; Dobbing, 1974; Sales et al., 1974; Thomas et al., 1980; Wiggins et al., 1976; Winick and Noble, 1966), pigs (Dickerson et al., 1967), and dogs (Platt et al., 1964; Widdowson and McCance, 1960) suggest that serious undernutrition during prenatal and lactational phases of development produces brain damage. Depending on the time of the insult, the result may be reduced neuronal or glial numbers, defective myelination, or defective synaptogenesis (Dickerson, 1981). In rats, the cerebellum is more vulnerable to nutritional deficits during the early weaning period than are the other brain regions (Dickerson, et al., 1972; Fish and Winick, 1969; Dobbing, 1974), although this cerebellum-specific effect does not appear to apply to myelination (Wiggins et al., 1976).

The most common nutritional problems facing the human fetus are inadequate supplies of energy and protein. So great are the needs of the growing fetus for nourishment, that nature has provided human mothers with specific physiological mechanisms to help ensure adequate neonatal nutrition. Thus, maternal blood volume increases to about 40% above the prepregnancy level, and maternal glucose and fat metabolism may be altered. Appetite also increases, thus ensuring maternal weight gain (Winick, 1989).

To meet the metabolic and nutritional demands of pregnancy and lactation, a woman whose weight is normal prior to pregnancy must gain approximately 25 pounds. This requires about 300 extra calories a day. The maintenance of lactation requires about 500 or 600 extra calories a day. In addition, to meet the protein needs of the growing fetus and child, pregnant women must increase their protein consumption by about 30 g. Lactating women must increase theirs by 20 g (Winick, 1989).

Studies from around the world indicate that severe maternal calorie restriction produces infants of lower birth weight, but that calorie supplements during pregnancy can reduce this problem (Habricht et al., 1974; Winick, 1976, 1989). Low birth weight is a potentially serious problem because small-for-dates infants are more likely to die in the early infantile period. In babies whose birth weight is low as a result of maternal nutritional deprivation, head size is smaller than expected for their gestational age, but normal for their body weight (Gruenwald, 1963; MacLean and Usher, 1970; Winick, 1976, 1989). Brain weight may also be low, and brain cell numbers and DNA content may be reduced (Chase et al., 1972; Sarma and Rao, 1974; Winick, 1989). The smaller the baby, the less the DNA content. Chase and his collaborators considered that the cerebellum, rather than the neocortex, was primarily affected, although Sarma and Rao found uniform deficiencies in DNA content throughout the brain. In addition, low-birth-weight infants may have brains that are less well myelinated than the brains of larger infants (Chase et al., 1972; Rorke and Riggs, 1969).

Postnatal Malnutrition

Two main forms of malnourishment have been identified in human children. Marasmus is a form of emaciation that results from an overall deficiency of calories and nutrients during the first year of life. Most marasmic infants have mothers who are severely undernourished and thus have inadequate breast milk (Winick, 1976). Kwashiorkor is a specific form of protein deficiency that mostly occurs in children 2–3 years old who have already been weaned and are following a high carbohydrate, but protein-deficient diet.

Studies of malnourished children indicate that malnutrition during the first 2–3 years of postnatal life may have a negative effect on brain growth (Brown, 1966; Chase, 1976; Rosso et al., 1970; Stoch and Smythe, 1963; Winick, 1976; Winick et al., 1970; Winick and Rosso, 1969). The earlier the malnutrition occurs, the greater the reduction in brain size. Further, the longer the period of severe malnutrition, the greater the effect (Morgan and Winick, 1985; Winick, 1976). Thus, both children suffering from marasmus and children suffering from kwashiorkor have significantly lower mean brain and body weights than well-nourished children. Further, children suffering from marasmus are more severely afflicted than those with kwashiorkor (Winick and Rosso, 1969). Brain/body weight ratios, however, are often normal or excessive for body size in these conditions.

The brains of severely malnourished children are not only smaller, but they contain less DNA, hence, fewer cells, in the cerebrum, cerebellum, and brain-stem (Chase et al., 1974; Rosso et al., 1970; Winick et al., 1970). DNA content, however, is in proportion to the overall brain size. Marasmic infants dying in the first year not only evidence decreased brain weight and cellularity, but decreased protein, RNA, and lipid contents. Chemical analysis suggests that such infants have reduced numbers of myelin sheaths, but the myelin sheaths they do have are normal in thickness (Chase et al., 1974; Dickerson, 1975; Rosso et al., 1970;

Winick, 1976). Reduced concentrations of gangliosides also occur in children malnourished after birth and indicate defects in dendritic growth. These defects in dendritic growth may actually exceed other neurological problems (Merat, 1971).

Catch-Up

The critical question is whether low-birth-weight infants or those who experience marasmus and kwashiorkor can ever catch-up and acquire normal brain sizes with mature cellular structures or whether their brains remain permanently damaged. Some animal studies indicate that severely undernourished pigs, rats, and dogs never achieve normal brain or body size even when subject to intensive nutritional rehabilitation during the post weaning period. Further, the earlier the nutritional deficit the more permanent the deficit in cell numbers (Dickerson, 1981; Winick, 1976; Widdowson and McCance, 1969). In addition, their brains may exhibit long-term deficits in myelin content (Wiggins and Fuller, 1979), although possibly not in synaptogenesis (Thomas et al., 1980). To a large extent, however, just as the effects of malnutrition vary with the timing of the insult, so do the effects of nutritional rehabilitation. If nutritional rehabilitation is begun early, when cell division is still occurring, catch-up growth may be possible (Winick and Noble, 1966).

The brains of malnourished children, while often small, may be of the appropriate size and chemical composition for their body weight. This opens the possibility that such children may simply be slow developers who will eventually catch-up to their peers, especially if provided with appropriate nutritional and environmental rehabilitation. In fact, many small-for-dates newborns do grow more rapidly in the neonatal period than infants of normal birth weight. Further, both children subject to intrauterine malnutrition and those recovering from marasmus and kwashiorkor may experience catch-up growth in head size. Children suffering from intrauterine malnutrition, however, usually experience less catch-up than those suffering from postnatal malnutrition (Davies, 1980; Engsner, 1974; Engsner et al., 1974; Morgan and Winick, 1985). The best chances for recovery are among those children who experienced nutritional deprivation after the first year of life and/or in whom nutritional therapy is begun early when cell division is still occurring and continued throughout the period of myelination and dendritic arborization.

When catch-up growth does occur, it is not known whether the cells formed are the same as those that would have formed initially (Chase, 1976). Most neurogenesis in the human species occurs at a specific time in the second trimester of pregnancy. There is no evidence that new cortical neurons can be formed after birth. Thus, in humans, the second trimester of pregnancy appears to be a "critical period" for the formation of cortical neurons. One would expect permanent deficits in neuronal numbers in human infants whose mothers experienced severe nutritional deficiency in the second trimester. This would be expected to have some effect on sensorimotor processes or intelligence.

The mediating factors in catch-up brain growth in humans also remain uncertain, but judging from animal data, both nutritional and environmental enrichment are involved. Thus, in rats considerable catch-up growth is possible when nutritional rehabilitation is combined with social and environmental enrichment during the immediate postweaning period. (Bell, 1975; Carughi, 1987; Diamond, 1988). In fact, in Carughi's studies, rats who were nutritionally deprived during pregnancy and lactation, but environmentally and nutritionally enriched during the postweaning period, developed larger brains than those who never suffered nutritional deprivation but who lacked environmental enrichment. These rats never, however, developed brains as large as those of rats who experienced enriched environments and a continuous period of appropriate feeding. Thus, they did experience some permanent deficit, but much less than if they had been subject to nutritional rehabilitation alone.

These studies strongly suggest that environmental enrichment can partially compensate for nutritional deprivation if the enrichment is initiated soon enough and occurs for a sufficient period of time. This suggests that both nutrition and environmental stimulation have a factor in common. Morgan and Winick (1980 a,b) have found that they do. Thus, both environmental stimulation and nutritional supplementation result in the elevation of particular neurochemical, *N*-acetylneuramic acid (NeuAc), which is a component of gangliosides. As stated earlier, ganglioside concentrations are thought to reflect dendritic arborization and synaptogenesis. In addition, several investigators have suggested a specific role for NeuAc in neural function and learning processes (Dunn and Hogan, 1975; Irwin and Sampson, 1971; Schengrund and Nelson, 1975; Weseman, 1969).

Intelligence

From the standpoint of human society, the primary question, of course, is not how large a person's brain is or how well myelinated. The critical question is, how well does the brain function? To some, it may seem self-evident that an unusually small brain will result in lowered intelligence. This is almost certainly true if the brain is more than two standard deviations below the human norm (Gabriel, 1974; O'Connell et al., 1965). In particular, those children weighing less than 2000 g at birth and with head circumferences below the 90th percentile have a relatively high incidence of microcephaly and neurological deficits with accompanying mental retardation and sensorimotor problems (Gross et al., 1978). Further, various studies have suggested that intelligence will be impaired when nutritional deprivation results in significant head size reductions (Lloyd-Still, 1976).

Within the more usual range of human brain sizes, however, no correlation between brain size and intelligence has ever been demonstrated in well-nourished populations (although such correlations have been claimed for malnourished populations, Stoch and Smythe, 1963). Further, in both humans and animals brain size correlates with body size, and cogent arguments have been made that brain size relative to body size is a more critical parameter than absolute brain size (Jerison, 1973). None of the studies demonstrating permanent reductions in brain size has demonstrated reductions in brain size/body size ratios.

Thus, the conclusion that early nutritional deficits produce intellectual deficits rests on behavioral rather than on anatomical data. Behavioral studies parallel those of brain development and suggest that nutritional deficiencies may indeed impact on later intelligence if they occur early in life. Considerable rehabilitation is possible, however, if begun early and continued for a long period of time, particularly if nutritional supplementation is combined with environmental stimulation and emotional support (Lloyd-Still, 1976; Yatkin, 1971).

Thus, studies of malnourished Serbians, Indonesians, South Africans, Mexicans, Guatemalans, and Americans have all indicated permanent deficiencies in intelligence as a result of early malnourishment (Winick, 1976). Small-for-dates infants manifest low average IQs, poor grades in school, and various behavioral problems (Fitzhardinge and Stevens, 1972). Children cured of kwashiorkor may show permanent signs of sensorimotor retardation and deficits in language, hearing, eye–hand coordination, interpersonal relationships, and problem-solving abilities (Cravioto and Delicardie, 1979; Pereira et al., 1979). The earlier the malnutrition, the greater the psychological retardation (Winick, 1976). Thus, Mexican children admitted to the hospital for malnutrition under 6 months of age did not recover; older children did (Cravioto and Robles, 1965).

Despite these negative findings, other work indicates that under the right conditions, even severely deprived infants can achieve normal IQs. Thus, no reductions in intelligence occurred among army inductees who had been fetuses or young infants during the Dutch famine of 1944–1945 (Stein and Susser, 1976). Similarly, children suffering from cystic fibrosis, coeliac disease, and pyloric stenosis experience severe malnourishment, yet such children often have normal IQs (Lloyd-Still, 1976).

A study of Korean War orphans adopted into middle-class American homes indicates interactions between the timing of nutritional deficits and timing and nature of rehabilitation (Lien et al., 1977; Winick et al., 1975). In this study, girls who were seriously malnourished as infants achieved IQ scores equivalent to or above the American norm provided they were adopted prior to 2 years of age. Those whose nutritional/environmental rehabilitation was begun at a later age, however, scored below the American norms. Thus, the earlier rehabilitation was begun, the more successful it was.

Even, however, when long-term nutritional and environmental rehabilitation result in normal intelligence, children may still fall short of their potential intelligence. Although severely malnourished children adopted at young ages achieved normal IQ scores, their scores were lower than those of other Korean orphans adopted into American homes who had not experienced malnutrition. In addition, although rehabilitation may result in normal intelligence, there are no data to indicate whether the sensorimotor and other neurological problems that may accompany early malnutrition are subject to rehabilitation. Some studies suggest that perhaps they are not, because upper and middle-class children may achieve normal IQs subsequent to nutritional deficits but still demonstrate deficits in fine motor control. This suggests that they may have permanent cerebellar damage (Lloyd-Still, 1976). In addition, McKay et al. (1974) found persistent memory defects in children subject to 2 years of nutritional and behavioral rehabilitation beginning at age 3. These children had shown clear signs of improvement in other intellectual functions.

Nutritional deprivation in infancy and prenatal life has the potential to seriously undermine the mental functions of the individuals experiencing it and of the societies and social classes in which severe undernutrition is rampant. This potential is especially strong when it occurs in situations that provide minimal intellectual stimulation. The achievement of genuine equality of opportunity for all of humanity must encompass serious attempts to eliminate undernutrition in pregnant women and in infants and to provide appropriate nutritional and environmental stimulation, when serious undernutrition does occur.

Summary

Early growth of the human brain is a chronologically programmed series of biochemical and physiological events. The long-term impact of nutritional deprivation depends on the timing of the deprivation with respect to developmental events. The earlier the deprivation, the greater the neurological deficit as measured by brain size, brain cellularity, and lipid deposition. Similarly, the earlier nutritional rehabilitation is begun the more favorable the prognosis. The best hopes for recovery occur when early and prolonged nutritional supplementation is combined with early and prolonged environmental stimulation and emotional support. The intellectual deficits resulting from prenatal nutritional deficits follow the same pattern. In the absence of nutritional or environmental rehabilitation, they will be permanent. With appropriate rehabilitation, however, even severely malnourished infants can often achieve normal IQs.

References

Aquilar, M. J., and Williamson, M. L. (1968). Observations on growth and development of the brain. In D. B. Cheek (Ed.), *Human growth* (pp. 592–605). Philadelphia: Lea & Febiger.

Bell, R. W. (1975). Interactive effects of population density and dietary protein sufficiency upon selected morphological, neurochemical and behavioural attributes in the rat. In G. Serban (Ed.), *Nutrition and mental functions* (pp. 91–97). New York: Plenum Press.

Benjamins, J., and McKhann, G. M. (1981). Development, regeneration and aging of the brain. In G. J. Siegel, R. W. Albers, B. W. Agranoff, and R. Katzman (Eds.), *Basic neurochemistry* (pp. 445–469). Boston: Little, Brown.

Brante, G. (1949). Studies on lipids in nervous system with special reference to quantitative chemical determination and typical distribution. *Acta Physiologica Scandanavica, 18* (Suppl. 63), 1–189.

Brown, R. E. (1966). Organ weight in malnutrition with special reference to brain weight. *Developmental Medicine and Child Neurology, 8,* 512–522.

Carughi, A. (1987). The effect of environmental enrichment during nutritional rehabilitation on certain parameters of cortical development. Ph.D. thesis, University of California, Berkeley.

Chase, H. P. (1976). Undernutrition and growth and development of the human brain. In J. D. Lloyd-Still (Ed.), *Malnutrition and intellectual development* (pp. 103–159). Littleton, MA: Publishing Sciences Group.

Chase, H. P., Welch, N. N., Dabiere, C. S., Vasan, N. S., and Butterfield, L. J. (1972). Alterations in human brain biochemistry following intrauterine growth retardation. *Pediatrics, 50,* 403–411.

Chase, H. P., Canosa, C. A., Dabiere, C. S., Welch, N. N., and O'Brien, D. (1974). Postnatal undernutrition and human brain development. *Journal of Mental Deficiency Research, 18,* 355–366.

Chugani, H. T., Phelps, M. E., and Mazziotta, J. C. (1987). Human brain functional development. *Annals of Neurology, 22,* 487–497.

Conel, J. L. (1939–1967). *The postnatal development of the cerebral cortex,* Vols. 1–8. Cambridge, MA: Harvard University Press.

Carvioto, J., and Delicardie, E. R. (1979). Nutrition, mental development and learning. In F. Falkner and J. M. Tanner (Eds.), *Human growth* (pp. 481–511). New York: Plenum.

Cravioto, J., and Robles, B. (1965). Evolution of adaptive and motor behavior during rehabilitation from Kwashiorkor. *American Journal of Orthopsychiatry, 35,* 449–472.

Cravioto, J., Delicardie, E. R., and Birch, H. G. (1966). Nutrition, growth and neurointegrative development. An experimental ecological study. *Pediatrics, 38,* 319–372.

Cummings, J. N., Goodwin, H., Woodward, E. M., and Curzan, G. (1958). Lipids in the brains of infants and children. *Journal of Neurochemistry, 2,* 289–297.

Davies, D. P. (1980). Some aspects of "catch-up" growth in "light-for-date" babies. In B. Wharton (Ed.), *Topics in pediatrics. Vol. 2. Nutrition in childhood* (pp. 72–80). Tunbridge Wells: Pitman Medical.

Davison, A. N., and Dobbing, J. (1966). Myelination as a vulnerable period in brain development. *British Medical Journal, 22,* 40–44.

Davison, A. N., and Dobbing, J. (1968). *Applied neurochemistry.* Philadelphia: Davis.

Diamond, M. C. (1988). *Enriching heredity: The impact of the environment on the anatomy of the brain.* New York: The Free Press.

Dickerson, J. W. T. (1975). Effect of growth and undernutrition on the chemical composition of the brain. In A. Chavez, H. Bourges, and S. Basta (Eds.), *Nutrition*

(Vol. 2. pp. 132–138). *Proceedings of the Ninth International Congress on Nutrition, Mexico*. Basal: S. Karger.

Dickerson, J. W. T. (1981). Nutrition, brain growth and development. In K. J. Connolly and H. F. R. Prechtl (Eds.), *Maturation and development: Biological and psychological perspectives* (pp. 110–130). Suffolk: The Lavenham Press.

Dickerson, J. W. J., Dobbing, J., and McCance, R. A. (1967). The effect of undernutrition on the postnatal development of the brain and cord in pigs. *Proceedings of the Royal Society of London Series, B, 166*, 396–407.

Dickerson, J. W. T., Hughes, P. C. R., and McAnulty, P. A. (1972). The growth and development of rats given a low protein diet. *British Journal of Nutrition, 27*, 527–536.

Dobbing, J. (1972). Vulnerable periods of brain development. In *Lipids, malnutrition and the developing brain*. CIBA Foundation Symposium.

Dobbing, J. (1974). The later growth of the brain and its vulnerability. *Pediatrics, 53*, 2–6.

Dobbing, J., and Sands, J. (1971). Vulnerability of the developing brain. IX. The effect of nutritional growth retardation on the timing of the brain growth spurt. *Biology of the Neonate, 19*, 363–378.

Dobbing, J., and Sands, J. (1973). The quantitative growth and development of the human brain. *Archives of Disease of Childhood, 48*, 757–767.

Dunn, J. A., and Hogan, E. L. (1975). Brain gangliosides: Increased incorporation of 1-3H-glucosamine during training. *Pharmacology and Biochemistry of Behavior, 3*, 605–612.

Engsner, G. (1974). Brain growth and motor nerve conduction velocity in children with protein calorie malnutrition. *Archives University of Uppsala, 180*, 1–60.

Engsner, G., Habte, D., Sjogren, I., and Vahlquist, B. (1974). Brain growth in children with kwashiorkor. A study using head circumference measurement, transillumination and ultrasonic echo ventriculography. *Pediatrica Scandinavica, 63*, 687.

Enesco, M., and Leblond, C. P. (1962). Increase in cell number as a factor in the growth of the organs of the young male rat. *Journal of Embryology and Experimental Morphology, 10*, 530–562.

Fish, I., and Winick, M. (1969). The effects of malnutrition on the developing rat brain. *Experimental Neurology, 25*, 534–540.

Fitzhardinge, P. M., and Stevens, E. M. (1972). The small for date infant. II. Neurological and intellectual sequelae. *Pediatrics, 50*, 50–57.

Flechsig, P. (1920). *Anatomie des Menschlichen Gehirns and Rueckenmarks auf myelogenetischer Grundlage*. Liepzig: George Thomas.

Gabriel, R. S. (1974). Malformations of the central nervous system. In J. H. Menkes (Ed.), *Textbook of child neurology* (pp. 161–237). Philadelphia: Lea & Febiger.

Gross, S. J., Kosmetatos, N., Grimes, C. T. and Williams, M. L. (1978). Newborn head size and neurological status. *American Journal Diseases of Children, 132*, 753–756.

Gruenwald, P. (1963). Chronic fetal distress and placental insufficiency. *Biology of the Neonate, 16*, 215–268.

Habicht, J. P., Yarbrough, C., Lechtig, A., and Klein, R. E. (1974). Relations of maternal supplementary feeding during pregnancy to birth weight. In M. Winick (Ed.), *Current Concepts in Nutrition. Vol. 2. Nutrition and Fetal Development* (pp. 127–146). New York: Wiley.

Huttenlocher, P. R. (1979). Synaptic density in human frontal cortex—developmental changes and effects of aging. *Brain Research, 163*, 195–205.

Irwin, L. N., and Samson, F. E. (1971). Content and turnover of gangliosides in rat brain following behavioural stimulation. *Journal of Neurochemistry, 18*, 203–211.

Jacobson, M. (1978). *Developmental neurology.* New York: Plenum.

Jerison, H. (1973). *Evolution of the brain and intelligence.* New York: Academic Press.

Kennedy, C., and Sokoloff, L. (1957). An adaptation of the nitrous oxide method to the study of the cerebral circulation in children: Normal values for cerebral blood flow and cerebral metabolic rate in childhood. *Journal of Clinical Investigation, 36*, 1130–1137.

Kennedy, C., Grave, G. D., Jehle, J. W., and Sokoloff, L. (1972). Changes in blood flow in the component structures of the dog brain during postnatal maturation. *Journal of Neurochemistry, 19*, 2423–2433.

Kinsbourne, M. (1974). Disorder of mental development. In J. H. Menkes (Ed.), *Textbook of child neurology* (pp. 636–666). Philadelphia: Lea & Febiger.

Klee, C. B., and Sokoloff, L. (1967). Changes in $D(-)$-β-hydroxybutyric dehydrogenase activity during brain maturation in the rat. *Journal of Biological Chemistry, 242*, 3880–3883.

Lajtha, A. L., Maker, H. S., and Clarke, D. D. (1981). Metabolism and transport of carbohydrates and amino acids. In G. J. Siegel, R. W. Albers, B. W. Agranoff, and R. Katzman (Eds.), *Basic neurochemistry* (pp. 329–353). Boston: Little, Brown.

Langworthy, O. L. (1928). Medullated tracts in the brain stem of the seventh month human fetus. *Carnegie Institute of Washington. Pub. 443. Contributions to Embryology, 27*, 37–52.

Lapham, L. W. (1968). Tetraploid DNA content of Purkinje neurons of human cerebellar cortex. *Science, 159*, 310–312.

Ledeen, R. W. (1978). Ganglioside structure and distribution. Are they localized at the nerve endings. *Journal of Supramolecular Structure, 8*, 1–17.

Lien, N. M., Meyer, K. K., and Winick, M. (1977). Early malnutrition and "late" adoption: A study of their effects on the development of Korean orphans adopted into American families. *American Journal of Clinical Nutrition, 30*, 1734–1739.

Lloyd-Still, J. D. (1976). *Malnutrition and intellectual development.* Littleton, MA: Publishing Sciences Group.

McKay, H., McKay, A., and Sinisterra, L. (1974). Intellectual development in preschool children in programs of stimulation and nutritional supplementation. In J. Cravioto, L. Hambraeus, and B. Vahlquist (Eds.), *Symposium of the Swedish nutrition foundation. XIII, Early malnutrition and mental development* (pp. 226–233). Uppsala, Sweden: Almqvist and Wiksell.

MacLean, F., and Usher, R. (1970). Measurement of liveborn fetal malnutrition infants compared with similar gestation and similar birth weight controls. *Biology of the Neonate, 16*, 215–221.

Merat, A. (1971). *Effects of protein-calorie malnutrition on brain gangliosides.* Ph.D. Thesis, University of Surrey.

Miller, S. A. (1969). Protein metabolism during growth and development. In H. N. Munro (Eds.), *Mammalian protein synthesis* (Vol. 3 pp. 183–236). New York: Academic.

Morgan, B. L. G. and Winick, M. (1980). Effects of administration of N-acetylneuraminic acid (NANA) on brain NANA content and behaviour. *Journal of Nutrition, 110,* 416–420.

Morgan, B. L. G., and Winick, M. (1980). Effects of environmental stimulation on brain N-acetylneuraminic acid content and behavior. *Journal of Nutrition, 110,* 425–443.

Morgan, B. L. G., Winick, M. (1981). The subcellular localization of administered N-acetylneuraminic acid (NANA) in the brains of well-fed and undernourished rats. *British Journal of Nutrition, 46,* 231–238.

Morgan, B. L. G., and Winick, M. (1985). Pathologic effects of malnutrition on the central nervous system. In H. Sidransky (Ed.), *Nutritional pathology— Pathobiochemistry of dietary imbalances* (pp. 161–206). New York: Dekker.

Nowak, T. S., and Munro, H. N. (1977). Effects of protein-calorie malnutrition on biochemical aspects of brain development. In R. J. Wurtman and J. J. Wurtman (Eds.), *Nutrition and the brain* (Vol. 2, pp. 194–260). New York: Raven Press.

Pereira, S. M., Sundaraj, S., and Begum, A. (1979). Physical growth and neurointegrative performance of survivors of protein-energy malnutrition. *British Journal of Nutrition, 42,* 165–171.

Platt, B. S., Heard, C. R. C., and Stewart, R. J. C. (1964). Experimental protein calorie deficiency. In H. N. Munro and J. B. Allison (Eds.), *Mammalian protein metabolism* (Vol. 2, pp. 445–522). New York: Academic Press.

O'Connell, E. J., Feldt, R. H., and Stickler, G. B. (1965). Head circumference, mental retardation and growth failure. *Pediatrics, 36,* 62–66.

Rorke, L. B., and Riggs, H. E. (1969). *Myelination of the brain in the newborn.* Philadelphia: Lippincott.

Rosso, P., Hormanzabal, J., and Winick, M. (1970). Changes in brain weight. cholesterol, phospholipid and DNA content in marasmic children. *American Journal of Clinical Nutrition, 23,* 1275–1279.

Salas, M., Dias, S., and Nieto A. (1974). Effects of neonatal food deprivation on cortical spines and dendritic development of the rat. *Brain Research, 73,* 139–144.

Sarma, M. K. J., and Rao, K. S. (1974). Biochemical composition of different regions in brains of small for date infants. *Journal of Neurochemistry, 22,* 671–677.

Schengrund, C. L., and Nelson, J. T. (1975). Influence of cation concentration on the sialidase activity of neuronal synaptic membranes. *Biochemical Research and Communications, 63,* 217–223.

Sokoloff, L. (1974). Changes in enzyme activities in neural tissues with maturation and development of the nervous system. In F. O. Schmitt and F. G. Worden (Eds.), *The neurosciences: Third study program* (pp. 885–898). Cambridge, MA: MIT Press.

Sokoloff, L. (1981). Circulation and energy metabolism of the brain. In G. J. Siegel, R. W. Albers, B. W. Agranoff, and R. Katzman (Eds.), *Basic Neurochemistry* (pp. 471–495). Boston: Little, Brown.

Stein, Z. A., and Sussner, M. W. (1976). Prenatal nutrition and mental competence. In J. Lloyd-Still (Ed.), *Malnutrition and intellectual development* (pp. 39–79). Littledon, MA: Publishing Sciences Group.

Stoch, M. B., and Smythe, P. M. (1963). Does undernutrition during infancy inhibit brain growth and subsequent intellectual development? *Archives Disease in Childhood, 38,* 540–552.

Suzuki, K. (1967). Formation and turnover of the major brain gangliosides during development. *Journal of Neurochemistry*, *14*, 917–925.

Svennerholm, L. (1974). Lipid biochemical changes of brain during development. In J. Cravioto, L. Hambraeus, and B. Vahlquist (Eds.), *Early malnutrition and mental development* (pp. 67–71). Uppsala, Sweden: Almqvist and Wiksell.

Thomas, Y. M., Bedi, K. S., Davies, C. A., and Dobbing, J. (1980). Deficits in synapse-to-neuron ratio due to early undernutrition show evidence of catch-up in later life. *Experientia*, *36*, 556–557.

Tingey, A. H. (1956). Human brain lipids at various ages in relation to myelination. *Journal of Mental Science*, *102*, 429–432.

Vanier, M. T., Holm, M., Ohman, R., and Svennerholm, L. (1971). Developmental profiles of gangliosides in human and rat brain. *Journal of Neurochemistry*, *18*, 581–592.

Wesemen, W. (1969). Isolation of 5-hydroxytryptamine-containing vesicles and of synaptic membranes from the rat brain. FEBS Letters, *3*, 80–84.

Widdowson, E. M., and McCance, R. A. (1960). Some effects of accelerating growth. I. General somatic development. *Proceedings of the Royal Society of London*, *152*, 188–206.

Wiggins, R. C., and Fuller, G. N. (1979). Relative synthesis of myelin in different brain regions of postnatally undernourished rats. *Brain Research*, *162*, 103–112.

Wiggins, R. C., Miller, S. L., Benjamins, J. A., Krigman, M. R., and Morell, P. (1976). Myelin synthesis during postnatal nutritional deprivation and subsequent rehabilitation. *Brain Research*, *107*, 257–273.

Winick, M. (1976). *Malnutrition and brain development*. New York: Oxford University Press.

Winick, M. (1989). *Nutrition, pregnancy and early infancy*. Baltimore: Williams & Wilkins.

Winick, M., and Noble, A. (1966). Cellular response in rats during malnutrition at various ages. *Journal of Nutrition*, *89*, 300–306.

Winick, M., and Rosso, P. (1969). Head circumference and cellular growth of the brain in normal and marasmic children. *Journal of Pediatrics*, *74*, 774–778.

Winick, M., Rosso, P., and Waterlow, J. (1970). Cellular growth of cerebrum, cerebellum, and brain stem in normal and marasmic children. *Experimental Neurology*, *26*, 393–400.

Winick, B., Meyer, K. K., and Harris, R. (1975). Malnutrition and environmental enrichment by early adoption. *Science*, *190*, 1173–1175.

Yakovlev, P. (1962). Morphological criteria of growth and maturation of the nervous system in man. *Proceedings A. Research in Nervous and Mental Disease*, *39*, 3–46.

Yakovlev P., and Lecours, A. R. (1967). The myelogenetic cycles of regional maturation of the brain. In A. Minkowski (Ed.), *Regional development of the brain in early life*. Oxford: Blackwell, pp. 3–65.

Yatkin, U. S., McLaren, D. S., Kanawati, A. A., and Sabbach, S. (1971). Undernutrition and mental development: A one year follow-up. In D. S. McLaren and N. J. Daghir (Eds.), *Proceedings of the 6th symposium on nutrition and health in the Near East*. Beirut: American University, pp. 277–281.

Yusof, H. K. M., Merat, A., and Dickerson, J. W. T. (1977). Effect of development on the gangliosides of human brain. *Journal of Neurochemistry*, *28*, 1299–1304.

Chapter 6

Environmental Influences on the Young Brain

Marian C. Diamond

Introduction

Wherever we are in the world from Berkeley to Nepal, developing neurons require the challenge of new and stimulating input. As the individual experiences a constant flow of new stimuli, what kind of changes are occurring in the brain cells within the skull? At birth, the brains of most mammals are structurally and functionally underdeveloped. During the early neonatal period, rapid development occurs, but rates of brain growth taper off in early life. Ideally, with controlled environmental input, one could identify detailed stages of development in the mammalian brain and delineate the so-called "normal stages" of growth and maturation. This requires examining the growth curve of the mammalian brain under a given set of circumstances and considering how changes in the environment can alter this basic pattern. Since it is the cerebral cortex that appears most responsive to changes in the external environment, this report will focus on this region of the brain.

Obviously, the knowledge we seek can best be attained by examining the brains of human beings. Because of ethical and practical considerations, however, we can neither control the environmental input into human brains nor make precise measurements over time of identical areas on fixed human cortices. Even CAT and PET scanning techniques lack the resolution to measure living human brains. For instance, we are unable to precisely differentiate the boundaries of the gray matter constituting the cerebral cortex from the underlying white matter. Consequently, we cannot follow the growth of human cortical thickness. In the future, however, we hope to be able to do so by means of more sensitive magnetic resonance technology. In the meantime, we must turn to animal models where we can control the environment and make precise measurements of cortical dimensions on preserved tissue.

Much of the work included in this report deals with the rat brain, a circumstance that evokes the usual cautions about extrapolating from rats to man. Neurologically, however, there is every reason to consider such extrapolations reasonable. The rat brain is very similar to the human brain in its developmental patterns and sequences. This, both human and rat brains experience a period of early neurogenesis. Once that period has passed, no new cerebral cortical neurons are formed (Winick, 1976). Rather, later developmental events include synaptogenesis, dendritic arborization, myelination, and the proliferation of glial cells (Jacobson, 1978). In both species, synaptogenesis first evidences a period of synaptic overproduction, followed by a period of synaptic pruning. Both species also exhibit highly similar patterns of myelination (Conel, 1939–1967; Flechsig, 1920; Jacobsen, 1963; see also review by Gibson, this volume). Thus, in both species, brain stem fiber tracts myelinate in advance of cortical regions. Within the cortex, sensorimotor areas myelinate in advance of association areas, and lower cortical layers myelinate in advance of higher cortical areas. During these periods of neurological development, both human and rat brains are highly vulnerable to insult as a result of nutritional or environmental deprivation. Both are less vulnerable later on (Winick, 1976). Thus, there is every reason to believe that the basic developmental processes that underlie neurological abilities to respond to environmental stimulation are similar in the two species.

The one major developmental difference lies in developmental timing. The human brain experiences a greater portion of its neurological maturation *in utero*, while at the same time having a more protracted period of postnatal maturation. Thus, both dendritic branching and myelination are almost entirely postnatal events in rats, but both are also well developed within the first 30 days after birth and environmental influences can govern their development or loss after that period. In the human, both dendritic branching and myelination begin before birth, but have been demonstrated to continue to at least 3 to 4 postnatal years and are, undoubtedly, environmentally influenced. So, the differences between human and rat brains may not be as great as once thought. In humans, at least five-sixths of dendritic development occurs postnatally (Dobbing and Sands, 1973), as does the major spurt of myelination (Chase, 1976). In one respect the somewhat lesser degree of maturity of the rat brain at birth is also a scientific plus, because the other common animal subject, the rhesus monkey, is more mature at birth than the human. Thus, the rat brain can provide information on developmental lability during cycles of neuronal maturation that are postnatal in both human and rat, but prenatal in the rhesus monkey.

Until the early 1960s, that brains could structurally change with experience was not generally accepted. In 1911, Ramon y Cajal, the great neurohistologist, stated that cerebral exercise affects neuronal structure. Nonetheless, scientists believed that after initial development, the brain became structurally stable. With aging it might decrease in size, but that it could grow with use and shrink with disuse was not widely recognized. Now, however, plasticity of the morphology of the cerebral cortex has been clearly demonstrated by several laboratories. Nonetheless, there are still many variables to be considered: age, duration of stimulation, sex, nutrition, brain regions involved, chemical supplements, sleep, etc.

Normal Cortical Development

To understand the brain's structural and chemical responses to alterations in the environment, it is essential first to examine the normal curve of development. In 1975, such a curve was published presenting the cerebral cortical thickness of the male rat (Diamond et al., 1975). In general, the whole cortex, whether frontal, parietal, occipital, medial, or lateral, grows very rapidly for the first 10 days postnatally, and then continues to grow more slowly until somewhere between 26 and 41 days of age. At this time a gradual decrease in cortical thickness begins and continues until death. These slopes were found in the brains of rats that lived six per cage ($32 \times 20 \times 20$ cm) with their mothers prior to weaning and three per cage subsequent to weaning at 23–25 days of age [This study is part of a larger histological exploration that has been ongoing for several years; it includes rats from the following age groups (with 15–25 rats per age group): 6, 10, 14, 20, 26, 41, 55, 77, 90, 108, 185, 300, 400, 650, and 904 days.]

Figure 1 shows a representative sample of a rat brain. This transverse section illustrates the method of measuring cortical thickness in the occipital cortex. Figure 2 presents the developing cortical curves for each of the areas measured from birth to 55 days of age, frontal cortex (M), somatosensory, ($S_{B', C', D'}$) and occipital ($V_{B', C', D'}$). These separate areas are offered because they indicate that although, in general, the total mantle increases in a similar fashion, certain areas do have different development patterns. For example, the frontal cortex develops similarly to the rest of the cortex until age 14 days; at that point its growth curve maintains a plateau until 20 days of age when once again the slope follows the pattern of the other cortical areas.

Because of the possible use of these neural developmental data as *guidelines* in the modern human educational system, the whole and the parts are presented separately. No comparable data are available on human brains. It has been proposed that "the brain grows in spurts" and that intellectual inputs are most effective during the growth spurts (Epstein, 1978). Our male rat data do not support this hypothesis of cycles of growth advances. Measuring skull dimensions alone is evidently not adequate to determine the dimensions of intracranial structures. By measuring roentgenograms of enriched and impoverished rats' skulls, we have found that the intracranial size was not significantly different between the two groups of animals, although the external cranial dimensions were (Diamond et al., 1965). Isolated rats with greater body weights had larger

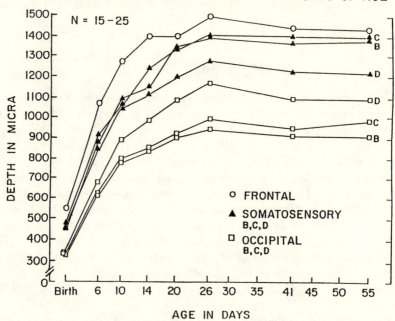

CORTICAL THICKNESS (IN MICRA) DEVELOPMENT
IN MALE LONG-EVANS RATS   Birth-55 DAYS OF AGE

Figure 1.   A transverse section of the rat brain indicating the method by which cortical thickness was measured.

external skull dimensions compared to the enriched rats but their cortical dimensions were less.

Our data suggest that for the first month postnatally the dimensions of the male rat's cerebral cortex increases rapidly and then decreases slowly thereafter. The next important question is whether one can accelerate maturation during the increasing slope of the curve or alter the curve during its decline. Before turning to environmental influences, however, we are aware that all of the above discussion has dealt with the male rat's cortex. What about the female cortex? The developmental curve of the cortical thickness for the female rat is still being determined. Nonetheless, it is of interest to point out one obvious difference in the developmental pattern of the female compared to the male. Between 7 and 14 days of age, area 39 (as identified by Krieg, 1946) grows at a much more rapid rate than do the other regions of the cortex. In fact, in the second postnatal week this area increases many fold. What determines the rapidity of this growth, so out of proportion to the rest of the cortex at this time, is not clear. Area 39 is reportedly a region where extensive sensory integration takes place. Is it possible

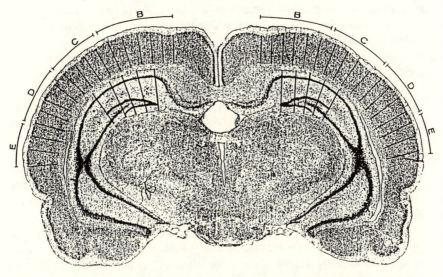

Figure 2. Cortical thickness growth curves from birth to 55 days of age.

that the eventual demands of child rearing by the female require early development of this integrative region to ensure her preparation for this role?

Investigators have reported concurrent maturational changes in the histology of the cortex (Schade and Ford, 1965) and in behavioral patterns (Tilney, 1934). Before 10 days of age, when cortical neuronal cell bodies are expanding but not sending out branches in any number, reflex actions are well developed. After 10 days of age, as the dendrites and axons increase richly and synaptogenesis proceeds rapidly, infant rats begin to crawl over their littermates and show signs of more mature behavior. By 30 days of age, the animals have attained adult behavior and the cortex has reached its maximum thickness. These observations were made while the animals were living in the uneventful laboratory environment.

Enriched Environments during the Preweaning Period

Cortical Thickness

Having established the developmental curve of the thickness of the male rat cerebral cortex, let us now explore how the external environment can modify this curve. The only available morphological work on the cortex of preweaned rats is that of Malkasian and Diamond (1971). The aims of these experiments were to determine the effects on cortical neurogenesis of an enriched condition combined with a multifamily environment as compared to nonenriched unifamily condition. An additional experiment examined the effect of a tranquilizer on the morphological cortical response in the enriched condition–multifamily environment. It was also of interest to compare the response of the preweaned rats' cortex to the environmental conditions with that of the adult animals.

The experimental conditions of these preweaned enriched and nonenriched environments were the following. At birth, all litters were reduced to three pups per mother. At 6 days of age, three conditions were established. (1) One mother and her three pups remained in the standard colony cage ($32 \times 20 \times 20 \times$ cm, unifamily nonenriched environment). (2) Three mothers with three pups each were placed in a single large cage ($70 \times 70 \times 46$ cm) (multifamily nonenriched environment). (3) Three mothers, each with three pups, were placed in a single large cage that contained objects to explore, climb, and sniff (multifamily enriched environment).

None of the pups was weaned at the usual time (between 21 and 23 days of age). Instead, they lived continuously with the mothers until autopsy at 26 days of age. No data are available about the direct effect of weaning on cerebral development.

Since the major thrust of the experiment was to determine whether stimulating living conditions could enhance brain development, more animals were studied in the experiment between the multifamily environmentally enriched (large cage and toys) and the unifamily nonenriched (small cage and no toys) environments than between the multifamily nonenriched (large cage and no toys) and the unifamily nonenriched (small cage and no toys) animals.

The results from these experiments indicated that when comparing the brains of the animals from the multifamily enriched conditions with those of the nonenriched group in small cages, the changes in cortical thickness were striking. As early as 14 days of age, i.e., 8 days after being placed in the enriched environment, the somatosensory cortex showed increases of 7–11% ($p < 0.001$) compared to the unifamily littermate controls. In particular, on the lateral aspect of the occipital cortical section, Area 39 increased as much as 16% ($p < 0.001$). It is noteworthy that during this early period, the primary visual cortex did not change, undoubtedly because the eyes had not as yet opened. By 19 days of age in response to the enriched conditions, most measured cortical areas showed significant increases in thickness with differences ranging from 7 to 12%. Statistically, these increases were highly significant.

There were no significant differences in cortical thickness, however, between the multifamily nonenriched and the unifamily nonenriched condition. Thus, it is the presence of the objects or toys, rather than grouped living in a large cage, that stimulates cortical changes. At the same time, it is not clear what aspect of the interaction with the toys is necessary, i.e., whether the cortical increase is due primarily to touch, pressure, temperature, vision, or other factors. Most likely, it is a combination of many varieties of incoming stimuli. Integration and sorting of stimuli are essential for priorities in responses.

These results clearly indicate that the maturation of the developing cerebral cortex can be accelerated by exposing an animal to reasonably stimulating environments. Many additional experiments are needed to answer the numerous questions that arise from these studies. For example, how much stimulation is optimal and at what point does it become excessive? Is there a ceiling that the cortex will reach with increased activity during this early developing period? Can one prevent normal neuronal cell loss by providing an enriched environment during this early period?

Needless to say, endless potential experiments could illuminate the optimum conditions for the growing cortex. Priority is a key issue. What are the most important questions to ask? What environmental input should be given and when? What is an optimal rate of input for optimal behavior? It is possible to stimulate one's children positively with enriched conditions and bring about negative effects . . . too much, too rapidly, and too soon.

As we are primarily interested in normal cortical development and aging in the laboratory, as a rule we do not study the effects of drugs on the brain. In the case, however, of these enriched preweaned rats, one group was given reserpine 0.1 mg injected subcutaneously each day from 6 to 28. This tranquilizer is a catecholamine depleting agent and was chosen for its possible effect on the increased cortical dimensions brought about by the enriched condition. In spite of the known tranquilizing effect of this drug, the medial cortical somatosensory cortex increased by as much as 7% ($p < 0.001$). Without the drug, this medial cortical area (area 4) increased by 8% ($p < 0.002$). In the more lateral portions of the somatosensory cortex (areas 3 and 2 of Krieg (1946), however, reserpine dampened the enrichment effects. Without the drug, areas 3 and 2 increases by 7 and 9%, respectively, but with the drug, the changes were only 5 and -1.5%. Evidently, different areas of the cortex respond individually to such a systemically introduced tranquilizer.

Cerebral Cortical Neuronal Area

One can ask at this time what intracortical structures change dimensions to create differences in cortical thickness? When the somatosensory cortex of the enriched pups was compared to that of the nonenriched, planimetric measurements of the mean neuronal nuclear and perikaryon areas indicated increases by as much as 19 and 15% in layers II and III, respectively. In the occipital cortex (area 18), the neuronal nuclear area of the enriched animals exceeded that of the nonenriched by as much as 25% ($p < 0.001$)!

Lateral Geniculate Neuronal Area

The lateral geniculate nucleus is a thalamic station for visual impulses; in the course of this study it, too, was examined for possible plasticity of response to an enriched environment. In the lateral geniculate nucleus there were no significant differences between the enriched and nonenriched animals, in the neuronal nuclear *area*, but the proportion of neuronal constituents was 20% ($p < 0.01$) less in the enriched than in the nonenriched rats. This means that when the lateral geniculate nucleus from the enriched animals was compared to that of the nonenriched, significantly more neuropil was present. Such results demonstrate one pathway that is involved in creating the enriched cortical differences, namely, the visual. These conclusions were not anticipated, for Krech et al. (1963) had shown that blind enriched rats or rats that had been raised in darkness during the experimental period developed increased occipital cortical weight. In other words, environmental enrichment actually enhanced the development of visual pathways that were not directly used by the animals.

Behavior

Some behavioral observations were made on these pups, but no specific maze tests were used as with the older animals. At the time of feeding and cleaning, no striking differences were noted between the enriched and nonenriched with respect to gregariousness or social behavior. Since, however, the enriched animals did have more room to explore, they interacted more frequently with their toys during the 12-hour dark period. Thus, the interaction with the toys was evidently an important factor in creating the brain changes.

Enriched Environments during the Postweaning Period

Cortical Thickness

As mentioned earlier, in the young male rat there are two slopes to the cortical thickness curve. For the first month of postnatal life the slope increases; for the remainder of the lifetime of the male rat, the slope decreases. Now that we have shown that the developing curve can be further accelerated, the next question is whether it is possible to counteract the decreasing slope by placing animals in enriched environments? For this group of experiments, the animals did not need to live with their mothers. Three basic experimental conditions were used (Rosenzweig et al., 1972): enriched, standard colony, and impoverished. The enriched environment consisted of 12 rats living in the large cage with stimulus objects or "toys"—the same objects used for the preweaned rats. To maintain the increased cortical dimensions, the objects must be changed frequently. The standard colony environment included three rats per small cage with no toys; and the impoverished, one rat per small cage also with no toys. Food, water, and lighting periods were available equally to all animals.

These experiments provided much new information. One, an enriched environment increased cortical thickness at any age from the very young to the extremely elderly rat. Significant morphological changes were noted as early as 4 days after exposure to an enriched condition. As mentioned above, it was found that continued substitution or replacement of the toys was essential. With constant exposure to the same objects, the rats' cortices decreased in size, the animals apparently becoming bored much as do people with the unchanging living conditions

If the rats separated immediately after weaning into enriched and impoverished conditions, the effects of the latter were stronger than the former. In other words, isolation immediately after weaning was markedly detrimental to cortical development. If after weaning, the rats were first placed into standard colony conditions for a month, and then transferred into either the enriched or impoverished conditions for 1 month, the enriched environmental input to the animals was more effective. Indeed this timing sequence established the largest overall cortical thickness increase encountered in these types of experiments. Also, isolation was not as detrimental to the cortex if the reduction in number of the animals into a single small cage took place gradually, i.e., from weaning to standard colony, and then finally to isolation for a short period (4 days). Isolation for as long as 30 days, however, produced a significant decrease in cortical structure, even if introduced gradually

Neuronal Size and Glial Measures

Once cortical structure had been shown to change with response to a positive environmental condition, many investigators, using various techniques and measurements, supported and expanded our basic findings. Thus, we now know that enrichment enhances the dimensions of the cerebral cortex (Altman et al., 1968; Walsh et al., 1971), enhances dendritic branching patterns (Conner et al., 1982; Greenough et al., 1973; Holloway 1966), alters the numbers and sizes of dendritic spines (Shapiro and Vukovich, 1970; Shapiro, 1971), changes synaptic length (Diamond et al., 1975b; Mollgaard et al., 1971; Walsh and Cummins, 1976; West and Greenough, 1972; Altschuler, 1976, in the hippocampus), and increases the numbers of glial cells (Altman and Das, 1964; Diamond et al., 1966).

These enriched and impoverished experiments have distinctly demonstrated that at any age, in response to the environmental input, the cerebral cortex can change its structure either positively or negatively (Diamond et al., 1985). Cummins and Livesey (1979) suggest that the primary cause of differential development is retarded neurological growth in the isolated animals. Jorgeson and Bock (1979), too, interpret their results as delayed development in the isolated rats. However, this theory has been refuted by the results of experiments of Uylings et al. (1979), which showed that in the adult, enriched rats, growth of dendrites had taken place compared with a baseline control. The baseline group was autopsied at 112 days of age. The enriched and controls were autopsied 30 days later. The enriched measurements were greater than those of the controls and baselines.

Chemical Changes due to Environmental Alterations

The studies on chemical changes in the brain in response to the environment have been carried out on postweaned rats. Brenner et al. (1983) experimented with pups placed into enriched environments at 1, 3, 5, and 7 days of age postnatally. If the pups received saline until 25 days of age, the cortical weight increased. If, however, they received 60HDA, cortical weight was lowered. The investigators concluded that norepinephrine influenced early cortical development. A very thorough review of the literature on chemical alteration with environment has been presented by Rosenzweig and Bennett (1978).

Findings due to Modifications of the Original Enriched Environmental Paradigm

Negative Air Ions

These experiments indicated that raising the level of small negative air ions (10^5 cm^3) while the preweaned animals lived in enriched or nonenriched conditions resulted in an increase in cerebral cortex wet weight and a decrease in amounts of endogenous serotonin and cyclic AMP. The cortical changes with ions were more marked if the rats lived in the enriched environmental conditions rather than in the nonenriched. This experiment shows the unusual sensitivity of the cerebral cortex to external environmental conditions such as air ions (Diamond et al., 1980).

Sleeping Patterns and the Environment

According to Mirmiran et al. (1983) if clonidine was given to rats from 8 to 21 days after birth, the amount of REM sleep was diminished. When this suppressing agent was employed, it prevented the usual enriched versus standard colony cortical weight increases. These authors reported that under enriched conditions active sleep and noradrenaline play a role in the growth of the cortex.

Tagney (1973) found that environmental conditions altered the sleeping patterns of postweaned rats. In the impoverished condition the rats spent only 45% of their time sleeping, as compared to 56% of the time in the enriched condition. For instance, if the animals were transferred from the impoverished to the enriched condition, the sleeping pattern of the rats followed those of the enriched rats.

Learning Ability after Enrichment

At every age at which they have been tested, enriched rats have run a maze better than the nonenriched animals. Forgays and Reed (1962) found improvement in learning at 123 days of age if the animals had begun an enriched condition at birth, 22, 44, or 66 days of age. Nyman (1967) found that from 30 to 40, 50 to 60, and 70 to 80 days, the rats given only 8 hours per day of environmental enrichment proved better at spatial learning than did nonenriched rats. An enriched environment after weaning improved problem-solving activity. Of course, one can always ask whether the laboratory-enriched environment is comparable to that of the wild rat's environment. The answer is simply and clearly "NO." The natural environment is more challenging because every moment is life preserving. The laboratory conditions, however, do provide a graded degree of stimulation whose effectiveness can be estimated from the results obtained from the reported cortical measurements.

Nutrition and Enriched Conditions

Bhide and Bedi (1984) concluded that 80 days of enriched environment could bring about changes in both undernourished and well fed pups. The pups were nutritionally deprived from day 16 of gestation until postnatal day 25. They were then divided into isolated or enriched conditions until 80 days later. These data are presented with some reservations because the usual cortical thickness changes with healthy nonnutritionally deprived rats in enriched and impoverished conditions were not obtained!

In another group of nutritionally deprived and normally fed animals followed by enriched conditions, the cerebrum of undernourished animals showed deficits in weight and size but not in cortical thickness (Davis and Katz, 1983). Changes in cerebral weight and size also occurred as a result of differential housing; relative to their impoverished littermates, the enriched rats showed increased values. A recent study on enriched conditions used to rehabilitate the cerebral cortex in "protein deprived" rats confirmed these findings (Carughi et al., 1989).

Sexual Maturation and Enriched Environment

Swanson and Poll (1983) handled rats from birth to 30 days of age before placing them in enriched, standard colony or isolated environments. Isolation advanced vaginal opening in both handled and nonhandled rats. Isolation also improved sexual performance more than either the standard or the enriched condition.

Implications for Human Brain Development and Evolution

Philosophers and scientists have long debated the question, "Which is more important, nature or nuture?" Both sides sometimes assume that the biological substrates of behavior, including brain structure, are imprinted in the genome, hence, immutable. Based on our studies, this premise is wrong. The structure of the brain is, in many ways, highly plastic. Thus, the quantity of neural tissue that a rat can bring to bear on its learning processes reflects its environmental history as well as its genetic heritage. Similarly, certain aspects of cortical structure including ratios of glial cells to nerve cells and the size and numbers of synapses are influenced by environmental parmeters. In rats, at least, behavior reflects the structure of the brain, but the converse is also true, the structure of the brain reflects past behavior and other environmental circumstances.

As discussed earlier, human and rat brains exhibit highly similar neural developmental processes and sequences. Given this overall resemblance, the most parsimonious hypothesis is that similar developmental mechanisms influence neural growth in both species. Thus, one would expect that human brain size and cortical structure would also be influenced by environmental stimulation, nutrition, sleeping patterns, chemical intake, and the ionic balance of the air.

We cannot section the brains of healthy humans to examine cortical structure. Nor can we arbitrarily divide humans into controlled groups varying in environmental stimulation and nutritive balance. Society, however, has performed many experiments of its own. For social, political, and economic reasons, people experience varying degrees of intellectual stimulation and nutritional enrichment. A number of investigators have studied brain size in nutritionally deprived groups (see review by Morgan and Gibson, this volume). Others have looked at the interactions of nutritional deprivation, environmental enrichment, and intelligence. Nutritional deprivation clearly impinges on human and rat brains in a very similar manner. Just as environmental enrichment can help mitigate the negative effects of nutritional deprivation in rats (Carughi, 1987), it can do the same in humans (Lien et al., 1977; Winick et al., 1970). Further, the concept that early intellectual stimulation improves later intellectual function is so firmly ingrained in the American mind, that we have initiated special social programs to enrich the minds of young children from impoverished environments. Many lines of evidence converge in supporting the concept that human brains are also malleable.

Determining precisely how malleable the human brain is and what types of intellectual stimulation best facilitate its growth are, of course, complex issues. We cannot answer these questions by extrapolating directly from rat studies. Based on our rat work, we can, however, suggest some hypotheses and lines of inquiry. First, we might note that the environmental enrichment provided to our rats consisted primarily of toys. The animals were free to interact with the toys or not to interact at will. Thus, our enriched environments more closely approximated playrooms equipped with a variety of toys and other objects, than they did classrooms or other organized activities that are often forced on modern human children.

In the early years of our work, we did examine the effects of specific training in maze learning on the rat's brain. Our results suggested that while such training does result in increased brain size, fewer areas of the brain are affected and the overall effect on brain size is less than in our environmentally enriched groups. While our work suggests that environmental enrichment is helpful to neural growth, it does not imply that long hours of formal study or practice that lead to exhaustion, boredom, or anxiety are necessarily the appropriate way to provide this stimulation. We believe that a wide range of activities that stimulate all five senses and many neural areas, interspersed with adequate sleep, rest, and relaxation will probably provide the greatest neural effect.

Perhaps one of the most important implications of our study is that environmental stimulation can have beneficial effects on the brain at any age. That this may also be true in humans is evident from a variety of recent studies suggesting that many elderly people do maintain excellent brain function, as measured by alertness and intelligence, into old age (Henig, 1981). In general, those older people who have remained active and whose environments have remained stimulating maintain their neural and intellectual functions, at least as long as they remain physically healthy. This does not mean that environmental stimulation in adulthood can totally mitigate against severe environmental deprivation in infancy. We have, for instance, no evidence that new cortical neurons can be generated in adult mammals. It does mean, however, that whatever one's neural endowment, frequent use of the mind may improve it even in old age.

As this book is intended for anthropological audiences, it is perhaps fitting that a few words be stated relative to the long standing issue of whether brain size or brain structure correlates with intelligence in humans. In the nineteenth century, many scientists thought that brain size determined intelligence. However, both their brain size data and their measures of intelligence were highly flawed (Tobias, 1970; Gould, 1981). In recent decades, many anthropologists have come to believe that brain size bears no relationship to intelligence, although few well-controlled studies of this issue exist. It is, for instance, impossible to examine brain weight or histology in healthy individuals in the prime of life, and many illnesses result in neural deterioration.

Our own laboratories have collected no data on human brain size. We were privileged, however, to examine portions of the brain of Albert Einstein. The left parietal association area (area 39) of Einstein's brain contained a significantly higher ratio of glial cells to neurons than does the average human brain ($N =$ 11). Thus, limited data from one individual tentatively support the concept that the high ratios of glial cells to neurons that are characteristic of enlarged rat brains may also be characteristic of portions of the brains of humans who make full use of their intellectual potential.

Most importantly, our data suggest that one basic premise underlying many arguments about the significance of human differences in brain size is wrong. Brain size is not fixed. Hence, brain size variations within a species do not necessarily reflect differences in genetic endowment except in cases in which all species members experience the same environment. Such environmental similarity cannot be postulated for the human species. Wide variations in nutrition, intellectual stimulation, drug use, and magnetic and ionic fields differentiate human individuals and populations from each other. Thus, differences in brain size may often reflect environmental history

From an evolutionary standpoint, a final critical question involves the extent to which brain size and structure are malleable. A number of investigators have suggested that the development of brain and behavior in humans and other animals reflects canalized epigenetic processes (Gibson, 1981; Fishbein, 1976; Wilson, 1978). In other words, the genome codes for a delimited range of behaviors and neural structures, but not every aspect of behavioral and natural development is directly written into the genome. Since most species members encounter roughly similar environmental conditions, the genome is programmed to interact with the environmental conditions usually encountered. Thus, species similarities in neural and behavioral structures result both from shared environments and from shared genes. Adele Diamond (this volume) supports this view and suggests that environmental variations are somewhat limited in their effects on monkey neural and cognitive development. She finds that enhanced environments may accelerate the development of cognitive structures in nonhuman primates but they do not produce unique behaviors or change basic developmental sequences.

Our own studies have not been designed to directly test canalization hypotheses. They do, however, strongly support one aspect of canalization theory. Brain size and brain structure reflect genetic and environmental interactions. Indirectly, our studies also accord with other aspects of canalization theory. Thus, we have no data that would suggest that environmental enrichment can turn a rat brain into a monkey brain. Nor do we have data that would suggest that potential brain size increases are unlimited. Our enriched rats remained rats in both their brain structure and in their behavior. They simply became smarter than average rats with larger than average brains. We expect the same is true of humans. Environmental enrichment will produce smarter than average humans. No evidence indicates that it can produce people with brains, behaviors, or abilities that lie outside the normal human range.

Conclusion

Plasticity of the cerebral cortex is evident in both preweaned and postweaned rats. Whether they are from rats or man, nerve cells are designed to receive stimuli, store information, and transmit impulses, and the environmental situations that they have encountered can enhance or depress their ability to do this. Thus, the results obtained from animal studies can be used as guidelines to help understand the human brain. Such questions as how much stimulation is beneficial or detrimental, the optimal timing of stimulation, and whether there is a ceiling to cortical growth are yet to be answered and will probably require specific human data.

References

Altman, J., and Das, G. D. (1964). Autoradiographic examination of the effects of enriched environment on the rate of glial multiplication in the adult rat brain. *Nature, (London), 204,* 1161–1163.

Altman, J., Wallace, R. B., Anderson, W. J., and Das, G. D. (1968). Behaviorally induced changes in length of cerebrum in rats. *Developmental Psychobiology, 1,* 112–117.

Altschuler, R. (1976). Changes in hippocampal presynaptic density with increased learning experiences in the rat. *Neurosciences Abstracts, 2,* 438.

Bhide, P. G., and Bedi, K. S. (1984). The effects of environmental diversity on well fed and previously undernourished rats: Neuronal and glial cell measurements in the visual cortex (area 17). *Journal of Anatomy, 138,* 447–461.

Brenner, E., Mirmiran, M., Uylings, H. B., and Van der Gusten, J. (1983). Impaired growth of the cerebral cortex of rats treated neonatally with 6-hydroxydopamine under different environmental conditions. *Neurosciences Letters, 42,* 13–17.

Carughi, A. (1987). The effect of environmental enrichment during nutritional rehabilitation on certain parameters of cortical development. Ph.D. thesis, University of California, Berkeley.

Carughi, A., Carpenter, K. J., and Diamond, M. C. (1990). The effect of environmental enrichment during nutritional rehabilitation on body growth, blood parameters and cerebral cortical development. *Journal of Nutritional Development, 119,* 2005–2016.

Chase, H. P. (1976). Undernutrition and the growth and development of the human brain. In J. Lloyd-Still, (Ed.), *Malnutrition and intellectual development* (pp. 13–38). Lancaster: M. T. P.

Conel, J. L. (1939–1967). *The postnatal development of the human cerebral cortex,* Vols. 1–8. Cambridge, MA: Harvard University Press.

Conner, J. R., Wang, E. C., and Diamond, M. C. (1982). Increased length of terminal dendritic segments in old rats' somatosensory cortex: An environmentally induced response. *Experimental Neurology, 78,* 466–470.

Cummins, R. A., and Livesey, P. J. (1979). Enrichment-isolation, cortex length and range order effect. *Brain Research, 178,* 89–98.

Davies, C. A., and Katz, H. B. (1983). The comparative effects of early-life undernutrition and subsequent differential environments on the dendritic branching of pyramidal cells in rat visual cortex. *Journal of Comparatiive Neurology, 218,* 345–350.

Diamond, M. C., Rosenzweig, M. R., and Krech, D. (1965). Relationships between body weight and skull development in rats raised in enriched and impoverished conditions. *Journal of Experimental Zoology, 160,* 29–36.

Diamond, M. C., Law, F., Rhodes, H., Lindner, B., Rosenzweig, M. R., Krech, D., and Bennett, E. L. (1966). Increases in cortical depth and glia numbers in rats subjected to enriched environment. *Journal of Comparative Neurology, 128,* 117–126.

Diamond, M. C., Johnson, R. E., and Ingham, C. A. (1975a). Morphological changes in the young, adult and aging rat cerebral cortex, hippcampus and diencephalon. *Behavioral Biology, 14,* 163–174.

Diamond, M. C., Lindner, B., Johnson, R., Bennett, E. L., and Rosenzweig, M. R. (1975b). Differences in occipital cortical synapses from environmentally enriched, impoverished, and standard colony rats. *Journal of Neuroscience Research, 1(2),* 109–119.

Diamond, M. C., Conner, J., Jr., Orenberg, E. K., Bissell, M., Yost, M., and Krueger, A. (1980). Environmental influences on serotonin and cyclic nucleotides in rat cerebral cortex. *Science, 210,* 652–654.

Diamond, M. C., Johnson, R. E., Protti, A. M., and Kjias, L. (1985). Plasticity in the 904-day-old male rat cerebral cortex. *Experimental Neurology, 87,* 309–317.

Dobbing, J., and Sands., J. (1973). Quantitative growth and development of the human brain. *Archives of Disease in Childhood, 48,* 757–767.

Epstein, H. T. (1978). Growth spurts during brain development: Implications for educational policy and practice. In J. S. Chall and A. F. Mirsky (Eds.), *Education and the brain.* Chicago, IL: University of Chicago Press.

Fishbein, H. D. (1976). *Evolution, development and children's learning.* Pacific Palisades: Goodyear.

Flechsig, P. (1920). *Anatomie des menschlichen Gehirns und Rueckenmark auf myelogenetischer Grundlage.* Liepzig: George Thomas.

Forgays, D. G., and Read, J. M. (1962). Crucial periods for free-environmental experience in the rat. *Journal of Comparative and Physiological Psychology, 55,* 816–818.

Gibson, K. R. (1981). Comparative Neuroontogeny: its implications for the development of human intelligence. In G. Butterworth (Ed.), *Infancy and epistemology* (pp. 52–82). Brighton, England: Harvester Press.

Gould, S. (1981). *The mismeasure of man.* New York: Norton.

Greenough, W. T., Volkmar, F. R., and Juraska, J. M. (1973). Effects of rearing complexity on dendritic branching in frontolateral and temporal cortex of the rat. *Experimental Neurology, 41,* 371–378.

Henig, R. M. (1981). *The myth of senility.* Garden City, NY: Anchor Press.

Holloway, R. (1966). Dendritic branching in rat visual cortex. Effects of extra environmental complexity and training. *Brain Research, 2,* 393.

Jacobsen, S. (1963). Sequence of myelinization in the brain of the albino rat. A: Cerebral cortex, thalamus and related structures. *Journal of Comparative Neurology, 121,* 5–29.

Jacobson, M. (1978). *Developmental neurology.* New York: Plenum Press.

Jorgenson, O. S., and Bock, E. (1979). Brain specific proteins in the occipital cortex of rats housed in enriched and impoverished environments. *Neurochemistry Research, 4,* 175–187.

Krech, D., Rosenzweig, M. R., and Bennett, E. L. (1963). Effects of complex environment and blindness on the rat brain. *Archives of Neurology, 8,* 403–412.

Krieg, W. (1946). Connections of the cerebral cortex. I. The albino rat B. Structure of the cortical areas. *Journal of Comparative Neurology, 84,* 278–323.

Lien, N. M., Meyer, K. K., Winick, M. (1977). Early malnutrition and "late" adoption: A study of their effects on the development of Korean orphans adopted into American famillies. *American Journal of Clinical Nutrition, 30,* 1734–1739.

Malkasian, D. R., and Diamond, M. C. (1971). The effects of environmental manipulation on the morphology of the neonate rat brain. *International Journal of Neuroscience, 2,* 161–170.

Mirmiran. M., Uylings, H. B., and Corner, M. A. (1983). Pharmacological suppression of REM sleep prior to weaning counteracts the effectiveness of subsequent environmental enrichment on cortical growth in rats. *Brain Research, 283,* 102–105.

Mollgaard, K., Diamond, M. C., Bennett, E. L., Rosenzweig, M. R., and Lindner, B. (1971). Quantitative synaptic changes with differential experience in rat brain. *International Journal of Neuroscience, 2,* 113–128.

Nyman, A. J. (1967). Problem solving in rats as a function of experience at different ages. *Journal of Genetic Psychology, 110,* 31–39.

Ramon y Cajal, S. (1911). *Histologie du Systeme Nerveux de l'home et des Vertebre.* Reprinted by Consojo Superior de Investigaciones Cientificas, Madrid.

Rosenzweig, M. R., and Bennett, E. L. (1978). Experimental influences on brain anatomy and brain chemistry in rodents. In G. Gottlieb (Ed.), *Studies on the development of behavior and the nervous system.* (Vol. 4, pp. 289–327). *Early influences.* New York: Academic Press.

Rosenweiz, M. R., Bennett, E. L., and Diamond, M. C. (1972). Chemical and anatomical plasticity of brain: Replication and extensions, 1970. In J. Caito (Ed.), *Macromolecules and behavior,* 2nd ed. (pp. 205–277). New York: Appleton-Century-Crofts.

Schade, J. P., and Ford, D. H. (1965). *Basic neurology.* New York: Elsevier.

Shapiro, S. (1971). Hormonal and environmental influences on rat brain development and behavior. In M. B. Sterman, D. J. McGinty, and A. M. Adinolfi (Eds.), *Brain development and behavior* (pp. 307–334). New York: Academic Press.

Shapiro, S., and Vukovich, K. R. (1970). Early experience effects upon cortical dendrites: A proposed model for development. *Science, 167,* 292–294.

Swanson, H. H., and Van de Poll, N. E. (1983). Effects of an isolated or enriched environment after handling on sexual maturation and behavior in male female rats. *Journal of Reproductive Fertility, 69,* 165–171.

Tagney, J. (1973). Sleep patterns related to rearing rats in enriched and impoverished environments. *Brain Research, 53,* 353–361.

Tilney, F. (1934). Behavior and its relation to the development of the brain. Part II. Correlation between the development of the brain and behavior in the albino rat from embryonic states to maturity. *Bulletin Neurological Institute of New York, 3,* 252–358.

Tobias, P. (1970). Brain size, grey matter and race—Fact or fiction? *American Journal of Physical Anthropology, 32,* 3–26.

Uylings, H. B. M., Kupers, K., Diamond, M. C., and Veltman, W. A. M. (1979). Dendritic outgrowth in the visual cortex of adult rats under different environmental conditions. *Experimental Neurology, 62,* 658–677.

Walsh, R. N., and Cummins, R. A. (1976). Effects of differential sensory environments on the electron microscopy of the rat occipital cortex. *Proceedings of the Society for Neuroscience: Annual Meeting, 2,* 839.

Walsh, R. N., Budtz-Olsen, O. E., Torok, A., and Cummins, R. A. (1971). Environmentally-induced changes in the dimensions of the rat cerebrum. *Developmental Psychobiology, 4,* 115–122.

West, R. W., and Greenough, W. T. (1972). Effect of environmental complexity on cortical synapses of rats: Preliminary results. *Behavioral Biology, 7,* 279–284.

Wilson, R. S. (1978). Synchronies in mental development: An epigenetic perspective. *Science, 202,* 939–948.

Winick, M. (1976). *Malnutrition and brain development.* London and New York: Oxford University Press.

Winick, M., Rosso, P., and Waterlow, J. (1970). Cellular growth of cerebrum, cerebellum, and brain stem in normal and marasmic children. *Experimental Neurology, 26,* 393–400.

PART III

PRIMATE AND HUMAN BEHAVIORAL DEVELOPMENT FROM A BIOSOCIAL PERSPECTIVE

Chapter 7

Frontal Lobe Involvement in Cognitive Changes During the First Year of Life

Adele Diamond

The period of 6–12 months of age is a time of major change in the behaviors and cognitive abilities of human infants. The same changes, at roughly the same age, are found in infants in diverse physical, cultural, and social environments. This has led many to speculate that these changes may be, at least in part, biologically based. This chapter reports evidence suggesting that maturation of the frontal lobe[1] may play a role in some of the cognitive changes occurring in human infants between 6 and 12 months of age.

This line of inquiry has involved (1) studying the developmental progression of human infants and infant monkeys on tasks thought to depend on frontal cortex function, and (2) taking those same tasks and determining directly whether they are linked specifically to frontal cortex through studies of brain function in adult and infant monkeys. It has been important to supplement work on brain function in adult animals with work on infant animals because of the possibility that different neural systems might underlie successful performance of the tasks at different ages.

One of the classic markers of developmental change between 6 and 12 months is improved performance on Piaget's $A\overline{B}$ task (pronounced ''A not B'') (Piaget, 1954 [1937]). Since the task was originally devised it has been used extensively with infants (for reviews see Gratch, 1975; Schuberth, 1982; Harris, 1987; Wellman et al., 1987). It turns out that $A\overline{B}$ is almost identical to the classic test for frontal lobe function in nonhuman primates, delayed response (DR). Although both $A\overline{B}$ and DR have been in use for half a century, the psychologists studying human infant development and the neuroscientists studying brain function did not know they were using essentially the same task and their work remained separate. The initial insight that frontal lobe maturation might underlie some of the behavior changes between 6 and 12 months was suggested by the similarity between $A\overline{B}$ and DR and the dependence of DR on frontal cortex.

In both $A\overline{B}$ and DR, the subject watches as a desired object is hidden in one of two identical wells, the wells are covered simultaneously, a delay of 0–10 sec is imposed, and then the subject is allowed to reach. Within-trial procedures are exactly the same on the two tasks. $A\overline{B}$ and DR differ only in how side of hiding is varied over trials. In DR, side of hiding is varied randomly; in $A\overline{B}$, the reward is consistently hidden on one side until the subject is correct, then side of hiding is reversed and the procedure repeated.

Evidence Linking Delayed Response to the Frontal Lobe

Success on DR has consistently been shown to depend on frontal lobe function (specifically, dorsolateral prefrontal cortex) by virtually every anatomical, physiological, and pharmacological technique in existence. DR was first used to study functions localized to frontal cortex by Jacobsen (1935, 1936), and scores of lesion studies have replicated Jacobsen's finding that animals fail DR following bilateral lesions of frontal cortex (major reviews include Nauta, 1971; Rosvold, 1972; Markowitsch and Pritzel, 1977; Rosenkilde, 1979; Fuster, 1980). Equally large lesions elsewhere in the brain, e.g., parietal cortex, do not produce deficits on DR (e.g., Jacobsen, 1936; Meyer et al., 1951; Harlow et al., 1952). Lesions of frontal cortex that produce deficits on DR do not produce deficits on other tasks, such as visual discrimination (e.g., Jacobsen, 1936; Harlow and Dagnon, 1943; Pohl, 1973). In short, DR appears to be sensitive to damage specifically to dorsolateral prefrontal cortex and damage to dorsolateral prefrontal cortex appears to produce deficits only on specific tasks, such as DR.

These results have been replicated with techniques that enable experimenters to temporarily and reversibly interrupt functioning of a localized neural region. Thus, DR has also been linked to the dorsolateral prefrontal cortex using localized cooling (Fuster and Alexander, 1971; Bauer and Fuster, 1976; Alexander and Goldman, 1978), localized electrical stimulation (Weiskrantz et al., 1962; Stamm, 1969; Stamm and Rosen, 1969), and localized dopamine depletion (depleted using 6-OHDA, deficits reversed by L-Dopa) (Brozoski et al., 1979). Because these techniques interrupt functioning only temporarily, they effectively eliminate neural reorganization or secondary degeneration as competing explanations for observed behavioral effects. Moreover, because animals can be tested before and after cooling, stimulation, or dopamine depletion, each animal can serve as his or her own control, eliminating concerns about between-group differences.

Inferring function from dysfunction can be problematic, however. Deficits resulting from permanent damage or temporary inactivation do not always give an accurate indication of the role played by a neural region in intact, normally functioning subjects. For this reason it is important that the link between DR and the frontal lobe has been confirmed by techniques that assess patterns of functioning in the intact brain. Stamm (1969) and Stamm and Rosen (1969) confirmed this link by measuring surface negative steady potential shifts. Niki (1974), Fuster and Alexander (1971), and Fuster (1973) implanted micro-electrodes and recorded single unit activity, demonstrating the importance of frontal lobe firing for correct performance of DR. DR trials on which monkeys reached correctly are most often those trials on which there has been increased firing of neurons in dorsolateral prefrontal cortex during the delay period of the trial. Finally, using 2-deoxyglucose metabolic labeling, Bugbee and Goldman-Rakic (1981) demonstrated that local glucose utilization is elevated in dor-solateral prefrontal cortex during performance of DR, while other areas (e.g., motor cortex) show no changes relative to baseline during DR performance.

All of this work taken together, representing as it does such diverse experi-mental approaches, makes the link between DR and dorsolateral prefrontal cortex essentially incontrovertible.

Evidence of the Similarity between the Performance of Human Infants on AB and the Performance of Monkeys with Lesions of Frontal Cortex on Delayed Response

The performance of infants from 7½ to 9 months on $\overline{AB}^2$ matches that of monkeys with lesions of dorsolateral prefrontal cortex in striking detail. At delays as brief as 1–5 sec, infants fail $\overline{AB}$ and frontally lesioned monkeys fail DR (*infants*: Evans, 1973; Gratch et al., 1974; Diamond, 1985; *monkeys:* Harlow et al., 1952; Battig et al., 1960; Goldman and Rosvold, 1970; Fuster and Alex-ander, 1971). This is true whether the hiding places differ in left–right location (*infants:* Gratch and Lander, 1971; Diamond, 1985; *monkeys:* Harlow et al., 1952; Goldman et al., 1970) or up–down location (*infants:* Butterworth, 1976; *monkeys:* Fuster, 1980). However, both groups of subjects succeed when there is no delay (*infants*: Gratch et. al., 1974; Harris, 1973; *monkeys*: Harlow et. al., 1952; Battig et. al., 1960; Goldman et. al., 1970; Fuster and Alexander, 1971), or when they are allowed to keep looking at, or orienting their body toward, the correct well during the delay (*infants:* Cornell, 1979; Fox et. al., 1979; Dia-mond, 1985; *monkeys:* Battig et. al., 1969; Miles and Blomquist, 1960; Pinsker and French, 1967). Both are able to learn to associate a landmark with the correct well, and to use that information to reach correctly even at long delays (*infants:* Butterworth et al., 1982; Diamond, 1983; *monkeys:* Pohl, 1973).

Another task closely linked to frontal lobe function is Spatial Reversal. Here, side of hiding is varied in a manner more similar to $\overline{AB}$: the reward is always hidden on one side until the subject is correct, then it is hidden on the other side and the procedure repeated. In $\overline{AB}$, side of hiding is reversed after the subject has reached correctly on two trials in a row. In Spatial Reversal, side of hiding is reversed after the subject has reached correctly on 90% of 30 or 100 trials, thus days of testing often occur before side of hiding is reversed. Although $\overline{AB}$ and Spatial Reversal are similar in the manner in which side of hiding is determined, they differ in an important within-trial procedure: in Spatial Reversal the subject does not see where the reward is hidden, whereas in A$\overline{B}$ and DR the hiding is done in full view.

Spatial Reversal requires the subject to deduce where the reward is hidden on the basis of feedback. Initially, the reward is always hidden in the same place. If the subject reaches there he gets the reward, if not he gets nothing. Animals with frontal lobe damage have no difficulty learning this initial spatial discrimination (e.g., Gross and Weiskrantz, 1962; Goldman and Rosvold, 1970). When side of hiding is reversed, however, frontally operated animals are impaired; they persist in reaching to the previously correct place (e.g., Butter, 1969; Mishkin et al., 1969; Goldman & Rosvold, 1970; Butters et al., 1969.)

This is very similar to the pattern of performance of infants on A$\overline{B}$: they are correct at the first place the reward is hidden, but when side of hiding is reversed errors appear; infants persist in reaching to the previously correct place (Harris, 1973; Gratch et al., 1974; Diamond, 1985).

Failure on DR and Spatial Reversal is the hallmark of lesions to the dorsolateral prefrontal region of the frontal lobe. A$\overline{B}$ appears to be a composite of DR and Spatial Reversal: identical to DR on within-trial procedures, similar to Spatial Reversal on between-trial procedures.

The Wisconsin Card Sorting Test was designed to be an adaptation of the Spatial Reversal task appropriate for human adults (Berg, 1948; Grant and Berg, 1948), and it has become the classic test for damage of the frontal lobe, especially dorsolateral prefrontal cortex (Milner, 1963, 1964). On this test, the subject is required to deduce the correct criterion (color, shape, or number) for sorting a deck of cards on the basis of feedback.

Adult patients with damage to frontal cortex learn the initial sorting criterion on the Wisconsin Card Sort normally but are impaired when the criterion is switched; nonhuman primates with frontal cortex damage learn the initial spatial discrimination normally on Spatial Reversal but are impaired when side of hiding is reversed; 7½- to 9-month-old infants are able to correctly find a toy at the first place it is hidden during A$\overline{B}$ testing, but err when side of hiding is reversed.

Statement of Hypothesis and Experimental Plan

Because (1) A$\overline{B}$ and DR are such similar tasks, (2) DR has been so firmly linked to frontal cortex function in nonhuman primates, and (3) the performance of human infants on A$\overline{B}$ is so similar to the performance of nonhuman primates with lesions of frontal cortex on DR, I hypothesized that maturation of frontal cortex might make possible the improved performance on A$\overline{B}$ observed in infants from 7½ to 12 months of age. Further support for this came from A$\overline{B}$'s similarity to another marker of frontal lobe function in the monkey, Spatial Reversal, and from A$\overline{B}$'s similarity to the best marker for frontal lobe function in human adults, the Wisconsin Card Sort. If maturation of the frontal lobe does underlie some of the cognitive advances between 7½ and 12 months, then infants should improve during that age range not only on A$\overline{B}$, but on other tests requiring cognitive abilities dependent on the frontal lobe.

To test this hypothesis infants were administered two tasks, both similar to ones linked to frontal cortex function, but otherwise very dissimilar from one another. Twenty-five full-term infants (11 male, 14 female) were studied longitudinally, with testing on both tasks every 2 weeks from roughly 6 to 12 months. To control for repeated testing, another 84 children were tested only once. One of the tasks on which the infants were tested was A$\overline{B}$ (Diamond, 1985). The second task was quite different from A$\overline{B}$ to eliminate the possibility that an apparent link to frontal cortex functioning might be due to some artifact of the A$\overline{B}$ paradigm. I called the second task "Object Retrieval" (Diamond, 1981, submitted).

Object Retrieval requires infants to retrieve a toy from a simple transparent box open on one side. Although the toy can be seen through the box, the infant must reach around to the opening to actually obtain the toy. The idea for Object Retrieval came from a task on which Moll and Kuypers (1977) had demonstrated impairments following lesions of the frontal lobe[3] in monkeys: food could be seen beneath the center of a transparent floor plate, but the only route to the food was through a hole in the plate's side. Monkeys with lesions of the frontal lobe reached straight for the food at the center of the plate, although normal monkeys and those with lesions elsewhere had no difficulty making the appropriate detour. When a unilateral frontal lobe lesion was combined with a commissurotomy, the hand contralateral to the lesioned hemisphere persisted in reaching at the plate's center, while the hand connected to the intact hemisphere of the same monkey reached through the hole to the food!

Testing infants on A$\overline{B}$ and Object Retrieval was only the first step toward testing the hypothesis, however. No direct evidence on brain function was obtained from the infants because of lack of safe, noninvasive techniques for studying the brain. Therefore, step 2 was to administer A$\overline{B}$ and Object Retrieval, the exact tasks on which developmental progressions had been charted in infants, to nonhuman primates with lesions of the frontal lobe (Diamond and Goldman-Rakic, 1985, 1989). The critical questions were would they be impaired on these tasks and would their errors be similar to those made by the younger infants. Nine adult rhesus monkeys *(Macaca mulatta)* were tested every weekday for 15 weeks. Three animals received bilateral lesions of dorsolateral prefrontal cortex (Brodmann's areas 8, 9, and 10), three received bilateral parietal cortex lesions (Brodmann's area 7B), and three were unoperated. All ablations were bilateral, symmetrical, and performed in one stage. The prefrontal and parietal lesions were comparable in size (see Figure 1). A minimum of 2 weeks was allowed for postoperative recovery.

The next most likely neural region to be related to A$\overline{B}$ and Object Retrieval performance was the hippocampus because of the importance of the hippocam-

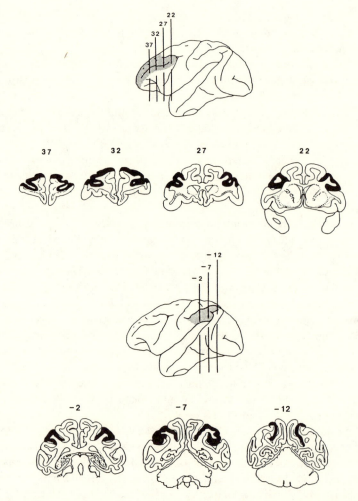

Figure 1. Diagram of intended lesions to dorsolateral prefrontal cortex and inferior parietal cortex, projected on the left hemisphere and in coronal sections. The prefrontal site is shown above and the parietal site below. The dorsolateral prefrontal lesions included cortex in both banks of the principal sulcus, the anterior bank of the arcuate sulcus, and all tissue on the dorsolateral surface rostral of the arcuate sulcus (Brodmann's areas 8, 9, and 10), similar to lesions reported in Goldman (1971). The parietal lesions included the posterior bank of the intraparietal sulcus, the anterior bank of the superior temporal sulcus for about 10 mm, and all cortex between the two sulci including roughly 4 mm of the Sylvian fissure (most of Brodmann's area 7B). All ablations were bilateral, symmetrical, and performed in one stage. These animals are still involved in behavioral experiments, and so histological verification of lesion sites is not yet available. (From A. Diamond and P. G. Goldman-Rakic, "Comparison of human infants and rhesus monkeys on Piaget's AB̄ task: Evidence for dependence on dorsolateral prefrontal cortex," *Experimental Brain Research, 74,* 24–40. Copyright © 1990. Reprinted with permission of Springer-Verlag, Heidelberg.)

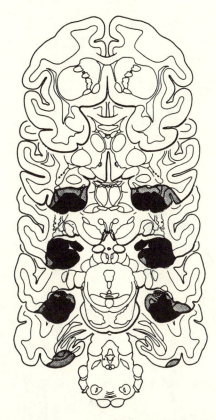

Figure 2. Representative coronal sections through the temporal lobe showing the extent of damage (shaded area) in a representative monkey in the hippocampal group. All three monkeys sustained extensive bilateral removal of the hippocampal formation. The hippocampus, including the dentate gyrus and subicular cortex, was removed for its entire extent, except for the most anterior 2–3 mm in two cases. In two monkeys, the removal also included over 90% of the parahippocampal gyrus (area TF-TH of von Bonin and Bailey) and the posterior half of the entorhinal cortex. In the third animal, damage to the parahippocampal gyrus was less extensive and the entorhinal cortex was only slightly involved. The second animal sustained slight direct damage to the amygdaloid complex, involving the ventral limit of the posterior border of the lateral nucleus. The amygdala was entirely spared in the other two animals. The caudate and the temporal stem were undamaged in all animals. The medial dorsal nucleus of the thalamus appeared normal during histological examination. Extensive gliosis was observed bilaterally throughout the fornix.

pus in memory and spatial functions. Since monkeys with lesions of the hippocampal formation could not be included in the first study, a second study was conducted with six adult cynomolgus monkeys *(Macaca fascicularis)*. Three received bilateral lesions of the hippocampal formation (see Figure 2) and three were unoperated (Diamond et al., 1989b). All six were tested on A$\overline{\text{B}}$ and Object Retrieval.

Table 1. Brain Lesions and Task Performance-Literature Summary

	$A\bar{B}$	Delayed Response	Object Retrieval
Human infants	Diamond (1985)	Diamond and Doar (1989)	Diamond (1990a)
Adult monkeys with lesions of frontal cortex	Diamond and Goldman-Rakic (1989)	Diamond and Goldman-Rakic (1989)	Diamond and Goldman-Rakic (1985)
Adult monkeys with lesions of parietal cortex	Diamond and Goldman-Rakic (1989)	Diamond and Goldman-Rakic (1989)	Diamond and Goldman-Rakic (1985)
Adult monkeys with lesions to the hippocampus	Diamond et al. (1989[b])	Squire and Zola-Morgan (1983)	Diamond et al. (1989[b])
Infant monkeys	Diamond and Goldman-Rakic (1986)	Diamond and Goldman-Rakic (1986)	Diamond and Goldman-Rakic (1986)
5-month-old infant monkeys, who received lesions of frontal cortex at 4 months	Diamond and Goldman-Rakic (1986)	Diamond and Goldman-Rakic (1986)	

The next step was to try to link developmental changes in performance of $A\overline{B}$ and Object Retrieval to maturational changes in the frontal lobe of infant monkeys. Four infant rhesus monkeys were studied longitudinally, with testing every weekday from 40 to 150 days. At the end of testing (4½ months), two of the infant monkeys received bilateral ablations of dorsolateral prefrontal cortex (Brodmann's areas 8, 9, and 10) (Diamond and Goldman-Rakic, 1986).

Finally, to complete the $A\overline{B}$–DR comparison, human infants were tested on DR. Twelve infants (six male, six female) were tested every 2 weeks and another 36 infants were tested only once on DR (Diamond and Doar, 1989) (see Table 1).

Testing Procedures

The $A\overline{B}$ Task

The $A\overline{B}$ apparatus consisted of a testing tray with embedded wells. All subjects were tested individually in the laboratory. For testing human infants, the subject was seated on the parent's lap facing the testing table, equidistant from the wells. The experimenter was seated across the table, facing parent and child. A trial began with the experimenter holding up a toy to catch the infant's attention. As the subject watched, the experimenter slowly hid the toy in one of two wells. Particular care was taken to ensure that the subject observed this.

Both wells were then covered simultaneously and the delay period began. Subjects were prevented from straining, turning, or looking at a well during the delay. The parent restrained the infant's arms and torso gently but firmly from the beginning of the trial until the end of the delay period. Parents were instructed to look straight ahead during the delay and to release the infant's hands as soon as the experimenter said "okay." Visual fixation of the wells was broken by the experimenter calling to the infant during the delay and counting aloud, which caused the infant to look up. After the delay, the subject was allowed to reach. A reach was defined as the removal of a cover. A typical sequence of trials during an AB testing session can be seen in Table 2. As illustrated there, trials can be characterized by whether the reward is hidden in the same well as on the previous trial or in the other well, and by whether the subject was correct on the previous trial or not.

The same $A\overline{B}$ task administered to the infants, given by the same experimenter, was administered to the monkeys. The only differences in procedures were (1) food was hidden instead of a toy, (2) visual fixation was broken by lowering an opaque screen rather than by calling to the subject and counting aloud, and (3) monkeys were not physically restrained from moving during the delay (although if they showed signs of position cueing this habit was broken).

The Delayed Response Task

The procedures used within a trial for DR were identical to those for $A\overline{B}$. The one difference between the testing procedures for DR and $A\overline{B}$ was in the rule for determining where the reward would be hidden. In DR, the hiding location was

Table 2. Typical AB̄ Testing Session Illustrating Types of Trials

| | | | Types of Trial[b] | | |
Trial No.	Side of Hiding[a]	Reach	Repeat Following Correct	Reversal Following Correct	Repeat Following Error
1	L	✓			
2		✓	 X		
3	R	errs		 X	
4		errs			X
5		errs			X
6		✓			X
7		✓	 X		
8	L	errs		 X	
9		errs			X
10		✓			X
11		✓	 X		
etc.					

| | Side of Hiding | |
Performance on Previous Trial	Same as on Previous Trial	Changed
Correct	Repeat-following-correct trials	Reversal-following-correct trials
Wrong	Repeat-following-error trials	Reversal-following-error trials

[a] Side of hiding = where toy is hidden. When toy is hidden in the same well as on the previous trial, this column is left blank. L, left well; R, right well.
[b] Type of trial is determined by whether side of hiding is the same as on the previous trial or not and by whether the subject was correct or not on the previous trial. Reversal-following-error trials occur in Delayed Response, but not in AB̄, as reversals are administered in AB̄ only following a correct reach. Thus, when discussing AB̄, the term "reversal trials" always refers to reversal-after-correct trials. Trial 1 above is not characterized by type of trial as there is no trial previous to it.

varied randomly, irrespective of the infant's response. In AB̄, on the other hand, the reward was always hidden in the same well until the subject reached correctly.

The Object Retrieval Task

Object Retrieval is a detour task with the goal object inside a rectangular box open on one side. Three Plexiglas boxes were used for human infant testing: (1) transparent, base 6 × 6 inches square, walls 2 inches high, (2) transparent, base 4½ × 4½ inches square, walls 2½ inches high, and (3) opaque, base 4½ × 4½ inches square, walls 2½ inches high.

As with AB̄, all subjects were tested individually in the laboratory. Each infant was seated on the parent's lap facing the testing table and experimenter. A trial began with the experimenter placing a toy in one of the boxes. The infant had simply to retrieve the toy. No time limit was imposed. A trial ended with retrieval or when the infant refused to try any longer. Considerable freedom of movement was permitted and if an infant became distracted, the experimenter tapped the box or toy to regain attention. The experimenter held the back of the box throughout each trial to prevent the infant from simply lifting the box off the toy.

Experimental variables included (1) side of box that was open (front, top, left, or right), (2) distance of toy from opening (ranging from partially outside the box to deep inside the box), and (3) position of box on the testing surface (near front edge of table or far; far to the left, midline, or far to the right). The bait was always visible when a transparent box was used, but the experimental variables jointly determined whether the toy was seen through a closed side of the box or through the opening. Order of conditions was counterbalanced across testing sessions.

The same Object Retrieval task administered to human infants, given by the same experimenter, was administered to rhesus and cynomolgus monkeys. The only differences in procedure were (1) food was placed in the box instead of a toy, and (2) the box was locked into position, rather than held by the experimenter. The Plexiglas boxes used with adult monkeys were (1) transparent, base 5 × 5 inches square, walls 2 inches high, and (2) transparent, base 3 × 3 inches square, walls 2 inches high. The Plexiglas box used for infant monkey was transparent, 3 × 3 inches square, 2½ inches high.

Results for Human Infants

$A\overline{B}$

Confirming and extending previous work (Gratch and Lander, 1971; Fox et al., 1979), a developmental progression in $A\overline{B}$ performance was found in infants between 7½ and 12 months of age (Diamond, 1985). The delay needed to produce the $A\overline{B}$ error increased continuously at an average rate of about 2 sec per month (see Figure 3). At 7½–9 months, the characteristic AB error pattern occurred at delays of 2–5 sec. By 12 months, infants reached correctly at delays as long as 10 sec.

Although delay remained constant across all trials within a testing session, performance did not. Infants erred only on certain kinds of trials (reversal trials and repeat-following-error trials), while in the same session, at the same delay, they reached correctly on another class of trials (repeat-following-correct trials) (Diamond, 1985). This is the classic error pattern from which the name $A\overline{B}$ is derived, for infants are correct at "A" but they err when side of hiding changes to "B" (reversal trial) and usually repeat that error over the next few trials (repeat following error trials) (see Figure 4a).

All children displayed the $A\overline{B}$ error throughout the months of testing. At each age, errors disappeared when the delay was reduced 2–3 sec, and reaching became random or severely perseverative when the delay was increased 2–3 sec above the level producing the $A\overline{B}$ error. Thus, at 7½–9 months a 10 sec delay

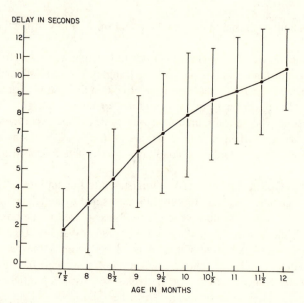

Figure 3. Delay at which the A$\overline{\text{B}}$ error occurs in human infants as a function of age. (From A. Diamond, "Development of the ability to use recall to guide action, as indicated by infants' performance on A," *Child Development, 56,* 868–883. Copyright © 1985 by The Society for Research in Child Development, Inc. Reprinted with permission.

produced "deteriorated performance," whose hallmarks are errors even on repeat-following-correct trials and overt signs of distress (Diamond, 1985). By 12 months, infants reached correctly even at delays as long as 10 sec. When a landmark indicated the toy's location, even young infants were able to use this to reach correctly even at long delays (Diamond, 1983).[4]

Infants in the longitudinal sample, tested every two weeks on A$\overline{\text{B}}$, were a few weeks ahead of infants tested only once. However, the same general developmental progression was found in infants tested cross-sectionally or longitudinally (Diamond, 1983).

Delayed Response

The developmental progression of human infants' performance in DR was almost identical to that for A$\overline{\text{B}}$ despite the fact that these two tasks were tested in different laboratories by different testers with infants from different parts of the country (see Figure 5). In all respects, the results for DR were comparable to those for A$\overline{\text{B}}$. For example, the delay infants could tolerate increased at a constant rate of approximately 2 sec per month. Infants of 7½–9 months failed DR at delays of 2–5 sec; by age 12 months infants succeeded on DR at delays over 10 sec. Individual differences between children of the same age were large, just as they had been on A$\overline{\text{B}}$. Girls could tolerate consistently longer delays than

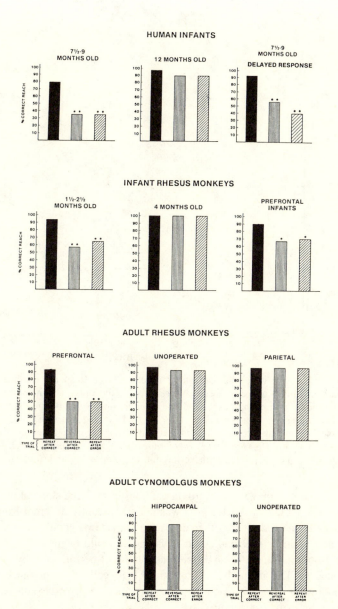

Figure 4. Percent correct by type of trial at delays of 2–5 sec. All results are for the ABtask, except where otherwise noted. The types of trials are repeat-after-correct, reversal-after-correct, and repeat-after-error. Top row: Human infants (7½–9 months and 12 months of age) on the AB̄ task and human infants (7½–9 months of age) on the Delayed Response task. Second row: Infant rhesus monkeys [1½–2½ months of age, 4 months of age, and those with lesions of dorsolateral prefrontal cortex (lesions at 4 months, testing at 5 months)] on the AB̄ task. Third row: Adult rhesus monkeys (with lesions of dorsolateral prefrontal cortex, lesions of inferior parietal cortex, and unoperated) on the AB̄ task. Bottom row: Adult cynomolgus monkeys (with lesions of the hippocampal formation and unoperated) on the AB̄ task.

139

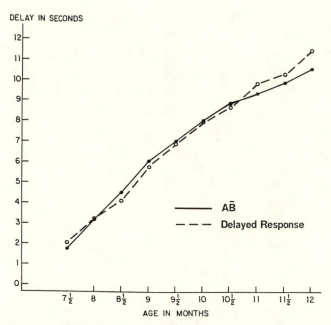

Figure 5. Delay at which human infants failed Delayed Response (dashed line) as a function of age, superimposed over Figure 3 (the delay at which the AB error occurred as a function of age; solid line). Failure on DR was defined as performance below the criterion of 88% correct. From A. Diamond and B. Doar "The performance of human infants on a measure of frontal cortex function, the delayed response task." *Development Psychobiology* 22: 278 Copyright © 1989, John Wiley and Sons, Inc. Reprinted with permission of John Wiley and Sons, Inc.

boys, not because they were improving at a faster rate (the slope of the delay × age function on DR or AB̄ for girls was not significantly different from that for boys), but because they got off to an earlier start. Girls could uncover a hidden object at a younger age than could boys and so could begin DR or AB̄ testing earlier. Importantly, the same differential pattern of performance by type of trial was found for DR as had been found for AB̄ [excellent performance on repeat trials following a correct reach; poor performance on reversals and repeat trials following an error (see Figure 4b)].

Object Retrieval

Infants were found to pass through a clear, tightly age-related series of phases in the performance of Object Retrieval (Diamond, 1981, submitted). All infants progressed through the same sequence of phases, in the same order, at approximately the same age (Diamond, 1981, 1990a) (see Figure 6). So rarely did infants deviate from this that the sequence of development fit a Guttman scale with a coefficient of reproducibility of .93. There was a small effect of repeated testing (infants in the cross-sectional sample lagged approximately 2–4 weeks behind infants tested longitudinally) but the same phases were found in the same order.

Infants 6½–8 months, like the monkeys with frontal lobe lesions studied by Moll and Kuypers, were unable to retrieve the reward if they saw it through a closed side. They banged and scratched with considerable effort and persistence, but if their line of sight did not happen to change they tried no other route to the toy. They insisted on reaching directly to where they saw the toy. The tendency to be guided only by visual information was so strong that it overrode available tactile information and the effect of repeated reinforcement. So totally controlled was their reach by their line of sight that a fraction of an inch difference in the height of the box or in how close the box was to the baby made the difference between success and failure—everything depended on whether the infant was looking through the opening. Even if an infant's hand was already inside the box en route to the toy, if line of sight changed, the infant withdrew the hand and reached to the side through which he or she now saw the toy (see Figure 7).

The first advance on Object Retrieval was seen at 7½–8 months. It was a small change and so is called Phase 1B, rather than Phase 2. The advance is that infants, for the first time, took active steps to look at the toy through different sides of the box (e.g., learning to look through a different side of the box or moving the box). However, 7½– to 8-month-old infants still reached only at the side of the box through which they were looking. When line of sight changed, the reach changed too. The onset of Phase 1B coincided almost exactly with when infants could first uncover a hidden object (see Table 3). Phase 1B and uncovering a hidden object both require a more active, or less passive and reactive, orientation than that seen in younger infants. This marks the first time infants take active steps to change the situation with which they are presented.

The means–end behavior seen here is quite rudimentary. For example, infants were permitted to raise the front of the box (with the experimenter holding the back of the box down on the table) so that the front opening of the bottomless box became quite large and the infant could see in. Often, a 7½– to 8-month-old infant would raise the front of the box with both hands, remove one hand from the box, and attempt to reach for the toy, but the box would come down halting the reach. The reach would halt and go back to the box top because once the box was down the infant saw the toy through the box top rather than through the open front, and reaches were made at this age only at the side through which the infant was looking (see Figure 8). But why did the box come down, after all the second hand was still holding on? The problem here was that when the infants lowered one hand to reach for the toy, they had great difficulty *not* lowering the other. They would repeatedly try to raise the front of the box, but the hand left to hold up the box repeatedly failed at its task. With both hands in the raised position, when one was lowered, the other came down too.[5]

At 8½–9 months (Phase 2), the first separation of line of sight and line of reach occurred. Infants leaned and looked through the front opening of the box, sat up, then reached into the front while looking through the top of the box. For

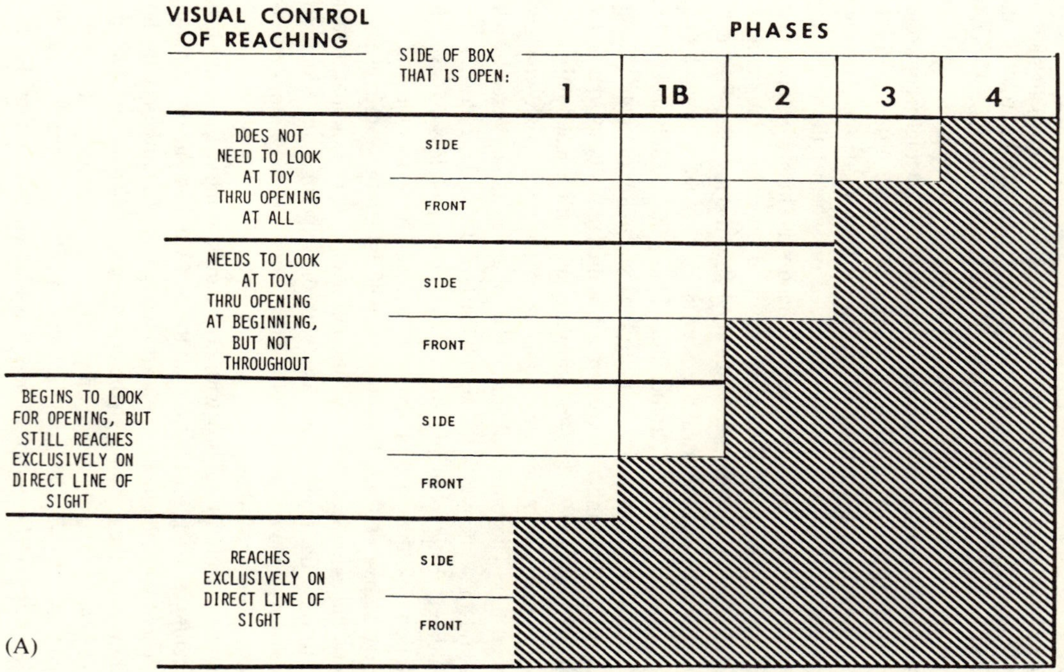

Figure 6. (A) The phases through which infants progress in performance on the Object Retrieval task. (From A. Diamond, 1990.) (B) Developmental progression of performance on the Object Retrieval task with transparent barrier, showing histograms for the age distribution of each phase. (From A. Diamond, 1990.)

PHASES

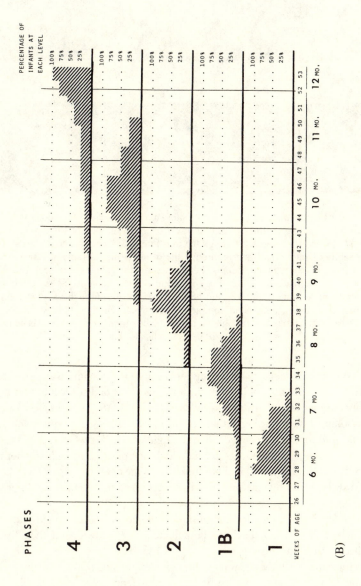

(B)

143

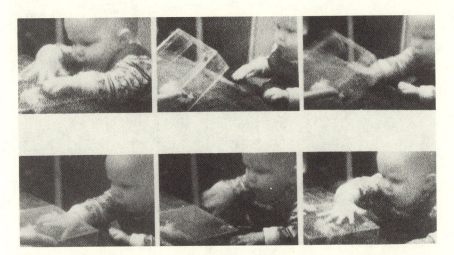

Figure 7. Infants in Phase 1 (6½–7½ months) reach at the side of the box through which they are looking. Frame 1: Front of box is open. Brian sees the toy through the top of the box and tries to reach through the top. Frame 2: Experimenter "raises" the box, enabling Brian to see the toy through the front opening. Frame 3: As soon as Brian sees the toy through the opening, he reaches into the opening. Frame 4: Experimenter lowers box back to its original position. Brian's hand is inside the box on an unobstructed line to the toy, but he now sees the toy through the closed top of the box. Frame 5: Rather than completing the reach, Brian withdraws his hand, and Frame 6: tries to reach through the top of the box to the toy. As soon as he is looking through a different side of the box, he reaches to that side. (From Diamond, 1990.)

the first time, the memory of having looked into the opening was sufficient. For the first time, infants could look through one side and reach through another. This is reminiscent of Millar and Schaffer's (1972, 1973) finding on an operant conditioning task requiring infants to push a lever to see a light display. Even 6-month-old infants succeeded when the lights and lever were in the same visual field, but not until 9 months could they look one place and reach another (Millar and Schaffer.) If the infant had not looked into the opening on that trial, he or she would still not reach there, but having once looked in, the infant did not need to continue to do so to succeed.

At 8½–9 months, the problem of raising the box was also solved sequentially. The infant first raised the box, both hands came down, and then the infant reached in and got the toy.

Performance with the opening at the left or right side of the box always lagged one phase behind performance at the front. Hence, at 8½–9 months, infants showed Phase 1B performance when the opening was on the left or right side of the box: they leaned and looked in the opening and needed to maintain this line of sight during the reach. This leaning and looking to the left or right was accompanied by an "awkward reach," i.e., a reach with the hand contralateral to the

Table 3. Comparison of the Age of Onset of Phase 1B in Object Retrieval and the Age When Infants Can First Uncover a Hidden Object[a]

	Onset of Phase 1B, Object Retrieval	First Able to Uncover a Totally Hidden Object
Jack	35 (3)	35 (3)
Lyndsey	33 (2)	33 (2)
Tyler	36 (2)	38 (4)
Jamie	34 (0)	34 (0)
Emily	34 (2)	34 (2)
Rachel	32 (4)	30 (6)
Brian	28 (3)	28 (3)
Ryan	33 (1)	33 (1)
James	28 (5)	28 (5)
Erin	30 (3)	32 (4)
Sarah	34 (6)	34 (6)
Julia	33 (2)	33 (2)
Mariama	34 (0)	36 (3)
Kate	31 (6)	33 (5)
Rusty	35 (6)	33 (5)
Todd	39 (4)	35 (1)
Nina	31 (0)	29 (0)
Isabel	32 (5)	32 (5)
Jennine	31 (4)	31 (4)
Jane	34 (5)	34 (5)
Bobby	33 (2)	33 (2)
Graham	34 (2)	34 (2)
Blair	35 (4)	35 (4)
Michael	34 (0)	36 (3)
Chrissy	32 (6)	32 (6)

[a]Results are for the 25 infants studied longitudinally at 2 week intervals. Age is given in weeks, with days in parentheses.

opening. Reaching thusly with the hand farthest from the opening made the action maximally contorted and awkward.

At 9½–11 months (Phase 3), infants succeeded when the front of the box was open without looking into the opening at all. Thus, 9½ months is the turning point where infants began to succeed on trials when they had not looked in the opening at all (see Figure 9a).[6] Infants of 9½–10 months were also able to raise the box with one hand and reach in with the other, or raise the box with both hands, lower one hand, and *keep the box raised* with the other. When the opening was on the left or right side of the box, 9½- to 11-month-old infants still needed to look in the opening, but they could then sit up, look through the top, and reach through the side. Awkward reaches disappeared.

Four of the 25 infants followed longitudinally departed from the typical picture of Phase 3. They reached to the left or right side opening *without* first looking in through that side. However, these four infants all failed to get their hand inside

Figure 8. Example of means–end behavior during Phase 1B (7½–8½ months). Whereas younger infants do not take any active steps to change line of sight, infants in Phase 1B begin to move themselves or the box to look at the toy through different sides of the box. However, infants in Phase 1B still reach only at the side of the box through which they are looking and have difficulty lowering one hand to reach without also lowering the other hand. Frame 1: Front of box is open. Nina raises the box. She can now see the toy through the front opening. (Experimenter is holding back of box, exerting downward pressure.) Frame 2: Nina lowered her left hand to reach for the toy. The right hand, holding onto the box, came down too, instead of remaining raised and thus keeping the box up so that she could continue to look through the opening. At this point her left hand is inside the box, a fraction of an inch from the toy, but she is looking at the toy through the closed top of the box. Frame 3: Nina withdraws her left hand from the box without having retrieved the toy, and reaches for the toy at the closed top of the box (the side through which she is looking). (From A. Diamond, 1990.)

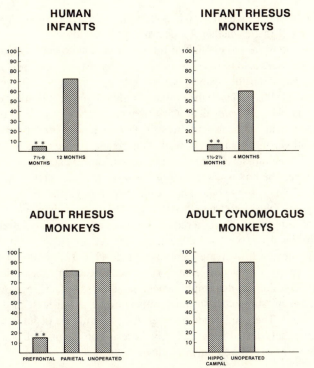

Figure 9. Percent of trials in the Object Retrieval task on which subjects reached to the box opening without having looked into the opening on that trial. (A) Human infants: 7½–12 months of age and 12 months of age. (B) Adult rhesus monkeys: those with lesions of dorsolateral prefrontal cortex, those with lesions of parietal cortex, and unoperated. (C) Adult cynomolgus monkeys: those with lesions of the hippocampal formation and unoperated. (D) Infant rhesus monkeys: 1½–2½ months of age and 4 months of age.

the opening. They misreached, going too high or too far, etc. For example, one child kept getting her thumb stuck on the top edge of the opening. To try to help her out, the experimenter tipped the box to enlarge the size of the opening, but then she reached much higher yet and still got her thumb stuck on the top edge of the opening! It was as if, although most infants appeared to attend only to vision, ignoring available tactile information, these four infants attended only to touch, ignoring the available visual information. They seemed to search for the opening the way a blind person would, by feeling for the edge. Therefore, when the opening was made very large, they still went for the edge.

Finally, by 11–12 months (Phase 4), infants were perfect at Object Retrieval. They did not need to look in the opening on any side to succeed. Their performance was efficient, quick, and accurate. One-year-old infants rarely returned to a side to which they had reached and found closed. A single touch sufficed to tell them whether a side was open or closed.

Once infants were old enough to retrieve a hidden object (approximately 7½ months) they were also tested with an opaque box. At each age, performance was one phase ahead on the opaque box compared with the transparent box (Diamond, 1981, 1990a). Thus, when infants could not see the toy at the outset of the trial, they performed *better* than when they could. Bruner et al., (1969), Lockman (1984), and Schonen and Bresson (1984) report similar results with an opaque wall versus a transparent wall. This counterintuitive finding that the task was easier when infants could not see their goal can be understood in light of the fact that when the box was opaque infants did not need to resist reaching along their line of sight; they could not see the toy through the box.

Testing on Object Retrieval, A$\overline{B}$, and DR thus yielded clear age-related patterns of improvement over a rather brief time period in all children. Although Object Retrieval is a very different task from A$\overline{B}$ or DR, improvement on all three tasks occurred over the same age range (7½–12 months of age). Since different experiences would seem to have been necessary for mastery of these different tasks, the fact that improvement on all these tasks is seen over the same age period suggests that these improvements may be, at least in part, maturationally based. The similarities between the performance of infants tested only once and infants tested longitudinally is also consistent with a maturational component to these developmental changes.

Results for Adult Monkeys

A$\overline{B}$

Adult rhesus monkeys with lesions of dorsolateral prefrontal cortex made the A$\overline{B}$ error at delays of 2–5 sec and reached randomly at delays of 10 sec (Diamond and Goldman-Rakic, 1989), just as did 7½- to 9-month-old human infants. Again, although delay was constant across trials, performance differed systematically by type of trial with errors restricted to reversal trials and to repeat-following-error trials (see Figure 4). Like 7½- to 9-month-old infants, frontally operated adult monkeys and reached randomly at delays of 10 sec.

Unoperated and parietally operated adult rhesus monkeys succeeded on A$\overline{B}$ at delays of 10 sec or more, and showed no pattern of differential performance by type of trial (Diamond and Goldman-Rakic, 1989; see Figure 4c). Similarly, unoperated and hippocampally operated adult cynomolgus monkeys performed correctly on A$\overline{B}$ at delays of 10 sec or more (Diamond et al., 1989; see Figure 4d). The excellent performance of monkeys with lesions of the hippocampal formation at short delays is consistent with extensive findings of good performance by hippocampal monkeys at delays of 10 sec or less, even on tasks particularly sensitive to damage of the hippocampus (Diamond, 1988; Squire and

Zola-Morgan, 1983; Zola-Morgan and Squire, 1986; Zola-Morgan et al., 1989). Amnesic patients, including patients with known hippocampal damage, similarly perform well at short delays provided that the material to be retained does not exceed short-term memory capacity (Squire, 1987; Zola-Morgan et al., 1986).

As the delay increased above 10 sec, monkeys with lesions of the hippocampal formation made progressively more errors on $\overline{AB}$. Finally, at delays of 30 sec they made roughly as many errors overall as frontally operated monkeys had made at delays of 2–5 sec. Monkeys with lesions of the hippocampal formation never showed the $\overline{AB}$ error pattern, however, not even at the 30 sec delay (see Figure 4d). The AB error pattern consists of errors confined to reversals and to the trials immediately following reversals. The performance of hippocampal monkeys was not significantly worse on reversal trials, even at the 30 sec delay, than on repeat-following-correct trials. Thus, they did not show the fundamental characteristic of the AB error. Their performance was significantly worse, however, on repeat-following-error trials than on repeat-following-correct trials. Were they perhaps showing some aspects of the AB error? The answer is no. Repeat-following-error trials simply indicate a string of errors. These can begin on a reversal trial or on a repeat-following-correct trial. Because errors on reversal trials are indicative of the AB error, a string of errors immediately following a reversal might reasonably be taken as further evidence of the AB error. A string of errors following a correct reach when side of hiding has not changed, however, would *not* be indicative of the AB error. Monkeys with lesions of the hippocampal formation performed roughly at chance on *both* kinds of repeat-following-error trials (46% correct on those following a reversal trial and 53% correct on those following an error on a repeat-following-correct trial). Their low score on repeat-following-error trials thus reflects poor performance in general, not a selective tendency to repeat errors after reversals. In contrast, at delays of 2–5 sec, monkeys with lesions of dorsolateral prefrontal cortex performed significantly worse on reversal trials and on repeat-following-error trials than on repeat-following-correct trials, and their errors on repeat-following-correct trials were largely confined to those trials immediately following a reversal (40% correct on repeat-following-error trials following an error on a reversal trial; 72% correct on repeat-following-error trials following an error on a repeat-following-correct trial). Thus, frontal monkeys showed the AB error at brief delays and hippocampal monkeys never showed the AB error at either brief delays or long delays. When frontal monkeys erred at brief delays they did so by reaching back to where they had previously been correct, and by repeating that error over the next several trials, as if the experience of successfully retrieving the reward at the old location was having more influence over their behavior than the sight of where the reward had just been hidden. Hippocampal monkeys, on the other hand, showed excellent performance at brief delays, and when they finally erred at long delays, they did so by reaching randomly, not by showing a preference for the previously correct location.

Thus, only lesions of dorsolateral prefrontal cortex produced the $\overline{AB}$ error. Prefrontal lesions produced the $\overline{AB}$ error pattern at *the same length of delay* as that seen in human infants of 7½–9 months (2–5 sec). In every way, the performance of human infants of 7½–9 months and of monkeys with lesions of dorsolateral prefrontal cortex was comparable: the errors of both groups were confined primarily to reversals and to the trials immediately following reversals; they performed well if allowed to circumvent the memory requirements by staring at, reaching toward, or positioning their body toward the correct well during the delay, and they immediately tried to correct themselves after an incorrect reach. At delays of 10 sec, their performance deteriorated: they showed overt signs of distress, and there was no longer a differential pattern of performance by type of trial; instead performance was poor on all types of trials.

It should be noted that the monkeys with lesions of the hippocampal formation exhibited the classic memory deficits associated with lesions to this region (e.g., they performed poorly both before and after AB testing on Delayed Nonmatch to Sample, a memory test often used to assess hippocampal deficits). Thus, their success on AB cannot be attributed to lack of impairment or to recovery of function, nor can the pattern of errors of infants and prefrontal monkeys be attributed solely to poor memory, for the hippocampal monkeys had a severe memory impairment and yet never showed the AB pattern of error.

Delayed Response

It was already known that the DR performance of monkeys with lesions of dorsolateral prefrontal cortex closely resembles the $\overline{AB}$ performance of human infants aged 7½–9 months. The same monkeys had never been tested on both DR and $\overline{AB}$, however. Diamond and Goldman-Rakic (1989) demonstrated that in the same monkeys performance on these two tasks are remarkably similar. Unoperated rhesus monkeys and those with parietal lesions showed excellent performance on both tasks at delays well over 10 sec. Monkeys with lesions of dorsolateral prefrontal cortex, on the other hand, failed DR and $\overline{AB}$ even at delays as brief as 2 sec. The performance of frontally operated monkeys on DR was fully comparable to the performance of 7½- to 9-month-old human infants on DR.

Object Retrieval

Adult rhesus monkeys with lesions of dorsolateral prefrontal cortex showed the same pattern of performance on Object Retrieval as 7½- to 9-month-old human infants (that is, they showed the behaviors characteristic of Phases 1B and 2) (Diamond and Goldman-Rakic, 1985). No monkeys displayed Phase 1 behavior (seen at 6½–7 months of age in human infants) as they all actively tried to look through more than one side of the Object Retrieval box. However, frontally operated monkeys, like human infants of 7½–9 months, needed to have seen the

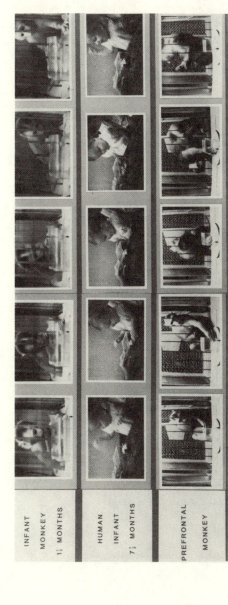

Figure 10. Failure after pushing the bait inside the box themselves: infant monkey of 1½ months, human infant of 7½ months, and adult monkey with lesion of dorsolateral prefrontal cortex. Frame 1: Bait is partially out of box, S reaches immediately for the part that is sticking out of the box. Frame 2: S accidentally pushes bait into the box. Once bait is inside the box, S is unable to retrieve it, even though S was touching the bait, S pushed the bait inside the box himself, and S was at the opening. Frame 3: S withdraws hand from opening and goes to the side of the box through which he sees the bait. Frame 4: S looks at bait through front of box and reaches to the front. Frame 5: Unable to retrieve the bait, S gives up.

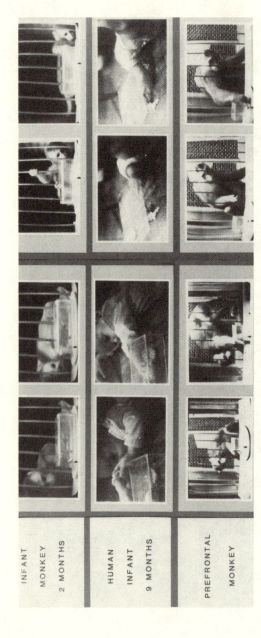

Figure 11. The "awkward reach" in infant monkey of 2 months, human infant of 9 months, and adult monkey with lesion of dorsolateral prefrontal cortex. Frame 1: S leans and looks at bait through opening of box. Frame 2: S reaches in awkwardly with the far hand. Frame 3: Opening is on the other side of the box. Performance is the same. S leans and looks into the opening. Frame 4: S reaches in awkwardly with the far hand.

bait through the opening of the box to reach in and retrieve it. When the bait (toy for children, food for monkeys) was partially out of the box they reached for it straightaway, but if in so doing they accidentally pushed the bait inside the box, they could no longer retrieve it. Deserting the opening, they tried to reach through the transparent wall of the box through which they now saw the bait, even though they had pushed the bait inside the box themselves! (see Figure 10).

Monkeys with lesions of dorsolateral prefrontal cortex also showed the "awkward reach": they reached to the left side of the box with their right hand and to the right side of the box with their left hand, seeming to make the task maximally difficult for themselves (see Figure 11).

In contrast, unoperated monkeys, and monkeys with lesions of parietal cortex or of the hippocampal formation reached to the opening on all trials straightaway, as do human infants of 11–12 months (see Figure 7b and c). They did not need to have looked through the opening and they reached into the left or right side effortlessly with the hand nearest the opening. A single touch served to tell them whether a side was open or closed; they did not persist at a closed side and did not return to sides already tried and found closed.

Thus, on all three tasks (Object Retrieval, A$\overline{\text{B}}$, and DR) monkeys with lesions of dorsolateral prefrontal cortex performed as do human infants of 7½–9 months. They failed under the same conditions and in the same ways. Monkeys with lesions of the hippocampal formation or parietal cortex performed well on all tasks, as do human infants of 12 months.

It should be noted that the monkeys with lesions of the hippocampal formation exhibited the classic memory deficits associated with lesions to this region (e.g., they performed poorly both before and after AB and Object Retrieval testing on Delayed Nonmatch to sample). Thus, their success on AB and Object Retrieval cannot be attributed to no loss of function or recovery of function, nor can the pattern of errors of infants and prefrontal monkeys be attributed solely to poor memory, for the hippocampal monkeys had a severe memory impairment and yet never showed the AB pattern of error.

Results for Infant Monkeys

A$\overline{\text{B}}$

Infant rhesus monkeys of 1½–2½ months made the A$\overline{\text{B}}$ error at delays of 2–5 sec (Diamond and Goldman-Rakic, 1986),[7] as do human infants of 7½–9 months and adult rhesus monkeys with lesions of dorsolateral prefrontal cortex (see Figure 12). The infant monkeys also showed the familiar A$\overline{\text{B}}$ error pattern: excellent performance on repeat following correct trials, with errors confined to reversals and repeat following error trials, even though the same delay was used on all three types of trials (see Figure 4, line 2). Like 7½- 9-month-old infants and frontally operated adult monkeys, infant monkeys of 1½–2½ months

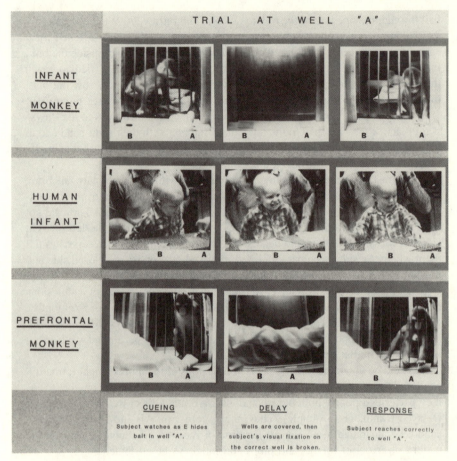

Figure 12. Comparison of performance of infant monkeys, human infants, and adult monkey with bilateral lesions of dorsolateral prefrontal cortex on the AB task. All succeed on the trial at A, but when the side of hiding is changed to well B, they all err by reaching back to A, even though they all saw the bait being hidden at B.

reached randomly at delays of 10 sec, but reached correctly if allowed to stare at the correct well, or sit in front of it, throughout the delay. By 4 months, infant monkeys reached correctly on $A\overline{B}$ even at delays of 10 sec or more, as do 12-month-old human infants.

Lesions in the infant do not always produce the same effect as lesions in the adult. If a neural region is late maturing, lesions of that region may produce deficits in the adult, but not in the infant (e.g., Goldman, 1971, 1974). It has been suggested that lower areas of the brain might mediate infants' performance on a task, even though performance of that task by adults is mediated by a later maturing area of the brain. Thus, although prefrontal cortex seems to mediate

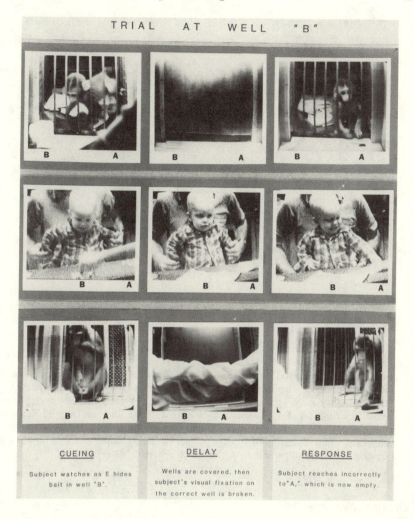

TRIAL AT WELL "B"

CUEING	DELAY	RESPONSE
Subject watches as E hides bait in well "B".	Wells are covered, then subject's visual fixation on the correct well is broken.	Subject reaches incorrectly to "A," which is now empty.

A$\overline{\text{B}}$ performance in the adult, it might not be involved in improved A$\overline{\text{B}}$ performance in the infant. To determine whether prefrontal cortex is necessary for success on AB in infant monkeys, two of the infant monkeys who had been tested longitudinally on A$\overline{\text{B}}$ from 1½ to 4 months of age received bilateral lesions of dorsolateral prefrontal cortex at 4½ months and were retested on A$\overline{\text{B}}$ at 5 months. Although these monkeys had considerable postoperative training on A$\overline{\text{B}}$, and had performed perfectly on A$\overline{\text{B}}$ at delays greater than 10 sec preoperatively at 4 months, after lesions of dorsolateral prefrontal cortex they failed A$\overline{\text{B}}$ at delays of 2–5 sec and showed the differential pattern of performance over trials characteristic of the A$\overline{\text{B}}$ error (see Figure 4, line 2). That is, the lesion produced the same effect in infant monkeys as it did in adult monkeys: the A$\overline{\text{B}}$ error at delays of 2–5 sec.

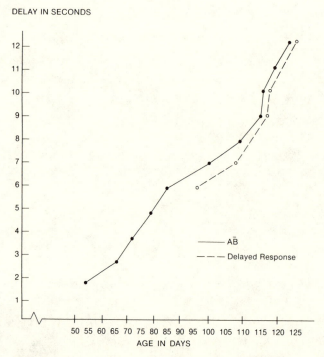

Figure 13. Developmental progression of infant monkeys' performance on Delayed Response and $A\overline{B}$. The delay at which infant monkeys failed Delayed Response as a function of age is shown by the dashed line, and the delay at which they made the $A\overline{B}$ error as a function of age is shown by the solid line. Failure on Delayed Response was defined as performance below the criterion of 88% correct. Testing on Delayed Response did not begin until 80 days of age, but note that performance on this task quickly became comparable to performance on $A\overline{B}$.

Delayed Response

The same infant monkeys tested longitudinally on $A\overline{B}$ were also tested longitudinally on DR during this same period (Diamond and Goldman-Rakic, 1986). The developmental progressions on both tasks were identical (see Figure 13). Infant monkeys improved in their performance of Delayed Response over the same age period and at the same rate as they did on the $A\overline{B}$ task. For example, they reached criterion on $A\overline{B}$ with a 10 sec delay at a mean age of 112.75 days and the reached criterion on Delayed Response with a 10 sec delay at a mean age of 113.80 days. They progressed on both tasks at the rate of approximately 1 sec a week.

Infant monkeys of 4 months succeeded on DR at delays over 10 sec. The two infant monkeys who received bilateral lesions of dorsolateral prefrontal cortex at 4½ months, following all of this longitudinal testing, once again failed DR at delays of 2–5 sec, despite their excellent performance on DR at delays over 10 sec just before surgery. Thus, lesions of dorsolateral prefrontal cortex appeared to have the same effect on DR performance at 4–5 months of age as they did in adult monkeys.

Object Retrieval

Infant monkeys of 1½–2½ months showed behaviors characteristic of Phases 1B and 2 on Object Retrieval. They needed to have seen the bait through the opening of the box to retrieve it. When the bait was partially out of the box, if they accidentally pushed it back inside the box, they were unable to retrieve it, even though they themselves had been the one to push the bait in the box (see Figure 10 above). When the opening was on the left or right side of the box, if they leaned and looked in the opening they could retrieve the bait, but in this position they reached with the hand contralateral to the opening, displaying the "awkward reach" (see Figure 11). These behaviors are the same as those shown on Object Retrieval by human infants of 7½–9 months and adult monkeys with lesions of dorsolateral prefrontal cortex.

No infant monkeys displayed Phase 1 behavior (characteristic of human infants at 6½–7½ months). From the start, infant monkeys actively tried to look through more than one side of the box (Phase 1B behavior). Whereas, human infants below 7½ months rather passively accepted the task as presented, infant monkeys of even 1½ months moved quite a bit. (Monkeys below the age of 1½ months cannot reach and retrieve a piece of food and so cannot be tested on Object Retrieval). Monkeys are more advanced at birth than are humans and very shortly become quite mobile and agile.

By 4 months, infant monkeys reached to the opening of the box on all trials straightaway. The task was trivially easy for them, just as it was for human infants of 12 months.

Thus, infant monkeys showed developmental progressions on all three tasks (Object Retrieval, A$\overline{B}$, and DR) between 1½ and 4 months quite comparable to that seen in human infants between 7½ and 12 months. Note that in monkeys, just as in humans, even though Object Retrieval is quite different from A$\overline{B}$ or DR, and so one might think different experiences would be relevant to acquiring mastery, improvement on all three tasks occurred over the same age period. This is consistent with there being a maturational component to these changes.

Monkeys are born more neurologically and physically mature than humans and show more rapid postnatal development. Hence, 1½- to 2-month-old monkeys performed on these tasks as do 7½- to 9-month-old human infants, and while human infants required roughly 5 months to attain mastery, infant monkeys required only about 2 months. The progression on Object Retrieval was truncated in the monkey: human infants progressed through Stages 1, 1B, 2, 3, and 4; infant monkeys progressed from Stage 1B–2 to Stage 4.

Lesions of dorsolateral prefrontal cortex in infant monkeys disrupted performance of these tasks, just as these lesions do in adult monkeys. Thus, these tasks appear to test an aspect of frontal lobe function that matures very early in life.

Indeed, many had believed that prefrontal cortex did not subserve any cognitive functions until much later in life.

Evidence of Maturation of the Frontal Lobe

The human nervous system is not fully mature at birth, and frontal cortex is one of the clearest examples of a structure that matures postnatally (e.g., Schade and van Groenigen, 1961; Yakovlev and Lecours, 1967; Dekaban, 1970).

Although all neurons in frontal cortex are generated before birth (Rakic, 1974), they remain immature for some time. The immaturity of frontal cortex early in life, like that of many other regions of the brain, has been shown by diverse indicators. For example, most of the layers of frontal cortex are narrower in the infant than in the adult and the subregions are cytoarchtectonically less distinct (Larroche, 1966). The dendritic systems of pyramidal neurons in layers 2, 3, and 5 are rudimentary and lack extensive branching (Schade and van Groenigen, 1961). Synaptic density in frontal cortex is low at birth, as is the number of synapses per neuron (Huttenlocher, 1979). Available staining methods have not been able to detect evidence of axonal myelin sheaths in frontal cortex during the early months of life (Yakovlev and Lecours, 1967).

Developmental changes in performance of $A\overline{B}$, DR, and Object Retrieval coincide with maturational changes in frontal cortex: (1) Neurons, at least in layer 3 of the middle frontal gyrus, have probably acquired their full complement of synapses by the end of the first year (Huttenlocher, 1979). (2) The mean number of synapses per neuron in this region increases rapidly from roughly 10,000 at birth to roughly 100,000 by 1 year of age; increase thereafter is much slower (Huttenlocher, 1979). (3) The density of neurons here declines markedly during the first year. After one year the decrease proceeds more gradually (Schade and van Groenigen, 1961; Huttenlocher, 1979). (The neonatal brain appears to have more neurons in regions such as frontal cortex than does the adult brain. Thus, neuronal loss is an aspect of maturation. For example, the average number of neurons per mm^3 in layer 3 of the middle frontal gyrus in the neonate is about 10^5, while in the adult it is only slightly over 10^4.) (4) The density of synaptic contacts across all layers of dorsolateral prefrontal cortex in the rhesus macaque increases during the first 1½–2½ postnatal months; thereafter density declines (Bourgeois et al., 1985). (2) The dopamine concentration in the brain increases during this period in rhesus macaques as well (Brown et al., 1979). Dopamine is particularly concentrated in frontal cortex. When levels of dopamine are low in dorsolateral prefrontal cortex, monkeys are unable to succeed at DR (Brozoski et al., 1979). Their performance returns to normal following a return to normal dopamine levels (Brozoski et al., 1979). Thus, increasing levels of dopamine with age may help make possible improved performance with age.

A potential mechanism by which frontal cortex maturation might result in improved Object Retrieval performance is through frontal inhibition of collicular mechanisms. The frontal lobe (including both dorsolateral prefrontal cortex and premotor cortex specifically) projects directly to the superior colliculus in monkeys and probably in humans (Goldman and Nauta, 1976; Kunzle, 1978) and indirectly via the substantia nigra. If the inhibitory projections to the colliculus are interrupted, frogs (who readily detour around a transparent barrier ordinarily) try to go straight through a transparent barrier to the reward instead of detouring around the barrier (Ingle, 1973).

Plans are now underway to explore this hypothesis in human infants. Interruption of inhibitory projections to the superior colliculus in monkeys results in saccadic intrusions during the smooth pursuit of a slow moving target (Hikosaka and Wurtz, 1983, 1984, 1985). That is, instead of the eyes smoothly following the target, they dart away momentarily and then continue tracking. Infants of 3–4 months show saccadic intrusions during smooth pursuit (Aslin, personal communication). If saccadic intrusions disappear because of frontal inhibition of the colliculus and if this inhibitory projection becomes functional between 7½ and 12 months of age in humans, then human infants of 5–7 months should still show saccadic intrusions during smooth pursuit, but infants of 12 months should not. This prediction will be tested in collaboration with Naomi Wentworth and Marshall Haith.

Performance of Brain-Damaged Human Adults on Tasks Similar to AB, Delayed Response, and Object Retrieval

Human adults with damage confined to dorsolateral prefrontal cortex have never been tested on any of these tasks. Human adults with more diffuse brain damage have, however, been tested on DR (Freedman and Oscar-Berman, 1986). Freedman and Oscar-Berman used DR with delays of "0",[8] 10, 30, and 60 sec, summing the results over all delays. Patients with bilateral frontal lobe damage, which included dorsolateral prefrontal cortex in some cases, failed DR, while amnesic patients (some of whom were reported to have signs of frontal lobe dysfunction) and alcoholic control subjects performed well. Performance on DR was correlated with performance on the Wisconsin Card Sort, as it should be if both are measures of dorsolateral perfrontal function.

Schacter et al. (1986) tested amnesic patients with signs of frontal lobe dysfunction on tasks similar to AB̄. In one task, an object was either hidden in a room rich in objects and landmarks ("Room Search") or in one of four drawers, each drawer being a different color ("Container Search"). The delay for both tasks was 150 sec (2½ min). The amnesic patients correctly retrieved the object from the first hiding place (location A), but when the object was hidden at a second location (B) they continued to search at A (similar to the AB̄ error). Unlike human infants, however, these patients were as likely to err when the object was uncovered as when it was covered. Human infants make very few errors when there are no covers (Butterworth, 1977). Patients with damage to *medial* frontal cortex succeeded on these tasks and perseverated less on the Wisconsin Card Sort than did the amnesic patients. This is as it should be if errors on AB and the Wisconsin Card Sort result from damage specifically to the dorsolateral region of frontal cortex.

The good performance of the amnesic patients in the Freedman and Oscar-Berman (1986) study and the poor performance of the amnesic patients in the Schacter et al. study (1986) may have been due to the difference in length of delay. The 150-sec delay used by Schacter and colleagues may have taxed the memory of the amnesic patients, while the shorter delays used by Freedman and Oscar-Berman did not. A second possibility is that the amnesic patients tested by Schacter et al. may have had more severe frontal lobe dysfunction than the amnesic patients studied by Freedman and Oscar-Berman.

Three points should be noted from these two studies. First, patients with dorsolateral prefrontal cortex damage failed DR even at relatively short delays (Freedman and Oscar-Berman, 1986), just as do monkeys with lesions of dorsolateral prefrontal cortex and as do infants. Second, the amnesic patients who failed tasks similar to $\overline{AB}$ had signs of frontal lobe dysfunction, as indicated by their poor performance on the Wisconsin Card Sort task (Schacter et al., 1986). Third, patients with medial frontal cortex damage succeeded on the $\overline{AB}$-like tasks (Schacter et al., 1986), as they should if the critical neural locus for the performance of AB is dorsolateral prefrontal cortex.

Adult patients with frontal lobe damage are also impaired on other delayed comparison tests (Prisko, cited in Milner, 1964). On one such test, patients were presented with a color or a sound, the stimulus was removed, then a second color or sound was presented and the patients were asked if that color was the same shade or the sound the same intensity as the first stimulus. Frontal lobe patients performed well when there was no delay between the stimuli, but failed when a delay of 60 sec was used.

Adults have never been tested on Object Retrieval. However, there is evidence that vision exerts a pull on the behavior of frontal patients similar to that seen in monkeys with lesions of dorsolateral prefrontal cortex and in infants. Vision exerts a strong pull in all of us (e.g., Rock and Harris, 1967), but most of us with intact frontal lobes are able to inhibit or counteract that tendency when necessary. The power of vision over the behavior of adult frontal patients can be seen, for example, if asked to hold up a finger when the examiner makes a fist, and to make a fist when the examiner holds up a finger. Most of us might be tempted to copy what we see but would manage to follow the instructions. A patient with frontal lobe damage, on the other hand, cannot resist mimicking what he sees and so upon seeing the fist, makes a fist, even though he can repeat the instructions back correctly (for other examples of echopraxia see Luria, 1966).

In short, although adults with damage restricted specifically to dorsolateral prefrontal cortex have not been tested on precisely the same tasks on which we have tested infants and monkeys, the performance of patients on similar tasks is fully consistent with the conclusions about brain function drawn from the work with monkeys.

Abilities Required for Success on A$\overline{B}$, Delayed Response, and Object Retrieval and Which Depend on the Frontal Lobe

Object Retrieval, on the one hand, and A$\overline{B}$ and DR, on the other, would appear to share little in common. Object Retrieval is a detour task with a transparent barrier so the bait is always visible. In A$\overline{B}$ and DR the bait is hidden. However, the fact that the human and simian infants improve on all three tasks over the same period and the fact that all three tasks have been linked to frontal cortex suggest that A$\overline{B}$, DR, and Object Retrieval probably require common abilities.

A$\overline{B}$ and DR have usually been thought to be measures of memory or perseveration (e.g., memory: Fox et al., 1979; Jacobsen, 1936; perseveration: Bremmer and Bryant, 1977; Mishkin, 1964). However, neither of these interpretations works very well for Object Retrieval. Object Retrieval does not appear to require memory as the box is transparent. Instead of infants perseveratively repeating what they did on the previous trial, they *fail* to repeat the previous trial's performance if a change is made in the variables controlling line of sight. For example, following three successful retrievals from the *front* of the box, if the box is moved forward 1 inch and the toy moved ½ inch deeper into the box (so that the infant now sees the toy through the top), infants below 8½ months reach only at the top of the box, although the perseverative response would be to reach at the front. Infants fail by not repeating their previous response (Diamond, 1981, submitted). Thus, the search for common abilities required for A$\overline{B}$, DR, and Object Retrieval required rethinking what might be involved in the A$\overline{B}$ and DR tasks.

It is suggested that the frontal lobe subserves two principal abilities that develop between 7½ and 12 months and are required for performance of A$\overline{B}$, DR, and Object Retrieval.

Relating Information Separated in Time or Space

Object Retrieval requires the subject to relate the box opening to the bait over a spatial separation. When bait and opening are superimposed (as when the bait is in the opening, partially out of the box) even the youngest infants succeed. However, as the spatial separation between bait and opening widens, the age at which infants succeed progressively increases.

A$\overline{B}$ and DR require the subject to relate two *temporally* separated events—cue and response. The subject watches as a bait is hidden in one of two identical wells, a brief delay follows, then the subject is allowed to reach. When there is no delay between hiding and retrieval even the youngest infants succeed. However, as the time interval between hiding and retrieval increases, the age at which infants succeed progressively increases.

It should be noted that the delays in AB and DR are very brief (e.g., 2–5 sec). Whereas the hippocampus appears to be required for information to be available beyond short-term memory, prefrontal cortex appears to be needed to use information effectively while it is within short-term memory, e.g., to keep information on-line for current use.

One challenge to the importance of the role of memory in the AB task has come from the fact that studies using multiple wells have typically found better performance on AB (especially on the trials at well B) than have studies using two wells (see, e.g., Wellman et al., 1987). We have recently demonstrated, however, that this is due to a difference in experimental procedure: *when two wells are used* both wells are uncovered, the reward is hidden, and then both wells are simultaneously covered; *when more than two wells are used,* on the other hand, only the correct well is uncovered, the reward is hidden, and then only the correct well is covered again. The latter procedure makes the task easier because it draws the subject's attention to the correct well. When multiple wells are used and all wells are covered simultaneously, infants perform worse with multiple wells than they do with only two wells (Diamond et al., 1989).

It might seem contradictory to argue that infants have difficulty remembering where the toy was hidden a few seconds ago, and yet can remember where they last found the toy on previous trials (which happened perhaps minutes ago). This is not contradictory because two different kinds of memory are involved, which rely on different neural systems. The kind of memory that shows up as a response bias is the kind of memory that has traditionally been assessed using conditioning paradigms. Studies that have used conditioning to assess memory in infants (the dependent measure being how long a response is retained) have typically found quite long memory in very young infants. For example, infants of only 2 months can remember a conditioned response for at least 3–5 days (Rovee-Collier, 1984). I would argue that this is the kind of memory called "implicit" or "procedural" (Cohen, 1984; Schacter, 1987; Squire and Cohen, 1984). It is the kind of memory that can be demonstrated in behavior without any conscious awareness of the "memory" on the part of the person. Adults with amnesia demonstrate similar robust memory on conditioning paradigms, even though they have no conscious recollection of having done the task and even though their conscious recall and recognition are very poor after a few minutes (Mishkin et al., 1984; Weiskrantz and Warrington, 1979). The areas of the brain required for implicit or procedural memory, i.e., required to show the effects of conditioning, are clearly subcortical and mature very early. For example, Thompson and colleagues (McCormick and Thompson, 1984; Thompson et al., 1984) have demonstrated the crucial involvement of the cerebellum in retention of the classically conditioned eyeblink response. $\overline{AB}$ and DR, on the other hand, require explicit recall of the hiding.

Conceiving of memory as one aspect of the ability to relate information over a separation, be it temporal or spatial, enables one to bring together literatures which are not usually discussed in the same breadth—conditioning in infants and the Piagetian AB task. Millar and Watson (1979) demonstrated that infants of 6–8 months could acquire a conditional response if the delay between response and reinforcement were 0 sec, but not if the delay were 3 sec. These results are quite comparable to those found for $A\overline{B}$ and DR. Infants of 8 months succeed on DR or $A\overline{B}$ when the delay between hiding and response is 0 sec, but not when the delay is 3 sec. The Millar and Watson task, like $A\overline{B}$ and DR, requires that memory be maintained on-line either to relate the response to the reward (Millar and Watson) or to relate the cue (site of hiding) to the response (site of retrieval) ($A\overline{B}$ and DR). These tasks all look at the ability to bridge a delay within a trial, the ability to integrate information over a temporal separation.[9] Whereas, Millar and Watson looked at the effect of a temporal separation between cue and reward, Millar and Schaffer (1972; 1973) looked at the effect of a spatial separation between cue and reward. They trained infants to push a lever to produce a visual light display. As long as cue and reward were in the same visual field, infants of 6–8 months succeeded, but when required to look one place and reach another, only infants of 9 months or older succeeded. This is reminiscent of the results on Object Retrieval. Only by 9 months (Phase 2) could infants look one place (through a closed side) and reach another (through the opening). Having looked through the opening, a Phase 2 infant could sit up, look through a closed side and reach into the opening.

The development of the ability to relate or integrate two or more items is an ever-present theme in the age progression in Object Retrieval performance. It is seen in the development of (1) the ability to reach through one side of the box while looking through a different side, (2) the ability to attend to both visual and tactile information, and (3) the ability to do different things with the two hands. When infants reach through the side they are looking, they can almost always reach the toy by a straight route. When they look through one side and reach through another, their reach is almost always two-directional, as when an infant sits up and looks through the top and then reaches away from the midline to get to the left or right opening and then directs the reach back toward the midline to get the toy. Here one sees the development of the ability to integrate two movements in opposing directions.

Tasks that require the simultaneous use of multiple facts prove very difficult for adults with frontal cortex damage. For example, they can solve math problems such as "What is 30 divided by 2?" and "What is 15 times 5?" But they cannot solve "If the price of 2 packages is $30, what is the price of 5 packages?" (Barbizet, 1970). Frontal patients also have unusually severe difficulty doing two things at once or attending to more than one thing at a time. When they are shown a pictorial scene suggesting a story, they typically fixate on one detail in the picture, missing the suggested story (Nichols and Hunt 1940).

Relating items in a sequence is also a problem. An expert cook, following frontal lobectomy, can still measure, pour, sift, and knead, but may not be able to put these together to bake a loaf of bread or to make a many course meal. Frontal patients have great difficulty keeping track of a temporal sequence. They can remember which of two pictures they saw before (unlike temporal lobe patients who cannot), but they cannot remember which of two pictures they saw most recently (Corsi, cited in Milner, 1974). When shown a page of words or pictures and instructed to touch all stimuli, one at a time, in any order, but without repeating a choice, frontal patients touch some stimuli more than once, never managing to touch them all (Petrides and Milner, 1982). They do not perseverate; rather they simply fail to sample all stimuli systematically. This is reminiscent of the behavior of 8- to 9-month-old infants who fail to systematically check all sides of the box; they reach back repeatedly to sides they have tried and found closed.

Inhibiting Prepotent Responses

In Object Retrieval, the tendency to reach straight to a visible target must be inhibited. Infants must instead reach around to the opening. Results when the box is opaque provide particularly strong evidence here: infants perform better with the opaque box, where the toy cannot be seen through a closed side (Diamond, submitted). The counterintuitive finding that the task becomes easier when the goal is not visible supports the hypothesis that *seeing* the goal through a closed side makes the task harder because the tendency to reach straight to the goal must then be inhibited.

Inhibition of the predominant response is to be distinguished from perseveration. The predominant response is often the response a subject has been making, in which case lack of inhibitory control will be manifest as perseveration. However, when the prepotent response is different from the response just made, lack of inhibitory control is manifest by a failure to perseverate (as seen in Object Retrieval). An example from work on the frontal lobe illustrating the distinction between inhibitory control and perseveration is as follows.

Jacobsen and colleagues (Jacobsen et al., 1935; Crawford et al., 1948) presented chimpanzees with a row of four pegs. The champanzees were taught to push on the first three pegs and pull the fourth to obtain a reward. Perseverative errors would have been to try to push peg 4, i.e., to repeat the response they had made at pegs 1, 2, and 3. The prepotent response, however, would be the one most closely associated with the reward. Since the reward was delivered after pulling the fourth peg, pulling would be prepotent here. Frontally lesioned chimpanzees did not try to push peg 4, instead they tried to pull pegs 2 and 3. These errors of "anticipation" were not overcome within the limits of testing.

Problems in the inhibitory control of behavior occur in all areas of life for frontal patients. Socially, they are "disinhibited," meaning that they lack the usual inhibitions about saying or doing inappropriate things (such as talking about sex in public). Frontal patients are easily distracted by irrelevant, but firmly established, connections. They are pulled by this free association or that. This makes it extremely difficult to obtain even a simple personal history from such patients because of the many associations to that history.

One of the classic tests for frontal lobe function is the Stoop test. Here, the names of colors are printed in the ink of another color (e.g., the word "blue" is printed in red ink). Patients are instructed to report the color of the ink as they look through the list of words. The customary response when reading, however, is to ignore the ink and attend to the meaning of the word. Frontal patients fail the test; they recite the words and not the color of the ink (Perret, 1974).

In $A\overline{B}$ and DR, a conditioned tendency or "habit" to reach to "A" (where the subject was rewarded) must be inhibited when the bait is hidden at "B." One would expect this tendency to be stronger, the greater the number of reinforced trials at A. Within a narrow range, more reinforced trials at A does *not* lead to more errors at B [one vs. three trials reinforced trials at A (Diamond, 1983), two vs. five trials (Evans, 1973), and three vs. five trials (Butterworth, 1977)], but when 2 vs. 8–10 consecutively correct reaches at A are compared, the expected result is found. Infants who reached correctly to A 8–10 times in a row made significantly longer strings of errors at B than infants who reached correctly at A only twice in a row before side of hiding was reversed (Landers, 1971).

If memory were the only requirement of $A\overline{B}$, errors should appear equally on all types of trials. The $A\overline{B}$ error, however, consists of good performance when reward is hidden where the subject just reached correctly, and repeated errors when the side of hiding is reversed. When the side of hiding changes, $A\overline{B}$ sets up a conflict between a subject's memory of where the reward was just hidden and the subject's tendency to repeat a rewarded response. To succeed on $A\overline{B}$, a subject must inhibit that tendency. Hippocampal monkeys, who have poor memory but can inhibit their response tendency, do not show the AB error pattern. At short delays they perform well and at long delays, where their performance is poor, they are no more likely to err on reversal trials than when side of hiding is unchanged.

Infants and prefrontal monkeys may sometimes reach back to well A *even when they know the toy's location*, because of difficulty inhibiting the habitual response. Baillargeon (Baillargeon et al., 1985; Baillargeon, 1987; Baillargeon and Graber, 1988) has shown by visual fixation measures that infants appear to know where the hidden toy is, even though they err when allowed to reach. Certainly, infants sometimes reach back to A when the toy is visible at B, as when the covers are transparent, and occasionally when there is no cover at all (Butterworth, 1977; Harris, 1974). Often infants will uncover A, *not look in*, then reach immediately to B and retrieve the toy (Diamond, 1985). It is as if they know the toy is at B even though they reach first to A. Most telling, an infant occasionally looks directly at B before, and throughout, the reach, even as the infant's hand goes to A.[10] If direction of gaze were the dependent measure, the infant would be scored as correct on such trials (see Figure 14).

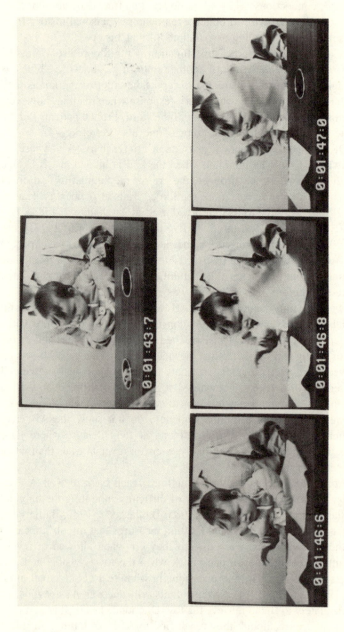

Figure 14. Instance of an infant looking at B while reaching to A. Infant had successfully retrieved the toy at well A. Side of hiding is now reversed to B. Frame 1: Infant clearly sees the hiding at B. After a brief delay, infant was allowed to reach. Frames 2–4: Although infant is looking fixedly at B, his hand reaches back to A.

This interpretation gains support from observations with the Wisconsin Card Sort: After having been rewarded for sorting the cards by one criterion, patients with damage to the frontal lobe have difficulty sorting the cards by a new rule. *However, these patients can sometimes tell you the new rule as they continue to sort the cards incorrectly.* Indeed, they sometimes say as they are sorting the cards by the old criterion, "This is wrong, and this is wrong" (Luria and Homskaya, 1964; Milner, 1964; Nauta, 1971).[11] Infants cannot tell you the correct answer verbally, but looking at A even as they reach to B may be the nonverbal equivalent.

Thus improved performance here may mark the emergence of the ability for a memory-based intention to override habit: the emergence of the ability to exercise choice. In $A\overline{B}$, DR, and the Wisconsin Card Sort, an initial response is strengthened by reinforcement. This effect of reinforcement on a response is evident in infants soon after birth (e.g., Papousek, 1961) and in the simplest organisms (e.g., Castellucci and Kandel, 1976; Carew et al., 1984). It develops early (in both phylogeny and ontogeny) and is robust, capable of surviving considerable neurological insult. A more fragile and later developing ability is the capacity to *resist* a dominant action tendency, whether it is innately strong or has been strengthened by reinforcement. It is this ability that is required when the correct well changes in $A\overline{B}$ or DR, the correct criterion changes in the Wisconsin Card Sort, or the subject sees the reward through one side of the Object Retrieval box but must reach through a different side. Although instinctual and habitual responses are very strong even in humans, we are capable, with effort, of breaking a habit, whereas organisms without frontal cortex may have no such option. This ability to resist the strongest response of the moment endows us with extraordinary flexibility and the freedom to choose and control our actions. Inhibitory control thus distinguishes us from lower organisms and is one of our highest accomplishments.

It is as much a developmental achievement to be able to inhibit unadaptive reactions as to acquire new behaviors and knowledge. Development proceeds both by the progressive acquisition of concepts and by the progressive inhibition of reactions that get in the way of expressing knowledge that is already present. To some extent, infants appear to know more than they can demonstrate in their behavior, as when they seem to know the location of a hidden toy, but are unable to demonstrate this in their reaching behavior (see also, Diamond and Gilbert, 1989).

In conclusion, I would like to suggest that a maturational change in frontal cortex underlies improved performance on $A\overline{B}$, DR, and Object Retrieval between 7½ and 12 months in human infants and 1½–2½ months in infant monkeys, and that the cognitive abilities subserved by frontal cortex and required for success on these tasks are (1) the ability to integrate information over a temporal or spatial interval, and (2) inhibitory control (the ability to resist a bias to make the prepotent response). These tasks are dependent on frontal cortex function because they require *both* of these abilities. If either ability is taxed alone some errors occur (e.g., a few errors occur at well A in the AB task when a delay is used, taxing only memory; a few errors occur at well B when transparent covers are used, taxing only inhibitory control), however, the vast majority of errors occur when both abilities are taxed (when the reward is hidden at well B with opaque covers and a delay).

This leads to the prediction that infants of 7½–9 months of age would succeed at Delayed Match to Sample [we already know that monkeys with lesions of dorsolateral prefrontal cortex perform well on this task (Passingham, 1975; Mishkin and Manning, 1978)], *but* that both these infants and monkeys would fail Delayed *Non*match to Sample. Delayed Match to Sample and Delayed *Non*match to Sample are formally similar. On both tasks the subject is shown a sample object, and then after a brief delay the subject is given the choice of reaching to the object that matches the sample or to a novel object. The crucial difference between the tasks comes from the fact that infants (e.g., Fantz, 1964; Fagan, 1970) and monkeys (e.g., Brush et al., 1961; Harlow, 1950) have a natural tendency to prefer novel stimuli over familiar ones. Thus, Delayed Match requires only memory (which object have I seen before?), whereas Delayed *Non*match requires both memory and inhibition of the tendency to reach to the new stimulus.[12] It is this combination of requirements that I believe is the hallmark of tasks dependent on prefrontal cortex.

Coda: Principles of Development as They Are Illustrated by A$\overline{B}$, Delayed Response, and Object Retrieval

It is of interest to consider the developmental progressions outlined here in light of the principles outlined by Gilbert Gottleib at the meeting and summarized in his 1983 paper.

Invariant Sequence

> Despite significant individual differences in the quantitative aspects of develop-ment, the *sequence* in which behavioral stages follow each other in any given species is remarkably constant when typical developmental conditions prevail. (Gottlieb, 1983, p. 8)

All infants progressed through the same series of phases in the same order on Object Retrieval. So consistent was this developmental sequence across infants that it fit a Guttman scale with a coefficient of reproducibility of 0.93. Although no infant of 7½ months had yet reached Phase 2, by 9 months no infant was still in Phase 1, and by 12 months *all* infants had reached Phase 4. No infant ever reached a later phase without having gone through the earlier phases.

On A$\overline{B}$, all infants showed an increase in the delay they were able to tolerate between hiding and retrieval. No 7-month-old infant was ready for A$\overline{B}$ testing with a delay even as long as 5 sec. Indeed, at 8 months most infants were still making the $A\overline{B}$ error at delays under 5 sec. By 12 months of age, however, only one infant was still making the $A\overline{B}$ error at a delay of 5 sec, and only three infants were still making the $A\overline{B}$ error at delays under *10 sec.*

There were also marked individual differences on $A\overline{B}$, however, as can be seen by the size of error bars in Figure 3. Children of the same age differed widely in the delay at which they made the $A\overline{B}$ error, so much so that age accounted for only 46% of the variance. For example, at 8 months, the range of delay at which the $A\overline{B}$ error occurred was 0–8 sec and at 11 months it was 2–12 sec. Some infants progressed gradually and continuously on $A\overline{B}$, others showed early precocious performance but then no further advance for months, and still others progressed in spurts where no change was seen for weeks and then suddenly there was a dramatic improvement.

There was less variability across infants in the age of attainment of the Object Retrieval phases. This was particularly true for the younger ages. With the later phases (Phases 3 and 4), however, individual differences in rates of attainment became more noticeable. Thus, the age range for Phase 3 was 9–11½ months and the age range for Phase 4 was 9½–12 months.

Although infants progressed through an invariant sequence of phases on Object Retrieval, there was still room for alternative developmental routes to successful performance in that the character of the phases did not always look the same for all infants. In particular, when 4 of the 25 infants followed longitudinally reached Phase 3, they did not conform to the pattern of Phase 3 behavior described above. When the left or right side of the box was open, most Phase 3 infants did not reach to the opening unless they had already looked into the opening, although this line of sight did not need to be maintained. However, four Phase 3 infants did not need to look in the left or right side of the box to reach there. They reached to a side opening without ever having looked into it. This was not yet Phase 4 performance, however, because these four infants never succeeded in getting inside the opening and retrieving the toy on these trials. Each of these infants failed because of an "aim problem" (e.g., reaching too high and getting their thumb caught on top edge of opening, or reaching too far back and reaching behind the box instead of into the opening). While most infants appeared to attend to visual information only, ignoring information available through touch, these four infants appeared to attend to tactile information only, ignoring information available through vision. These infants seemed to tactily search for the opening by feeling for an edge. It was striking to see an infant feel the back wall of the opening then reach behind the box as if it were the opening. The two infants who kept getting their thumb caught did so even when the box was tipped, greatly increasing the size of the opening, because they kept adjusting their reach upward so that their thumb kept hitting the top edge of the opening. Thus, no infant at Phase 3 was yet fully integrating visual and tactile information. However, while most infants attended to vision, a few directed their attention to touch. This latter strategy may have been superior because all 4 infants who chose this route reached Phase 4 at an earlier age than did the other 21 infants.

Critical Periods

> There are prenatal and postnatal periods or stages in development when the organism is dependent on certain forms of stimulation for subsequent normal (typical) development. Other ways of viewing these stages are that they are ones in which the organism is maximally susceptible to certain kinds of stimulation, or when ease of mastering certain behavioral tasks is much higher than at other times in the life cycle. These stages are sometimes referred to as critical periods of development. . . . On its weakest interpretation, the concept of an optimum or critical stage implies that the development of particular abilities or endpoints is not equipotential over the lifespan; on its strongest interpretation, the critical period concept means that certain experiences must occur during a delimited period early in development if subsequent development is to be normal (species typical). (Gottlieb, 1983, p. 7)

There is no evidence that there is a critical period for attainment of $A\overline{B}$ or Object Retrieval. There is no evidence that if some critical experience does not occur by a certain stage, infants will be impaired on $A\overline{B}$ or Object Retrieval. On the other hand, there *is* evidence that infants cannot benefit from certain experiences *before* certain ages. Although the term "optimum" or "critical" stage is usually meant to imply that it is best if some experience occurs before a certain age, it is suggested here that a point of development might also be "optimum" or "critical" in that a given experience will have little or no effect if it occurs before that point. On Object Retrieval, the critical points were transitions between phases. Experience with the opaque box often aided an infant in moving to the next higher phase with the transparent box when that infant was at the border of moving to that next higher phase. However, if an infant had just entered a particular phase, experience with the opaque box did not improve performance with the transparent box. Having looked through the opening did not aid a Phase 1 or 1B child if this line of sight was broken, however, it greatly aided older infants. The results on Object Retrieval yield countless examples of experiences or information that did not aid performance until infants reached a certain age.

Limits to the Role of the Environment

> It is the developmental geneticist Waddington's (1942) notion that early normal or species-typical physiological and anatomical development can withstand great assaults or perturbations and still return to (or remain on) its usual developmental pathway, thus producing the normal phenotype. Waddington's concept of canalization is one that says that usual developmental pathways are buffered and thus normal (typical) development can be only temporarily derailed. (Gottleib, 1983, p. 9)

The abilities required for Object Retrieval and A$\overline{B}$ appear to be well canalized (to use Waddington's terminology) or characterized by a narrow range of modifiability (to use the terminology of Lorenz, 1965), at least over the ranges of experience thus far investigated. Infants tested longitudinally do perform better than infants tested only once. But the differences are small and are as easily attributed to familiarity with the tester and laboratory as to practice. The same developmental progression on A$\overline{B}$ is found in lower and upper middle class children (lower middle class: Gratch and Landers, 1971; upper middle class: Diamond, 1985), although preliminary results suggest that very poor children may be more significantly behind their attainment of milestones on the task. On Object Retrieval, exposure to the opaque box aided performance with the transparent box if an infant was almost ready to move on to the next phase. However, experience with the opaque box never aided infants who had just entered a phase and it never enabled infants to move up more than one phase. Thus, its effects were limited both in terms of when they could occur and in magnitude.

Facilitation Versus Induction

Facilitation acts as a temporal regulator of achievements which will nonetheless eventually be reached even if the organism is deprived of the normally occurring experience. *Induction* represents experience that is essential if the species typical endpoint is to be fully achieved. (Gottlieb, 1983, p. 15)

Performance on Object Retrieval and A$\overline{B}$ can be facilitated by experience to a small extent, but success on both is achieved regardless of the infant's experience, at least within the range of experience thus far investigated. Repeated testing and exposure to the opaque box are two experiences that appear to have salutary effects. However, infants of 1 year who were tested only once and who were never exposed to the opaque box performed perfectly on A$\overline{B}$ even at delays as long as 10 sec and succeeded on all Object Retrieval trials, displaying sophisticated Phase 4 behavior. Thus, A$\overline{B}$ and Object Retrieval would appear to be dependent on abilities so fundamental to the human organism that given the normal range of experience these abilities will be acquired by all infants.

Acknowledgements

The work summarized here was carried out at: (a) Harvard Univeristy, in the laboratory of Jerome Kagan, with funding from NSF (Doctoral Dissertation Grant BNS-8013-447) and NICHD (HD-10094), and support to the author from NSF and Danforth Graduate Fellowships, (b) Yale University School of Medicine, in the laboratory of Patricia Goldman-Rakic, with funding from NIMH (MH-00298 & MH-38456), and support to the author from a Sloan Foundation award and NIMH Postdoctoral Fellowship (MH-09007), (c) University of California, San Diego, in the laboratory of Stuart Zola-Morgan, with funding from the Medical Research Service of the Veterans Administration, NIH, and the Office of Naval Research, and support to the author from a grant from Washington University, and (d) Washington University, St. Louis, and the University of Pennsylvania, in the laboratories of the author, with funding from the McDonnell Center for Studies of Higher Brain Function at Washington University School of Medicine, NIMH (MH-41842), & BRSG (RR07054 & RR07083).

Notes

1. "Frontal lobe" is used in this paper to refer to that portion of frontal cortex rostral to the precentral gyrus. It includes association cortex (prefrontal, supplementary motor, and premotor), but not primary motor cortex. The frontal lobe is the largest and most prominent functional subdivision of cortex in the human brain. It is also the area that has undergone the most dramatic increase in size over the course of human evolution. Thus, for example, not only is the human brain larger than the cat brain, but the frontal lobe occupies 25% of this larger human brain whereas it occupies only 3% of the cat brain.

2. Infants do not reach for hidden objects until about 7½ months of age. Since the AB task requires the subject to uncover a hidden object, infants younger than 7½ months cannot be tested on the task.

3. The lesion used by Moll and Kuypers was unusually large, extending from the posterior two-thirds of the principal sulcus to the rostral portion of the precental gyrus. Thus, it included the posterior portion of dorsolateral prefrontal cortex, the entire periarcuate region, the supplementary motor area (SMA), and premotor cortex.

4. As there has been some misunderstanding about the characteristics of "deteriorated performance," some clarification is in order. Deteriorated performance is seen when the task has become so difficult that the subject becomes distressed and does not want to remain in the situation. Sometimes subjects react by reaching randomly; other times they exhibit exceedingly long error strings. Always they show overt signs of distress, such as crying or fussing (or, in the case of monkeys, agitated circling); and often they fail to self-correct. This is the only time that performance on repeat-following-correct trials (roughly equivalent to trials at well A) is as poor as performance on reversal trials (roughly equivalent to trials at well B) and as performance on repeat-following-error trials.

The progression from accurate performance, to the the AB error, to deteriorated performance is not curvilinear, as Wellman et al. (1987) thought I was saying. As illustrated in Figure 6, during accurate performance subjects are correct at both wells A and B. The defining characteristic of the AB error is significantly worse performance at B than at A. Empirically, subjects perform at roughly chance on the trials at B, and significantly better than chance on trials at A. During deteriorated performance subjects perform poorly on trials on both A and B; there is no longer any differential pattern of performance by type of trial.

5. A similar observation was made by Bruner (1970). Here the task consisted of a box with a transparent lid mounted on sliding ball bushings. To retrieve the toy, the child had to slide the lid up its track, which was tilted 30° from the horizontal and would fall back down if not held. "A seven month old has great difficulty holding the panel with one hand while reaching underneath with the other. Indeed, the first compromise solutions to the problem consist of pushing the panel up with both hands, then attempting to free one

hand in order to slip it under the panel. One notes how often the infant fails because the two hands operate in concert'' (Bruner, 1970, p. 71).

6. It is important to note that although developments in Object Retrieval performance have been discussed here in terms of no longer needing to look through the opening, it is equally accurate to describe these developments in terms of being able to relate two movements to one another. When infants could see the toy through the opening they could reach straight for the toy. When infants were looking through a closed side of the box, they usually needed to reach in one direction to clear the opening and then change direction to retrieve the toy.

Younger infants almost always reached on a straight line. Two-directional reaches were seen in older infants and emerged as infants began to reach into the opening without simultaneously looking into the opening. In part, progress on Object Retrieval over age appears to be progress in executing reaches that change direction, i.e., reaches with two vector components.

7. Infant monkeys do not reach for hidden objects until about 1½ months of age. Since the AB task requires the subject to uncover a hidden object, monkeys younger than 1½ months cannot be tested on the task.

8. After the covering of the wells, a curtain was quickly lowered and raised between the wells and the subject. Thus, the ''0'' sec delay was probably at least 1–2 sec long.

9. Note how different the results are if a conditioning paradigm is used to determine how long a delay between response and reward the subject can withstand within a trial (as done by Millar and Watson) as opposed to how long the subject can retain a response once it is learned.

10. It should be emphasized that such dissociation of looking and reaching is uncommon in infants; infants, especially at 7½–9 months, almost always look where they are reaching. However, laboratories all over the country who have studied AB have seen this behavior, and it is particularly dramatic because it goes counter to the strong tendency of infants to direct their eyes and their hands to the same place.

11. Such dissociations between frontal patients' verbal and motor behavior are common. One such example is provided by Teuber: The patient "has in many ways what people call a classical frontal lobe syndrome. . . . He was put to work in the garden where he was assigned to another man who was digging ditches; our patient had a big pair of shears with which to cut roots . . . And while a ditch was opened, a huge thing appeared; four black strands lying side by side. The patient was standing there, and the subsequent episode was described by both the patient and his companion. He said, "Ha, ha, it's not a root. It looks like a root (going through the motions of cutting). It looks like a root. It's not a root. Why are the fire alarms ringing?" By cutting the strands he had sorted out all the cables that led to the alarms all over the camp." (Teuber, in discussion of Konorski and Lawicka, 1964, pp. 287–288).

12. Neither monkeys with lesions of dorsolateral prefrontal cortex nor human infants have been tested on Delayed *Non*match to Sample with the modern procedure of trial-unique stimuli. This procedure is critical because if the same stimuli are used repeatedly over trials, then no stimulus is new, and the tendency to reach to the new stimulus does not need to be inhibited.

References

Alexander, G. E., and Goldman, F. S. (1978). Functional development of the dorsolateral prefrontal cortex: An analysis utilizing reversible cryogenic depression. *Brain Research, 143*, 233–250.

Baillargeon, R. (1987). Object permanence in 3½- and 4½-month-old infants. *Developmental Psychology, 23,* 655–664.

Baillargeon, R., and Graber, M. (1988). Evidence of location memory in 8-month-old infants in a non-search task. *Developmental Psychology, 24,* 502–511.

Baillargeon, R., Spelke, E. S., and Wasserman, S. (1985). Object permanence in five month old infants. *Cognition, 20,* 191–208.

Barbizet, J. (1970). Prolonged organic amnesias. In J. Barbizet (Ed.), D. K. Jardine (trans.), *Human memory and its pathology* (pp. 25–93). San Francisco: Freeman.

Battig, K., Rosvold, H. E., and Mishkin, M. (1960). Comparison of the effects of frontal and caudate lesions on delayed response and alteration in monkeys. *Journal of Comparative and Physiological Psychology, 4,* 400–404.

Bauer, R. H., and Fuster, J. M. (1976). Delayed-matching and delayed-response deficit from cooling dorsolateral prefrontal cortex in monkeys. *Journal of Comparative and Physiological Psychology, 90,* 293–302.

Berg, E. A. (1948). A simple objective technique for measuring flexibility in thinking. *Journal of Genetic Psychology, 39,* 15–22.

Bourgeois, J.-P., Goldman-Rakic, P. S., and Rakic, P. (1985). Synaptogenesis in the prefrontal cortex: Quantitative EM analysis in pre- and postnatal rhesus monkeys. *Society for Neuroscience Abstracts, 11,* 501.

Bremner, J. G., and Bryant, P. E. (1977). Place versus response as the basis of spatial errors made by young children. *Journal of Experimental Child Psychology, 23,* 162–171.

Brown, R. M., Crane, A. M., and Goldman, P. S. (1979). Regional distribution of monoamines in the cerebral cortex and subcortical structures of the rhesus monkey: Concentrations and in vivo synthesis rates. *Brain Research, 168,* 133–150.

Brozoski, T., Brown, R. M., Rosvold, H. E., and Goldman, P. S. (1979). Cognitive deficit caused by depletion of dopamine in prefrontal cortex of rhesus monkey. *Science, 205,* 929–931.

Bruner, J. S. (1970). The Growth and Structure of Skill. In K. J. Connolly (Ed.), *Mechanics of Motor Skill Development* (pp. 63–94). NY: Academic Press.

Bruner, J. S., Kaye, and Lyons, K. (1969). *The growth of human manual intelligence: III. The development of detour reaching.* Unpublished manuscript, Center for Cognitive Studies, Harvard University.

Brush, E. S., Mishkin, M., and Rosvold, H. E. (1961). Effects of object preferences and aversions on discrimination learning in monkeys with frontal lesions. *Journal of Comparative and Physiological Psychology, 54,* 319–325.

Bugbee, N. M., and Goldman-Rakic, P. S. (1981). Functional 2-deoxyglucose mapping in association cortex: Prefrontal activation in monkeys performing a cognitive task. *Society for Neuroscience Abstracts, 7,* 416.

Butter, C. M. (1969). Perseveration in extinction and in discrimination reversal tasks following selective frontal ablations in *Macaca mulatta. Physiology and Behavior, 4,* 163–171.

Butters, N., Pandya, D., Sanders, K., and Dye, P. (1969). Behavioral deficits in monkeys after selective lesions within the middle third of sulcus principalis. *Journal of Comparative and Physiological Psychology, 76,* 8–14.

Butterworth, G. (1976). Asymmetrical search errors in infancy. *Child Development, 47,* 864–867.

Butterworth, G. (1977). Object disappearance and error in Piaget's stage IV task. *Journal of Experimental Child Psychology, 23,* 391–401.

Butterworth, G., Jarrett, N., and Hicks, L. (1982). Spatiotemporal identity in infancy: Perceptual competence or conceptual deficit? *Developmental Psychology, 18,* 435–449.

Carew, T. J., Abrams, T. W., Hawkins, R. D., and Kandel, E. R. (1984). The use of simple invertebrate systems to explore psychological issues related to associative learning. In D. L. Akron and J. Farley (Eds.), *Primary neural substrates of learning and behavioral change* (pp. 169–184). Cambridge: Cambridge University Press.

Castellucci, F., and Kandel, E. R. (1976). Presynaptic facilitation as a mechanism for behavioral sensitization in *Aplysia. Science, 194,* 1176–1178.

Cohen, N. J. (1984). Preserved learning capacity in amnesia: Evidence for multiple memory systems. In L. R. Squire and N. Butters (Eds.), *Neuropsychology of memory* (pp. 83–103). New York: Guilford.

Cornell, E. H. (1979). The effects of cue reliability on infants' manual search. *Journal of Experimental Child Psychology, 28,* 81–91.

Crawford, M. P., Fulton, J. F., Jacobsen, C. F., and Wolfe, J. B. (1948). Frontal lobe ablation in chimpanzee: A resume of 'Becky' and 'Lucy.' *A.M.A. Research Publications of Association for Research in Nervous and Mental Disease, 27,* 3–58.

Dekaban, A. (1970). *Neurology of early childhood.* Baltimore: Williams & Wilkins.

Diamond, A. (1981). Retrieval of an object from an open box: The development of visual-tactile control of reaching in the first year of life. *Society for Research in Child Development Abstracts, 3,* 78.

Diamond, A. (1983). Behavior changes between 6 to 12 months of age: What can they tell us about how the mind of the infant is changing? Unpublished doctoral dissertation, Harvard University.

Diamond, A. (1985). Development of the ability to use recall to guide action, as indicated by infants' performance on AB. *Child Development, 56,* 868–883.

Diamond, A. (1988). The abilities and neural mechanisms underlying $\overline{AB}$ performance. *Child Development, 59,* 523–527.

Diamond, A. (1990). Retrieval of an object from an open box: The development of visual-tactile control of reaching in the first year of life. *Monographs of the Society for Research in Child Development.*

Diamond, A. (in press). Frontal lobe involvement in cognitive changes during the first year of life. In K. Gibson, M. Konner, and A. Patterson (Eds.), *Brain and behavorial development.* Hillsdale, NJ: Lawrence Erlbaum Associates.

Diamond, A., and Doar, B. (1989). The performance of human infants on a measure of frontal cortex function, the delayed response task. *Developmental Psychobiology, 22,* 271–294.

Diamond, A., and Gilbert, J. (1989). Development as progressive inhibitory control of action: Retrieval of a contiguous object. *Cognitive Development, 12,* 223–249.

Diamond, A., and Goldman-Rakic, P.S. (1985). Evidence for involvement of prefrontal cortex in cognitive changes during the first year of life: Comparison of human infants and rhesus monkeys on a detour task with transparent barrier. *Society for Neuroscience Abstracts (Part II), 11,* 832.

Diamond, A., and Goldman-Rakic, P. S. (1986). Comparative development in human infants and infant rhesus monkeys of cognitive functions that depend on prefrontal cortex. *Neuroscience Abstracts, 12,* 742.

Diamond, A., and Goldman-Rakic, P. S. (1989). Comparison of human infants and rhesus monkeys on Piaget's abä task: Evidence for dependence on dorsolateral prefrontal cortex. *Experimental Brain Research, 74,* 24–40.

Diamond, A., Cruttenden, L., and Neiderman, D. (1989a). Why have studies found better performance with multiple wells than with only two wells on AB? *Society for Research in Child Development Abstracts, 6,* 227.

Diamond, A., Zola-Morgan,, S., and Squire, L. (1989b). Successful performance by monkeys with lesions of the hippocampal formation on AB and Object Retrieval, two tasks that mark developmental changes in human infants. *Behavioral Neuroscience, 103,* 526–537.

Evans, W. F. (1973). The stage IV error in Piaget's theory of concept development: An investigation of the rise of activity. Unpublished doctoral dissertation, University of Houston.

Fagan, J. F. (1970). Memory in the infant. *Journal of Experimental Child Psychology, 9,* 217–226.

Fantz, R. L. (1964). Visual experience in infants: Decreased attention to familiar patterns relative to novel ones. *Science, 146,* 668–670.

Fox, N., Kagan, J., and Weiskopf, S. (1979). The growth of memory during infancy. *Genetic Psychology Monographs, 99,* 91–130.

Freedman, M., and Oscar-Berman, M. (1986). Bilateral frontal lobe disease and selective delayed response deficits in humans. *Behavioral Neuroscience, 100,* 337–342.

Fuster, J. M. and Alexander, G. E. (1970). Delayed response deficit by cryogenic research of frontal cortex. *Brain Research, 20,* 85–90.

Fuster, J. M. (1973). Unit activity in prefrontal cortex during delay-response performance: Neuronal correlates of transient memory. *Journal of Neurophysiology, 36,* 61–78.

Fuster, J. M. (1980). *The prefrontal cortex.* New York: Raven Press.

Fuster, J. M., and Alexander, G. E. (1971). Neuron activity related to short-term memory. *Science, 173,* 652–654.

Goldman, P. S. (1971). Functional development of the prefrontal cortex in early life and the problem of neuronal plasticity. *Experimental Neurology, 32,* 366–387.

Goldman, P. S. (1974). Recovery of function after CNS lesions in infant monkeys. *Neuroscience Research Progress Bulletin, 12,* 217–22.

Goldman, P. S., and Nauta, W. J. H. (1976). Autoradiographic demonstration of a projection from prefrontal association cortex to the superior colliculus in the rhesus monkey. *Brain Research, 116,* 145–149.

Goldman, P. S., and Rosvold, H. E. (1970). Localization of function within the dorsolateral prefrontal cortex of the rhesus monkey. *Experimental Neurology, 27,* 291–304.

Gottlieb, G. (1983). The psychobiological approach to development issues. In M. M. Haith and J. J. Campos (Eds.), *Infancy and developmental psychobiology,* Vol. II. (pp. 1–26). New York: Wiley.

Grant, D. A., and Berg, E. A. (1948). A behavioral analysis of degree of reinforcement and ease of shifting to new responses in Weigl-type card-sorting problem. *Journal of Experimental Psychology, 38,* 404–411.

Gratch, G. (1975). Recent studies based on Piaget's view of object concept development. In L. B. Cohen and P. Salapatek (Eds.), *Infant perception: From to cognition* (vol. 2). New York: Academic Press.

Gratch, G., Appel, K. J., Evans, W. F., LeCompte, G. K., and Wright, N. A. (1974). Piaget's stage IV object concept error: Evidence of forgetting or object conception? *Child Development, 45,* 71–77.

Gratch, G., and Landers, W. F. (1971). Stage IV of Piaget's theory of infant's object concepts: A longitudinal study. *Child Development, 42,* 359–372.

Gross, C. G., and Weiskrantz, L. (1962). Evidence for dissociation of impairment on auditory discrimination and delayed response following lateral frontal lesions in monkeys. *Experimental Neurology, 5,* 453–476.

Harlow, H. F. (1950). Analysis of discrimination learning by monkeys. *Journal of Experimental Psychology, 40,* 26–39.

Harlow, H. F., and Dagnon, J. (1943). Problem solution by monkeys following bilateral removal of prefrontal areas: I. Discrimination and discrimination reversal problems. *Journal of Experimental Psychology, 32,* 351–356.

Harlow, H. F., Davis, R. T., Settlage, P. H., and Meyer, D. R. (1952). Analysis of frontal and posterior association syndromes in brain-damaged monkeys. *Journal of Comparative and Physiological Psychology, 54,* 419–429.

Harris, P. L. (1973). Perseverative errors in search by young infants. *Child Development, 44,* 28–33.

Harris, P. L. (1974). Perseverative search at a visibly empty place by young infants. *Journal of Experimental Child Psychology, 18,* 535–542.

Harris, P. L. (1987). The development of search. In P. Salapatek and L. B. Cohen (Eds.), *Handbook of Preception* (Vol. 2, pp. 155–207). New York: Academic Press.

Hikosaka, O., and Wurtz, R. H. (1983). Visual and oculomotor functions of monkey substantia nigra pars reticulata. IV. Relation of substantia nigra to superior colliculus. *Journal of Neurophysiology, 49,* 1285–1301.

Hikosaka, O., and Wurtz, R. H. (1984). Modification of saccadic eye movements by GABA-related substances. II. Effect of muscimol and bicuculline in the monkey superior colliculus. *Journal of Neurophysiology, 52,* 266–291.

Hikosaka, O., and Wurtz, R. H. (1985). Modification of saccadic eye movements by GABA-related substances. II. Effects of muscimol in monkey substantia nigra pars reticulata. *Journal of Neurophysiology, 53,* 292–308.

Huttenlocher, P. R. (1979). Synaptic density in human frontal cortex—developmental changes and effects of aging. *Brain Research, 163,* 195–205.

Ingle, D. (1973). Disinhibition of tectal neurons by pretectal lesions in the frog. *Science, 180,* 422–424.

Jacobsen, C. F. (1935). Functions of frontal association areas in primates. *Archives of Neurology & Psychiatry, 33,* 558–560.

Jacobsen, C. F. (1936). Studies of cerebral functions in primates. I. The function of the frontal association areas in monkeys. *Comparative Psychology Monographs, 13,* 1–60.

Jacobsen, C. F., Wolfe, J. B. and Jackson, T. A. (1935). An experimental analysis of the frontal association areas in primates. *Journal of Nervous and Mental Disease, 82,* 1–14.

Konorski, J., and Lawicka, W. (1964). Analysis of errors by prefrontal animals on the delayed response task. In J. M. Warren and K. Akert (Eds.), *The frontal granular cortex and behavior* (pp. 271–312). New York: McGraw-Hill.

Kunzle, H. (1978). An autoradiographic analysis of the efferent connections from premotor and adjacent prefrontal regions (areas 6 and 9) in *Macaca fascicularis*. *Brain. Behavior, and Evolution, 15,* 185–234.

Landers, W. F. (1971). The effect of differential experience in infants' performance in a Piagetian stage IV object-concept task. *Developmental Psychology, 5,* 48–54.

Larroche, J. C. (1966). The development of the central nervous system during intrauterine life. In S. Faulkner (Ed.), *Human development* (257–276). Philadelphia: Saunders.

Lockman, J. J. (1984). The development of detour ability during infancy. *Child Development, 55,* 482–491.

Lorenz, K. (1965) *Evolution and modification of behavior.* Chicago: University of Chicago Press.

Luria, A. R. (1966). *The higher cortical functions in man.* New York: Basic Books.

Luria, A. R., and Homskaya, E. D. (1964). Disturbance in the regulative role of speech with frontal lobe lesions. In J. M. Warren and K. Akert (Eds.), *The frontal granular cortex and behavior* (pp. 353–371). New York: McGraw-Hill.

Markowitsch, H. J., and Pritzel, M. (1977). Comparative analysis of prefrontal learning functions in rats, cats, and monkeys. *Psychological Bulletin, 84,* 817–837.

McCormick, D. A., and Thompson, R. F. (1984). Cerebellum: Essential involvement in the classically conditioned eyelid response. *Science, 223,* 296–299.

Meyer, D. R., Harlow, H. F., and Settlage, P. H. (1951). A survey of delayed response performance by normal and brain-damaged monkeys. *Journal of Comparative and Physiological Psychology, 44,* 17–25.

Miles, R. C., and Blomquist, A. (1960). Frontal lesions and behavioral deficits in monkey. *Journal of Neurophysiology, 23,* 471–484.

Millar, W. S., and Schaffer, H. R. (1972). The influence of spatially displaced feedback on infant operant conditioning. *Journal of Experimental Child Psychology, 14,* 442–453.

Millar, W. S., and Schaffer, H. R. (1973). Visual-manipulative response strategies in infant operant conditioning with spatially displaced feedback. *British Journal of Psychology, 64,* 546–552.

Millar, W. S., and Watson, J. S. (1979). The effect of delayed feedback on infant learning reexamined. *Child Development, 50,* 747–751.

Milner, B. (1963). Effects of brain lesions on card sorting. *Archives of Neurology, 9,* 90–100.

Milner, B. (1964). Some effects of frontal lobectomy in man. In J. M. Warren and K. Akert (Eds.), *The frontal granular cortex and behavior* (pp. 313–334). New York: McGraw-Hill.

Milner, B. (1974). Hemispheric specialization: Scope and limits. In F. O. Schmitt and F. G. Worden (Eds.), *The neurosciences: Third study program* (pp. 75–89). Cambridge, MA: MIT Press.

Mishkin, M. (1964). Perseveration of central sets after frontal lesions in monkeys. In J. M. Warren and K. Akert (Eds.), *The frontal granular cortex and behavior* (pp. 219–241). New York: McGraw-Hill.

Mishkin, M., and Manning, F. J. (1978). Nonspatial memory after selective prefrontal lesions in monkeys. *Brain Research, 143,* 313–323.

Mishkin, M., Vest, B., Waxler, M., and Rosvold, H. E. (1969). A reexamination of the effects of frontal lesions on object alternation. *Neuropsychologia, 7,* 357–364.

Mishkin, M., Malamut, B., and Bachevalier, J. (1984). Memories and habits: Two neural systems. In G. Lynch, J. L. McGaugh, and N. M. Weinberger (eds.), *Neurobiology of learning and memory* (pp. 65–77). New York: Guilford.

Moll, L., and Kuypers, H. G. J. M. (1977). Premotor cortical ablations in monkeys: Contralateral changes in visually guided reaching behavior. *Science, 198,* 317–319.

Nauta, W. J. H. (1971). The problem of the frontal lobe: A reinterpretation. *Journal of Psychiatric Research, 8,* 167–187.

Nichols, I. C., and Hunt, J. McV. (1940). A case of partial bilateral frontal lobectomy: A psychopathological study. *American Journal of Psychiatry, 96,* 1063–1087.

Niki, H. (1974). Differential activity of prefrontal units during right and left delayed response trials. *Brain Research, 70,* 346–349.

Papousek, H. (1961). Conditioned head rotation reflexes in infants in the first months of life. *Acta Paediatrica (Stockholm), 50,* 565–576.

Passingham, R. E. (1975). Delayed matching after selective prefrontal lesions in monkeys *(macaca mulatta). Brain Research, 92,* 89–102.

Perret, E. (1974). The left frontal lobe of man and the suppression of habitual responses in verbal categorical behaviour. *Neuropsychologia, 16,* 527–537.

Petrides, M., and Milner, B. (1982). Deficits on subject-oriented tasks after frontal- and temporal-lobe lesions in man. *Neuropsychologia, 20,* 249–262.

Piaget, J. (1954). *The construction of reality in the child.* New York: Basic Books. (Original French edition, 1937.)

Pinsker, H. M., and French, G. M. (1967). Indirect delayed reactions under various testing conditions in normal and midlateral frontal monkeys. *Neuropsychologia, 5,* 13–24.

Pohl, W. (1973). Dissociation of spatial discrimination deficits following frontal and parietal lesions in monkeys. *Journal of Comparative and Physiological Psychology, 82,* 227–239.

Rakic, P. (1974). Neurons in rhesus monkey visual cortex: Systematic relation between time of origin and eventual disposition. *Science, 183,* 425–427.

Rock, I., and Harris, C. S. (1967). Vision and Touch. *Scientific American,* 96–104.

Rosenkilde, C. E. (1979). Functional heterogeneity of the prefrontal cortex in the monkey: A review. *Behavioral and Neural Biology, 25,* 301–345.

Rosvold, H. E. (1972). The frontal lobe system: Cortical-subcortical interrelationships. In J. Konorski, H.-L. Teuber, and B. Zernicki (Eds.), *Functions of the septo-hippocampal system* (pp. 439–460). Warsaw: Polish Science Publishers.

Rovee-Collier, C. (1984). The ontogeny of learning and memory in human infancy. In R. Kail and N. E. Spear (Eds.), *Comparative perspectives on the development of memory* (pp. 103–134). Hillsdale, NJ: Erlbaum.

Schacter, D. L. (1987). Implicit memory: History and current status. *Journal of Experimental Psychology: Learning, Memory & Cognition, 13,* 501–518.

Schacter, D. L., Moscovitch, M., Tulving, E., McLachlan, D. R., and Freedman, M. (1986). Mnemonic precedence in amnesic patients: An analogue of the AB error in infants? *Child Development, 57,* 816–823.

Schade, J. P., and van Groeningen, W. B. (1961). Structural organization of the human cerebral cortex. I. Maturation of the middle frontal gyrus. *Acta Anatomica, 47,* 74–85.

Schonen, S. de, and Bresson, F. (1984). Development de l'atteinte manuelle d'un objet chez l'enfant. *Omportements, 1,* 99–114.

Schuberth, R. E. (1982). The infant's search for objects: Alternatives to Piaget's theory of object concept development. In L. P. Lipsitt and C. K. Rovee-Collier (Eds.), *Advances in infancy research* (Vol. 2) (pp. 137–182). Norwood, NJ: Ablex.

Squire, L. R., and Cohen, N. J. (1984). Human memory and amnesia. In G. Lynch J. L. McGaugh, and N. M. Weinberger (Eds.), *Neurobiology of learning and memory* (pp. 3–64), New York: Guilford.

Squire, L. R., and Zola-Morgan, S. (1983). The neurobiology of memory: The case for correspondence between the findings for human and non-human primates. In J. A. Deutsch (Ed.), *The physiological basis of memory* (pp. 199–268). New York: Academic Press.

Stamm, J. S. (1969). Electrical stimulation of monkeys' prefrontal cortex during delayed response performance. *Journal of Comparative and Physiological Psychology, 67,* 646–546.

Stamm, J. S. & Rosen, S. C. (1969). Electrical stimulation and steady potential shifts in prefrontal cortex during delayed response performance by monkeys. *Acta Biologicae Experimentalis, 29,* 385–399.

Thompson, R. F., Clark, G. A., Donegan, N. H., Lavond, D. G., Madden, J., IV, Mamounas, L. A., Mauk, M. D., and McCormick, D. A. (1984). Neuronal substrates of basic associative learning. In L. R. Squire and N. Butters (Eds.), *Neuropsychology of memory* (pp. 424–442). New York: Guilford, Press.

Waddington, C. H. (1942). Canalization of development and the inheritance of acquired characteristics. *Nature, (London) 150,* 563–564.

Weiskrantz, L., and Warrington, E. K. (1979). Conditioning in amnesic patients. *Neuropsychologia, 17,* 187–194.

Weiskrantz, L., Mihailovic, L., and Gross, C. G. (1962). Effects of stimulation of frontal cortex and hippocampus on behavior in the monkey. *Brain, 85,* 487–504.

Wellman, H. M., Cross, D., and Bartsch, K. (1987). A meta-analysis of research on Stage 4 object permanence: A-not-B error. *Monographs of the Society for Research in Child Development, 5*(3).

Yakovlev, P. I., and Lecours, A.-R. (1967). The myelogenetic cycles of regional maturation of the brain. In A. Minkowski (Ed.), *Regional development of the brain in early life* (pp. 3–70). Oxford: Blackwell.

Zola-Morgan, S., and Squire, L. R. (1986). Memory impairment in monkeys following lesions limited to the hippocampus. *Behavioral Neuroscience, 100,* 155–160.

Zola-Morgan, S., Squire, L. R., and Amaral, D. G. (1989). Lesions of the Hippocampal Formation, but not lesions of the fornix or mammillary nuclei, produce long-lasting memory impairments in monkeys. *Journal of Neuroscience, 9,* 1922–1936.

Chapter 8

Universals of Behavioral Development in Relation to Brain Myelination

Melvin Konner

Introduction

Pediatrics, neurology, and psychiatry assume that key elements of normal psychological and behavioral development are understood (Rudolph and Hoffman, 1982, Chap. 4; Adams and Victor, 1981, Chap. 27; Nicholi, 1978, Chap. 23). In part, these assumptions form the basis for clinical assessment and treatment, including recommendations about primary prevention that are staples of pediatric and psychiatric advice. Some presumed "facts" of early development, however, are based on minimal data. For example, some clinicians believe that immediate postnatal contact between mother and infant is essential for "mother–infant bonding" (Klaus and Kennell, 1976), but the evidence for this assertion is at best very weak (Svejda et al., 1982). Similarly, many Western clinicians believe that infants should outgrow night-waking after about 3 months of age and assume that this transition reflects patterns of neurological maturation (Spock, 1976). Elaborate treatment programs may be instituted to extinguish night-waking after this time. Many of the world's cultures, however, consider night-waking to be normal and expectable until as late as 3 years of age and make no attempt to extinguish it at earlier ages (Konner and Worthman, 1980).

Recently, doubt has even been cast on one of the most fundamental beliefs about human psychological development (Kagan et al., 1978; Kagan, 1984). A substantial body of opinion holds that the importance of infancy has been greatly exaggerated. Despite much evidence from animal models showing lasting effects of early experience, decisive clinical evidence of comparable effects in humans has been difficult to find. Early experience has not been clearly shown to have lasting important, or even measurable, effects on the course of psychological development. This recent viewpoint, if true, must jeopardize some of what is now common clinical practice in psychiatry and behavioral pediatrics.

Cross-cultural and cross-population studies of psychological development have had, as a main purpose, the demonstration of flexibility of the human psychological repertoire and, by inference, of the underlying neural and endocrine functions. Few studies have attempted to delineate cultural universals of development. Yet, it is increasingly recognized that much of psychological development is inflexible in the face of marked variation in environment of rearing (e.g., Eibl-Eibesfeldt, 1971a,b, 1983; Kagan, 1976; Konner, 1982; Super, 1981).

Developmental studies have also lacked a clear delineation of the underlying events of regional neurological and neuroendocrine development. In past decades, this lack was generally attributed to the absence of adequate studies of structure–function relationships and of brain development itself, particularly in humans, and, particularly, in the late prenatal and early postnatal periods. Recent work, however, has produced great advances in relevant fields, including neuroanatomy (e.g., Nauta and Domesick, 1980), neurophysiology (Evarts, 1975; Waxman, 1977, 1982), behavioral neurology (Heilman and Valenstein, 1979; Geschwind and Galaburda, 1985), neuroethology (MacLean, 1978), and developmental neurology (Brody et al., 1984; Geschwind and Galaburda, 1985; Gilles et al., 1983; Yakovlev and Lecours, 1967). We now know that changes in brain structure and function during the first few years of postnatal life are rapid and large. In the first year of life the brain more than doubles in volume, reaching 60% of its adult size. Growth rate declines only gradually during the second year (Yakovlev, 1962; Blinkov and Glezer, 1968). This high rate of postnatal volumetric increase in brain tissue may be unique to our species among the higher primates and has been viewed as one of the most distinctive advances of human evolution (Gould, 1977).

In the course of this growth, profound structural changes occur in the nervous system. Some basic processes are almost complete by birth. Most neurons, for instance, have already formed, and their cell bodies have migrated to their destined places. Other processes, however, proceed in extrauterine life: proliferation of synapses, branching of dendrites, changes in the density of dendritic spines, changes in connectivity, proliferation of glial support cells through cell division, and the formation of myelin sheaths around axons in the white matter of the central nervous system (Jacobson, 1978). These processes involve attendant and/or underlying neurochemical changes. They are influenced by experience, but to a large extent proceed independently of experience. Each year a considerable literature increases our understanding of these developmental events.

Advances in our knowledge of behavioral development have paralleled those of neural development. Behavioral studies have become increasingly systematic and precise in their methods of measurement and have taken advantage of modern computers to analyze large volumes of behavioral data in an unprecedentedly sophisticated way (Osofsky, 1979; Field et al., 1981; Mussen, 1983). Most behavioral studies, however, fail to consider neurological development.

The persistent lag in incorporating advances in neuroscience into explanations of early psychological development may result from the difficulty of mastering both the language of behavioral development and that of neuroscience, as well as from the reluctance of some students of behavioral and psychological development to come to terms with the existence and nature of fixed maturational sequences. Such sequences have long been known and accepted in the realm of motor development, and have become increasingly established in the realm of cognitive and social development.

This chapter reviews evidence for fixed sequences of behavioral and psychological development drawing on cross-cultural and cross-population studies throughout the world, and relates these behavioral data to brain development in infants and children. Based on these data, a model is proposed to account for certain universals of psychological behavioral development in infancy in terms of maturing brain function.

Assessment of Behavioral and Neuroanatomical Development

Assessment and Observation of Infant Behavior

During the 1960s and 1970s, new methods of assessment led to rapid advances in the study of infant behavior. Anthropologists, cross-cultural psychologists, pediatricians, and psychiatrists readily adopted these methods and applied them to populations throughout the developing world. The result is a new body of knowledge pertaining to cross-cultural and cross-population maturational variations and constancies. This chapter draws on data derived from several of these assessment methods including tests of neurological maturation, motor development, and social development.

Neurological and Behavioral Assessment of Neonates. Two neurological assessment techniques widely used in cross-cultural studies are the Prechtl procedure (Prechtl and Beintema, 1964; Beintema, 1968) and the Brazelton Behavioral Assessment Scale (BNBAS; Brazelton, 1973).

The Prechtl procedure is rigidly standardized and controls for behavioral state of the infant, time since last fed, nonneurological health status, age in days, order of examination, and other variables. The infant is numerically scored on more than 150 assessment items, including behavioral observations, color, muscle tone, joint mobility, a wide variety of specific signs (e.g., hiccups and cough) and, in particular, a comprehensive array of neurological reflexes, both normal (e.g., the Moro reflex elicited by three different stimulus procedures) and abnormal (e.g., Chvostek's sign). The examination generally takes about an hour and requires some training to learn. This procedure has satisfactory interobserver and test–retest reliability if done after 3 days of age with proper attention to state variables.

The Brazelton Neonatal Assessment Scale (BNBAS; Brazelton, 1973) consists of 27 subscales on which the infant is scored from one to nine, with each level defined in detail. The subscales include such items as "alertness," "irritability," and "hand-to-mouth facility." Despite the greater difficulty of obtaining agreement on such measures, this scale has also proved to have satisfactory interobserver and test–retest validity after proper training.

Assessment of Motor Development. Cross-cultural data on motor development derive primarily from four tests: the Bayley scale of infant development (Bayley, 1965, 1969), a similar test used in Britain (Griffiths, 1954), the Gesell scales (Gesell and Amatruda, 1947; Knobloch, 1958), and the McGraw scale (McGraw, 1943). Bayley norms exist and have been validated for large samples of both the white and the black population in the United States. The Griffiths test has been less well validated, but has been more frequently used throughout the British colonial network. The Gesell scales leave much to be desired in terms of standardization but are acceptable for crude comparison. Although standardized on much smaller samples, the McGraw scale renders a more sophisticated assessment of motor development than is possible with the other scales. Rather than assessing broad developmental milestones, the McGraw scale follows the gradual emergence of specific motor skills such as sitting or walking throughout infancy.

Observation and Assessment of Social Development Systematic, timed observations with standardized settings and clearly defined codes for the recording of behavior make reliable and valid measurements of social development possible. Modern electronic recording equipment and computers make possible the collection and analysis of unprecedented volumes of behavioral data, and remove much of the subjective even from categories of behavior such as social interaction. Some items of social behavior, such as smiling and crying, can be assessed and recorded with as much or greater accuracy than neurological reflexes or motor milestones.

Such methods of observation and analysis have been frequently reviewed (e.g., Whiting and Whiting, 1975; Cairns, 1974). In the typical study a preset sample of the infant's time (usually 15–90 min) is recorded in a predetermined setting (e.g., with mother in nonfeeding interaction) and with a list of behaviors of established observational reliability. Initial state is usually defined as alert, not hungry, not irritable, and free of illness, among other constraints. In the best studies, repeated samples of the infant's time minimize transient variation, and, ideally, the order of observations is generated from a random number table. Analysis may include calculation of frequency and duration of events, contingency of some events on others, lag sequence analysis designed to reveal complex causal interaction chains, and other approaches.

Cross-population comparisons using these methods of observation must carefully control for cultural variations in setting, response to observations, and other extraneous sources of variance. In any case, these methods represent a great technical improvement over the methods of two or three decades ago, and are greatly superior to the methods of screening for social maturation in common use in pediatric practice.

Specific tests of social responsiveness are numerous and varied. Three tests that have been applied cross-culturally figure in the model of social development presented here: Gewirtz's test of the development of social smiling (Gewirtz, 1965), tests of the development of stranger reactions (Ricciuti, 1974; Konner, 1972; Chisholm, 1983), and Bretherton's and Ainsworth's test for the infant attachment (1974). Gerwirtz's method appraises the development of social smiling in early infancy by beginning with the infant in a quiet alert state and presenting the face of a live, but impassive, adult in a face-to-face juxtaposition with that of the infant. The number of smiles seen in a period of 1 min is recorded.

Ricciuti (1974), Konner (1972), Chisholm, (1983) and others appraise the development of stranger reactions during the period after 6 months of age using minor variations of the following paradigm. The infant or toddler is sitting near the mother and is approached slowly, in a nonthreatening way, by a completely unknown adult who often speaks in a designated manner intended to evoke a positive reaction. Specific behaviors both positive and negative are recorded, including, among others, smiling, approaching the stranger, gaze aversion within 2 sec, withdrawing, and crying. Positive responses are summed arithmetically or weighted according to intensity of response (i.e., more points for crying than for gaze aversion). The sum provides a score for a given infant at a given age in response to this stimulus.

Bretherton and Ainsworth's (1974) test for the evaluation of attachment involves a defined set of behaviors of the infant toward the mother or other primary caretaker in a novel situation. Briefly, the infant and mother are brought into a room with toys on the floor. The infant is given 3 min to acclimatize to the room, whereupon a stranger enters, chats with the mother, and interacts with the infant for 1 min each. The mother then leaves the room for 3 min, or until the infant cries for 30 sec, and returns for 3 min with the stranger absent. Similar staged events, including leaving the infant alone, follow for a total of eight episodes. The infant's behavior is recorded according to a predetermined list of items, with an emphasis on crying and other protest behavior on mother's departure, and on behavior at reunion.

Myelination and Myelination Cycles

Myelin Structure and Function.   Myelin, apparently first named by Virchow in 1864, is a fatty sheath that insulates a large proportion of mammalian nerve fibers, both peripheral and central. This insulation is a space saving and energy-efficient adaptation that provides for rapid impulse conduction without necessitating the great fiber size characteristic of rapidly conducting fibers in inverte-brate nervous system.

The composition of myelin is grossly similar to that of typical cell membranes, but with a higher ratio of lipid to protein and a larger proportion of glycolipids relative to phospholipids and cholesterol. The proteins, embedded in the lipid bilayer in a manner common in other plasma membranes, include, among others, myelin basic protein, proteolipid protein, and glycoprotein and enzymes (Peters et al., 1976; Raine, 1984a).

Myelination Sequences in Development. Since the introduction of the Weigert stain in the late nineteenth century, myelin-stained sections of brain and spinal cord have been a mainstay of neuroanatomic research and teaching. The Weigert stain and its successors, the Loyez stain (Yakovlev, 1970) and the Luxol fast blue stain, are relatively easy to make and to interpret. Thus they permit easy visualization and tracing of fiber pathways.

For example, the projection of optic radiation from the lateral geniculate body of the thalamus to area 17 of the occipital cortex becomes stainable (acquires myelin) during the immediate postnatal months in the human brain, making it stand out at that time from the background of unstained (unmyelinated) pathways in most other parts of the cortical radiations. The vivid stainability of the myelin sheath together with the regionally specific timing of myelination made studies of Weigert-stained sections of fetal and young postnatal brains of various species a mainstay of neuroanatomical tracing in the era when neural circuits were first being delineated.

In the peripheral nervous system, myelin is the product of the Schwann cell, while in the central nervous system it is produced by another glial cell type, the oligodendrocyte. Under the light microscope, the developmental process of myelination has several distinct phases (Yakovlev and Lecours, 1986; Gilles et al., 1983). Some time after the extension of axions toward or, more likely, to their sites of termination, marked glial cell hyperplasia occurs in the vicinity of the axon. This process has been termed "myelination gliosis" by analogy (technically inappropriate) with gliosis that occurs in the vicinity of injured neurons. The glial cells so generated accumulate myelin lipid components ("premyelin lipids") cytoplasmically before the actual appearance of myelin. Following myelination gliosis there are at least three recognizable phases of myelination in appropriately stained sections: (1) myelin visible only micro-scopically, (2) myelin visible to the naked eye, but faintly in comparison to the ultimate or mature level, and (3) mature level of myelin density.

Although the progress from myelination gliosis to grossly visible myelin is complete in a matter of weeks in most systems, the attainment of the mature level of density may take months or even years in some systems. Central nervous system pathways, in particular, myelinate at distinctly different times during development, and despite some significant timing differences along the course of a given pathway (a cephalocaudal direction of myelin deposition seems to be a regular feature), there are greater timing differences between than within pathways.

Myelination as an Index of Regional Brain Development. Originally, myelination studies focused on the more central purpose of using immature brains to illuminate connections. Ever since the pioneering work of Flechsig (1920), however, myelination has been used to illuminate developmental sequences and attempts have been made to correlate myelination and behavioral maturation. These attempts have engendered some controversy and criticism because the interrelationships between myelination, maturation, and behavior are not transparently obvious.

Encyclopedic treatments of the development of the human cortex by Conel (1939–1967) and his successor, Rabinowicz (1979), however, have shown that various aspects of cortical development exhibit considerable synoptic growth: e.g., width of the cortex and its layers; number, size, and density of neurons; condition of intercellular components such as chromophil substance and neurofibrils; number and size of extrinsic fibers; and number, size, and form of neuronal processes, including the density of "pedunculated bulbs" (now called thorns or spines) on the dendrites. These data suggest the validity of myelination sequences as a crude general index of regional brain development. A rank ordering of the relative maturity of a series of cortical regions at a given age would be quite similar whichever of Conel's indices were used. Although Conel's work has been criticized for methodological inadequacies (Purpura and Reaser, 1974), these inadequacies appear to affect the materials he studied uniformly, so that at worst the timing, but not the sequence, of developmental events may have been inaccurately described. The consistency of rank order should and does survive uniformly expressed difficulties of method.

Experimental animal studies also demonstrate correlations between myelination sequences and other indices of regional brain development. Numerous changes occur in cell bodies during myelination of their axons. For instance, quantities of cytoplasm and axoplasm increase in direct proportion to each other and changes occur in neuronal packing density, nuclear and nucleolar diameters, and distribution of chromophil substance within the cell (Martinez and Friede, 1970). In addition, the extent of myelination correlates with the growth of axon diameter, so much so that axon diameter has been proposed as the trigger for myelination (Friede and Samorajski, 1967; Matthews, 1968), although this view may be oversimplified (Moore et al., 1976). It thus appears that myelination sequences can serve provisionally as a crude index of regional brain development.

Myelination and Nerve Function. Whether myelination can serve as an index of behavioral capability is a separate issue. Early investigators thought that it could (Tilney and Casamajor, 1924; Windle et al., 1934; Keene and Hewer, 1931; Langworthy, 1933). It is now clear, however, that myelination cannot be considered "an absolute index of behavioral capability" (Angulo y Gonzalez, 1929).

In both rats and humans, neurological function begins before myelin appears. In many species critical functions in the adult, such as those of the autonomic nervous system, occur in normally unmyelinated fibers. Many invertebrate nervous systems function without myelin, and anatomically specific demyelination does not invariably result in the expected loss of function in clinical syndromes such as multiple sclerosis. For these reasons, some modern authors consider myelination sequences irrelevant to the development of behavior (e.g., see Kinsbourne and Hiscock, 1983, with special reference to the role of myelination of the cerebral commissures in the development of lateralized hemispheric function).

Such cautionary remarks have validity, but they represent only one side of a complex set of questions about the role of myelination in nerve function. On the other side are arrayed a large body of clinical data from the study of a variety of syndromes involving demyelination or delayed myelination, mounting evidence from experimental animal models of demyelination and delayed myelination, and theoretical and experimental considerations relating to membrane function with and without myelin, all of which support a significant, if imperfect, relationship between myelination and function (Ritchie, 1984; Waxman, 1977, 1982).

Nerve fibers subjected to a pathological or experimentally induced loss of myelin share certain functional alterations. These include (1) decreased conduction velocity, (2) increased refractory period, (3) more frequent conduction failure, (4) temporal dispersion of impulses, (5) increased susceptibility to inadvertent electrical modification by neighboring axons, and (6) increased susceptibility to mechanical, thermal, and other extraneous influences (McDonald and Sears, 1970; Rasminsky and Sears, 1972; Ritchie, 1984; Waxman, 1977, 1982). These effects are listed in Table 1, and some of the studies demonstrating them are listed in Table 2.

In addition, studies of remyelination have demonstrated convincing correlations between reacquisition of myelin and reappearance of normal or approximately normal conduction latency and refractory period in the remyelinating fibers (Smith, et al., 1981).

It is not clear, however, that evidence about demyelination or remyelination, even when consistent across different clinical and experimental models, can be transferred to the normally unmyelinated condition. There may be abnormalities of the membrane underlying damaged or diseased myelin that do not characterize the membrane of developing not-yet-myelinated cells. The few existing studies of functional consequences of lack of myelin in normal systems appear to corroborate these findings, however.

In the best study of this nature, Huttenlocher (1970) followed the developing cat pyramidal tract from 3 to 5 weeks of postnatal life and found that several functional capabilities precede myelination. The ability of the fiber to conduct

Table 1. Consequences of Demyelination[a]

Increased conduction latency (up to 30×)
Increased refractory period
Impairment at higher frequencies
Conduction block more likely
Temporal dispersion of impulses
Ephaptic communication ("cross-talk")
Temperature and mechanical sensitivity

From Ritchie (1984) and Waxman (1977, 1982).

Table 2. Correlates and Consequences at Myelination and Demyelination

Study	Model System	Finding
Selected landmark studies		
Huxley and Stämpfli (1949)	Frog myelinated nerve fiber	First demonstration of saltatory conduction, restriction of ion flow to node of Ranvier
McDonald and Sears (1970)	Cat dorsal column, diphtheria toxin demyelination	Decreased conduction velocity, increased refractory period, high-frequency block
Rasminsky and Sears (1972)	Rat ventral root, diphtheria toxin demyelination	Internodal conduction time increased from 20 to 600 μsec
Rasminsky (1973)	Rat ventral root, diphtheria toxin demyelination	Exquisite temperature sensitivity (block with increase of 0.5°C)
Raminsky (1980)	Dystrophic mice, spinal nerve roots	Ephaptic transmission ("cross-talk") among single fibers
Developmental studies		
Huttenlocher (1970)	Cat pyramidal tract, 3 days to 5 weeks	Myelination makes repetitive firing possible
Martinez and Friede (1970)	Rat sciatic nerve, 1–16 weeks	Multiple correlates in axon and cell growth
Freeman (1978)	Cat optic nerve, adult, no treatment	Myelin sheath thickness predicts conduction latency in mature fibers
Recovery studies		
Smith et al. (1981)	Cat dorsal, column, adult, LPC demyelination	Remyelination restores experimentally blocked conduction
Bostock et al. (1981)	Cat dorsal column, adult, LPC demyelination	Conduction precedes remyelination due to nodal aggregation of Na$^+$ channels

impulses under the stimulus of a high-frequency train, however, was absent before myelination. Rates of repetitive firing as low as 40/sec resulted in conduction block. Since rates of 50–100/sec have been shown to be involved in the normal course of pyramidal tract function during voluntary contraction of hand and forearm muscles in monkeys, the limitations of premyelinated neurons would have functional significance. Metabolic considerations support this interpretation. The active membrane surfaces of unmyelinated axons is two to three orders of magnitude greater than that of myelinated axons. The energy expenditure required to maintain the same rate of firing in the unmyelinated condition would be formidable.

Experience Effects on Myelination. Although much is known about the events leading up to and associated with early myelination (Peters et al., 1976; Raine, 1984a; Sidman and O'Gorman, 1981), there is not yet a convincing account of what causes it. Possibly, function not only precedes but also causes myelination. This hypothesis is consistent with findings that experience or exercise affect brain development. Early experience, for instance has dramatic effects on the structure and function of neurons in the visual cortex of cats and monkeys (Wiesel and Hubel, 1965; LeVay et al., 1980). Although less dramatic, consistent effects have been demonstrated of environmental enrichment on the thickness, neuronal density, dendritic branching complexity, dendritic spine counts, synaptic density, acetylcholine level, cholinesterase activity level, and glia-to-neuron ratio in the cerebral cortex of the rat (Globus et al., 1973; Diamond et al., 1964, 1985).

Studies of the effects of experience and exercise on myelination have not been as numerous or impressive as these classic studies, but they have shown a moderately consistent effect of experience, as indicated in Table 3 (Gyllenstein and Malmfors, 1963; Wendell-Smith, 1964; Kingsley et al., 1970; Moore et al., 1976; Sammeck, 1975; Samorajski and Rolsten, 1975; Tauber et al., 1980).

Although these studies show that there is a significant effect of experience on myelination, these effects are either transient or, if permanent, relatively small—on the order of 10–20%. The most severe procedures of stimulus deprivation, such as rearing in darkness, total occlusion of an eye, or sciatic neurectomy, are compatible with the eventual acquisition of normal myelin in the great majority of fibers in the deprived nerves or tracts. This strongly suggests an underlying process whose timing is under genetic control.

A considerable literature supports this suggestion. Among the infantile diseases of the cerebral white matter at least six, known as dysmyelinating leucodystrophies and resulting in specific retardation syndromes, have been shown to have simple Mendelian inheritance patterns (Carter and Gold, 1974; Raine, 1984b; Traugott and Raine, 1984). Clinical syndromes of specifically peripheral hypomyelination in infants suggest a genetic basis as well. These syndromes are characterized by global delays in motor development that are unresponsive to exercise and consistent with the delay or insufficiency of myelination (Ono et al., 1982).

Table 3. Experience Effects on Myelination

Study	Model System	Finding
Gyllensten and Malmfors (1963)	Mice reared in darkness, birth to 30 days	12% reduction in number of myelinated fibers in optic nerve
Wendell-Smith (1964)	Mice, one eye occluded, birth to 75 days	"Visual impression" of decreased sheath thickness in optic nerve
Kingsley et al. (1970)	Rats, sciatic neurectomy, birth to 21 days	10–20% reduction in number of myelinated fibers in dorsal funiculus
Sammeck (1974)	Rats, swimming 2–4 h/day, from "adolescence" for 12–16 days	"Considerable increase" in number of myelinated axons in sciatic nerve
Samorajski and Rolsten (1975)	Mice, activity wheel running 2–4 h/day from 3 to 24 months	No effect on posterior tibial nerve myelin despite fiber hypertrophy
Moore et al. (1976)	Cats reared in darkness, birth to 4 weeks	No effect on percentage of myelinated axons
Tauber et al. (1980)	Rabbits, artificial eye opening at 5 days (vs. 10 days)	Myelin-specific proteins double at 7–10 days, but equal at 20 days

Animal models have been more directly supportive of a primarily genetic control of myelination, since they permit deciphering some of the details of development control (Hogan and Greenfield, 1984; Carnow et al., 1984). For example, two mutants of the mouse affecting myelination—"jimpy," an X-linked mutation that causes severe CNS hypomyelination while sparing the PNS, and "quaking," an autosomal recessive allele on chromosome 17 causing global hypomyelination—have been studied with respect to myelin basic protein (MPB) gene expression. Messenger RNA transcription is normal in both cases, but MPB-related translation products are altered in the proportions of different molecular weight species that become particularly relevant at different stages of myelin synthesis (Carnow et al., 1984). Such studies, carried out in parallel with continued ultrastructural examination of the myelination process, should lead to a general characterization of the genetic control of myelination in the not too distant future.

Myelination, then, whether pre- or postnatal, must be considered to be a genetically controlled process largely intrinsic to the growth and differentiation of the brain. Its influence on developing behavior is likely to be large compared with the reciprocal influence of experience on myelination, although the latter is certainly significant, and mutual interaction of biology and experience must always be considered to be the rule.

Human Myelination Data. Paul Flechsig (1920) was the first to provide detailed descriptions of the sequence of myelination in humans. His reputation is closely associated with the mapping of the sequence of myelination within the cerebral cortex. During the 1920s and 1930s, Flechsig's work inspired a number of studies directed toward correlating myelination sequences with the development of behavioral capability, particularly during fetal development (Tilney and Casamajor, 1924; Windle et al., 1934; Keene and Hewer, 1931; Langworthy, 1933).

In the modern period, several investigations have expanded and confirmed the work of Flechsig. Yakovlev and Lecours (1967) studied a total of 200 brains, ostensibly neurologically normal, ranging from early gestation to late in the senium. The unique value of their series is that all the brains were uniformly preserved, cut, and stained.[1] The brains were fixed with formalin, imbedded in celloidin, and serially sectioned at 20–40 um. Every tenth section was then strained according to the Loyez modification of the Weigert hermatoxylin stain for myelin sheaths, and the adjacent section stained with the Bielschowsky–Plien cresyl violet stain for cell bodies. (All details of method are given in Yakovlev, 1970.) Yakovlev and Lecours (1967) then studied the myelin-stained sections with the light microscope using nonquantitative methods of description and comparison. The essence of this method is the preservation of whole brain serial sections giving the opportunity to reconstruct the main elements of three-dimensional brain anatomy, including all circuitry distinguishable with the myelin stain.[2]

Rorke and Riggs (1969) conducted a study specifically directed to the perinatal status of the brains of infants of varying birthweight (from 740 to 3910 g) to represent a range of gestation lengths from quite premature to full-term. The entire sample consisted of 107 infants of which 23 were considered to be full-term and normal sized. Death occurred within 7 days of birth (96% were either stillborn or died within 3 days), and was, in most cases, a result of hyaline membrane disease, pneumonia, or pulmonary hemorrhage. After celloidin-embedding, a limited but representative number of sections (around 30) of each brain were taken at 20 um and stained with luxol fast blue and cresyl violet according to the technique of Klüver–Barrera. As was the case in the Yakovlev and Lecours study, assessment was made by careful visual inspection and description rather than by morphometric or other quantitative methods. These authors were the first to introduce the refinement of recognizing and describing individual variation at a given age. However, for the ostensibly full-term normal-sized infants, 87% of the specimens showed "essentially similar" myelination, with the other 13% showing lesser degrees of development.

Gilles et al. (1983 see Table 4) conducted their study of myelination as part of the National Collaborative Perinatal Project (NCPP) of the National Institute of Neurological and Communicative Disorders and Strokes. They used 323 cases from NCPP collection, most of which were Loyez stained (see above), ranging in estimated age from 20 to 48 postconceptual weeks. They introduced a number of refinements of method compared with prior investigators. First, they declined to

Table 4. Comparison of Several Estimates of Ages of Onset of Myelination in the Human Fetal Nervous System[a]

	Gilles, et al. 1983 (Microscopic Myelin)	Yakolve and Lecours (1967)	Larroche (1966)	Langworthy (1933)
Spinal cord				
Fasciculus gracilis	< 20	—	28	28
Dorsal spinocerebellar	< 20	—	26	20
Spinothalamic	< 20	—	26	28
Brainstem				
Medial longitudinal fasciculus	< 20	20–22	24	20
Medial lemniscus	23–25	24	26–28	28 and 36
Acoustic	23–24	20–24	24–28	38
Inferior cerebellar peduncle	24	24	28	—
Superior cerebellar peduncle	26	32	32	28
Corticospinal	32–35	38	28–36	4 PN
Transpontine	35	4 PN	—	—
Middle cerebellar peduncle	35	8 PN	PN	4 PN
Cerebellum				
Parasagittal	27	—	32	—
Hemispheral	38	PN	40	—
Prosencephalon				
Habenulointerpeduncular	28	28	34	28
Ansa lenticularis	28	28	26	—
Optic chiasm	32	—	32	—
Optic tract	29	36	32	36
Optic radiation	38–39	38–40	38	—
Internal capsule, posterior limb	32	36	36	—
Corona radiata	34	30	—	—
Corticopontine	Latl. ped.–38 Medl. ped.–46	8 PN	—	8 PN
Cingulum	38	8 PN	—	—
Fornix	39	16 PN	PN	8 PN
Callosum	46	12 PN	PN	4 PN
Anterior commissure	46	12 PN	—	—
Mammilothalamic	48	36	—	8 PN

[a] All figures are in weeks of gestational age or postnatal age (PN) as indicated by each author. This table is reproduced with permission from Gilles, Leviton and Dooling Eds., copyright © 1983. The *Developing Human Brain*, Littleton, MA: John Wright.

distinguish "normal" from "abnormal" specimens, viewing all these pathological materials as abnormal to one degree or another. Second, they used a
quantified scale of degree of myelination instead of qualitative description (0 =
no myelin, 1 = microscopic only, 2 = just visible, 3 = intensity approaching
mature myelin). Third, at every age they made assessments of a number of cases
in identical fashion, and reported the results according to the satistical distribution of quantitative scale scores, thus incorporating the realities of individual
variation into the basic presentation of the data. Finally, two observers systematically assessed each of 53 carefully defined sites in each specimen, yielding a
total of nearly 70,000 scores for analysis.

Most recently, Brody et al. (1984) extended this painstaking method of
assessment to the first 2 postnatal years. They studied 171 cases, a sample with
no overlap with the Gilles et al. sample described above. Differences in method
included the use of the luxol fast blue stain instead of a hematoxylin stain for
visualization of myelin, and the use of standard neuropathological blocks taken
from strategically chosen brain regions including a sample of the most important
structures. [Gilles et al. (1983) apparently used some specimens cut in such
blocks and some whole brain sections.] In other respects their method followed
that of Gilles et al. This material is not yet fully reported, but it promises to
greatly extend and refine the findings of Yakovlev and Lecours (1967) on the
first 2 postnatal years. Fortunately, a preliminary account of their findings is
available.

With the exception of Lecours (1975; Lecours et al. 1983), none of the modern
investigators has had a direct interest in correlating myelination sequences with
behavioral maturation, and it would be unfair to impute any such intention to
them. Nevertheless, their work provides a basis for speculation of this kind.
Their data, as well as that of the older investigators, will be used in the remainder
of this study. As noted by Gilles et al. (1983), these studies demonstrate a
substantial degree of agreement, certainly in the sequence of myelination and, to
a lesser extent, in its precise timing, across studies done at different times, by
different investigators, using different methods, and with different purposes.

Parallels in Behavioral and Neuroanatomical Development

Myelination and the Development of Behavior

Several investigators have suggested that specific events and sequences of
myelination have specific behavioral consequences. For example, the system
subserving detection of postural orientation and vestibular stimulation (Figure 1,
line 3) is fully myelinated before birth. As Korner (1972) has noted, this may
explain the unique effectiveness of rocking stimulation in quieting the newborn,
as well as the apparent positive effect of upright posture on alertness at this age.
A more mundane consequence of this state of myelination of the vestibular

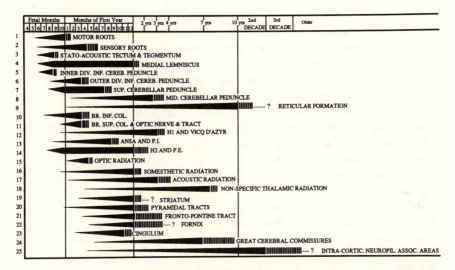

Figure 1. Cycles of myelination, adapted from Yakovlev and Lecours (1967). Widening of the bars indicates progressive intensity of staining and density of myelinated fibers. Interrupted bars to the right indicate approximate age range of termination of myelination process. From Yakovlev, P. I. and Lecours, A. R. "The myelogenetic cycles of regional maturation of the brain" in Minkowski, A. (Ed.) *Regional Development of the Brain in Early Life*, F. A. Davis Co., Phila., Pa., 1967, pp. 4–5. Copyright © Blackwell Scientific Publications, Ltd., Oxford.

system may be the concatenation of vestibular reflexes elicitable at birth (Peiper, 1963; Prechtl and Beintema, 1964; see next section for further discussion).

The major tracts of the visual system begin to show evidence of myelin staining just before birth and complete their myelination rapidly in the first few months of life (Figure 1, lines 11 and 15) (Brody et al., 1987; Yakovlev and Lecours, 1967). This corresponds to the rapid attainment of visual maturity in the same epoch. A detailed attempt to relate the maturation of visual perceptual capacity in early infancy to myelination sequences in the visual system constitutes one of the more convincing models of this kind in the literature (Bronson, 1974, 1982).

This pattern in the visual system contrasts markedly with the sequence of myelination of the auditory system, as noted by Lecours (1975; Lecours et al., 1983). The acoustic radiation to the cerebral cortex (Figure 1, line 17) has a very protracted course of myelination. It requires at least 1, possibly 2 years, corresponding to the pace of growth of the major function of the human auditory analyzer, namely language comprehension (Brody et al., 1987).

In general, the longer the axon, the more the cell gains by myelination. Thus, the myelination of the very long neurons of the pyramidal tracts (Figure 1, line 20) predicts quite well the dramatic gains in neuromuscular function during the first year of life (Brody et al., 1987; Yakovlev and Lecours, 1967). A section through the spinal cord of a human newborn resembles sections seen in a patient with spinal transection (Rorke and Riggs, 1969). Further, the development of reflexive and sensorimotor behavior in the normal newborn resembles in several respects what would be expected in a neurological patient recovering from such an injury. These correspondences are discussed at some length below.

Finally, the great cortical association areas (Figure 1, line 25) may continue to gain myelin up to the age of 30 years. The increase in staining density in these areas is of a magnitude consistent with that of the known effects of experience on myelination (discussed previously) and may in fact represent such an effect, although the argument for a correlation is weakest with subtler degrees of change.

In a more sophisticated analysis of the myelination of the cortex, Gibson (1977, 1981) compared the myelination of afferents and efferents to different cortical layers in both rhesus monkeys and humans, in relation to the known facts about cognitive development in these two species. She noted that there is a reliable sequence of myelination among the six cortical layers in any given region of cortex, although the sequence occurs more rapidly in some areas than others. Specifically, just as the primary sensory and motor projection areas of cortex develop in advance of the association areas, the layers subserving communication with brainstem and spinal cord (I, IV, V, and VI) myelinate in advance of the layers subserving communication within the cortex itself (II and III). In particular, layers IV, V, and VI in the association cortex become myelinated between 15 and 24 months of age in humans, or later at a time when great advances in cognitive functioning, plausibly described as requiring intermodal integration of a high order, are taking place.

Other equally impressive correspondences between myelination sequences and behavioral development have received little or no attention in the literature. Some of the major tracts of the limbic system, which mediate the emotions, do not begin to myelinate until weeks or months after birth. The cingulum, linking the frontal lobe to the limbic system (Nauta, 1971), myelinates between 2 and 10 months (Figure 1, line 23); 4 months according to Brody et al., 1984). The fornix, a massive fiber bundle leaving the hippocampus, myelinates in the second half of the first year and later (Figure 1, line 22). Other major connection tracts of the limbic system myelinate in the first, second, third, and later years (Brody et al., 1987; Yakovlev and Lecours, 1967).

Finally, the corpus striatum and globus pallidus, as well as their fiber tracts, myelinate postnatally in the first and second years. These structures, long thought of as mere modulators of movement, are now known to participate intimately in the initiation of movement (Evarts, 1975). More interesting for present purposes, stimulation of sites within them has been shown to produce highly ritualized species-specific fixed action patterns that serve as social displays in squirrel monkeys (MacLean, 1978). This raises the possibility that if there are any fixed action patterns in human social behavior, they may be controlled in part from homologous sites. None of these various tracts and structures is principally concerned with human information processing and problem solving with the possible exception of the fornix. All, however, are crucial to human social behavior, and all undergo dramatic changes during infancy.

The Neonatal Neurobehavioral Baseline

Neonatal neurological and behavioral assessment scales have produced a detailed characterization of human neurological status at birth. This characterization has served as the basis for analyses of the state of development of the neonatal nervous system (Minkowski, 1955; Peiper, 1963; Bronson, 1982). The peculiar concatenation of reflexes and movements, some essential for survival and continuous with mature functions (for example, the sucking and withdrawal reflexes), others precisely reminiscent of the signs of some neurological disorders and destined to wane with normal growth (such as athetoid movements and the plantar extensor reflex), has suggested to various observers that the neonate resembles a decorticate, decerebrate, midbrain, or even spinal organism in its level of function.

Prior to considering how best to model neonatal behavior in terms of neuroanatomical development, it is necessary to establish the fixed features of human neurobehavioral status at birth. This requires going beyond the European and American populations that have formed the basis of most generalizations. Occasional reports in the literature claim marked population-wide departures from what Europeans and Americans consider fundamental aspects of human neurological status at birth. Most notable among these was the report by Geber and Dean (1957) purporting to show that neonates of the Baganda population in Kampala, Uganda lacked certain reflexes considered obligatory in healthy European neonates: the automatic march reflex, the stepping reflex, the placing reflex, and the scarf sign. This lack was interpreted by the authors, and by many others who have cited their findings, as being indicative of precocity in African neonates. That is, they claimed that African neonates had already developed past the point at which these reflexes are elicitable, and they estimated the difference in developmental status to be on the order of 4 to 6 weeks.

Whatever the interpretation, this absence of major reflexes in a group of neonates would, if true, require rethinking of the status of the nervous system at birth. This finding, however, has not received confirmation from other studies. Warren (1972) reviewed the subject through the 1960s, and concluded that no such phenomenon had been shown in African neonates, citing three nonconfirmatory studies and noting a number of defects in the original study. Super (1981) reviewed the subject more recently and concluded that "there is no reliable corroboration of Geber and Dean's claim of neurological precocity in African newborns. Substantial contradictory evidence now exists, as well as doubt about the original methodology" (p. 188).

This is not to say that there are no differences in the neonatal behavior and responsiveness of different racial groups. The possibility remains that the Moro reflex and the plantar extension reflex have higher thresholds and lower amplitudes in African than in European newborns. There is also some evidence of temperamental differences between Oriental and European newborns, with the Oriental infants showing less activity and less irritability (e.g., Freedman, 1974). Finally, there are numerous reports of statistically significant, but minor differences, in neonatal neurobehavioral status of different populations as measured by the Brazelton scale (Sameroff, 1979). These results, however, do not alter the general impression that a characteristic repertoire of reflexes and behavioral capabilities applies to the neonates of all human groups. (For detailed review see Super, 1981.)

Illustrative of the similarities are the results of the Prechtl neonatal neurological examination (discussed above) for a small sample of neonates in one African population, the !Kung San. Nine infants were examined between 8 and 12 days of age. During the examination, subtleties of threshold and amplitude of response were recorded, but for comparison purposes only the percentage of infants who unambiguously exhibited the reflex in response to the given stimulus, regardless of threshold amplitude, were used. Many of these responses are difficult to elicit in any neonate under the best of conditions. The proportions of infants responding among the !Kung San are within the range expected by chance for European and American samples. In particular, the reflexes reported by Geber to be absent in Baganda neonates after 4 days of age are present in !Kung neonates at 10 days of age.

Other investigators have obtained similar results within our African populations based on larger samples of neonates, and on samples representing several Asian populations, Australian aborigines, and New World Indians (Super, 1981). Thus, the general neurobehavioral capacity of human neonates appears adequately characterized by the normal expectable repertoire obtained through standard procedures for neurological examination in European and American populations (Prechtl and Beintema, 1964).

These behavioral and myelination data suggest that the neonate functions at a level consistent with full development of the peripheral nervous system, extensive development of the spinal cord and medulla, substantial development of the mesencephalon, and partial development of the prosencephalon, almost all below the cortical level.

Individual reflexes can be explained with reference to the state of development of specific structures (Minkowski, 1955; Peiper, 1963). For example, the tonic deviation of the head and eyes in the direction of body displacement, the doll's eye reflex, and the labyrinthine righting reflex owe their presence to the relative maturity of the vestibular portion of the eighth cranial nerve and its communications with the brainstem nuclei of the cranial nerves effecting the responses. The stepping and automatic march reflexes directly parallel similar reflexes in both decorticate and decerebrate animal preparations, and are interpretable as reflecting the relatively advanced state of development of the spinal cord and medulla, with the exception of the descending cortical efferents, which provide inhibitory control. Finally, the best-studied neonatal reflex is the plantar extensor or Babinski reflex, which consists of a splaying outward and upward of the toes when the sole of the foot is stroked. This appears homologous to the same reflex in adult patients who have suffered damage to the corticospinal (pyramidal) tracts. In the neonate, this reflex almost certainly reflects the absence of myelin from the same tracts (Brain and Wilkinson, 1959; Ghez, 1981). Many similar arguments are possible with respect to sensory capacity at birth, for example, in the visual system (Bronson, 1974, 1982).

As noted by Bronson (1982), it is reasonable to think of the neonate as functionally subcortical. Although some potential for function exists in cortical systems, behavioral and physiological data suggest that this function is extremely rudimentry. An ingenious series of experiments, however, has shown that neonates are, to a limited extent, capable of intermodal transfer—exchange of information among different sensory modalities—a capability they were long thought to lack (Meltzoff and Moore, 1977; Meltzoff and Borton, 1979). Whether this reflects an unexpected level of functioning for unmyelinated intracortical association areas, or an unexpected role for subcortical structures in intermodal transfer, is impossible to determine at present (but see Gibson, 1981).

The Growth of Bipedal Locomotion: A Paradigmatic Case

Motor development sequences are largely genetically programmed. Research in the 1930s and 1940s by Gesell (Gesell and Amatruda, 1947), McGraw (1943), and others noted, and, in some instances, showed effects of experience, but such effects were invariably minor against the background of the temporal map of developmental milestones. McGraw explicitly embraced the notion of a species-specific neuromuscular development sequence and described it in detail for a longitudinally studied sample. Gesell and his colleagues made similar descriptions, supported by photographs, for a wider range of infant behavior patterns.

Shortly after his initial publications, Conel (1939–1967) began to rely on these two sets of behavioral descriptions in making functional interpretations of his large body of data on the regional maturation of the cerebral cortex. For example, he noted that by all measures area FA gamma of the precentral gyrus (the motor cortex), in the region of the hand, is, at 6 months of age, developmentally advanced compared to other areas of the motor strip. This corresponds well with behavioral evidence on the earlier maturation of hand control compared with control of other body parts. Another part of area FA gamma, the region of the lower extremities, is, in contrast, developmentally behind the rest of the motor cortex even at 15 months, corresponding to the continuing weakness of behavioral control of the lower limbs at that age.

To be sure, there are interesting variations in the timing of motor and sensorimotor milestones within and among populations (Super, 1981; Werner, 1972, 1979). At present it is not possible to partition such variation, whether within or between populations, into genetic, environmental, and genotype–environment interaction components. Nevertheless, the range of variation among individuals within samples considerably exceeds that among population means for the appearance of these milestones world-wide, despite much greater variation in environmental influences among populations. This consistency among population means suggests a species-specific and species-wide timing of events in motor and sensorimotor development. For example, independent sitting and visually directed reaching appear in the middle of the first year, independent rising to stand later that year, and independent walking and thumb-to-finger fine grasp early in the second year.

A useful paradigmatic case is provided by the emergence of bipedal locomotion, a species typical, centrally organized neuromotor action pattern shown by all normal adults—indeed by all normal 2 year olds—in our species. The mean age of attainment of one useful criterion, three steps taken without hands held, hovers around a year of age in many samples, usually falling between 11 and 14 months. Large samples studies in five European cities had means with 6 weeks of each other at the extremes (Hindley et al., 1966). Precocity for infants in developing countries, especially Africa, has frequently been claimed (Super, 1981; Werner, 1972, 1979). Some carefully designed and conducted studies, however, fail to show any difference, and one critical review of a large number of studies concluded that African infant precocity has not been demonstrated (Warren, 1972).

The claims for greatest precocity center on the early part of the first year of life. The means for African and other samples in developing countries for age at independent walking typically fall within the American and European range mentioned above. To take only one example, among the !Kung San, hunter-gathers of the Kalahari Desert in Botswana, deliberate efforts are made to accelerate the development of walking by means of seemingly appropriate tactics. These include extensively holding the infant in a sitting or standing posture long before independent maintenance of these postures is possible, exercising rudimentary walking capabilities, and so on. The curve for development of independent walking in these infants falls within the range of the corresponding curves for American infants (Konner, 1973, 1977).

Other cross-cultural variations in infant care that might be expected to alter the rate of development of this behavior also have little effect. The Hopi (Dennis, 1940; Dennis and Dennis, 1940) and Navajo Indians (Chisholm, 1983), for instance, traditionally restricted their infants much of the time by tightly swaddling them against cradleboards. This procedure did not substantially delay the age of first walking.

Finally, deliberate attempts to accelerate this maturational pattern experimentally under relatively controlled conditions usually met with little success (e.g., McGraw, 1935). One intervention study (Zelazo, et al., 1972) did succeed in producing an 8 week advancement of first independent walking by systematically exercising the neonatal automatic march reflex for the first 8 weeks of life. Although this suggests that extraordinary environmental modifications may alter the rate of development, more typical variations in rearing conditions do not have this effect.

In addition to regularities of developmental rate, a preponderance of evidence points to the existence of a species-typical developmental sequence. From the neonatal automatic march reflex, a centrally organized subcortical motor stereotype, to the mature gait of the 2 year old, with heel–toe progression directly under the hips and synchronous alternate arm swinging, the developmental history of the bipedal locomotor pattern is for the most part characteristic and universal, and the timing of its major transition is narrowly defined.

Underlying this developmental history is a fairly clear plan of neural development. Classical studies linked the waning of the automatic march reflex as well as the ascendance of true walking to progressive development (including myelination, hypertrophy, and other growth changes) in the corticospinal tract from later prenatal life to the end of the second postnatal year (Minkowski, 1955; André-Thomas, 1960). These changes result in increasing cortical inhibition of primitive spinal reflexes, stabilization of the postural stretch reflex, and voluntary control of coordinated limb movements. Accompanying the myelination of the corticospinal tracts are associated changes in the precentral (motor) gyrus, particularly the lower limb regions of the gyrus, over a similar developmental time course (Conel, 1939–1967). Functional evidence from clinical lesions shows that adults suffer profound loss of lower limb control in disease of the corticospinal tracts. Specifically, they exhibit the extensor plantar reflex of the neonate, known since Babinsky's 1896 description to be pathognomic of corticospinal tract conduction failure (see Ghez, 1981 for review). Thus, the development of improved function in this tract as a result of myelination is a likely candidate for a neural basis of the maturation of walking, and of the waning of the extensor plantar, or Babinsky reflex.

Modern concepts of the cortical and subcortical control of voluntary movement, however, have greatly expanded the range of neuroanatomical structures that may be involved in maturing locomotor skills. According to these concepts (Evarts, 1975; Allen and Tsukahara, 1974) both the basal ganglia and the cerebellum are implicated in goal corrected movement. Briefly, nonmotor cortex (i.e., the great majority of the cortex) initiates voluntary movement not primarily through a direct communication to the motor cortex (although such a connection may still play a role) but through transstriatopallidal and transcerebellar circuits. Nonmotor cortex projects to the basal ganglia and cerebellum, which project, via way-stations in the ventral anterior and ventral lateral thalamus, back to the motor and premotor cortex, respectively.

This widely accepted model must direct our attention to the myelination sequences of the major efferent pathways from the globus pallidus [the ansa lenticularis (Figure 1, line 13) and field H1 of Forel (line 12)], of the middle cerebellar peduncle (line 8), which carries cerebral cortical information to the cerebellum, and of the intrinsic fibers of basal ganglia (line 19). Collectively these structures exhibit a course of myelination that is highly consistent and as protracted as that of the corticospinal tract (line 20) and its somatosensory feedback pathway, the somesthetic radiation (line 16). This complex proposed circuitry of independent bipedal locomotion thus exhibits a cycle of myelination consistent with the use of the cycle to explain the maturation behavior.

Psychosocial Maturation during the First Year

Among many motoric, perceptual, and cognitive changes occurring during the first year of life are some transformations that are specifically social or emotional (Bowlby, 1969, 1973, 1980; Emde et al., 1976; Lewis and Rosenblum, 1978; Campos et al., 1983). Although all development is continuous, two critical transitions in infant psychosocial growth occur during the first year.

The first, achieved during the first 3 months of life, is characterized by a marked increase of social competence, from a neonatal level that is basically asocial or presocial, to a level of relatively advanced social expressiveness including mutual gaze interactions, contingent responsiveness in dyadic exchanges (Stern, 1974; Stern and Gibbon, 1977), and, most notably, the easily elicited social smile. Much data of a cross-cultural nature are available for one of these, the social smile (e.g., Gewirtz, 1965; Kilbride and Kilbride, 1975; Kilbride, 1980).

The second transition is slower, extending from about 5 to at least 15 months, with the most dramatic transformation taking place during the third quarter of the first year. It consists of the development of what is usually called attachment or attachment behaviors. One hallmark of this complex is crying or protest when the mother leaves the infant alone in a strange place, although numerous other specific behaviors with respect to the mother (or other primary caretaker) appear earlier, such as preferential greeting, approaching, and following. A related developmental phenomenon, the fear of strangers or stranger protest, also occurs during the second half of the first year.

The Emergence of Social Smiling.   An early maturational development of a specifically social nature is the smile in response to a human face. In the human adult, smiling in greeting is universal, or at least exists universally as an option. It has been filmed and measured in the same form and context in societies on all continents, primitive and modern, some remote from the influence of the others (Eibl-Eibesfeldt, 1971a,b, 1983). Similarly, adults in widely distributed societies interpret pictures of smiles as signaling friendliness or happiness (Ekman, 1973). Young children exhibit the social smile in typical form and context and make the usual interpretation (Izard, 1977).

Quantitative variation in form and function of the smile may reflect the influence of learning, but such variation does not bear on the fundamental qualitative constancy of the behavior. It is as close as we are likely to come to a human fixed action pattern, or to a human species-specific social display. The smile evidently relates to the primate "playface," an open mouthed smile occurring during social play, and to the primate submissive closed-mouth grin shown in greeting a dominant animal (Van Hooff, 1972; Andrew, 1963), but the relaxed friendly smile in social greeting is characteristically human (Blurton Jones, 1971).

For practical purposes, smiling is absent at birth and emerges during the first few months of postnatal life. Incidence of smiling in naturalistic social contexts or in experimental settings in which the infant is presented with a face is two orders of magnitude higher at 4 months of age than at term, and the response cannot be indisputably identified until some time in the second month (Ambrose, 1959; Emde, et al., 1976; Emde and Harmon, 1972; Spitz and Wolf, 1946; Sroufe and Waters, 1976). There is some variation in the early incidence and rate of emergence of smiling among samples in different environments. This variation is statistically significant but quantitatively minor (Gewirtz, 1965). Comparisons of infants among the Baganda of Uganda, the Samia of Kenya, and other cultures with American infants show little difference in the age of emergence of social smiling (Kilbride and Kilbride, 1975; Kilbride, 1980).

This growth process produces a marked change in parent–offspring relations. Mothers may report that they did not subjectively sense the existence of a relationship, or even that they did not love the infant, before the emergence of gaze fixation and competent social smiling (Robson, 1967; Robson and Moss, 1970). The absence of this care-eliciting behavior at birth is an evolutionary puzzle, the solution of which probably lies in the phylogenetic constraint on gestation length imposed by a narrowing birth canal on a slowing rate of growth (Konner, 1979, 1981).

A convincing developmental explanation of the emergence of social smiling has also eluded investigators. Well-formed nonsocial smiles occur regularly in neonates during rapid eye movement (REM) sleep and may be observed from 30 weeks of gestational age (Emde and Harmon, 1972; Emde et al., 1976; Wolff, 1963). Anencephalic infants with a mesencephalic level of functioning exhibit such smiles (Monnier, 1956), making telencephalic or diencephalic involvement in their regulation unlikely or at least not essential. Painstaking videotape studies of normal neonates show that highly coordinated and specific facial expressions, involving a number of sometimes widely separated elements of facial musculature acting in concert, are present at birth (Oster, 1978). Thus, at birth, with only lower brain functions mature, intricately timed facial muscle action patterns are already under complex central control. Also at birth, gaze fixation and even visual following of a face by the infant can be elicited, suggesting the existence of some underlying perceptual–cognitive capacity (Als, 1977; Brazelton, 1973).

Since blind infants develop reliable social smiling only a month or two later than sighted infants (Fraiberg, 1977; Freedman, 1964; see also Thompson, 1941), a crucial role for visual perception in the growth of the behavior can be ruled out. Since the mean age of the onset of social smiling in samples of low-risk mature infants can be better predicted from their postmenstrual than from their postnatal age (Brachfeld et al., 1980), a key role for associative or operant conditioning, both readily demonstrated later in infancy (Ahrens, 1954; Ambrose, 1959; Brackbill, 1958), also seems unlikely. Finally, since monozygotic twins are significantly more concordant in the rate of emergence of social smiling than dizygotic twins (Freeman, 1974), some genetic contribution to the individual variation is probable.

Thus, some central connection between the perceptual mechanism and the already well-formed motor output matures during the growth of this socially functional behavior. Some of the change may be perceptual and cognitive, rather than social or emotional. For example, by 2 months of age, visual following of eyes and faces substantially improves (Haith et al., 1977). By 3 months, an infant is most attracted to stimuli whose changes it can control ("contingently responsive stimuli" (Watson, 1972; Watson and Ramey, 1972)) or at least to stimuli (such as are provided by an indulgent caretaker) that change at a pace ideally suited to challenge infant attention (Stern, 1974; Stern and Gibbon, 1977)—faculties that are largely absent earlier. By 4 months, visual pattern memory emerges (Super et al., 1972). In addition to these essentially cognitive changes, some aspects of the maturing competence are undoubtedly specifically social, perhaps even in the ethological sense of the word, that is, "wired-in" for social functions.

Initial approaches to a developmental neurology of smiling must be indirect, but the following facts are noteworthy. Myelination of the motor roots of the fifth and seventh cranial nerves is completed prenatally (Langworthy, 1933; Rorke and Riggs, 1969). This finding is consistent with the mature form of nonsocial smiling even in premature neonates. The motor nuclei of these nerves are in close proximity to the pontine neurons believed to control REM sleep (McCarley and Hobson, 1975), which is the context in which these early nonsocial smiles most frequently occur.

In adults, voluntary and emotional control of the smile can each be lost separately as the result of regionally localized brain damage (Brain and Walton, 1969; Monrad-Krohn, 1924, 1927; Rinn, 1984). In facial paralysis from a corticospinal lesion above the level of the motor nuclei, voluntary retraction of the corners of the mouth is weak or absent, while smiling in appropriate emotional contexts is preserved. "Mimic" paralysis (the emotional form) is less clear in origin, but is believed to result from lesions of the basal ganglia (see Rinn, 1984 for review).

This notion receives strong support not only from stroke and injury studies but from the "masked face" syndrome of Parkinson's disease. This syndrome, which occurs early in the disease, consists of a marked facial unresponsiveness in the presence of emotion, but a preservation of voluntarily assumed facial expression. Since Parkinson's disease primarily affects the basal ganglia (or, more properly, the substantia nigra that projects to them), the masked face syndrome lends credence to the notion of regulation of social smiling from this part of the brain (Rin, 1984).

In view of these findings—particularly if it is accepted that smiling is a species-typical social display—certain neuroethological concepts that would otherwise seem remote become relevant. MacLean and his colleagues have long maintained that the striatopallidal complex (the major part of the basal ganglia) plays a key role in the control of fixed social displays (MacLean 1978, 1985). They note the prominence of these structures (or their homologies) in birds and reptiles, taxa that (more exclusively than mammals) use fixed displays in their social behavior. More important, they have found and repeatedly confirmed that electrocoagulative lesions of the pars interna of the globus pallidus specifically abolish a species-typical fixed action pattern (genital presentation) that serves as a social display in the squirrel monkey, *Saimiri sciureus* (MacLean, 1978). No other deficits are observable in these monkeys, although these are assiduously sought, particularly in the realm of motor function, which is traditionally associated with striatopallidal circuits. This has led MacLean to redefine the striatopallidal complex as a regulator of species-specific displays, and to identify the globus pallidus as a particularly essential way-station for such displays.

From these findings, the following model of the growth of social smiling may be tentatively advanced. In late prenatal life the smile appears in mature form, during the high level of development of the fifth (trigeminal) and seventh (facial) nerves and their motor nuclei, but it does not appear in mature context. Its association with REM sleep perhaps bears some relationship to the relatively easy access of the pontine reticular formation to those motor nuclei.

In the course of the first few postnatal months, the response is brought into the realm of social control. Regional brain growth changes likely to be involved in this change are (1) sensory changes, perhaps, especially tectal (Figure 1, lines 10, 11, and 15); (2) motor changes, especially cerebellar (lines 5 and 6); and, most importantly, (3) changes in the striatopallidal complex, especially the globus pallidus and its efferents, and ansa lenticularis and the fields of Forel (lines 12–14), with the ansa and pars interna showing the most rapid change at this age (line 13).

The Growth of Social Fears.   At the end of this phase transition, the social interaction is well established but relatively undiscriminating. It appears to the observer to be associated with positive emotion, but the emotion seems impersonal; almost anyone can elicit it and, despite subtle signs of discrimination of primary caretakers, strong emotional bonds do not appear to exist. This situation changes markedly in the second half-year. Strangers begin to be discriminated in social responding, often negatively, and increasingly so through the course of the second 6 months (Morgan and Ricciuti, 1969; Tennes and Lampl, 1964; Lewis and Rosenblum, 1974); crying when left by the mother in a strange situation, with or without a strange person, becomes common, although it is certainly not universal (Bretherton and Ainsworth 1974; Ainsworth et al., 1978); vulnerability to the adverse effects of separations of substantial duration from primary caretakers becomes demonstrably more marked (Bowlby, 1973); and "attachment behaviors" such as following, clinging, and cuddling become frequent in relation to the primary caretaker(s), especially in strange situations or in the presence of strange persons (Ainsworth et al., 1978).

Such changes are, to be sure, not all functions of the growth of fear. They represent changes in the emotional valence of the interpersonal space of the infant that make certain key individuals very attractive while rendering the rest of the species less so, if not actually repelling. These changes are often characterized by primary caretakers as indicative of a deepening of the emotional bond they feel they share with the infant, and by theorists of affective development such as Bowlby (1969, 1980) and Ainsworth (Ainsworth, et al., 1978) as signaling the onset of the capacity for attachment, a major event in the growth of emotional and social competence.

Non-Western cultures exhibit similar behavioral patterns (Kagan, 1976; Super, 1981). Thus, the growth of social fears and the concomitant growth of attachment, as defined by these and related measures, appear to be universal features of the second half-year of human life (with much individual variation in the degree of overt expression). It is, at least in its ontogenetic timing, a species-specific feature of human behavioral organization. The percentage of infants who withdraw, fret, or cry when a stranger appears, who cry when left by the mother either alone or with a stranger, or who go to the mother rather than a stranger or a secondary caretaker when mildly apprehensive (Kagan et al., 1978) rises steadily from the middle of the first to the middle of the second year, whether the sample is drawn from the !Kung San of Botswana (who have 24-hour mother–infant physical contact in a dense social context), traditional Navajo Indians (who strap their infants into cradleboards much of the time), a remote Guatemalan Indian village (who have high mother–infant contact), an Israeli kibbutz (infant separated from the mother in a nursery except on afternoons and weekends), or various subcultures of the United States, including professional and working class socioeconomic levels (Konner, 1982; Chisholm, 1983; Kagan, 1976; Super, 1981). Among Chinese–American and Caucasian–American subcultures in Boston, infants who have 8 hours a day of day-care separating them from the mother do not differ significantly from control infants who have had no such separation on measures of social fear and attachment at any age, despite the fact that the day-care regime began before 4 months of age (Kagan et al., 1978). This latter finding is confirmed by similar studies of the effects of day-care on social behavior in other cities (Caldwell et al., 1970; Ricciuti, 1974; Brookhart and Hock, 1976; Blanchard and Main, 1979; Campos et al., 1983).

Similarly organized behavioral patterns, with species-typical motor components and ontogenetic timing, may be seen in the early postnatal development of higher primates (Blurton Jones, 1972; Rosenblum and Alpert, 1974) and other mammals (Scott, 1962). Analogous, although probably not homologous, events may be seen in the very early posthatching development of precocial birds (Sluckin, 1970). Observation in the environments of evolutionary adaptedness (Rheingold, 1963; Altman, 1979), including one such environment for humans (Konner, 1972, 1977, 1981), clearly suggests an adaptive role for such behaviors in two ways: prevention of predation and intergenerational transfer of adaptively relevant, acquired formation. The ontogenetic association of independent locomotion and active imitation with the growth of social fear and attachment behavior (in several species) supports, respectively, the two putative adaptive significances postulated for these infant emotions. The concatenation of fixed-action-pattern-like components with one another, and with apparently innate releasing mechanisms, in an organized, goal-corrected, predictable, "driven" fashion resembles, in important respects, other patterns that are usually called instincts.

Some evidence suggests that individual variation in the precise ontogenetic timing and in the degree of expression of the social fears is under genetic influence. In at least two studies, fear of strangers in infancy has been shown to have significantly higher concordance in identical than in fraternal twin pairs. One of these studies focused on the longitudinal pattern of growth of fear (Freedman, 1974), and the other on specific behaviors toward the stranger (Plomin and Rowe, 1978). No evidence exists for similar heritability of positive behavior toward caretakers, but little work has been done on this question. Possibly only the negative aspects of the fear/attachment complex have their individual variation under significant genetic influence.

For present purposes, however, it is the control not of individual variation but of universal features of maturation that is of interest. In view of the known facts relating fear and other strong emotions to the nuclei and pathways of the limbic system (see Isaacson, 1974, for review), it would be appropriate to examine this system for developmental events that might help to dispel the mystery of the rise of the social fears. In Papez's original formulation, the burden of the "stream of feeling" was laid for the first time on a core of circuitry, including especially the hippocampus, the fornix, the mammillary body, the mammillothalamic tract, the anterior nucleus of the thalamus, the cingulum bundle, and the cingulate cortex (Papez, 1937). It subsequently became clear that the main outgoing pathways of the amygdala—the ventral amygdalofugal path and the stria terminals, various parts of the hypothalamus, and the septal area—also belong in the proposed emotional circuitry (MacLean, 1952; Nauta and Domesick, 1980).

In addition, Nauta delineated three major extensions of the system beyond these primarily diencephalic and older cortical nuclei and circuits: (1) a two-way communication with the frontal lobes as "the neocortex of the limbic system"

(Nauta, 1971); (2) direct fiber connections with the striatopallidal circuitry, via the ansa lenticularis and fields of Forel (Nauta and Mehler, 1966), perhaps providing a basis for species-specific displays of the emotions as proposed by MacLean (1978); and (3) various connections with the "limbic mid-brain," over the mammillary peduncle, the dorsal longitudinal fasciculus, the habenulointer-peduncular tract, and other pathways (Nauta, 1958; Nauta and Domesick, 1978), which probably constitute an important part of the nonendocrine effector output of the system, especially, but not exclusively, in the visceral realm. The connections of the limbic system and its relations with other brain circuitry have been authoritatively reviewed (Nauta and Domesick, 1980).

Turning to Figure 1, we note that at 3 months of age there is little or no myelin in the striatum, the fornix, and the cingulum (lines 19, 22, and 23), but that these have achieved almost the adult level of staining by the end of the first year (Yakovlev and Lecours, 1967). The mammillothalamic tract (bundle of Vic d'Azyr, line 12) also gains heavily in staining density during this period. Although there are other dramatic changes during the second half-year of life, they mainly relate to the neocortical and cerebellar control of movement (see above); as such they are likely to be less relevant to the growth of the emotions than are the structures just mentioned. With the absence of myelin on the fornix, the cingulum, and to a lesser extent the mammillothalamic tract, it is probable that the level of functioning in the Papez circuit is very poor at 3 months compared to its level of functioning at the end of the first year. Thus, it is not surprising to find that the emotional competence of the older infant is much greater, and it seems likely that more than an increase in information processing ability (an explanation offered by Kagan et al., 1978) is involved. Furthermore, the gains in myelin staining in the striatum and in the fiber fields of Forel (H1 and H2, lines 12 and 14) suggest the possibility that not only emotional competence, but also the ability to express emotion in motor action, are maturing at this age.

In addition, data from stimulation studies, lesion studies, and to a lesser extent, psychosurgical practice (for reviews see Gray, 1971; Valenstein, 1973; Isaacson, 1974) indicate the involvement of portions of the amygdala, the cingulum, the hypothalamus, and the limbic midbrain in the mediation of fear and anxiety. In the original classic experiments on the consequences of temporal lobe lesions, Klüver and Bucy found that removal of large portions of the temporal lobe in monkeys resulted in a syndrome including fearlessness, tameness, tendency to approach objects indiscriminately, mouthing of objects indiscriminately, and hypersexuality (Klüver and Bucy, 1937, 1939). With the exception of hypersexuality, which may require previously mature reproductive competence, the syndrome is in some respects reminiscent of behavior of normal human infants in the 4–5 month age range. Perhaps the absence of myelin in the limbic circuitry gives them a partial temporal lobe disconnection syndrome that mimics physiologically as well as phenomenologically the Klüver–Bucy syndrome in postoperative adult monkeys.

Whether or not these specific explanations relating infant emotionality to lesion studies are correct, no account of the striking changes in infant emotional competence during the second half-year of life will be satisfactory without an account of the relationship to the equally striking changes in limbic system structures know to underlie emotional behavior.

Discussion

This model is based on correlations, some of which are rather general in nature. Eventually, improvements in the methodology of relating myelination sequences to behavioral development will result from application of magnetic resonance imaging (MRI) to the maturing brain. MRI (also known as nuclear magnetic resonance, NMR) is demonstrably superior to computed tomography and other brain imaging methods, particularly in its ability to discriminate white from gray matter in the central nervous system, and is, for this reason, showing itself to be particularly useful in following demyelinating disorders such as multiple sclerosis. This imaging modality has the potential to produce quantified determinations of the degree of myelination in anatomically specific regions of the living, developing brain. Thus, the potential for correlations with developing behavior is extraordinary. Although strictly speaking these will still be mere correlations, they will be so much more precise and dynamic than the ones considered here as to constitute a completely new body of data against which to test these hypotheses. No matter how fine the correlations, however, such models will always be subject to criticism on the grounds that other structures that mature at the same time may be responsible for the behaviors in question.

One way to confirm the correlational models is to remove the pertinent developing structures and to observe the resulting behavioral deficits. These procedures generally rely on clinical materials that do not precisely parallel the desired lesion or on animal models that do not precisely parallel the function of the human brain. In one of the most impressive studies of this kind, Diamond (1985, and this volume) demonstrated a developmental sequence for perfor-n.ance on an object-retrieval task that matures during the second half of the first year in human infants. She attributed this development to maturation of the frontal cortex during the same time period, citing clinical and experimental lesion studies. She went on to show that rhesus monkeys exhibit the same sequence of development between 2 and 4 months of age and, most importantly, that the ability can be eliminated in adult rhesus monkeys by specific ablation of the dorsolateral prefrontal cortex, which is developing in both species at the ages at which they respectively develop the behavior (Diamond and Goldman-Rakic, 1983). This sequence of investigations provides a model for future research on the neuroanatomical bases of behavioral development. [Incidentally, the object retrieval task in question, which is, in effect, the object permanence task of

Piaget, has been shown to develop according to a pattern that deserves the status of a cross-cultural universal (Werner, 1979; Dasen and Heron, 1981).]

The model proposed in this chapter is also subject to criticism on the grounds that infant behavior has been properly studied in only a handful of the thousands of known human cultures. Although the cross-cultural studies reviewed are not exhaustive, they do sample a widely representative selection of human populations around the world. These populations are mutually independent. Some are essentially independent of Western influence. Most are very different from one another in culture, ecology, nutrition, child training, and other characteristics of the environment that might jeopardize the hypothesis of universality. These systematic studies of a few populations draw support from descriptive and anecdotal materials from a much larger range of cultures. At this point, the burden of proof rests on whose who assert the possibility of a marked cultural departure in infant behavior or developmental sequence. Fortunately, the field of cross-cultural psychology is developing rapidly, and will in the near future settle the question for many behaviors (Triandis and Lambert, 1980–1981).

In the model of social development proposed here, an essentially presocial phase during the neonatal period is followed within 3 months by a highly, but indiscriminately, social phase of which the hallmarks are effective sustained gaze contact and reliable social smiling. This, in turn, is followed, by the last quarter of the first year, by a type of sociability the very essence of which is discrimination. It is characterized by preferential direction of positive social behavior toward one of a few individuals with an absence of response toward others and frequently negative responses toward strangers. This is usually called the attachment phase of infant social development. Finally, the maturation of higher cognitive functions, particularly, but not exclusively, in the realm of language, serves by around age 3 years to begin to terminate the intense phase of attachment to the primary caretaker and to deliver the child into a wider social and cultural world (Lenneberg, 1967; Lecours, 1975; Lecours et al., 1983).

It is interesting to note some parallels between this sequence of three phases of social development and the three phases in the evolutionary sequence postulated by MacLean (1973, 1995). Briefly, MacLean has argued that the human brain consists of at least three levels of systemic functioning that, while certainly not separate in their ongoing activity, are usefully separated for heuristic purposes. Each represents the contribution made to brain structure by a major epoch of phylogeny: the reptilian brain, or "R-complex," roughly corresponding to the level of the basal ganglia in humans; the paleomammalian brain, representing the major neuroanatomical advance of the early mammals over the reptiles, and corresponding to the level of the limbic system in humans; and the neomammalian brain, corresponding to the level of the neocortex, which has increased steadily, especially in certain lines, throughout mammalian evolution.

The concept of recapitulation of phylogeny by ontogeny has been frequently criticized, and at one time was certainly exaggerated by evolutionary biologists, but it may remain valid to a limited extent (Gould, 1977; Konner, 1981; Gibson,

1981, 1983; Parker and Gibson, 1979). As applied to the proposed sequence of psychosocial development, it is reasonable to hypothesize the following. The human neonate has a severely restricted social repertoire, consisting mainly of expressions of distress that are probably not, strictly speaking, social. Within a few months the infant is capable of engaging adults in compelling social interactions, utilizing "wired-in" ritualized motor patterns, notably the social smile. Smiling as a social display may be functionally similar to the social display behaviors of other animals, including reptiles, which MacLean has shown to be mediated by the basal ganglia (MacLean, 1978, 1985), just as emotional smiling appears to be in humans (Monrad-Krohn, 1924, 1927; Rinn, 1984).

By the end of the first years, at the latest, social behavior has taken on a much more complex emotional depth, including such phenomena as attachment, fear of separation, and fear of strangers. This developmental sequence depends, in large part, on the maturation of the major fiber tracts of the limbic system, and on the development of their nuclei of origin and destination. This corresponds closely to the evolutionary advance represented by the paleomammalian brain in MacLean's model, both at neuroanatomical and behavioral levels. In fact, what MacLean views as the crucial functions of the paleomammalian brain are exemplified best by the very social capacities, summarized by a term attachment, that emerge in the human infant at this time (MacLean, 1985).

Finally, the maturation of higher neocortical and cognitive functions (Gibson, 1981; Parker and Gibson, 1979), ultimately including language (Lecours, 1975; Lecours et al., 1983), provides a reasonable correspondence with the phylogenetic emergence of the neocortex, MacLean's neomammalian brain, superimposing on the two older systems a series of new neurobehavioral functions, but without eliminating or suppressing completely the older functions of the other systems. Thus, the model proposed here, although conceived independently of MacLean's "triune brain" model, appears to have something in common with it as a recapitulation, in part, of the proposed events of phylogeny.

Finally, from a psychiatric viewpoint, it is interesting to note that this model in a sense attempts what Freud tried unsuccessfully to do at a much earlier stage in the history of neuroscience—to provide an account of the fixed features of neurological development that could be used as a basis for the interpretation of psychosocial development. Freud's theory of libidinal energy, which he postulated as migrating from one part of the central nervous system to another according to an orderly development plan (Freud, 1905), can, it is to be hoped, soon be replaced by an account of the actual features of nervous system development, as a basis for the analysis of psychosocial growth.

Summary and Conclusions

A number of universals of behavior and developmental sequence in infancy exist that appear to be independent of variations in cultural and environmental context within the normal human range. These universals may relate the underlying species-typical sequences of regional maturation of the brain. Myelination sequences, in particular, serve as a useful index of regional brain maturation and, with some reservations, are an important basis for developing function. The neurobehavioral status of the neonate is subject to modeling with reference to the degree of myelination and other aspects of neural developmental status at birth. In the realm of motor development, particularly with reference to the maturation of bipedal walking, enough is known to give a fairly convincing explanation by relying on myelination sequences in the corticospinal tract, the postthalamic somesthetic radiation, and selected features of the extrapyramidal and cerebellar systems. Finally, in the realm of psychosocial development, it is possible to propose a tentative explanation of the two main transitions of the first year of life, the emergence of social smiling and the emergence of attachment, by reference to developmental events indicated by the myelination of the circuitry of the basal ganglia and of the limbic system, respectively. Further research can be expected to expand and improve these models by providing a broad-based assessment of patterns of regional brain maturation and by further elucidating, through clinical and experimental studies, the neuroanatomical bases of complex behavior.

This model of the development of social behavior in infancy is related to the evolutionary model proposed by MacLean (1973, 1985) and commonly known as "the triune brain." Interesting parallels are drawn between the major events of psychosocial development in infancy and the phylogenetic sequence of Mac-Lean, with the suggestion that ontogeny in this area of development recapitulates, to a limited extent, phylogeny. The model also has the interesting property of serving the function that was meant to be served by Freud's theory of libidinal development, but using known facts of nervous system development instead of dubious and speculative theory.

It is concluded that the strategy proposed has been successfully pursued, and that the model outlined has conceptual and heuristic value. Further research will undoubtedly improve the model by broadening the base for generalization about regional brain maturation and by elucidating the neuroanatomical bases of complex behavior.

Acknowledgments

The author thanks B. A. Brody, I. Devore, K. Gibson, J. Kagan, A. R. Lecours, W. Nauta, C. Super, and the late P. I. Yakovlev for valuable discussions. B. A. Brody generously provided access to unpublished data from her study of postnatal myelination. P. I. Yakovlev, with his characteristic gracious generosity, acted as a guide through the great maze of the Yakovlev Collection during four visits and facilitated the interpretation and photography of specimens relevant to normal postnatal myelination. Mohamed Haleem, Curator of the

Collection, was also of great help. The late Norman Geschwind commented helpfully in writing on the proposal for this review. Earlier work on the !Kung San frequently referred to here was made possible by the help of I. DeVore, N. Howell, R. B. Lee, and M. Shostak, and by the support of the National Science Foundation, the National Institute of Mental Health, the Harry Frank Guggenheim Foundation, the Spencer Fund, and the Milton Fund. Earlier work leading more directly to this review was supported by the Social Science Research Council and the John Simon Guggenheim Memorial Foundation.

Notes

1. This uniformity also applies to several hundred other brains in the Yakovlev collection with specific neuropathological abnormalities.
2. The method is extremely expensive and considered prohibitive for most purposes today. Thus the Yakovlev Collection, located at the Armed Forces Institute of Pathology in Washington, D.C., remains a major resource for studies requiring whole brain reconstruction, whether for tracking of long fiber tracts, supplying the larger context of a focus of interest, or other reasons. Many further studies on this same material are possible. An up-to-date and independent reappraisal of the method and the current status and potential of the Collection is given by Kretschmann et al. (1979).

References

Adams, R. D., and Victor, M. (1981). *Principles of neurology, 2nd ed.* New York: McGraw-Hill.

Ahrens, R. (1954). Beitrag zur Entwicklung des Physiognomie und Mimmerkennens. *Zeitschrift für experimentell und angewandte Psychologie, II*(3), 412–454 and II(4), 599–633.

Ainsworth, M. D. S., Blehar, M. C., Waters, E., and Wall, S. (1978). *Patterns of attachment: A psychological study of the strange situation.* Hillsdale N.J.: Lawrence Erlbaum.

Allen, G. I., and Tsukahara, N. (1974). Cerebrocerebellar communication systems. *Physiological Review, 54*, 957–1006.

Als, H. (1977). The newborn communicates. *Journal of Communication, 27*(2), 66–73.

Altman, J. (1979). *Baboon mothers and infants.* Cambridge, MA: Harvard University Press.

Ambrose, J. A. (1959). The development of the smiling response in early infancy. In B. M. Foss (Ed.), *Determinants of infant behavior I.* London: Methuen.

André-Thomas, Chesni, Y., and St. Anne-Dargassies, A. (1960). *The neurological examination of the infant. Little Club Clinics in Developmental Medicine, No. 1.* London: Heinemann.

Andrew, R. J. (1963). Evolution of facial expressions. *Science, 142*, 3595, 1034–1041.

Angulo Y Gonzalez, A. W. (1929). Is myelinogeny an absolute index of behavioral capability? *Journal of Comparative Neurology, 48* 459–464.

Bayley, N. (1965). Comparisons of mental and motor test scores for ages 1–15 months by sex, birth order, race, geographical location and education of parents. *Child Development, 36,* 379–411.

Bayley, N. (1969). *Manual for the Bayley Scales of Infant Development.* New York: The Psychological Corporation.

Beintema, D. J. (1968). *A neurological study of newborn infants. Clinics in Developmental Medicine No. 28.* London: Heinemann.

Blanchard, M., and Main, M. (1979). Avoidance of the attachment figure and socioemotional adjustment in day-care infants. *Developmental Psychology, 4,* 445–446.

Blinkov, S. M., and Glezer, I. I. (1968). *The human brain in figures and tables: A quantitative handbook.* New York: Basic/Plenum.

Blurton Jones, N. G. (1971). Criteria for use in describing facial expressions. *Human Biology, 43*(3), 365–413.

Blurton Jones, N. G. (1972). Comparative aspects of mother-child contact. In N. G. Blurton Jones (Ed.), *Ethological studies of child behavior.* New York: Cambridge University Press.

Bostock, H., Hall, S. M., and Smith, K. H. (1981). Demyelinated axons form "nodes" prior to remyelination. *Journal of Physiology (London), 308,* 21P.

Bowlby, J. (1969). *Attachment.* New York: Basic Books.

Bowlby, J. (1973). *Separation: Anxiety and anger.* New York: Basic Books.

Bowlby, J. (1980). *Loss: Sadness and depression.* New York: Basic Books.

Brackbill, Y. (1958). Extinction of the smiling response in infants as a function of reinforcement schedule. *Child Development, 39,* 114–124.

Brachfeld, S., Goldberg, S., and Sloman, J. (1980). Parent infant interaction in free play at eight and twelve months: Effects of prematurity and immaturity. *Infant Behavior and Development, 3,* 289–305.

Brain, L., and Walton, J. N. (1969). *Brain's diseases of the nervous system.* Oxford: Oxford University Press.

Brain, R., and Wilkinson, M. (1959). Observations on the extensor plantar reflex and its relationship to the functions of the pyramidal tract. *Brain, 82,* 297–320.

Brazelton, T. B. (1973). *Neonatal behavioral assessment scale. Clinics in Developmental Medicine, No. 50.* London: Heinemann.

Bretherton, I., and Ainsworth, M. (1974). Response of one-year-olds to a stranger in a strange situation. In M. Lewis and L. Rosenblum (Eds.), *The origins of fear.* New York: Wiley.

Brody, B. A., Kinney, H. C., Kloman, A. S., and Gilles, F. H. (1984). Sequences of human postnatal myelination. Paper presented at the American Association of Neuropathologists, 60th Annual Meeting, November.

Brody, B. A., Kinney, H. C., Kloman, A. S., and Gilles, F. H. (1987). Sequence of central nervous system myelination in human infancy. 1. An autopsy study of myelination. *Journal of Neuropathology and Experimental Neurology, 46,* 283–301.

Bronson, G. W. (1974). The postnatal growth of visual capacity. *Child Development, 45,* 873–890.

Bronson, G. W. (1982). Structure, status and characteristics of the nervous system at birth. In P. Stratton (Ed.), *Psychobiology of the human newborn.* New York: Wiley.

Brookhart, J., and Hock, E. (1976). The effects of experimental context and experimental background on infant's behavior toward the mother and a stranger. *Child Development, 47,* 333–340.

Cairns, R. B. (Ed.). (1974). *Social interaction: Methods, analysis and illustration.* New York: Lawrence Erlbaum.

Caldwell, B. M., Wright, C., Honig, A., and Tannenbaum, J. (1970). Infant day-care and attachment. *American Journal of Orthopsychiatry, 40,* 397–412.

Campos, J. J., Barrett, K. C., Lamb, M. E., Goldsmith, H. H., and Stenberg, C. (1983). Socioemotional development. In P. H. Mussen (Ed.), *Handbook of child psychology,* 4th ed., Vol. 2: *Infancy and development psychobiology* (pp. 783–916). New York: Wiley.

Carnow, T. B., Carson, J. H., Brostoff, S. W., and Hogan, E. L. (1984). Myelin basic protein gene expression in quaking, jimpy, and myelin synthesis-deficient mice. *Developmental Biology, 106,* 38–44.

Carter, S., and Gold, A. P. (1974). *Neurology of infancy and childhood.* New York: Appleton-Century-Crofts.

Chisholm, J. (1983). *Navajo infancy: An ethological study of child development.* New York: Aldine.

Conel, J. (1939–1967). *The postnatal development of the human cerebral cortex,* Vols. I–VIII. Cambridge, MA: Harvard University Press.

Dasen, P. R., and Heron, A. (1981). Cross-cultural tests of Piaget's theory. In H. C. Triandis and A. Heron (Eds.), *Handbook of cross-cultural psychology,* Vol. IV: *Developmental psychology* (pp. 295–341). Boston: Allyn and Bacon.

Dennis, W. (1940). Does culture appreciably affect patterns of infant behavior? *Journal of Social Psychology, 12,* 305–317.

Dennis, W., and Dennis, M. G. (1940). The effect of cradling practices upon the onset of walking in Hopi children. *The Pedagogical Seminary and Journal of Genetic Psychology, 56,* 77–86.

Diamond, A. (1985). Development of the ability to use recall to guide action, as indicated by infants' performance on A$\overline{B}$. *Child Development, 56,* 868–883.

Diamond, A., and Goldman-Rakic, P. (1983). Comparison of performance on a Piagetian object permanence task in human infants and rhesus monkeys: Evidence for involvement of prefrontal cortex. *Neuroscience Abstracts* (Pt. I), *9,* 641.

Diamond, M. C., Krech, D., and Rosensweig, M. R. (1964). The effects of an enriched environment on the histology of the rat cerebral cortex. *Journal of Comparative Neurology, 123,* 111–120.

Diamond, M. C., Johnson, R. E., Protti, A. M., Ott, C., and Kajisa, L. (1985). Plasticity in the 904-day-old male rat cerebral cortex. *Experimental Neurology, 87,* 309–317.

Eibl-Eibesfeldt, I. (1971a). Vorprogrammierung in menschlichen Sozialverhalten. *Mitteilungen an die Max-Planck-Gessellschaft, 5,* 307–338.

Eibl-Eibesfeldt, I. (1971b). Zur Ethologie menschlichen Grussverhaltens: II. Das Grussverhalten und einige andere Muster freundlicher Kontaktaufnahme der Waika-Indianer (Yanoama). *Zeitschrift für Tierpsychologie, 29,* 196–213.

Eibl-Eibesfeldt, I. (1983). Patterns of parent-child interaction in a cross-cultural perspective. In A. Oliverio and M. Zappella (Eds.), *The behavior of human infants.* New York: Plenum.

Ekman, P. (1973). Cross-cultural studies of facial expression. In P. Ekman (Ed.), *Darwin and facial expression*. New York: Academic Press.

Emde, R. N., and Harmon, R. J. (1972). Endogenous and exogenous smiling system in early infancy, *Journal of the American Academy of Child Psychiatry, 11*(2), 177–200.

Emde, R. N., Gaensbauer, T. J., and Harmon, R. J. (1976). Emotional expression in infancy: A biobehavioral study: *Psychological Issues Monograph,* 10(37) 1–192.

Evarts, E. B. (1975). The third Stevenson lecture. Changing concepts of central control of movement. *Canadian Journal of Physiology, 53,* 191–200.

Field, T. M., Sostek, A. M., Vietze, P., and Leiderman, P. H. (Eds.). (1981). *Culture and early interactions*. Hillsdale, N.J.: Lawrence Erlbaum Associates.

Flechsig, P. (1920). *Anatomie des Menschlichen Gehirns und Rückenmarks auf myelogenetischer Grundlage*. Leipzig: Georg Thieme.

Fraiberg, S. (1977). *Insights from the blind: Developmental studies of blind children*. New York: Basic Books.

Freedman, D. G. (1964). Smiling in blind infants and the issue of innate vs. acquired. *Journal of Psychology and Psychiatry, 5,* 171–184.

Freedman, D. G. (1974). *Human infancy: An evolutionary perspective*. New York: Wiley.

Freeman, B. (1978). Myelin sheath thickness and conduction latency groups in the cat optic nerve. *Journal of Comparative Neurology, 181,* 183–196.

Freud, S. (1905). *Three essays on the theory of sexuality*. Standard edition of the complete psychological works of Sigmund Freud, (Vol. 7, pp. 135–245). London: Hogarth.

Friede, R., and Samorajski, T. (1967). The relation between the number of myelin lamellae and the axon circumference in fibres of vagus and sciatic nerves of mice. *Journal of Comparative Neurology, 130,* 223–232.

Geber, M., and Dean, R. F. A. (1957). The state of development of new born African children. *Lancet, 1,* 1216–1219.

Geschwind, N., and Galaburda, A. (1985). Cerebral lateralization and cortical dominance. Parts I, II and II. *Archives of Neurology, 42*(5, 6, and 7).

Gesell, A., and Amatruda, C. S. (1947). *Developmental diagnosis* 2nd ed. New York: Hoeber.

Gewirtz, J. L. (1965). The course of infant smiling in four child-rearing environments in Israel. In B. M. Foss (Ed.), *Determinants of infant behavior III* (p. 161–180). London: Metheun; New York: Wiley.

Ghez, C. (1981). Cortical control of voluntary movement. In E. R. Kandel and J. H. Schwartz (Eds.), *Principles of neural science* (pp. 323–333). New York: Elsevier.

Gibson, K. R. (1977). Brain structure and intelligence in macaques and human infants from a Piagetian perspective. In S. Chevalier-Skolnikoff and F. E. Poirer (Eds.) *Primate biosocial development* (pp. 113–157). New York: Garland.

Gibson, K. R. (1981). Comparative neuro-ontogeny: Its implications for the development of human intelligence. In G. Butterworth (Ed.), *Infancy and epistemology* (pp. 52–82). Brighton, England: Harvester.

Gibson, K. R. (1983). Comparative neurobehavioral ontogeny: the constructionist perspective in the evolution of language, object manipulation and the brain. In E. DeGrolier (Ed.), *Glossogenetics* (pp. 41–46). New York: Harwood Academic Press.

Gilles, F. H., Leviton, A., and Dooling, E. C. (1983). *The developing human brain: Growth and epidemiologic neuropathology.* Boston: John Wright/PSG.

Globus, A., Rosensweig, M. R., Bennett, E., and Diamond, M. C. (1973). Effects of differential experience on dendritic spine counts. *Journal of Comparative and Physiological Psychology, 82,* 175–181.

Gould, S. J., (1977). *Ontogeny and phylogeny.* Cambridge, MA: Harvard University Press.

Gray, J. A. (1971). *The psychology of fear and stress.* New York: McGraw-Hill.

Griffiths, R. (1954). *The abilities of babies.* London: University of London Press.

Gyllensten, L., and Malmfors, T. (1963). Myelination of the optic nerve and dependence on visual function. *Journal of Embryology and Experimental Morphology, 11,* 255–266.

Haith, M. M., Bergman, T., and Moore, M. J. (1977). Eye contact and face scanning in early infancy. *Science, 198,* 853–855.

Heilman, K. M., and Valenstein, E. (Eds.). (1979). *Clinical neuropsychology,* New York: Oxford.

Hindley, C. B., Filliozat, A. M., Klackenberg, G., Nicolet-Meister, D., and Sand, E. A. (1966). Differences in the age of walking in five European longitudinal samples. *Human Biology, 38,* 364–379.

Hogan, E. L., and Greenfield, S. (1984). Animal models of genetic disorders of myelin. In P. Morell (Ed.), *Myelin,* 2nd ed. (pp. 489–534). New York: Plenum.

Huttenlocher, P. R. (1970). Myelination and the development of function in immature pyramidal tract. *Experimental Neurology, 29,* 405–415.

Huxley, A. F., and Stämpfli, R. (1949). Evidence for saltatory conduction in peripheral myelinated nerve fibres. *Journal of Physiology, 108,* 315–339.

Isaacson, R. L. (1974). *The limbic system.* New York. Plenum Press.

Izard, C. E. (1977). *Human Emotions.* New York: Plenum Press.

Jacobson, M. (1978). *Developmental neurobiology.* New York: Plenum Press.

Kagan, J. (1976). Emergent themes in human development. *American Scientist, 64*(2), 186–196.

Kagan, J. (1984). *The natural child.* New York: Basic Books.

Kagan, J., Kearsley, R., and Zelazo, P. (1978). *Infancy: Its place in human development.* Cambridge, MA: Harvard University Press.

Keene, M. F. L., and Hewer, E. E. (1931). Some observations on myelination in the human central nervous system. *Journal of Anatomy, 66,* 1–13.

Kilbride, J. E., and Kilbride, P. L. (1975). Sitting and smiling behavior of Baganda infants: The influence of culturally constituted experience. *Journal of Cross-Cultural Psychology, 6,* 88–107.

Kilbride, P. L. (1980). Sensorimotor behavior of Baganda and Samia infants: A controlled comparison. *Journal of Cross-Cultural Psychology, 11,* 131–152.

Kingsley, J. R., Collins, G. H., and Converse, W. K. (1970). Effect of sciatic neurectomy on myelinogenesis in the rat spinal cord. *Experimental Neurology, 26,* 498–508.

Kinsbourne, M., and Hiscock, M. (1983). The normal and deviant development of functional lateralization of the brain. In P. Mussen (Ed.), *Handbook of child psychology,* 4th ed., Vol. II. New York: Wiley.

Klaus, M., and Kennell, J. (1976). *Maternal infant bonding.* St. Louis: Mosby.

Klüver, H., and Bucy, P. C. (1937). "Psychic blindness" and other symptoms following bilateral temporal lobectomy in Rhesus monkeys. *American Journal of Physiology*, *119*, 352–353.

Klüver, H., and Bucy, P. C. (1939). Preliminary analysis of functions of the temporal lobes in monkeys. *Archives of Neurological Psychiatry*, *42*, 979–1000.

Knobloch, H. (1958). Precocity of African children. *Pediatrics*, *22*, 601–604.

Konner, M. J. (1972). Aspects of the developmental ethology of a foraging people. In N. G. Blurton Jones (Ed.), *Ethological studies of child behavior*. Cambridge: Cambridge University Press.

Konner, M. J. (1973). Newborn walking: Additional data. *Science*, *179*, 307.

Konner, M. J. (1974). Relations among infants and juveniles in comparative perspective. In M. Lewis and L. Rosenblum (Eds.), *Friendship and peer relations*. New York: Wiley. (Reprinted in *Social Science Information*, 1976, *15*(2), 371–402.)

Konner, M. J. (1976). Maternal care, infant behavior and development among the !Kung. In R. B. Lee and I. Devore (Eds.), *Kalahari hunter-gatherers*. Cambridge, MA: Harvard University Press.

Konner, M. J. (1977). Infancy among the Kalahari Desert San. In H. Liedermawn, S. Tulkin, and A. Rosenfeld (Eds.), *Culture and infancy*. New York: Academic Press.

Konner, M. J. (1979). Biological bases of social development. In M. W. Kent and J. E. Rolf (Eds.), *Primary prevention of psychopathology*. Vol II: *Social competance in children*. Hanover: New England University Press.

Konner, M. J. (1981). Evolution of human behavior development. In R. H. Munroe and B. B. Whiting (Eds.), *Handbook of cross-cultural development*. New York: Garland.

Konner, M. M., and Worthman, C. (1980). Nursing frequency, gonadal function and birth spacing among !Kung hunter-gatherers. *Science*, *207*, 788–791.

Korner, A. (1972). State as variable, as obstacle and as mediator of stimulation in infant research. *Merrill-Palmer Quarterly*, *18*, 77–94.

Kretschmann, H. J., Schleicher, A., Grottschreiber, J. F., and Kullmann, W. (1979). The Yakovlev Collection: A pilot study of its suitability for the morphometric documentation of the human brain. *Journal of the Neurological Sciences*, *43*, 111–126.

Langworthy, O. (1933). Development of behavior patterns and myelination of the nervous system in the human fetus and infant. *Contributions to Embryology*, *139*, 1–57.

Lecours, A. R. (1975). Myelogenetic correlates of the development of speech and language. In E. H. Lenneberg and E. Lenneberg (Eds.), *Foundations of language development*, (Vol. 2, pp. 75–94). New York: Academic Press.

Lecours, A. R., Lhermitte, F., and Bryans, B. (Eds.). (1983). *Aphasiology*. London: Balliere Tindall.

Lenneberg, E. H. (1967). *Biological foundations of language*. New York: Wiley.

LeVay, S., Wiesel, T. N., and Hubel, D. H. (1980). The development of ocular dominance columns in normal and visually deprived monkeys. *Journal of Comparative Neurology*, *191*, 1–51.

Lewis, M., and Rosenblum, L. A. (Eds.). (1974). *The origins of fear*. New York: Wiley.

Lewis, M., and Rosenblum, L. A. (Eds.). (1978). *The development of affect*. New York: Plenum.

MacLean, P. D. (1952). Some psychiatric implications of physiological studies on frontotemporal portion of limbic system (visceral brain). *Electroencephalography and Clinical Neurophysiology, 4,* 407–418.

MacLean, P. D. (1973). *A triune concept of brain and behavior. The Hincks Memorial Lectures.* Toronto: University of Toronto.

MacLean, P. D. (1978). Effects of lesions of globus pallidus on species-typical display behavior of squirrel monkeys. *Brain Research, 149,* 175–196.

MacLean, P. D. (1985). Brain evolution relating to family, play and the separation call. *Archives of General Psychiatry, 42,* 405–417.

Martinez, A. J., and Friede, R. L. (1970). Changes in nerve cell bodies during the myelination of their axons. *Journal of Comparative Neurology, 138,* 329–338.

Matthews, M. A. (1968). An electron microscopic study of the relationship between axon diameter and the initiation of myelin production in the peripheral nervous system. *Anatomical Record, 161,* 337–352.

McCarley, R. W., and Hobson, J. A. (1975). Discharge patterns of cat brain stem neurons during desynchronized sleep. *Journal of Neurophysiology, 38,* 751–766.

McDonald, W. I., and Sears, T. A. (1970). The effects of experimental demyelination on conduction in the central nervous system. *Brain, 93,* 583–598.

McGraw, M. (1935). *Growth: A study of Johnny and Jimmy.* New York: Appleton-Century.

McGraw, M. (1943). *The neuromuscular maturation of the human infant.* New York: Columbia University Press.

Meltzoff, A., and Borton, R. W. (1979). Intermodal matching by human neonates. *Nature (London), 282,* 403–404.

Meltzoff, A., and Moore, M. K. (1977). Imitation of facial and manual gestures by human neonates. *Science, 198,* 75–78.

Minkowski, M. (1955). Quelques réflexions sur la neurophysiologie du nouveau-né et du nourrisson et ses relations avec celle du foetus. *Revue Neurologique, 93,* 247–256.

Monnier, M. (1956). The behaviour of newborn anencephalics with varying degrees of anencephaly. In J. M. Tanner and B. Inhelder (Eds.), *Discussion on child development* (Vol. 2, pp. 237–239). London: World Health Organization/Tavistock.

Monrad-Krohn, G. H. (1924). On the dissociation of voluntary and emotional innervation in facial paralysis of central origin. *Brain, 47,* 22–35.

Monrad-Krohn, G. H. (1927). A few remarks on the question of dissociation between voluntary and emotional innervation in peripheral facial paralysis. *Acta Psychiatrica et Neurologica, 3,* 35–39.

Moore, C. L., Kalil, R., and Richards, W. (1976). Development of myelination in optic tract of the cat. *Journal of Comparative Neurology, 165,* 125–136.

Morell, P. (Ed.). (1984). *Myelin* 2nd ed. New York: Plenum.

Morgan, G. A., and Ricciuti, H. N. (1969). Infants responses to strangers during the first year. In B. M. Foss (Ed.), *Determinants of infant behavior* (Vol. 4, pp. 253–272). London: Methuen.

Mussen, P. H. (Ed.). (1983). *Handbook of child psychology,* 4th ed., Vols. I–IV. New York: Wiley.

Nauta, W. J. H. (1958). Hippocampal projections and related neural pathways to the midbrain in the cat. *Brain, 81,* 319–340.

Nauta, W. J. H. (1971). The problem of the frontal lobe: A reinterpretation. *Journal of Psychiatric Research, 8,* 167–187.

Nauta, W. J. H., and Domesick, V. B. (1978). Crossroads of limbic and striatal circuitry:

Hypothalamonigral connections. In K. E. Livingston and O. Hornykiewicz (Eds.), *Limbic mechanisms* (pp. 75–94). New York: Plenum.

Nauta, W. J. H., and Domesick, V. B. (1980). Neural associations of the limbic system. In A. Beckman (Ed.), *Neural substrates of behavior* (pp. 173–206). New York: Spectrum.

Nauta, W. J. H., and Mehler, W. R. (1966). Projections of the lentiform nucleus in the monkey. *Brain Research, 1*, 3–42.

Nicholi, A. M. (Ed.) (1978). *The Harvard Guide to Modern Psychiatry*. Cambridge, MA: Harvard University Press.

Ono, J., Senba, E., Okada, S., Abe, J., Futagi, Y., Shimizu, H., Sugita, T., Hashimoto, S., and Yabuuchi, H. (1982). A case report of congenital hypomyelination. *European Journal of Pediatrics, 138*, 265–270.

Osofsky, J. D. (1979). *Handbook of infant development*. New York: Wiley-Interscience.

Oster, H. (1978). Facial expression and affect development. In M. Lewis and L. A. Rosenblum (Eds.), *The development of affect*. New York: Plenum.

Papez, J. W. (1937). A proposed mechanism of emotion. *Archives of Neurology and Psychiatry*, 38, 725–743.

Parker, S., and Gibson, K. R. (1979). A model of the evolution of language and intelligence in early hominids. *The Behavioral and Brain Sciences, 2*, 367–407.

Peiper, A. (1963). *Cerebral function in infancy and childhood*, 3rd ed. New York: Consultants Bureau.

Peters, A., Palay, S. F., and Webster, H. deF. (1976). *The fine structure of the nervous system: The neurons and supporting cells*. Philadelphia: Saunders.

Plomin, R., and Rowe, D. C. (1978). Genes, environment and development of temperament in young human twins. In G. M. Burghardt and M. Bekoff (Eds.), *The development of behavior: Comparative and evolutionary aspects* (pp. 279–296). New York: Garland.

Prechtl, H., and Beintema, D. (1964). The neurological examination of the full-term newborn infant. *Little Club Clinics in Developmental Medicine No. 12*. London: Heinemann.

Purpura, D. P., and Reaser, G. P. (1974). *Methodological approaches to the study of brain maturation and its abnormalities*. Baltimore: University Park Press.

Rabinowicz, T. (1979). The differential maturation of the human cerebral cortex. In F. Falkner and J. M. Tanner (Eds.), *Human growth* (Vol. III pp. 97–123). New York: Plenum.

Raine, C. S. (1984a). Morphology of myelin and myelination. In P. Morell (Ed.), *Myelin*. New York: Plenum, pp. 1–50.

Raine, C. S. (1984b). The neuropathology of myelin diseases. In P. Morell (Ed.), *Myelin* (pp. 259–310). New York: Plenum.

Rasminsky, M. (1973). The effects of temperature on condition in demyelinated single nerve fibers. *Archives of Neurology (Chicago), 28*, 287–292.

Rasminsky, M. (1980). Ephaptic transmission between single nerve fibres in the spinal nerve roots of dystrophic mice. *Journal of Physiology (London), 305*, 151–156.

Rasminsky, M., and Sears, T. A. (1972). Internodal conduction in undissected demyelinated nerve fibers. *Journal of Physiology, 227*, 323–350.

Rheingold, H. (Ed.). (1963). *Maternal behavior in mammals*. New York: Wiley.

Ricciuti, H. N. (1974). Fear and the development of social attachments in the first year of life. In M. Lewis and L. A. Rosenblum (Eds.), *The origins of fear* (pp. 73–106). New York: Wiley.

Rinn, W. E. (1984). The neuropsychology of facial expression: A review of the neurological and psychological mechanisms for producing facial expressions. *Psychological Bulletin, 95*, 52–77.

Ritchie, J. M. (1984). Pathophysiology of conduction in demyelinated nerve fibers. In P. Morell (Ed.), *Myelin* 2nd ed. New York: Plenum.

Robson, K. S. (1967). The role of eye-to-eye contact in maternal-infant attachment. *Journal Child Psychology and Psychiatry, 8*, 13–25.

Robson, K. S., and Moss, H. A. (1970). Patterns and determinants of maternal attachment. *Journal of Pediatrics, 77*(6), 976–985.

Rorke, L. B., and Riggs, H. E. (1969). *Myelination of the brain in the newborn.* Philadelphia: Lippincott.

Rosenblum, L. A., and Alpert, S. (1974). Fear of strangers and attachment in monkeys. In M. Lewis and L. A. Rosenblum (Eds.), *The origins of fear* (pp. 165–190). New York: Wiley.

Rudolph, A. M., and Hoffman, J. I. E. (1982). *Pediatrics*, 17th ed. Norwalk, CT: Appleton-Century-Crofts.

Sameroff, A. (Ed.). (1979). Organization and stability of newborn behavior: A commentary on the Brazelton Neonatal Behavioral Assessment Scale. *Monographs of the Society for Research in Child Development, 43*, 5–6 (Serial No. 177).

Sammeck, R. (1975). Training-induced myelination in peripheral nerves of the rat. *Journal of Physiology, London, 244*, 7P.

Samorajski, T., and Rolsten, C. (1975). Nerve fiber hypertrophy in posterior tibial nerves of mice in response to voluntary running activity during aging. *Journal of Comparative Neurology, 159*, 533–558.

Scott, J. P. (1962). Critical periods in behavioral development. *Science, 138*, 949–958.

Sidman, R. L., and O'Gorman, S. V. (1981). Cellular interactions in Schwann cell development. In V. M. Riccardi and J. J. Mulvihill (Eds.), *Advances in neurology*, Vol. 29: *Neurofibromatosis (von Recklinghausen Disease)* (pp. 213–236). New York: Raven.

Sluckin, W. (1970). *Early learning in man and animal.* Cambridge: Schenkman.

Smith, K. J., Blakemore, W. F., and McDonald, W. I. (1981). The restoration of conduction by central remyelination. *Brain, 104*, 383–404.

Spitz, R. A., and Wolf, K. M. (1946). The smiling response: A contribution to the ontogenesis of social relations. *Genetic Psychology Monographs, 34*, 57–125.

Spock, B. (1976). *Baby and child care*, 4th ed. New York: Pocket Books.

Sroufe, L. A., and Waters, E. (1976). The ontogenesis of smiling and laughter: A perspective on the organization of development in infancy. *Psychological Review, 83*(3), 173–189.

Stern, D. (1974). Mother and infant at play: The dyadic interaction involving facial, vocal, and gaze behaviors. In M. Lewis and L. A. Rosenblum (Eds.), *The effect of the infant on its caregiver* (pp. 187–214). New York: Wiley.

Stern, D., and Gibbon, J. (1977). Temporal expectancies of social behaviors in mother-infant play. In E. Thoman (Ed.), *The origins of the infant's responsiveness* (pp. 409–430). New York: Lawrence Erlbaum.

Super, C. S. (1981). Behavioral development in infancy. In R. H. Munroe, R. L.

Munroe, and B. B. Whiting (Eds), *Handbook of cross-cultural human development* (pp. 181–270). New York: Garland.

Super, C., Kagan, J., Morrison, F., Haith, M., and Weiffenbach, J. (1972). Discrepancy and attention in the five-month infant. *Genetic Psychology Monographs, 85*, 305–331.

Svejda, M. J., Pannabecker, B. J., and Emde, R. (1982). Parent-to-infant attachment: A critique of the early "bonding" model. In R. N. Emde and R. J. Harmon (Eds.), *The development of attachment and affiliative systems* (pp. 83–94). New York: Plenum.

Tauber, H., Waehneldt, T. V., and Neuhoff, V. (1980). Myelination in rabbit optic nerves is accelerated by artificial eye opening. *Neuroscience Letters, 16*, 235–238.

Tennes, K. H., and Lampl, E. E. (1964). Stranger and separation anxiety in infancy. *Journal of Nervous and Mental Disorders, 139*, 247–254.

Thompson, J. (1941). Development of facial expression of emotion in blind and seeing children. *Archives of Psychology, 264*, 1–47.

Tilney, F., and Casamajor, L. (1924). Myelinogenesis as applied to the study of behavior. *Archives of Neurology and Psychiatry, 12*, 1–66.

Triandis, H. L., and Lambert, W. W. (1980–1981). *Handbook of cross-cultural psychology*, Vols. I–VI. Boston: Allyn and Bacon.

Traugott, U., and Raine, C. S. (1984). The neurology of myelin diseases. In P. Morell (Ed.), *Myelin*, 2nd ed. (pp. 311–336). New York: Plenum.

Valenstein, E. S. (1973) *Brain control*. New York: Wiley.

Van Hooff, J. A. R. A. M. (1972). A comparative approach to the phylogeny of laughter and smiling. In R. A. Hinde (Ed.), *Non-verbal communication* (pp. 209–242). Cambridge: Cambridge University Press.

Warren, N. (1972). African infant precocity. *Psychological Bulletin, 78*, 353–367.

Watson, J. S. (1972). Smiling, cooing and "the game." *Merrill-Palmer Quarterly, 4*, 323–339.

Watson, J. S., and Ramey, C. P. (1972). Reactions to response contingent stimulation in early infancy. *Merrill-Palmer Quarterly, 18*, 219–228.

Waxman, S. G. (1977). Conduction in myelinated, unmyelinated and demyelinated fibers. *Archives of Neurology, 34*, 585–589.

Waxman, S. G. (1982). Membranes, myelin, and the pathophysiology of multiple sclerosis. *New England Journal of Medicine, 306*, 1529–33.

Wendell-Smith, C. P. (1964). Effects of light deprivation on the postnatal development of the optic nerve. *Nature (London), 204*, 707.

Werner, E. E. (1972). Infants around the world: Cross-cultural studies of psychomotor development from birth to two years. *Journal of Cross-Cultural Psychology, 3*, 111–134.

Werner, E. E. (1979). *Cross-cultural child development*. Monterrey, CA: Brooks/Cole.

Whiting, B., and Whiting, J. (1975). *Children of six cultures*. Cambridge, MA: Harvard University Press.

Wiesel, T., and Hubel, D. (1965). Extent of recovery from the effects of visual deprivation in kittens. *Journal of Neurophysiology, 28*, 1060–1072.

Windle, W. F., Fish, M. W., and O'Donell, J. E. (1934). Myelogeny of the cat as related to development of fiber tracts and prenatal behavior patterns. *Journal of Comparative Neurology, 59*, 139–165.

Wolff, P. H. (1963). Observations of the early development of smiling. In B. M. Foss (Ed.), *Determinants of infant behavior II* (pp. 113–134). London: Methuen.

Yakovlev, P. I. (1962). Morphological criteria of growth and maturation of the nervous system in man. *Mental Retardation, 39*, 3–46.

Yakovlev, P. I. (1970). Whole brain serial histological sections. In C. G. Tedeschi (Ed.), *Neuropathology: Methods and diagnosis* (371–378). Boston: Little, Brown.

Yakovlev, P. I., and Lecours, A. R. (1967). The myelogenetic cycles of regional maturation of the brain. In A. Minkowski (Ed.), *Regional development of the brain in early life* (pp. 3–70). Oxford: Blackwell Scientific.

Zelazo, P., Zelazo, N., and Kolb, S. (1972). "Walking" in the newborn. *Science, 176*, 314–315.

Chapter 9

Developmental Transitions of Cognitive Functioning in Rural Kenya and Metropolitan America

Charles M. Super

Psychological theories of cognitive development are generally vertical. By examining the way subjects of different ages deal with a particular set of tasks, psychologists have derived generalizations about how thinking changes as children mature. The tasks on which these analyses are based have been carefully selected to draw out the distinctions that seem to mark growth. Whether they speak of stage or accretion, differentiation or integration, structure, content, or process, such theories are directed toward describing the ways in which our children do not think like us, but eventually come to do so. The vertical growth paradigm has long dominated psychological thought about thinking; Binet, Piaget, Pavlov, Vygotsky, Freud, Wechsler, Werner, the Kendlers, Flavell, all have looked at cognitive development as growing up.

Changes in thinking that are closely linked with age—the landmarks of growing up—have been of special interest. More or less explicitly, the regularity of cognitive changes is usually attributed to biological maturation of the neural substrate. The work of Gesell, who emphasized the "unfolding" of predetermined capabilities, is perhaps prototypical in this regard. "How does the mind grow? It grows *like* the nervous system; it grows *with* the nervous system. Growth . . . produces patterned changes in the nerve cells; it produces corresponding changes in patterns of behavior" (Gesell and Ilg, 1943, p. 18). This general model, of brain development driving mental growth, can also be seen in Freud's belief that psychosexual development is largely a predetermined process of maturation (see Baldwin, 1967) and in Piaget's discussion of cognitive development being an epigenetic system resting in part on the maturation of the nervous system (Piaget, 1964, p. 10).

In all major theories of development the period around age 6 years assumes particular importance (White, 1965, 1970). This age therefore appears to be an attractive candidate for relating changes in brain and behavior. The behavioral evidence is both broad and detailed. Piaget and his associates (e.g., Inhelder and Piaget, 1964), for example, locate the beginnings of rational, operational thought at this time. Similarly, Soviet psychologists emphasize that higher order processes overlay the mechanisms of classical conditioning beginning around 6 years of age. This concept dates back to Pavlov's "second signal system," and both Vygotsky (1962) and Luria (1961) preserve the shift as the central feature of adult cognitive functioning. The American mediation theorists, in their expansion of traditional learning theory, point to a similar process in the sixth year, as language plays an increasing role in conceptual learning (Kendler, 1963). Even Freud, for whom cognition was not a central concern, saw in the resolution of the Oedipal conflict the emergence of inhibitory systems in the superego, and thus a new level of cognitive control. For each theorist, in different languages and from different data, the period around 5 to 7 years is seen as the beginning of a dramatically more mature organization of the mind.

More recent theorizing, of less sweeping design than that of earlier generations, preserves the period of about 6 or 7 years as one of particular significance. Watson's (1981) analysis of children's understanding of social roles, for example, finds a full representational system at age 7. Siegler (1981) comments, on the basis of studies of within- and between-concept sequences of development, that children under age 6 may reason about diverse concepts in similar ways, while older children's reasoning becomes increasingly differentiated. Case's (1984) reformulation of Piagetian theory, although differing from some others in the kind of demarcation seen between ages 5 and 7 years, nevertheless emphasizes major developmental changes in this period. Fischer and Silvern (1985) have recently reviewed the concept of developmental stages and the evidence for such structure; they conclude that "there is strong research evidence to indicate a major change in capacity at (age 6 or 7 years) that fits all six empirical criteria" of true developmental stages (Fischer and Silvern, 1985, p. 635).

Perhaps because the characteristics of change around age 6 are so broad and, depending on their exact measurement, so widely spread across a span of several years, most psychologists have been content with a vague assumption that profound changes in the brain underlie the cognitive shifts. Linked with the complex difficulties of studying brain development in human children, this has resulted in relatively little direct research on the nature of the brain development and cognitive growth at this age.

The present study is no exception to the lack of neurological specificity, for neurological growth remains here a vague hypothesis. The purpose, however, is closely related: to explore the similarity of developmental changes in cognition under divergent environmental conditions, with the supposition that strong parallels in growth under these circumstances are evidence of a genetically based, species-specific program for developmental transitions. The data presented here demonstrate that some patterns of cognitive change in relation to age are, in fact, remarkably similar in rural African and suburban American children. To the degree that the similarities cannot be related to similarities in the children's environments, the data support the hypothesis that some cognitive changes in early and middle childhood are so highly canalized by the epigenetic system that they occur at similar points in development in all normal human environments. To that degree, the pattern of cognitive growth is driven by biology and the assumption of underlying neurophysiological change is made easier.

The utility of cross-cultural comparisons for exploring hypothesized universals is best appreciated in light of the growing realization that theory and data from a single culture are inherently uninterpretable. Because children's environments undergo regular changes with age (such as school entry at 6 years), the shape of developmental change in children's functioning cannot be logically attributed solely to maturational changes in the children, although this error is sometimes made. Comparative research on cognition, in turn, has focused on differences in absolute level of attainment of specific intellectual skills located from mono-cultural studies. In part because of this focus, year-by-year data were rarely collected or analyzed in a way that permitted attention to more discrete trends with age. More often, the central question was, for example, "When do children in this place master concrete operations," rather than "What skills are these children mastering at the same time our children are mastering concrete operations?" It is, of course, a complex issue to disengage cognitive theory from the particular tricks of Western industrial culture, but cross-cultural psychological research over the past two decades has demonstrated its necessity. The present results indicate that children in a variety of settings undergo many of the same kinds of change in thinking at about the same age, even though the new abilities may be applied to different tasks and refined to divergent skills.

The anthropological literature has offered little help in understanding universals of cognitive development, for in contrast to the vertical theories of psychology, anthropology has tended to look across horizontally at thinking, peering over the heads of children to examine the adult mind in foreign cultures. The vast majority of this work is concerned with myth and symbol, the historically elaborated products of everyday thinking. There are in addition some good accounts of mature problem solving in distinctly nonacademic settings. Both kinds of studies are relatively unconcerned, however, as is anthropology in general, with how adults in other societies have come to think as they do. The anthropological studies present, instead, a panorama of adult thinking and yield horizontal theories that relate characteristics of "thought" to characteristics of the society (for the cultural relativist), or to presumed universals of adult humanity (for the universalist).

The horizontal ad vertical perspectives ought to intersect, and at that point will lie a more general theory of the cultural expressions of cognitive growth. The present report narrows to some degree the project of understanding cognitive enculturation, for it clearly indicates that at least some of the major transitions in thought are based on broadly similar patterns of growth.

Sample and General Method

The data presented in this chapter come primarily from two communities: the village of Kokwet in rural Kenya, and the town of Duxbury in metropolitan America.

The Kipsigis of Kokwet. The Kipsigis people of Kenya number about 500,000. They refer to themselves as members of the larger Kalenjin grouping, the third largest in Kenya, and are Highland Nilotic in foreign taxonomies (Sutton, 1968). They emerged as an identifiable group around the end of the seventeenth century, coming southward from Mt. Elgon. Traditionally semi-nomadic, the early Kipsigis shifted pasture and field in response to the land, their cows and simple crops, and sporadic raiding to and from neighboring groups. In the early part of this century permanent residence and land tenure became more common, encouraged by increasing economic, and occasionally military, contact with the British settlers and colonial administrators (Manner, 1967). Today the Kipsigis are primarily farmers, living in the western part of the country, but with substantial representation in all quarters of national life, including business, the military, academics, and government.

Kokwet, where the present work was carried out during 1972–1975, was at that time a community of 54 Kipsigis homesteads stretching 3 miles along a low ridge formed by two streams that drain the Mau forest of the Western Highlands. To the North and East lie rich, rolling farmland and forest, and the tea estates of Kericho. The land dries to the South and West, sloping down to savannah, zebra, and lion.

The people of Kokwet were successful farmers for themselves and the national economy. They grew their daily diet of maize (white corn), and small herds of cattle provided milk for yoghurt-like drink and the ubiquitous tea (normally made with more milk than water, strong tea and sugar all boiled together). Milk, maize, and pyrethrum (a daisy-like flower used in "natural" insecticides) were marketed through national cooperatives. Each family—typically husband, wife and five children, often grandparents or a second wife and her children—had about 18 acres of useful land, a somewhat unusual circumstance created by the agreements with the British at the time of national independence (1963). The land was purchased by the new Kenyan government from a departing British settler and distributed to Kipsigis of the surrounding area who applied for its purchase. The relative abundance of fertile land in Kokwet permitted, at the time of this field work, a continuation of the agricultural adaptation to modern life without severe population pressure to leave the farm and seek wages in towns or plantations.

There was no village center to Kokwet, but mud-walled and straw-roofed houses often clustered near the homestead boundaries to form small groups within the community. Despite enormous change in Kipsigis life brought on by agricultural, radios, national government, metal teapots, and hybrid cattle, many traditional features persisted in Kokwet. Social organization of the community continued to operate at the face-to-face level, with disputes confronted and resolved in this context (Harkness et al., 1981). Age and sex were strong determinants of role in family relations and the household economy of chores, agricultural labor, and tending of cattle. Households worked together for ceremonies, harvesting and weeding, and community projects such as a dip to rid cattle of ticks. Most adults had little or no formal education. Christian missions had been active in the district for half a century, but most men and many women of Kokwet were, in their words, "not yet" converted from the more traditional, less formal system of spiritual beliefs. Few children under 9 years attended, school, and more traditional forms of preparation for adult life persisted in the home and the community. Children contributed early to household chores, and virtually all adolescents chose to participate in initiation and circumcision rites. The work reported here is part of a larger study of child development and family life in Kokwet (see Harkness, 1977; Harkness and Super, 1982, 1983, 1985, 1986; Super, 1976, 1983, 1988; Super and Harkness, 1982, 1986).

The New Englanders of Duxbury.   Scientific reports focus so thoroughly on middle class American children that one can be lulled into a false impression of Americans, the people of behavioral science, as a relatively homogeneous group. In world historical perspective they probably are. Nevertheless, the power of culturally comparative research is dissipated when results from a vastly different culture are compared to scattered findings from undifferentiated "American" children. Measures of development may be taken unknowingly from divergent subsamples. More critically, when the goal is to relate patterns of development to patterns of environment, general notions of the life-space of "the American child" may not be adequate. A particular community was therefore selected in America, as one had been in Kenya, to serve as a specific point of comparison. The middle and upper-middle class families in which the sample children lived are by no means a representative cross section of the nation, as Kokwet does not represent all ways of life in Kenya. Together, however, the two samples provide a rich base for examining similarities and differences in development under rather different conditions.

About the time the Kipsigis people began to migrate southward from Mt. Elgon, a small group of English families sailed westward across the Atlantic to seek a freer life for their religious beliefs and greater opportunity for economic advancement. Settling in what is now Plymouth, Massachusetts, they fared well enough to need larger fields and pastureland only a few years later. The first European family moved to Duxbury, across Plymouth Bay, in 1638.

Today Duxbury is a prosperous distant suburb of Boston. It affords comfortable housing, excellent public schools, diverse recreational facilities, and one of the finest ice-cream parlours in the world. The families in the neighborhood studied here (1976–1977), virtually all white, Anglo-Saxon Protestants, were highly educated, and most of the fathers commuted daily to white-collar and executive jobs in Boston and the high-technology industries in the metropolitan area. All children attended school at age 5, by law; many participated in nursery school or formal play groups before that. At home, they had room to play both outside and in the house, and the affluent American childhood cornucopia of games, television, comics, bicycles, and toys was available to occupy their time.

General Procedure

The children of Kokwet and Duxbury were given a battery of cognitive tests to assess their growth with identical measures. In Kokwet, 165 boys and girls from 3 to 9 who did not attend school were selected for study. At the youngest ages, randomized selection was used to choose 12 boys and 12 girls per year; with increasing age the appropriate pool decreased as some children attended school, so a few children from a neighboring community were drawn on as well. Even at the oldest ages unschooled children comprised a majority available for testing in Kokwet; nevertheless, they became less representative as children of more "modern" parents (who had been to school themselves and were at least nominal members of a Christian church) were more likely to go to school (r about .35, $p < .05$).

Ascertaining the age of children in Kokwet was problematic because written birthdates were rarely available. The ages used for sample selection were derived from parental reports with reference to a local calendar of events. Final estimates for analysis were assigned after testing using results from a multidimensional scaling of adult judgments of relative age in pairs of children (Super, 1986). Hence, the number of subjects of each age and sex varies slightly from the original intent. Anthropometric measures (height, weight, and dental eruption) were used to identify extreme errors or abnormal children, who were removed from the analysis. Two groups of adults were also given the cognitive test battery, 8 men and 8 women with no schooling, and 16 others with 4 or more years of education, matched for sex and religion with the unschooled group.

Testing was carried out by a local woman with 4 years of education and 2 months of training and practice specific to this project. The full battery of 24 tests typically required three or four separate sessions, spread out over a week or so. A small house on the investigators' compound was used for the testing. Constructed like others in the community, the hut was often used by female research staff during the workday and was the scene of familiar activities such as making tea. Every effort was made to keep the surroundings and atmosphere of testing comfortable for the children. Nevertheless, the very concept of being tested by an adult in a one-to-one relationship was not familiar to the children of Kokwet; it was, rather, intimidating (Harkness and Super, 1982). The children were polite and obedient in following directions so useful material was obtained, but it must be emphasized that the social interaction of testing is not equally meaningful to the two samples.

Children in Duxbury ($n = 112$) were recruited through neighborhood networks of friendships and acquaintances. Virtually all of the appropriately aged children in several residential areas were included. Testing was carried out in the children's homes by two trained, local women who were familiar to most of the children. The process was more rapid than in Kokwet, requiring only two or there session of about 30 to 45 min. The children approached the tests as a game or contest and were generally enthusiastic about participating. As in Kokwet, a small gift was presented to each child at the end of the last session. Sixteen adults were also tested with an abbreviated form of the procedures.

Topics and Results

Visual Analysis and Construction

Of the many changes in test performance that occur in middle childhood, one of the best established is an increase in ability to copy simple geometric figures—to examine and analyze the stimulus and reconstruct it with pencil and paper. It has been known for decades that young children score poorly on the Bender Gestalt test (Bender, 1938), and there are several reports indicating the greatest improvement occurs between 5 and 7 years (Koppitz, 1960), or at least under age 7 (Keogh and Smith, 1968). It may be reasonable to assume that the increase in test scores after age 5 reflects brain maturation, and there is evidence of errors similar to those of young children in adult patients with damage in the parietal lobe (e.g., Marley, 1982). It is also true, however, that the children studied by Koppitz and others prepared for and started school during this same period, and the role of increased exposure and practice with geometric forms and letters cannot be independently evaluated. In addition, beyond the particulars of discrete stimuli and responses, White (1970) argues than a more general factor underlies the growth of competence in analysis and construction of geometric forms: the ability to form and execute over time a plan of behavior (e.g., drawing a diagonal) in accord with a proposition offered to the child by others (e.g., an examiner). White lists this larger development as one of six fundamental changes in cognition occurring in middle childhood.

Test procedure. Only the first design ("A") of the Bender Gestalt test was used, a circle and a diamond (square rotated 45°) placed next to each other, just touching. Drawn in black ink on a white card about 5 inches by 7 inches, the figure was placed in front of the child with the instructions: "Here is a picture. Take this pencil and draw another like it on your paper. Make yours exactly like the one you see." No time limit was imposed. Protocols were scored according to a variation of Koppitz' system (Koppitz, 1960), yielding a three-point scale for each of five kinds of errors. Scoring reliability was established at .94, based on 20 protocols. The five kinds of errors are

Shape (e.g., extra or missing angles in the diamond, failure to close the
    circle);
Lack of Proportion of the two parts of the figure (diamond and circle);
Internal Rotation (one part relative to the other, 45° or more);
Overall Rotation (of the gestalt relative to the frame of the paper, 45° or more);
    and
Integration (topological placement of the circle and diamond more than ⅛ inch
    apart or overlap).

Results. Average scores for each age and sample are presented in Figures 1
through 5. The most striking similarity between the two samples is the timing of
reduction in distortions of Shape (Figure 1), Proportion (Figure 2), Internal
Rotation (Figure 3), and to a lesser degree Integration (Figure 5). For the first
two measures, the majority of development occurs between 2 and 5 years in both
communities. For Integration the curve of improvement appears somewhat
extended in Kokwet. Analysis of variance of all four scores in the age range of 3
to 9 years indicates the effect of Age is highly significant ($p< .0001$). For the
improvement in Shape, ages 3, 4, and 5 are statistically different from each other
and from 6, 7, 8, and 9 years; the latter four are statistically indistinguishable
(Duncan's multiple range test, alpha = .05). For Proportion scores, Duncan's
test yields a more complex overlapping of ages, namely (3) (4,5) (5,6,7)
(6,7,8,9). On Internal Rotation ages 3, 4, and 5, stand statistically alone, while

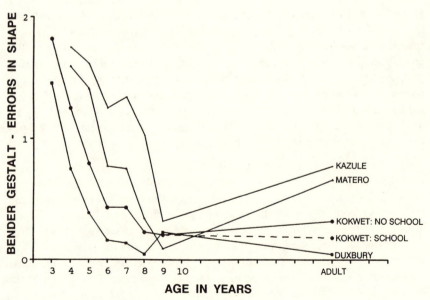

Figure 1. Errors in shape on the Bender Gestalt test.

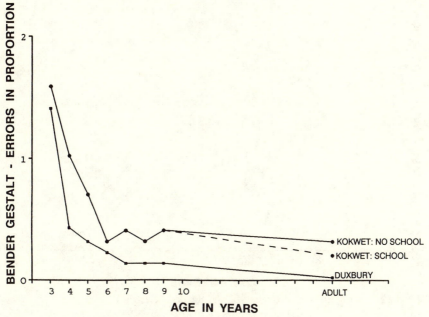

Figure 2.   Errors in proportion on the Bender Gestalt test.

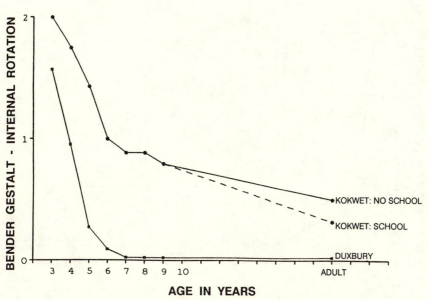

Figure 3.   Errors in internal rotation on the Bender Gestalt test.

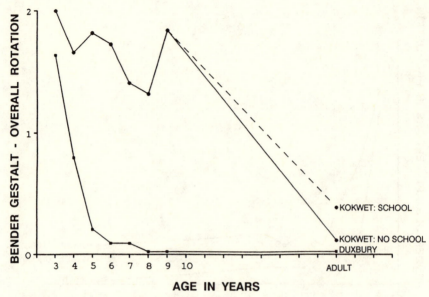

Figure 4.   Errors in overall rotation on the Bender Gestalt test.

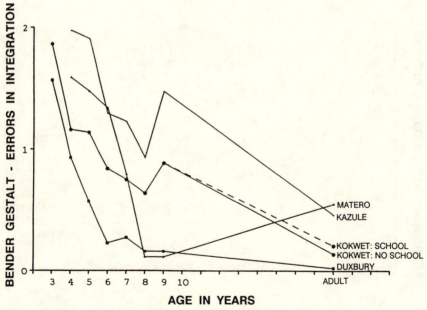

Figure 5.   Errors in integration on the Bender Gestalt test.

(6,7,8) and (7,8,9) overlap. The ages are grouped on Integration as (3) (4,5) and (6,7,8,9).

The Group differences in average score are also reliable in the 3- to 9-year age range ($p < .0001$), with the children in Duxbury performing better. For Shape, Proportion, Internal Rotation, and Integration there is no significant interaction of Age and Group, indicating the development of these skills follows the same pattern in both groups.

Differences in mean score among adult subjects on these four measures, like those for children, are understandable in terms of cultural relevance and experience. The adult differences are not significant overall, although the unschooled Kokwet adult versus Duxbury adult difference is reliable by a *t* test ($p < .05$) for Shape, Proportion, and Internal Rotation (not reliable for Integration).

Errors in Overall Rotation (Figure 4), that is altering the horizontal alignment of the gestalt, present more divergent curves. In addition to the Group and Age differences, the interaction of Age and Group is also highly reliable ($p < .0001$). As is evident from the curves, the timing and rate of growth in Duxbury follow closely the other measures, while in Kokwet there is no single period of a few years that shows particular gains. The adult scores are not reliably different, although the Duxbury vs. unschooled Kokwet comparison alone borders on statistical significance ($p = .06$).

Discussion. It is important to recall in interpreting these results that the children in Kokwet do not have school or literacy experience during the "preschool" period of 3 to 6 years. Yet the shape of their improvement by most measures is essentially the same as that of their counterparts in Duxbury who are watching Sesame Street, coloring preschool workbooks, and receiving at least informal tutoring in visual analysis (e.g., learning the letters of the alphabet).

Similarity in the shape of the developmental curves is further emphasized by comparison with two other samples from Africa. These data are reproduced from a preliminary study carried out in the communities of Kazule and Matero, Zambia (Super, 1972). Kazule was a rural farming area, more isolated and less prosperous than Kokwet. Very few of the children attended school at the time of testing. Matero was a working-class housing development in Lusaka, the capitol of Zambia, inhabited primarily by families who had recently migrated from rural areas. Children above the age of 6 years were attending school. Testing procedures were essentially the same as in Kenya, except that the author carried out the actual test sessions, and two other, more difficult, cards from the original Bender Gestalt were included. The developmental curves for improvement in Shape (Figure 1) from these two Zambian groups are very similar to the Kenyan and American ones, excepting again the difference in absolute value: There is a rapid decrease in errors up to age 6, a lack of change from 6 to 7, and then further progress toward good performance. Most striking is the pause in improvement at 6 years in all four samples. For Integration (Figure 5) there is greatest similarity in the curves between the two rural samples, with an apparent effect of schooling in Matero at age 7. In all samples, however, little improvement occurs after age 8.

The group differences in absolute level are important; Sesame Street does help, along with other elements of the cultural context that shape literacy skills. These include, apparently, the exposure to written materials that occurs incidentally in the urban environment of Matero. Differences in adulthood, on the other hand, are relatively small for the rudimentary skills involved in drawing the initial figure of the Bender Gestalt.

The singular developmental difference in maintaining the overall alignment of the two elements (Figure 4) suggests that this aspect of the figure is more arbitrary, that is, is defined more by cultural factors than developmental ones. Again, the Zambian results support this interpretation, for there are no strong age trends there. By adulthood most Kipsigis are sensitive to the issue of angular orientation, but its emergence is not so tightly canalized that the environmental differences have no effect on development. Orientation of geometric figures is a strongly marked aspect of the environment for children in Duxbury and they apply their analytic skills to this feature as they develop.

It is important, as others have pointed out, to distinguish conceptually the subjects' level of performance from their level of competence. In the case of Overall Rotation it is possible that the Kipsigis children become competent at reproducing this dimension at the same rate as American children, but they are simply not aware of the way their answers will be scored. Is it only that they do not realize that Rotation "counts?" Results from a related task in the Zambian study lends some support to this interpretation (Super, 1972). Children and adults alike did not reveal any inclination to distinguish the orientation of a geometric figure. When told, however, that orientation was important, the adults were able immediately to provide the correct answers. As age decreased, so did the ability to use this correction procedure. By age 7 years, no improvement was noted. Thus it seems likely in the present sample that the flatter Kipsigis curve reflects both poor competence by the younger children as well as a culturally based "misunderstanding" by the older children about what the experimenter wants. In addition, it is possible that the relevant competencies do emerge at a similar rate in Kokwet, but are not practiced in application to this feature, and thus the growth of skill in handling rotation appears truly slower.

Categorical Clustering

A central theme in psychological theories about thinking contrasts organization based on abstracted structural categories with organization based on physical features or function. The more formal and abstract organization is always considered more "mature," "normal," or "civilized" (e.g., Werner, 1961). The topic appears with various labels in different parts of the scientific literature.

In research on word associations, paradigmatic responses, such as the noun *cat* to the stimulus word *dog*, are contrasted with the syntagmatic responses more typical of children, who may respond *barks* or *brown*, as if to make a functional sentence (Brown and Berko, 1960; Ervin, 1961, McNeill, 1966; Nelson, 1977). A related body of literature examines the way people actively (but not necessarily consciously) restructure lists of words presented for memorization. Given "orange, ax, knife, tree," for example, one might later recall them as "ax and knife, tree and orange" (putting together the tools and then the plant matter); or as "ax and tree, knife and orange" (making two functional pairs). Active structuring around taxonomic class is more commonly found among adults than children (Rossi, 1964; Moley et al., 1969), and among normal adults than retarded persons. The abstract-similarity versus concrete-relational distinction in category formation (Inhelder and Piaget, 1964) and in intelligence testing (Wechsler, 1944) is essentially the same. Theories of conceptual style draw the same contrast under the terms "analytic" versus "relational" (e.g., Kagan et al., 1963). Each of these contrasts has a large literature of experimental dissection and theoretical explication, and each finds that the mentally more competent use taxonomic or semantic class as the criterion of organization rather than functional relatedness. By and large, approximately 6 years is seen as an important turning point for that competence.

Nevertheless, it is also clear that specific demand characteristics of the task and the nature of the stimuli (e.g., familiarity of the words: Ingersoll, 1974) influence the kinds of cognitive organization demonstrated. An important feature of recent work (e.g., Gollin and Garrison, 1980; Scott et al., 1985) is the suggestion that both types of cognitive organization are available to young children, and that differential environmental activation of the two types is an important developmental question in its own right.

Studies of clustering in free recall of word lists illustrates nicely the usual developmental trend. Initially, it was thought that young children were not able, or at least not disposed, to cluster the words in memory at all. Using lists of words with carefully selected associations, early studies (e.g., Rossi, 1964) tended to find an increase in clustering with age. Denney and Ziobrowski (1972), however, demonstrated that this result was an artifact of criteria that acknowledged only the kind of associations preferred by adults. When the potential clusters, scattered through the word list, were organized around complementary or functional pairs (e.g., pipe and tobacco) rather than similar or taxonomic ones (e.g., king and ruler), first-graders were found to use more clustering than college students, a reversal of previous findings. It is the *basis* of clustering, not the proclivity to do so, that appears to change.

Procedure. Following Denney and Ziobrowski, two lists were prepared, one containing words related by function, the other by taxonomic similarity. The lists used here contained 10 words, adapted from Denney and Ziobrowski's list to facilitate use in the two samples. The functional list was

fire–burn
path–walk
bird–fly
shovel–dig
food–eat

The list of taxonomically related words was

come–go
cold–hot
calf–cow
man–woman
king–ruler (for Kokwet: maize–millet)

The subject was told, "I have some words on this paper and I am going to read them to you. See how many you can remember. After I read them, you tell me back all the ones you remember." The words were then read at a rate of about 1 per second, in a predetermined pseudorandom order (no paired words adjacent). After the child completed answering, the procedure was repeated two more times with different word orders. Scoring consisted of computing for each subject the conditional probability of listing the second word of a pair immediately following the first, if the first was recalled (reversals of order were counted equally).

Results. Figure 6 presents the average clustering probability at each age for the functional (syntagmatic) list; Figure 7 gives results for the categorical (paradigmatic) list. Three aspects of the results deserve note. First, Denney and Ziobrowski's findings are weakly confirmed, if one assumes 6 year olds to be the equivalent of first-graders, and adults to be as college students. In Duxbury the "first-graders" clustered more than the adults on the functional list, while the reverse is true for the category pairs. In Kokwet, the same contrast holds, though more weakly, for the category pairs only, that is, adults do somewhat better; on the functional list however, the adults and "first-graders" perform essentially the same. As in the American data, the adults fail to show superiority by this measure, but it is not true in Kokwet that the 6 year olds cluster more in the functional list.

Second, it can be seen that in both samples this result depends on the choice of age 6 for the comparison—it is the peak, in childhood, of functional clustering and the nadir (or very close to it) of categorical clustering. The trends within childhood are in fact remarkably parallel in the two samples despite great and unanticipated year-to-year variability. This is emphasized in Figure 8, which presents the ratio of paradigmatic to syntagmatic clustering. Similarity of the age trends is also indicated by analysis of variance, which finds highly significant Age effects in Figure 6 ($p = .002$), the functional measure, but no reliable Group differences (or Group $\times$ Age interaction) in the 3- to 9-year period. For

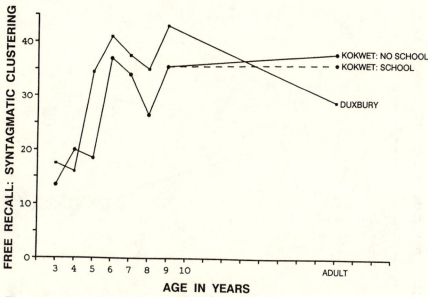

Figure 6. Syntagmatic ("functional") clustering in free recall.

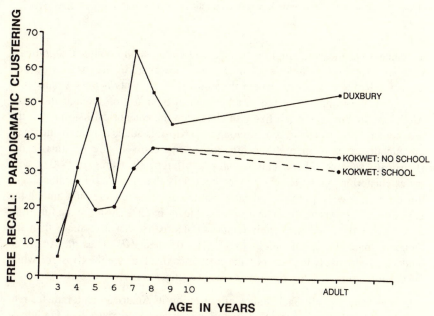

Figure 7. Paradigmatic ("taxonomic") clustering in free recall.

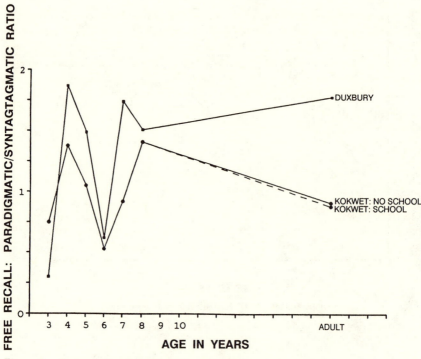

Figure 8.   Ratio of Paradigmatic to Syntagmatic scores in free recall.

the categorical measure (Figure 7), Age and Group both command significant variance ($p < .001$); there is no interaction, however, if one omits a deviant mean for Kokwet at age 9, where the number of subjects is very small.

Finally, the samples diverge in adulthood in their use of syntagmatic cues. Adults in Duxbury are more likely to cluster on the categorical list than are the unschooled Kipsigis ($p = .05$). Although the Kipsigis adults appear to cluster on the functional basis more frequently than Americans (Figure 6), this is not statistically reliable. There is an overall sex difference in scores ($p = .05$), with males clustering syntagmatically more frequently than females. Examination of this difference within groups indicates that the effect is reliable only among the unschooled Kipsigis adults. The unschooled men, in fact, cluster in the functional list not only more than their female counterparts, but also more than the Duxbury male and female adults ($p = .01$, .03, and .07). Thus the American adults are more likely to cluster on the categorical list than are the Kipsigis, while on the functional list the reverse is true, for males only.

Discussion.   Traditional studies of clustering in American children, for reasons that probably have more to do with logistics and economics than a failure of theory, have not examined year-to-year changes in clustering strategy. Rather, they pool several young ages (e.g., 3, 4, and 5 years) or choose one to compared with older groups. It is not possible to know, therefore, whether the pattern of change found in Duxbury, even, is an artifact of some unknown detail in the procedures used here, or whether it is generally true. Finding a similar pattern in Kokwet of course removes a large number of possible explanations, both methodological and environmental. If further study were to replicate the developmental pattern, it would be an instance of canalization of the timing of a cognitive change remarkable for its complexity.

The Verbal Transformation Effect

The verbal transformation effect (VTE) occurs when a word or simple phrase seems to change or lose its meaning when it is repeated over and over. Warren (1968, p. 262) cites one subject, for example, who listened to a recording of the stimulus *tress* played repeatedly for 3 min. During this time the subject reported the tape to include 16 transformations and 8 different forms: stress, dress, stress, dress, Jewish, Joyce, dress, Jewess, Jewish, dress, floris, florist, Joyce, dress, stress, dress, and purse. The phenomenon was known to early experimental psychology (Tichener, 1915, p. 26), and probably for centuries before as an oddity. More recently it has been explored by Warren to shed light on fundamental processes in auditory and especially speech perception (Warren, 1961a, b, 1968; Warren and Warren, 1966).

Two findings are of particular relevance here. First 5 year olds do not experience verbal transformations when hearing a recorded word repeatedly. The effect begins to appear at age 6 and is reportedly experienced by all children 8 years and older. (The effect declines during middle adulthood and is largely absent in those over 65 years.) Second, not only the rate but also the quality of transformations changes with age: when children report transformations, they include English words, English nonwords (nonsense words with speech sounds ordered according to the rules of English), and English nonsyllables (English speech sounds grouped in an order not permitted in English, e.g., the initial *sr* in *srime*). Older subjects show different patterns, leading Warren (1968, p. 265) to conclude that the "perceptual units appear to be individual phonemes for children, English phoneme clusters for young adults, and English words for the aged."

Several features of the VTE recommend it for cross-cultural replication, including its apparent reflection of central speech perception mechanisms and the organization of meaning. Many of the changes around 6 involve language-related phenomena (White, 1970), and some theorists consider changes in language as the essential component of cognitive change at this age (e.g., Vygotsky, 1962).

Procedure. Two tape loops were prepared, one in each language. The Kipsigis tape contained the phrase *"Tuga en mbar"* ("The cow [is] in the garden"), while the English was "Bring it now." During testing, the subject was told "This tape recorder has a lot of things on it, some are words, and some are just sounds that are not real words. You listen to it and tell me everything you hear it say; every time it says something new, you tell me.'' The tape loop was played for 3 min, through earphones worn by the subject. Every 30 sec the experimenter inquired "What is it saying now?" in order to obtain definite reports from younger subjects, a problem especially encountered in Kokwet (Harkness and Super, 1982). Responses were written down by the experimenter and later tabulated.

Results. Figure 9 displays the percentage of subjects at each age who, having correctly reported the recorded phrase, subsequently reported at least one other phrase (i.e., experienced a VTE). The results in Duxbury replicate the most relevant aspect of Warren's reports, namely a low rate of VTE experienced by younger children compared to older. In Kokwet, far fewer subjects at all ages meet the criterion for VTE; nevertheless, the shape of the curve is largely the same as in Duxbury. Nonparametric analysis (chi-square) confirms the significance of age effects in Duxbury ($p < .001$) and Kokwet ($p < .05$). Analysis of variance also suggests a significant effect of Age within the childhood years ($p = .0001$), as well an effect of Group ($p = .001$). The interaction is not significant. The sample difference among adults is highly significant ($p = .002$), but the effect of schooling is not. There are no significant effects or interactions involving sex of the subject.

Some children in Kokwet, and a few of the younger subjects in Duxbury, are not included in the above analysis because they did not initially identify the

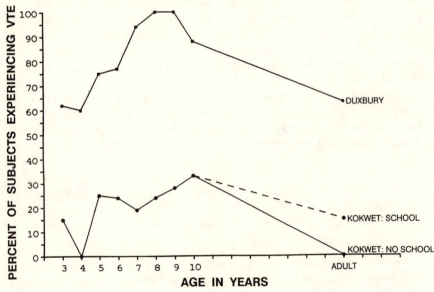

Figure 9. Percentage of subjects experiencing the Verbal Transformation Effect.

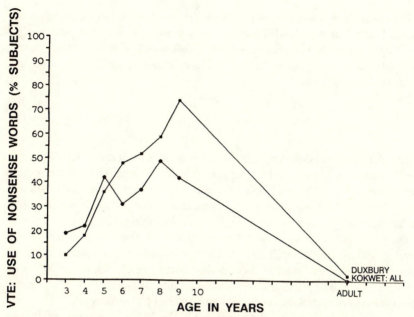

Figure 10. Percentage of subjects reporting nonsense words in the Verbal Transformation Effect.

recorded phrase correctly. They often did report other words and phrases, however, and Figure 10 presents the percent of subjects at each age who gave at least one nonsense word. Again the two curves are similar, rising to a peak at 8 or 9 years, and dropping to virtually zero among the adults. Chi-square analysis yields significant effects for Age ($p < .001$), as does analysis of variance ($p < .0001$). There is no reliable effect of Group, nor is the interaction of Group and Age significant.

The use of nonpermitted sequences of phonemes was rare (not shown). The few instances, usually one or two children per age, occurred at 5, 6, 7, and 8 years, in both samples.

Discussion. The results in Duxbury replicate Warren's findings in the two most relevant respects: younger children experience the VTE less frequently than older children, and children, unlike adults, may report nonsense words. In addition, only younger children (except the very youngest) report nonsyllables that violate permitted phoneme sequences. The decline in rate of VTE among adults, on the other hand, and the absolute rate (over 50%) among children under 6, are contrary to Warren's reports. Warren has demonstrated that procedural details, including the exact instructions, can influence the outcome, and the particular techniques used here might possibly account for these facts.

The results in Kokwet are essentially the same with regard to age effects, even though the overall rate of VTE is much lower in Kokwet. It is tempting to relate the sample difference to differences in the daily use of language—the simple rate of words per minute seems vastly greater in Duxbury—but there is no real evidence to bring to the issue.

Discussion

The data on visual-motor skills, clustering in free recall, and the verbal transformation effect all yield related common conclusions: The shape of cognitive growth in middle childhood is remarkably similar in the quite different settings of rural Kenya and suburban America; at the same time, it is evident that the application and use of the emerging abilities diverge in the two cultures.

The first conclusion is an unusual demonstration of regularity in the behavioral development of our species. There are a few other such cross-cultural demonstrations in the literature, most of them during infancy (e.g., Kagan, 1976, 1982; Konner, 1982). The similarity in both the quality of changes shown here and their timing is perhaps best considered an instance of "canalization." This term was elaborated initially by Waddington (1957, 1962) to discuss genotype–environment interactions in which patterns of development (e.g., sequences of growth, breathing reflexes) are relatively stable across a broad range of specific individual variance (e.g., in rate of growth, absolute size of anatomical parts) and under conditions of moderate environmental or genetic stress. Waddington's "epigenetic landscape" (see for example Fishbein, 1976, p. 36) has become familiar to developmentalists of several disciplines as a visual, topographic metaphor for the channeling of development toward particular, evolutionarily selected paths (e.g., Lumsden and Wilson, 1981; McCall, 1981; Parker and Gibson, 1979; Scarr-Salapatek, 1976). Although such use of Waddington's model has been criticized by Gottlieb (1983) as a distortion of the original concept, what is so attractive to developmentalists is the integration of a sense of genetic determination with the recognition of environmental guidance, or "induction" to use Spemann's (1938) embryonic term. Human cognitive abilities, like breathing, digestion, and motor skills, are universal under a range of normal circumstances, but they do not appear entirely of their own accord, without formative environmental interaction. Given an adequate environment, the cognitive competencies sampled here emerge at similar points in middle childhood.

The second conclusion, regarding the application and refinement of emerging abilities, brings to mind recent evolutionary literature concerning the relationship of species and their environments, in particular the concept of "exaptation." The term was coined by Gould and Vrba (1982) in recognition of the often unknown relationships between present functioning and past history. It contrasts (1) species characteristics whose current utility was synthesized through natural selection by the same external forces (predators, climate, etc.) that currently maintain its utility, with (2) those characteristics whole current utility is unrelated to the initial synthesis fostered through natural selection. The former group are true adaptations because selection led toward (*ad*) the fitness. The utility of exaptation, in contrast, is derived from (*ex*) the existing form, which may or may not be adaptive itself. Feathers, for example, probably served initially for heat insulation in a predecessor of birds, and their basic structure later became useful for flight. Other exaptations may take advantage of features that are initially useless by-products of existing systems; secondary effects of circulating hormones in the female hyena and "junk" DNA are examples presented by Gould and Vrba (1982).

Modern use of the visual and language systems for reading demonstrates a cultural version of exaptation. It seems reasonable to speculate that at no time in the evolutionary history of our species was the ability to learn to read, especially in childhood, of significance for reproductive success. Hence, reading is not an adaptation at the species level. Yet the skill is developed in many societies as a critical behavior for modern life. In America and many other countries, the emergence of learning to read is monitored with great concern; a delay of one or two years from the population standard can mobilize considerable social resources for intervention—pediatricians, psychologists, psychiatrists, family counselors, and neighborhood networks of advice and referral. The particular integration and application of cognitive skills for reading are cultural constructions. At the same time, the building blocks of reading appear to be strongly canalized features of our species, that is, their emergence is strongly favored under a variety of circumstances. The similarity of scores on the Bender Gestalt item in Kokwet and Duxbury presumably reflects such canalization, and the integration of related abilities into reading in Duxbury (and for those Kipsigis who attend school) is a cultural exaptation.

It is no accident that American theories and tests of cognition concern areas of growth, such as reading, that we see as important for successful passage toward maturity. The cultural specificity of tests, their "culture boundedness" or "culture bias," is now widely known and many psychologists are prepared to see earlier quests for a culture-free test of intelligence, for example, as akin to seeking a nutrition-free test of digestive capacity. The profundity of culture boundedness derives not only from the particular information proffered about Shakespeare, social mores, Newtonian physics, and geometric progression. The kind of thinking that "makes sense," the personal interaction of being tested, and the meaning of decontextualized questions are culturally constructed as well (e.g., Cole et al., 1971). Cognitive tests, including the ones adapted here, were designed to be diagnostic for particular theories of thinking. The tests and the theories—be they tests of IQ, Piagetian operations, or perceptual organization—coevolved, their meanings and workings closely woven from the threads of Western culture.

What is less obvious, in the absence of cross-cultural comparison, are the many ways in which American culture indirectly shapes and encourages these abilities. The visual-motor skills needed for reading and writing are also used in preschool games and toys. The geometry of letters is available in the design of houses, "stop" signs on the street, and advertisements on television. More abstractly, even the linear organization of the printed word is available in Western music.

The same cultural embeddedness exists for the tests of clustering and tax-onomic organization (Super et al., 1977). Look, with your mind's eye, around your kitchen. If you (or your spouse or mother) had a few minutes today to "put things away," there will be in one place all the dinner plates, and next to them eight or a dozen salad plates. There might be a separate set of fancy dinner plates. A variety of drinking containers might be organized by size, type of liquid, and possibly age of intended user. In a drawer is a set of little compart-ments, each with one category of tableware: knives here, teaspoons there, soup spoons, forks, and butter knives separately. Out of all this, a small number of elements of each class—plate, glass, knife, fork, and spoon—is chosen for each person at mealtime; it does not matter which dinner plate or which water glass as long as it is the right type. After the meal, as the objects lie in the dish drainer clean but all mixed up, someone has to put them in their proper place, that is to sort them by taxonomic class. Similarly, products are clustered by category in the supermarket, the hardware store, and the haberdashers; nails and tools are sorted in the shop, pencils and papers in the office.

Enormous energy goes to keeping things in their place and the reason is not difficult to see. When there are many identical or functionally equivalent mem-bers of a category, and several categories from which elements are chosen in varying combinations, life is simpler at the point of search if all the objects are arranged by class. The work of maintaining the organization is more than offset by the gain in access time. The exceptions prove the rule. The carving knife is kept with the carving fork, not with everyday table knives, because it is not interchangeable with the other knives and because whenever one of the carving tools is used so is the other. Similarly the tennis shirt may be kept with the tennis shorts and not with other shirts, and the soy sauce is on the same shelf in the grocery store as the Chinese noodles, not with other sauces. If there are few members of each class and little recombining, it is not worth fighting the taxonomic entropy, and the most efficient organization puts together those things that are used together.

The tests used here were designed to assess features of cognitive growth identified by Western psychologists as important for mature functioning in their environment. Underlying the particular expressions sampled by these tests are broader potentials of human conduct. The Kipsigis made different use of the growing competencies. Most salient to the American eye was the rapid integration of the child into the household economy and the social reality of a small, face-to-face community. By age 4 children were found to spend more of their available time in economically meaningful work than in play or resting; by age 6 years work was fully half of their waking activity (Harkness & Super, 1986). The actual tasks were of course adjusted to the capabilities of the child, and started with collecting small amounts of firewood, keeping calves from the drying pyrethrum, and hauling water from the stream. By age 6 or 7, the typical girl was in immediate charge of a baby or toddler for substantial blocks of time, and a boy would spend a major portion of his day herding cows. Both sexes participated in planting, weeding, and harvesting, as well as in carrying messages to neighboring homesteads and occasionally running an errand beyond the neighborhood borders.

Kipsigis parents were attentive to the growing abilities of their children and organized their perceptions of development in childhood around competence, particularly self-directed competence, in economic chores. Indeed they saw in their children around age 6 years the emergence of a mature quality essential to responsible participation in family and social life, the quality of being *ng'om*. The word is universally translated as "intelligent" by bilinguals, but detailed study of the word and its use suggests richer connotations of "responsible" and "obedient" (Super, 1983). A child was considered *ng'om* when he or she was old enough to understand how to behave in a helpful and responsible manner, but parents recognized that not all children do so to an equal extent. Because of the cultural emphasis on responsible helpfulness as the central element in development as well as a most desired personal quality, the Kipsigis concepts of intelligence and personality were tied to a developmental shift around age 6 when the child becomes mature enough to exhibit this kind of behavior (Super, 1983; Super and Harkness, 1986). Kipsigis parents, like Western psychologists, see around age 6 years the emergence of mature thought and behavioral regulation. Ethnographic material from other cultures around the world suggest this is a nearly universal belief (Rogoff et al., 1975).

The Kipsigis child did not live in a physical environment of multiple identical exemplars of hierarchically organized classes. Nor did the child in Kokwet have daily experience with coloring books, board games, cross-word puzzles, Sesame Street, or formal education. Nevertheless, some of the underlying changes in cognition that have been identified for American children were found to proceed among the Kipsigis at similar rates in the years around age 6. Changes in elementary visual analysis and construction, in the clustering of items in free recall, and in the rate and type of illusions in the Verbal Transformation Effect are highly canalized growth patterns of middle childhood. Also highly canalized is the openness of those abilities to application in the culturally defined developmental niche. To see essentials of cognitive growth behind the variety of their cultural exaptations adds a broader and more stable base to our picture of growing up.

Acknowledgments

This research was supported in part by funds granted by the Carnegie Corporation of New York, the William T. Grant Foundation, the Spencer Foundation, and the National Institute of Mental Health (Grant 33285). All statements made and opinions expressed are the sole responsibility of the author.

References

Baldwin, A. L. (1967). *Theories of child development*. New York: Wiley.

Bender, L. A. (1938). A visual motor Gestalt test and its clinical use. *Research Monograph of the American Orthopsychiatric Association*, no. 376.

Brown, R., and Berko, J. (1960). Word association and the acquisition of grammar. *Child Development 31*, 1–14.

Case, R. (1984) *Intellectual development: A systematic reinterpretation*. New York: Academic Press.

Cole, M., Gay, J., Glick, J. A., and Sharp, D. W. (1971) *The cultural context of learning and thinking*. New York: Basic Books.

Denney, N. W., and Ziobrowski, M. (1972). Developmental changes in clustering criteria. *Journal of Experimental Child Psychology, 13*, 275–282.

Ervin, S. (1961). Changes with age in the verbal determinants of words association. *American Journal of Psychology, 74*, 361–372.

Fischer, K. W., and Silvern, L. (1985). Stages and individual differences in cognitive development. *Annual Review of Psychology, 36*, 613–648.

Fishbein, H. D. (1976). *Evolution, development, and children's learning*. Pacific Palisades, California: Goodyear.

Gesell, A. and Ilg, F. L. (1943). *Infant and child in the culture of today*. New York: Harper.

Gollin, E. S., and Garrison, A. (1980). Relationships between perceptual and conceptual mediational systems in young children. *Journal of Experimental Child Psychology, 30*, 325–335.

Gottlieb, G. (1983). The psychobiological approach to developmental issues. In M. M. Haith and J. J. Campos (Eds.), *Infancy and developmental psychobiology*, Vol. 2 of P. Mussen (Ed.), *Handbook of child psychology* (pp. 1–26). New York: Wiley.

Gould, S. J., and Vrba, E. (1982). Exaptation—A missing term in the science of form. *Paleobiology, 8*. 4–15.

Harkness, S. (1977). Aspects of social environment and first language acquisition in rural Africa. In C. Snow and C. Ferguson (Eds.), *Talking to children: Language input and acquisition*, (pp. 309–361). Cambridge, England: Cambridge University Press.

Harkness, S. and Super, C. M. (1982). Why African children are so hard to test. In L. L. Adler (Ed.), *Cross-cultural research at issue*, (pp. 145–152). New York: Academic Press.

Harkness S., and Super, C. M. (1983). The cultural construction of child development: A framework for the socialization of affect. *Ethos, 11*(4), 221–231.

Harkness, S., and Super, C. M. (1985). Child-environment interactions in the socialization of affect. In M. Lewis and C. Saarni (Eds.), *The socialization of emotions* (pp. 21–36). New York: Plenum.

Harkness, S., and Super, C. M. (1986). The cultural structuring of children's play in a rural African community. In K. Blanchard (Ed.), *The many faces of play*, (pp. 96–103). Champaign, IL: Human Kinetics.

Harkness, S., Edwards, C. P., and Super, C. M. (1981). Social roles and moral reasoning: A case study in a rural African community. *Developmental Psychology, 17*, 595–603.

Ingersoll, G. M. (1974). Effects of age, form class, and word frequency on homogeneous work associations. *Psychological Reports, 35*(1, part 1), 59–64.

Inhelder, B., and Piaget, J. (1964). *The early growth of logic in the child*. London: Routledge & Kegan Paul.

Kagan, J. (1976). Emergent themes in human development. *American Scientist, 64*, 186–196.

Kagan, J. (1982). Canalization of early psychosocial development. *Pediatrics, 70*(3), 474–483.

Kagan, J., Moss, H., and Sigel, I. (1963). Psychological significance of styles of conceptualization. *Monographs of the Society for Research in Child Development, 28*, 73–112.

Kendler, T. S. (1963). Development of mediating responses in children. In J. C. Wright and J. Kagan (Eds.), Basic cognitive processes in children. *Monographs of the Society for Research in Child Development, 28*(2), 33–51.

Keogh, B. K., and Smith, C. E. (1968). Changes in copying ability of young children. *Perceptual and Motor Skills, 26*(3, part 1), 773–774.

Konner, M. J. (1982). Biological aspects of the mother-infant bond. In R. N. Emde and R. J. Harmon (Eds.), *The development of attachment and affiliative systems*, (pp. 137–159). New York: Plenum.

Koppitz, E. M. (1960). The Bender Gestalt test for children, a normative study. *Journal of Clinical Psychology, 16*, 432–435.

Lumsden, C. J., and Wilson, E. O. (1981). *Genes, mind, and culture: The coevolutionary process*. Cambridge, MA: Harvard University Press.

Luria, A. R. (1961). *The role of speech in the regulation of normal and abnormal behavior*. New York: Liveright.

Manners, R. A. (1967). The Kipsigis of Kenya: Culture change in a "model" East African tribe. In J. H. Steward (Ed.), *Three African tribes in transition*, (pp. 207–359). Urbana, IL: University of Illinois Press.

Marley, M. L. (1982). *Organic brain pathology and the Bender-Gestalt Test*. New York: Grune & Stratton.

McCall, R. B. (1981). Nature-nurture and the two realms of development: A proposed integration with respect to mental development. *Child Development, 52*, 1–12.

McNeill, D. A. (1966). A study of word association. *Journal of Verbal Learning and Verbal Behavior, 5,* 548–557.

Moley, B., Olson, F., Hawles, T., and Flavell, J. (1969). Production deficiency in young children's clustered recall. *Developmental Psychology, 1,* 26–34.

Nelson, K. (1977). The syntagmatic-paradigmatic shift revisited: A review of research and theory. *Psychological Bulletin, 84*(1), 93–116.

Parker, S. T. and Gibson, K. R. (1979). A developmental model for the evolution of language and intelligence in early hominids. *Behavioral and Brain Sciences, 2,* 367–408.

Piaget, J. (1964). Development and learning. In G. R. Ripple and V. N. Rockcastle (Eds.), *Piaget rediscovered.* Ithaca, NY: Cornell University Press, pp. 1–23.

Rogoff, B., Sellers, M. J., Pirrotta, S., Fox, N., and White, S. H. (1975). Age of assignment of roles and responsibilities to children: A cross-cultural survey. *Human Development, 18,* 353–369.

Rossi, E. L. (1964). Development of classificatory behavior. *Child Development, 36,* 137–142.

Scarr-Salapatek, S. (1976). An evolutionary perspective on infant intelligence: Species patterns and individual variations. In M. Lewis (Ed.), *Origins of intelligence: Infancy and early childhood,* (pp. 165–198). New York: Plenum.

Scott, M. S., Greenfield, D. B., and Urbano, R. C. (1985). A comparison of complementary and taxonomic utilization: Significance of the dependent measure. *International Journal of Behavioral Development, 8,* 241–256.

Siegler, R. (1981). Developmental sequences within and between concepts. *Monographs of the Society for Research in Child Development, 46*(2, Ser. No. 189).

Spemann, H. (1938). *Embryonic development and induction.* New Haven, CT: Yale University Press.

Super, C. M. (1972). *Cognitive changes in rural and urban Zambian children in the late preschool years* (HDRU *Reports* No. 22). Lusaka: University of Zambia.

Super, C. M. (1976). Environmental effects on motor development: The case of "African infant precocity." *Developmental Medicine and Child Neurology, 18,* 561–567.

Super, C. M. (1983). Cultural variation in the meaning and uses of children's "intelligence." In J. B. Deregowski, S. Dziurawiec, and R. C. Annis (Eds.), *Expiscations in cross-cultural psychology,* (pp. 199–212). Lisse: Swets & Zeitlinger.

Super, C. M. (1986). The use of multi-dimensional scaling techniques to assess children's ages in a field setting. Unpublished manuscript.

Super, C. M. (1988). Culture, temperament, and behavior problems in infancy. Submitted for publication.

Super, C. M., and Harkness, S. (1982). The development of affect in infancy and early childhood. In D. Wagner and H. Stevenson (Eds.), *Cultural perspectives on child development,* (pp. 1–19). San Francisco: Freeman.

Super, C. M., and Harkness, S. (1986). The developmental niche: A conceptualization at the interface of child and culture. *International Journal of Behavioral Development, 9,* 545–570.

Super, C. M., Harkness, S. and Baldwin, L. M. (1977). Category behavior in natural ecologies and in cognitive tests. *The Quarterly Newsletter of the Institute for Comparative Human Development,* Rockefeller University, *1*(4), 1–7.

Sutton, J. E. G. (1968). The settlement of East Africa. In B. A. Ogot (Ed.), *Zamani: A survey of East African History*, (pp. 70–97). Nairobi, Kenya: East African Publishing House and Longman Group.

Tichener, E. B. (1915). *A beginner's psychology*. New York: Macmillan.

Vygotsky, L. S. (1962). *Thought and language*. Cambridge, MA: MIT Press.

Waddington, C. H. (1957). *The strategy of genes*. London: Allen & Unwin.

Waddington, C. H. (1962). *New patterns in genetics and development*. New York: Columbia University Press.

Warren, R. M. (1961a). Illusory changes of distinct speech upon repetition—The verbal transformation effect. *British Journal of Psychology, 52,* 249–258.

Warren, R. M. (1961b). Illusory changes in repeated words: Differences between young adults and the aged. *American Journal of Psychology, 74,* 506–516.

Warren, R. M. (1968). Verbal transformation effect and auditory perceptual mechanisms. *Psychological Bulletin, 70*(4), 261–270.

Warren, R. M., and Warren, R. P. (1966). A comparison of speech perception in childhood, maturity, and old age by means of the verbal transformation effect. *Journal of Verbal Learning and Verbal Behavior, 5,* 142–146.

Watson, M. W. (1981). The development of social roles: A sequence of social-cognitive development. In K. W. Fischer (Ed.), *Cognitive development. New Directions for Child Development, 12,* 33–42.

Wechsler, D. (1944). *The measurement of adult intelligence*, 3rd ed. Baltimore: Williams & Wilkins.

Werner, H. (1961). *Comparative psychology of mental development*. New York: Science Edition, (originally published in 1948).

White, S. H. (1965). Evidence for a hierarchical arrangement in learning processes. In L. P. Lipsitt and C. C. Spiker (Eds.), *Advances in child development and behavior*, (pp. 187–220). Vol. 2. New York: Academic Press.

White, S. H., (1970). Some general outlines of the matrix of developmental changes between five and seven years. *Bulletin of the Orton Society, 20,* 41–57.

Chapter 10

Cognitive Changes at Adolescence: Biological Perspectives

Julia A. Graber and Anne C. Petersen

There has been an explosion of research recently on brain development, and on neurocognitive development. In addition, research on cognitive development has continued actively since the major stimulation to this field from Piaget. The research on brain development permits more adequate hypothesis formulation of factors influencing cognition and achievement during development. In this chapter, we will review research on cognitive development during adolescence, with particular emphasis on biological and experiential influences on gender differences in development. Gender is used as a convenient variable to examining biological and experiential factors effecting individual development. We also sketch a hypothesis for gender-differential brain and cognitive development.

Models of Development

The life-span perspective on development (e.g., Baltes, 1987) provides an important contribution to consideration of development and growth. In particular, it calls attention to important context effects especially from social groups such as family and friends. Such factors are particularly important when considering development during adolescence, a time of life characterized by change in every aspect of individual development and in every major social context (Peterson, 1987). Figure 1 shows one picture of the contexts for development across the life course. This figure also portrays some levels of influence within the individual, such as endocrine change. This perspective has been termed biopsychosocial development (e.g., Petersen, 1980), and emphasizes the role of biological and social factors. The life-span perspective focuses more on cumulative effects over life and less on the sources of variation. These perspectives are

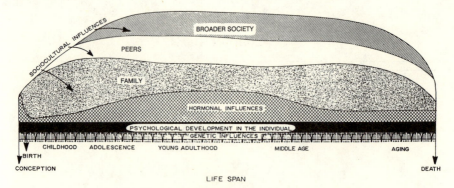

Figure 1.   Some factors hypothetically influencing psychological development over the
life-span. From Petersen, ''Biosocial processes in the development of sex related
differences.'' In J. E. Parsons Ed., *The psychology of sex differences and sex roles.*
Copyright © 1980 by Hemisphere Publ. Co. Reprinted with permission.

easily integrated and together provide a comprehensive description of individual
development.

Although wee have some knowledge of general developmental trends in
cognition, significant individual differences also exist. The examination of sex
differences can serve as a model for individual differences more generally,
although we note that other important sources of variation beyond whether the
individual is male or female also play a role. The development of sex differences
in cognition, often thought to merge in adolescence, has been attributed to a
variety of influences (e.g., Wittig and Petersen, 1979). One model, portrayed in
Figure 2, categorizes these influences into two groups: experiential and biological. Biological beliefs predominate as explanations for the development of
gender differences in cognition and for cognitive changes in adolescence (e.g.,
Petersen and Wittig, 1979).

This emphasis on biological causation in development is also seen with
adolescent development more generally. A common explanation for behavioral
changes seen in adolescence is that puberty causes great upheaval in adolescent
behavior (e.g., Kestenberg, 1968). Pubertal changes are controlled by the activity of an endocrine system initially influential prior to birth. Prenatal hormones
have an organizing effect on development at the time when the internal and
external sex organs develop, resulting in either male or female characteristics.
This systems remains dormant or at least predominately dormant until middle or
late childhood. At puberty, the system is activated for the development of adult
reproductive functioning. (See Brooks-Gunn and Reiter, 1990, or Petersen,
1980, for summaries of these processes.) Psychical changes at puberty are
brought about by a complex interaction of genetics, hormones, and environmental factors such as nutrition. Marshall and Tanner (1969, 1970) have described

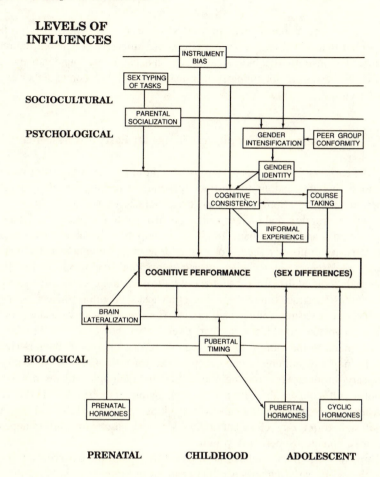

LEVELS OF INFLUENCES

SOCIOCULTURAL

PSYCHOLOGICAL

BIOLOGICAL

PRENATAL   CHILDHOOD   ADOLESCENT

PHASES OF DEVELOPMENT

Figure 2. A model for biopsychosocial influences on sex differences in cognition. (Adapted from Petersen, 1979.)

the typical patterns of pubertal changes for boys and girls in growth spurt, genital development, and other physical changes. They note the substantial range of variation in physical development among individuals.

The prevalent cultural belief that these changes cause an upheaval in behavior is quite interesting to compare with the data. Puberty is only one of the many changes that take place in early adolescence (Petersen, 1987). There has been little research examining pubertal effects in early adolescence until very recently (e.g., Brooks-Gunn and Petersen, 1983; Brooks-Gunn et al, 1985). The preliminary results of this research suggest that specific aspects of puberty (e.g., maturing earlier than one's peers) may affect some specific behaviors (e.g., body image) but that global and pervasive effects are unlikely. In general, the recent research demonstrates that biological effects on behavior are found; however, the specific processes are not simple, but instead, interact with contextual or experiential factors.

Explanations of Cognitive Change in Early Adolescence

In the early adolescent years, there is thought to be a major transformation in cognitive thought leading to abstract reasoning (Inhelder and Piaget, 1958; Super, this volume). Some researchers even characterize cognitive change at this time as a disruption and/or reorganization of cognition (Carey and Diamond, 1980; Merola and Liederman, 1985). It is important to note, however, that change is not uniformly seen. For example, abstract thought is not ubiquitous among adolescents, at least as measured by Piagetian tasks (Dulit, 1972). Indeed, data on adults suggest that about half of adults, even in our society, do not manifest abstract thinking on Piagetian tasks (Tomlinson-Keasey, 1972). Whether these results reflect task effects (i.e., inadequate measures) or real deficits in abstract thinking is unclear. Even Piaget, however, wrote of the need for a demand in the culture to elicit the emergence of some behaviors (Piaget, 1972). In many cultures some facets of abstract thinking are probably not necessary for mature functioning, thus explaining their apparent absence in some samples. Of course, the alternative explanation may be inadequacy of the measures; it is possible that abstract thinking appears in all cultures but is manifested differently cross-culturally as is the case with earlier appearing cognitive change (Super, this volume).

Three major hypotheses have been posed to explain the emergence of cognitive change in early adolescence: (1) changes in brain growth, (2) differential growth rates, and (3) differential socialization pressures in early adolescence. Each of these hypotheses will be described in turn.

Epstein (1978) attempted to relate developmental changes in brain growth to the development of cognitive abilities. By examining major longitudinal studies of physical and cognitive development, and using head circumference as an index of brain size, he found growth increments in head circumference that showed distinctive accelerations and declarations. Epstein (1978) argued that during times of rapid brain (i.e., head circumference) growth, learning is less likely. On the basis of this argument, Toepfer (1976, 1980) developed a curriculum for the middle schools, which involves no new learning during early adolescence; this curriculum has been widely adopted throughout the country.

Somewhat similar to the question of brain growth effects is that of whether pubertal development results in changes in the brain that have a disruptive effect on cognitive processing (Carey and Diamond, 1980; Merola and Liederman,

1985). If Epstein's hypothesis, or a pubertal disruption hypothesis were correct, we would expect to see a dip in cognitive performance at the time of puberty.

The second hypothesis explaining cognitive changes emerging in early adolescence is perhaps related to the one just described but was developed independently. This hypothesis posited that the rate or timing of maturation was related to the development of specific cognitive abilities, such as spatial skills and verbal skills (Waber 1976, 1977). Timing of pubertal maturation was originally hypothesized to be a possible cause for gender differences in spatial skills, which were thought to emerge in early adolescence. Gender-related differences in spatial ability are well established in the literature (Maccoby and Jacklin, 1974; Harris, 1978). The strong consensus is that sex-related differences increase with age and that early adolescence, when pubertal change occurs, is the crucial time period for the substantive differentiation of the sexes in performance on spatial tasks, with males performing better on most tasks.

Waber's hypothesis for cognitive change in early adolescence focused less on gender per se but rather on the fact that girls mature earlier than boys. Waber (1976) proposed that timing of pubertal maturation and subsequent hormonal shifts explain both the gender differences in spatial ability and the nature of its marked increase during puberty. This hypothesis proposes a process that conceptually parallels what is known about height differences in adults; that is, adult differences in height between men and women result from the earlier initiation of the growth spurt in women compared to men. The growth achieved during the pubertal growth spurt involves, as the term "growth spurt" suggests, a period of rapid growth terminated by fusion of the ends of long bones. This growth is added onto a shorter individual in the case of women and a taller one for men because men have had more time—2 years, on average—for the linear, prepubertal growth prior to the spurt. Using a similar developmental model, Waber proposed that the mechanism by which timing of maturation influences cognitive performance is brain lateralization. As is the case with height, the onset of puberty was hypothesized by Waber to curtail the process of lateralization in girls; later puberty in boys, in contrast, would permit a longer process of hemispheric specialization. Hypothetically, if brain lateralization continues developing until curtailed by the termination of pubertal growth, boys would have 2 additional years for further lateralization of function in their brains. More hemispheric specialization and later maturation are hypothesized to lead to better spatial skills relative to verbal skills; conversely, less specialization and earlier maturation are thought to result in better verbal skills relative to spatial skills. Thus, females would exhibit lower spatial abilities on the average because they mature earlier than males and are therefore less lateralized. Based on this hypothesis, late-maturing females should perform similarly to males on spatial tasks and early-maturing males should perform more similarly to the average female.

Socialization is the third hypothesis for cognitive change in early adolescence.

Hill and Lynch proposed a gender-intensification hypothesis for development that results from "acceleration of gender-differential socialization during adolescence" (Hill and Lynch, 1983, p. 201). Beginning in early adolescence, expectations for conformity to traditional gender roles intensify. For cognitive areas like mathematics and spatial representation, gender difference favoring boys would be expected to emerge at this time as girls comply with social pressure to excel in interpersonal skills and boys comply with pressure to pursue instrumental areas, often academic achievement. Typically, traditionally male careers (e.g., engineer) use spatial and mathematical skills more often than do traditionally female careers (e.g., secretary). Thus, gender-appropriate performance would be encouraged by parents and peers to ensure that the adolescent was prepared for his or her gender-specific adult role.

An Examination of the Data

Cognitive Changes in Early Adolescence

Within the framework of examining specific cognitive changes during adolescence, we present findings from the Adolescent Mental Health Study in which abstract reasoning, verbal skills, and spatial skills were measured longitudinally over sixth, seventh, and eighth grades. The subjects were 253 adolescents randomly drawn from two suburban school districts in the Chicago area (Petersen, 1984).

As previously mentioned, abstract reasoning exhibits an increase over the adolescent years (Inhelder and Piaget, 1958). In our research, formal reasoning was assessed with the Equilibrium in Balance Test, a paper and pencil version of Piaget's Proportional Reasoning Task (see sample item in Figure 3). This test correlates highly with the Piagetian task and follows the same increase in performance over time observed in the Piagetian task (Linn and Swiney, 1981). Because age was closely associated with grade in school for this sample (e.g., the average age in January of sixth grade was 11.6 years, with a standard deviation of 0.3), performance trends were analyzed by grade. Reasoning ability increased linearly from sixth to eighth grade for both boys and girls, with boys scoring significantly higher than girls at each grade (Dubas et al., 1990) (see Figure 4). As can be seen in the figure, the amount of increase is similar for boys and girls.

Other cognitive abilities examined were fluent production and spatial ability measured with the Clerical Speed and Accuracy subtest of the Differential Aptitude Test (DAT; Bennett et al., 1973) and the Space subtest of the Primary Mental Abilities test (PMA; Thurstone and Thurstone, 1941), respectively. The PMA requires mental manipulation of objects. Again, significant linear increases in performance over grades six to eight were found on these tasks for both boys and girls. Gender effect were significant on each as well with a grade by gender

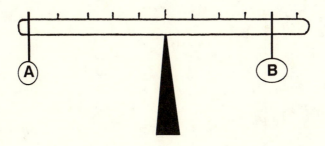

TO MAKE THE BEAM BALANCE, THE WEIGHT

OF A AND B SHOULD BE

a) A = 3 gms. AND B = 4 gms.

b) A = 12 gms. AND B = 15 gms.

c) A = 1 gm. AND B = 5 gms.

d) A = 17 gms. AND B = 17 gms.

Figure 3. A sample item from the Equilibrium in Balance Test.

interaction for AMA space, with girls showing superiority on fluent production all 3 grades and boys on spatial ability in sixth and seventh grades (see Figure 5a and b). No interaction effects were found for the DAT, demonstrating that the amount of change over time was similar for boys and girls.

These results raise two important points. First, there was no evidence for cognitive disruption over early adolescence for these cognitive abilities. Second, the data address the issue of whether gender differences arise in early adolescence. Gender differences were present by sixth grade with parallel developmental trends for boys and girls, except on the PMA, which showed convergence rather than divergence of males' and females' scores. Because ceiling effects on the PMA appeared for boys by eighth grade in this sample, the trend toward convergence may have been an artifact.

As a possible indicator of broader range cognitive change in early adolescence, we also examined grades in school. Figure 6 shows that grades decline from sixth to eighth grades. Although this finding might be construed as consistent with Epstein's hypothesis (1978) of deficits in cognitive processing during early adolescence, the fact that cognitive abilities increase over early adolescence in this sample suggests that neither cognitive ability nor achievement perfor-

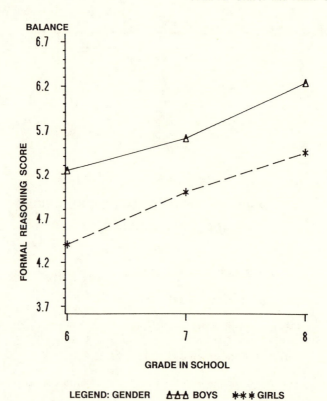

Figure 4. Increases in formal reasoning during early adolescence.

mance declines at this age. Instead, we found evidence that the decline in grades results at least in part from increasingly more difficult grading practices in middle or junior high school, particularly more use of lower grades.

Existence and Emergence of Gender Differences

Since Maccoby and Jacklin (1974) conducted their review of the literature, research on spatial ability, in particular, has flourished. Conclusions that are drawn from any particular sample with any one test may not be generalizable, however. The sample for the Adolescent Mental Health Study, for example, is different from average in that the mean IQ of subjects was 115. To overcome the problems arising from sample variation in the literature, Linn and Petersen (1985) conducted a meta-analysis of spatial data reported since the 1974 Maccoby and Jacklin volume.

Linn and Petersen (1985) analyzed these studies to find homogeneous groups of spatial skills, test whether a reliable gender difference in performance was

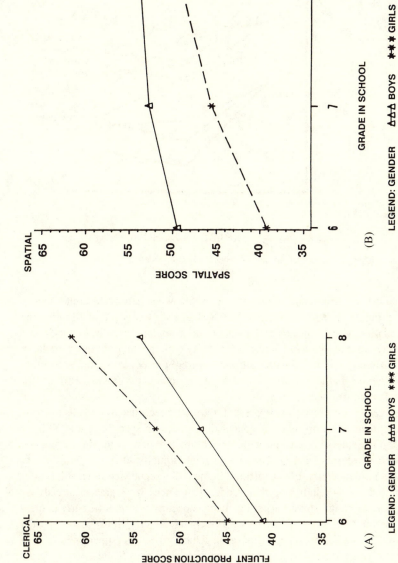

Figure 5a. Changes in fluent production over early adolescence.

Figure 5b. Changes in spatial ability over early adolescence.

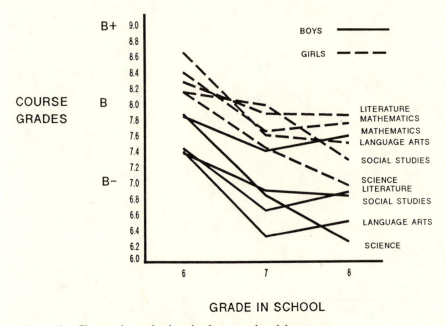

GRADE IN SCHOOL

Figure 6. Changes in grades in school over early adolescence.

observed in each group, and, if present, determine when gender differences arose in each group (Linn and Petersen, 1985). Spatial ability was classified into three areas: spatial perception, mental rotation, and spatial visualization. Gender differences were not uniform across areas. Only with mental rotations were large gender differences found; smaller differences were present for spatial perception tasks. Overall, spatial visualization tasks were apparently equally difficult for both males and females.

When gender differences were present, they were recorded as early as the tests could be given . The presence of gender differences on specific spatial abilities across the life span is consistent with Newcombe's review of the developmental literature (Newcombe, 1982). The lack of longitudinal studies of spatial ability may have influenced these conclusions. In the Adolescent Mental Health Study, the longitudinal data indicated that gender differences were present already by sixth grade, although some intriguing changes occurred during the early adolescence period (Dubas et al., 1990). Block and Block (1982) also reported longitudinal data for spatial perception in which girls were superior in performance at 4 years of age but were surpassed by boys at ages 5 and 7. By 11 years of age, the magnitude of differences in performance favoring males had attained adult levels. This suggests that some process affects performance prior to adolescence rather than during adolescence.

Pubertal Disruption of Cognition?

Epstein's assertions led to the assumption that education of postpubertal individuals would be relatively ineffective (e.g., Toepfer, 1980). This view, however, contrasts sharply with what we know about cognitive development in the early adolescent years. Data from the Berkeley Growth Study (Eichorn and Bayley, 1962) report spurts of growth in mental age (Figure 7). In addition, data on the same subjects indicate that a peak in head circumference growth in coincident with the pubertal growth spurt, with the predictable gender difference in timing of growth (see Figure 7). In contrast, Epstein (1978) does not report a gender difference in timing of growth. In addition, efforts to link head circum-

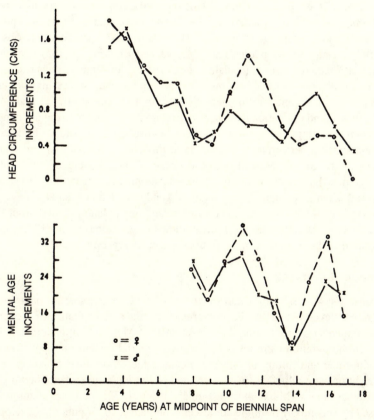

Figure 7. Increases in head circumference and in mental age. From H. T. Epstein, "Growth spurts during brain development: Implications for educational policy and practice." In J. S. Chall and A. F. Mirsky Eds., *Education and the Brain.* Copyright © 1978. Reprinted with permission of NSSE.

ference to measures of intelligence have yielded negative results (McCall et al., 1977).

Subsequent studies (Crey and Diamond, 1980; Carey et al, 1980) noted that investigating general cognition may be ineffective; instead, specific cognitive abilities may parallel physical growth patterns of spurts and plateaus. In their studies, Carey and Diamond (1980) focused on the development of the ability to recognize unfamiliar faces. Children showed an increase in ability to recognize unfamiliar faces from ages 6 to 10 but exhibited a decline in performance at ages 12 and 14, with recovery at age 16. These researchers proposed that pubertal maturation disrupted encoding of facial stimuli and compared performance among prepubescent and pubescent adolescents. Their results confirmed the hypothesis that puberty had a disruptive effect on face encoding.

Whereas other research (Flin, 1980) replicated this finding, for this specific task only, Merola and Liederman (1985) suggested that pubertal disruption of cognition may explain developmental changes in task processing they observed in children and young adolescents. Merola and Liderman (1985) investigated interhemisphere functional insulation and its effects on simultaneous task performance. With age, children become better at simultaneous processing and on task processed in different cerebral hemispheres. In a sample of 10, 12, and 14 year olds, they found dramatic differences between 10 year olds who did not benefit at all from targeting the tasks to different hemispheres and older children who demonstrated a performance advantage in this condition. Although no pubertal effects were found, Merola and Liederman (1985) concluded that pubertal change may have been involved in this developmental transition. However, if pubertal change explained the data, a gender difference should have been observed, with boys making this transition later due to later pubertal onset. What was observed is congruent with other studies (e.g., Dubas et al., 1990); that is, cognitive abilities showed a continuous linear increase over early adolescence.

Pubertal Effects

Since the Waber studies and other work, the role of pubertal maturation on cognitive development has been examined in areas other than face recognition and hemispheric processing. In the Adolescent Mental Health Study, pubertal effects on cognition were measured on two pubertal dimensions, pubertal status within grade and timing of puberty. Because the school districts either refused outright or were reluctant to allow trained pediatricians to make pubertal ratings of Tanner stages (Marshall and Tanner, 1969, 1970), pubertal status was assessed by self-report from the adolescents on their level of pubertal development on several dimensions (Peterson, et al., 1988). Based on these self-reports, subjects were classified as prepubertal, beginning pubertal, mid-pubertal, advanced pubertal, and postpubertal at the time of each interview. Pubertal development followed the expected trend on this measure; pubertal status increases over sixth, seventh, and eighth grades with both boys and girls more likely to be classified in more mature categories by eighth grade (Table 1). Table 1 also depicts the expected gender difference in timing of maturation with girls developing earlier than boys. Based on this cross-sectional grouping over sixth, seventh, and eighth grades, the highest percentage of boys shift from early to mid-pubertal status while the highest percentage of girls shift from mid- to late pubertal status (Crockett and Petersen, 1987). The entire pubertal process is difficult to track due to variations and asynchronies in timing and rate of development; furthermore, it would take 10 years to follow an entire birth cohort through puberty (Eichorn, 1975).

Timing of maturation was estimated by age at peak height velocity in the adolescent growth spurt. In one of the school districts, growth data were collected every year by the school nurse; these data produced comparable results to those on self-reported height, obtained every 6 months from all subjects (Petersen and Crockett, 1985). Age at peak height velocity was estimated from height data using a function derived from major national growth studies (Bock et al., 1973). From the growth spurt estimation, subjects were classified as early, on-time, and late compared to their same-sex peers.

Cognitive measures were, again, the Space subtest of the PMA, the Clerical Speed and Accuracy subtest of the DAT, and Equilibrium in a Balance. Pubertal

Table 1.   Frequency Distributions of Boys and Girls across Pubertal Categories[a]

	Grade–Season				
Category	6 Spring (%)	7 Fall (%)	7 Spring (%)	8 Fall (%)	8 Spring (%)
Boys					
1 = prepubertal	17	11	11	3	2
2 = early pubertal	60	51	44	35	13
3 = mid pubertal	23	36	38	49	57
4 = late pubertal	0	2	7	13	27
5 = post pubertal	0	0	0	1	1
M(SD)	2.06(.64)	2.29(.69)	2.41(.77)	2.74(.75)	3.12(.71)
Girls					
1 = prepubertal	5	9	3	1	0
2 = early pubertal	16	7	5	2	0
3 = mid pubertal	58	60	54	35	25
4 = late pubertal	18	21	29	43	45
5 = post pubertal	4	3	9	19	30
M(SD)	2.89(.83)	3.03(.88)	3.36(.83)	3.76(.81)	4.05(.74)

[a] Data for sixth-grade spring and seventh-grade fall are from Cohort II only ($n = 113$); otherwise, the two cohorts were pooled ($n = 240$). Adapted from Crockett and Petersen (1987).

status within grade revealed no multivariate effect on cognition. A subsample of boys and girls were matched on their age at peak height velocity in order to see if timing of maturation mediated gender differences. Previously significant gender differences for equilibrium in balance were no longer significant. Gender differences on the DAT were somewhat reduced and only significant at sixth and eighth grades. Gender differences for the PMA were still significant at sixth and seventh grades (Dubas et al., 1990). Timing of maturation did have a moderated effect on cognitive performance.

We also related pubertal status and timing of pubertal maturation to grades in school (Crockett and Petersen, 1987; Petersen and Crockett, 1985), another indicator of cognitive performance. When grades in school were examined in relation to pubertal timing, no multivariate effect was found. The only univariate effect was for grades in literature class, with early maturers receiving higher grades than on-time and later maturers. In looking at effects across courses, it was interesting that social studies and science grades do show the same pattern but were not statistically significant. (see Figure 8). Oddly, all of the other timing-of-maturation results considered in our sample (for noncognitive measures) found earlier maturers doing worse than their peers; in this case, early

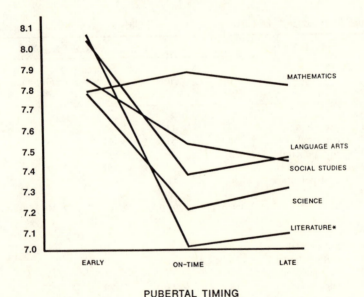

MEAN GRADES

PUBERTAL TIMING

NOTE: STARRED (*) COURSES SHOW SIGNIFICANT EFFECTS

Figure 8.   The effects of pubertal timing on course grades. Starred courses shows significant effects.

maturers received better grades. One hypothesis for this result is that teachers' grading is influenced by appearance and maturation. Other researchers (Duke et al., 1982) reported similar results form the National Health Examination Survey, a nationally representative sample. They found that earlier maturers did better on achievement tests but the effect occurred before the children were pubertal as well as later. Newcombe and Dubas (1987), in a meta-analysis of timing of maturation effects on cognitive abilities, obtained consistent support for the hypothesis that early maturers have a small advantage in IQ over late maturers. Possibly, this is a factor in the two aforementioned results.

Waber (1976, 1977) found that within sex, later maturers had higher spatial scores than earlier maturers; but no effect of pubertal timing was noted on verbal ability. She also found that late-maturing girls fit the spatial pattern more typical of boys. Although timing of maturation but not pubertal status was found to influence some cognitive measures in the Adolescent Mental Health Study (Crockett and Petersen, 1987; Dubas et al., 1990; Petersen and Crockett, 1985), a summary of the relevant literature illustrates the inconsistency of results on this topic. Linn and Petersen (1985) noted that timing of maturation does not explain gender differences in spatial ability. However, timing of maturation has been investigated to determine whether it has any influence on spatial ability.

Success in replicating Waber's original hypothesis (1976, 1977) has been mixed. Petersen (1976) found no significant association between timing of maturation and spatial performance in longitudinal data obtained at 13, 16, and 18 years of age. In fact, five of six correlations were negative. However, subsequent studies have replicated Waber's findings of a maturational effect on cognitive performance (Carey and Diamond, 1980; Newcombe and Bandura, 1983). In most cases, investigators have reported only a small effect.

Meta-analysis of timing of maturation effects on spatial ability suggested a small effect was possible, particularly on tasks that required disembedding (Newcombe and Dubas, 1987). One explanation for the inconsistency of results may be sampling strategy. Waber (1977) selected subjects from extreme maturational groups. Herbst and Petersen (1980) replicated her results with subjects who were differentiated into extreme groups based on spatial ability. This oversampling of the tails of the distributions has the effect of emphasizing an association, if one exists. In samples that were normally distributed for spatial ability or timing of maturation, as was the case in most studies, the effect was too weak to emerge.

Even studies that sampled from extreme groups have not uniformly replicated Waber's hypothesis. Rovet (1983) examined verbal and spatial skills and IQ in children with idiopathic precocious puberty, adolescents with clinically delayed puberty, and controls matched for age, sex, and IQ. With the exception of spatial ability in precocious females and verbal skills in delayed pubertal males, all comparisons revealed poorer performance by off-time pubertal groups than controls. However, other research (Meyer-Bahlburg, et al., 1985) did find subjects with idiopathic precocious puberty to have lower spatial skills than matched controls. In this study, in contrast to Rovet's sample, all subjects were postpubertal at the time of testing.

Subsequently, Waber et al. (1985) found that maturation rate was related to gender differences in cognitive process tasks, or those processes underlying cognitive skills (e.g., selective attention), but not in the actual cognitive ability tests. These results indicated that not only is the effect slight and difficult to encounter unless sampling from extremes but also shows, in concurrence with Newcombe and Dubas (1987), that the effect is dependent on the nature of the task and possibly on the strategies employed in task solution.

In summary, pubertal effects on cognition were not found in many studies. Puberty did not have a disruptive effect on cognitive abilities, but rather most cognitive abilities exhibited a linear increase over early adolescence. In addition, pubertal timing did not explain gender differences in performance on spatial tasks because gender differences were present as early as the tasks could be measured in the cases where they were present at all. Because pubertal effects were demonstrated in some cases and because these cases occurred in limited but replicable circumstances, the effect is probably small and accounts for some of the variance but is not the dominant factor influencing gender differences in cognitive skills.

Experiential Effects on Cognition

A clear factor in success on cognitive tasks is experience. It has been proposed that experience leading to skill development is influenced by gender-role stereotypes and expectations (Newcombe, et al., 1983; Tobin-Richards and Petersen, 1981). Although adolescence has been proposed as a time when sex-role stereotyping increases (Hill and Lynch, 1983), sex-role typing of behaviors such as toy choice (Connor and Serbin, 1977; Serbin and Connor, 1979) has been demonstrated from very early ages (see Huston, 1983, 1985; and Fagot, 1985, for reviews of this area).

Figure 9 compares the effect sizes for several constructs showing sex differences in adolescence. Gender differences on the masculinity scale of the Bem Sex-Role Inventory (Bem, 1979) are smaller than expected in adolescence. Gender differences on femininity show larger changes over adolescence. In a different research project focused on cognitive performance, experience effects on gender differences were examined (Peterson and Gitelson, unpublished data). When sex-typing was considered as a causal mechanism for course performance, only 0.6 of a standard deviation effect was associated with gender differences (Tobin-Richards and Petersen, 1981). A much larger effect, though, occurred for preferred activities of the adolescent. Although boys and girls engaged in some similar activities, many activities were clearly preferred by boys or by girls but not by both boys and girls. One inference from this study was that cognitive

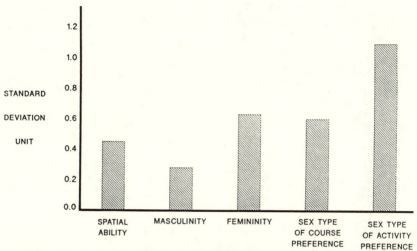

Figure 9. Effect sizes of several aspects of sex differences.

skills were channeled into activities that were gender appropriate; for example, girls who were good spatial visualizers frequently selected activities such as art or fashion design, which they considered acceptable for females, rather than engineering or other activities, which they sex-typed as male (Petersen and Gitelson, unpublished data).

A study using data from the Adolescent Mental Health Study, described earlier, investigated athletic experience effects on spatial ability in early adolescence (Richards, 1980). Boys and girls do not participate equally in the same sports. Hypothetically, if an athletic activity involves field play, it facilitates spatial development. Characteristic activities would be having to throw an object through space (e.g., a ball) to a particular point or player while monitoring where several players are on the field. Coaches rated adolescents on the kinds of skills demonstrated during field play and subjects were tested on spatial visualization skills. Richards (1980) reported an effect on spatial skills for boys but not for girls (see Figure 10). Basically, girls were less likely to engage in this type of activity, thus coaches had difficulty rating their performance. A confound of the effect for boys was clear. It was impossible to determine whether boys with good spatial visualization skills were better athletes due to spatial ability or whether athletic experience helped to develop better spatial skills.

Certainly, a substantive body of literature has demonstrated that spatial skills improve with practice (Connor et al., 1978; Goldstein and Chance, 1965; Kato, 1965; Vandenberg, 1975). Given clear gender-differentiated preferences in activities leading to different experiences, socialization patterns rather than sex per se would be more influential in explaining cognitive gender differences. We are

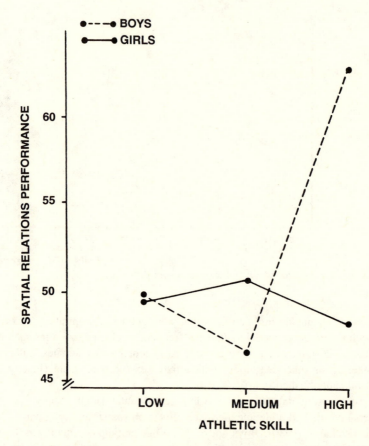

Figure 10.   Athletic skill and spatial performance. From Petersen, A. C. Sex differences
in performance on spatial tasks: Biopyschosocial influences. In A. Ansara, N.
Geschwind, A. Galburda, M. Albert, and N. Gartrell (Eds.), *Sex Differences in
Dyslexia.* Copyright © 1979. The Orton Dyslexia Society. Reprinted with permission.

not asserting that socialization is the sole determinant of gender-differential
behavior. For example, prenatal hormones, which play an organizational role in
brain development, have been linked to sexually differential behavior in primates
(Young et al, 1964). Possibly, the socialization of experiences to gender-
appropriate domains interacts with prenatal-hormone-based differences in the
brain to produce the gender differences reported in the literature (Linn and
Petersen, 1985, 1986).

A Model of the Development
of Individual Differences in Cognition

Prior research results have led us to propose that cognitive performance is influenced by two sources: biological propensities and experience. Biological propensities surely have a genetic basis (see Plomin and Ho, this volume) and are manifested through such aspects of biological development as brain development, endocrine change, and overall physical growth. The extent of growth, the timing of spurts, and overall rates of change are likely to be important components of any aspect of biological development.

Experience is the term used to convey not only formal learning but all experience that could affect brain development, and therefore cognitive development. Experience includes the variety of activity in which the developing individual engages, from exercise and play to interactional and emotional experiences. From this perspective, nutrition, for example, also plays an experiential role because it results in different nutrients reaching the developing brain. Evidence of gender-differential experience indicates that boys more than girls prefer foods that were shown to enhance neurotransmitters concentrated in sensorimotor areas of the primate brain (Lewis et al., 1986). This enhanced neural activity may facilitate other types of experiences.

We propose that the individual's biological potentials are differentially developed by the variety of experiences encountered from conception onward. Thus, an individual with such biological potential who encounters enhancing experiences could develop to full potential. The same individual biologically could also experience depriving situations and fail to develop fully. Conversely, one with more limited biological endowment could exceed the richly endowed but experientially deprived individual, if he or she developed in a context of enhancing experiences. As will be seen in the next section, maximal plasticity exists prior to the completion of puberty, and some brain growth continues throughout life. This provides a framework in which the biological development of boys and girls could influence and be influenced by gender differential experiences resulting in differences in cognitive skills between boys and girls.

A Brief Overview of Neurological Development

Although it has been established that the human brain doubles in mass over the first 2–3 years of life, some disagreements have arisen as to the extent of later development and, in particular, of cortical development after age 5 (Feinberg, 1987; Yakovlev and Lecours, 1967). Myelination, which provides for rapid neural transmission, continues at least to puberty. Some evidence indicates that it continues into the seventh and eighth decades of life (Yakovlev and Lecours, 1967). More recently, Feinberg (1987) has synthesized several areas of research to provide a picture of neural changes in the second decade of life. Feinberg (1987) noted that the developmental decline in cerebral oxygen consumption (Chugani et al., 1988) was coincident with the decline in synaptic density (Huttenlocher, 1979), with both exhibiting the steepest declines between 10 and 15 years of age. Overproduction of neuronal pathways occurs by 5 years of age and is maintained usually until age 10. The subsequent decline in neural pathways appears to be a fine tuning of the neurological system. As previously noted, formal operational thought is coincident with this fine tuning of the cerebral cortex in early adolescence. [See Gibson (this volume) for more information on neurological development.]

Thatcher et al. (1987) documented developmental changes in neural activity patterns that mirror Piagetian cognitive changes. They examined electroencephalography (EEG) coherence and phase measures in 577 children and adolescents with normal neurological histories. Differences in head size and IQ were controlled and comparisons were made for 17 successive 1-year age groups. Results indicated differential patterns of development for different cerebral lobes within the left and right cerebral hemispheres. Cerebral activity from birth to 3 years was scattered and similar for both hemispheres. Frontal–occipital connections achieved 90% of adult activity by 5 years of age in the left hemisphere, while change in the right hemisphere occurred more slowly. A similar pattern was true for the left and right temporal–frontal regions, with temporal–frontal connections reaching 90% of adult level of activity by age 5 in the left hemisphere and age 9 in the right hemisphere. Subsequent bilateral changes during adolescence were noted for the frontal region in particular. Whether these variations are biologically or experientially limited is unclear.

Thatcher et al. (1987) suggested that these changes were patterned similarly to Piaget's stage theory of development but say little about this theory. However, such changes clearly fit the established literature. Hahn (1987), in a review of the literature on the development of cerebral specialization, reported that linguistic functions are localized in the left hemisphere as early as can be tested. The marked changes in left temporal and frontal lobe activity around the age of 5 are congruent with the literature on language development and with the "5-to-7 shift" period of cognitive development (White, 1970).

The link in the literature between the right hemisphere and spatial processing (Harris, 1978) makes the differential developmental findings particularly intriguing in the area of development of spatial ability. Unfortunately, there is no indication that the data of Thatcher et al. were analyzed by gender. Given the literature on gender differences in spatial skills reviewed earlier, either a confirmatory or null finding of a gender difference in development or timing of development of adult level of activity in the right hemisphere would have been informative. As yet, the development of processing specialization of cognitive tasks in the right hemisphere is not well understood and appears to be task dependent (Hahn, 1987). A gender difference in development could be hypothesized given the aforementioned results by Block and Block (1982) that a significant gender difference on spatial tasks was not present at ages 5 and 7, prior to completed development of temporal and frontal lobe activity patterns, but was found by age 11, after adult activity level was attained.

The substantial evidence that neurological development continues at least until puberty indicates that plasticity in development may also occur until this time. Thus, neurological development may be strongly influenced by experiential factors and these factors may exert differential influence on certain subsets of individuals, for example, boys versus girls.

Experiential Interactions with Neurological Development

Substantial evidence suggests experiential influences on neural transmission and pathways (M. C. Diamond, this volume; Hubel and Weisel, 1970; Volkmar and Greenough, 1972). Recently, Greenough et al. (1987) proposed two types of neural pathway development, each depending on different categories of behaviors: (1) experience-expectant behaviors for which pathways are overproduced for behaviors where the species has at least some preprogramming for that path to develop, provided the necessary environmental stimulation occurs (e.g., pattern recognition), and (2) experience-dependent behaviors for which preprogramming has not occurred and new connections are formed in response to events (e.g., the development of higher cognitive skills). Indications that neurological changes could be produced in mature animals (i.e., rhesus monkeys) by social factors (Reite, 1987) broadened the scope of experiential influences and disputed the proposal of critical periods for neurological influence.

This type of research strengthens our model as it establishes possible mechanisms for experiential influences on the brain that could produce gender differences in cognition. An alternative hypothesis that anatomical differences would explain differences in cognitive performance is not well supported, as anatomical differences in the brain are found predominately in areas associated with sexual behavior rather than cognitive processing (Goy and McEwen, 1980; Swaab and Fliers, 1985). Corpus callosum differences have been proposed (de Lacoste-Utamsing and Holloway, 1982) but later research questioned the reliability of earlier data and reported contradicting results (Bleier et al., 1986; Witelson, 1985).

Conclusion

Biological influences on experience have been well documented. However, the reverse effect has not been considered as frequently, although there are some very notable exceptions (e.g., M. C. Diamond, this volume; Greenough et al.,

1987). Recent advancements as well as interdisciplinary collaboration have increased our understanding of the interaction of biological and experiential development and of the range of variations in individual development that is possible. The available evidence from neuropsychological research supports the concept of plasticity in most aspects of brain development, at least through puberty. This means that experience is likely to have a major impact on developing youngsters through this period.

Given that significant changes occur in cognitive functioning, physical development, and social experience during adolescence, the early adolescence years exemplify a period when differential physical and social development could lead to multiple cognitive outcomes. It is important to emphasize that overall cognitive functioning increases for adolescents. Single abilities or constellations of skills are more susceptible to specific biological and/or experiential influences than other abilities; for example, spatial skills are more susceptible than verbal skills. The literature is replete with evidence for differential experience, especially for boys and girls. This different experience could shape brain development, and then cognitive development in ways resulting in tremendous individual variability, with some effect for specific characteristics such as gender. Research examining the interaction between experience and neurological development is important for identifying which experiences may be most salient for understanding the development of individual differences occurring in some areas of cognition.

Acknowledgments

Some research described herein was supported by Grant MH 30252/38142 to A. Petersen from the National Institute of Mental Health; research supported by the Spencer Foundation is also mentioned. We thank Judith Dubas for her comments.

References

Baltes, P. B. (1987). Theoretical proposition of life-span developmental psychology: On the dynamics between growth and decline. *Developmental Psychology, 23,* 611–626.

Bem, S. L. (1974). The measurement of psychological androgyny. *Journal of Consulting and Clinical Psychology, 42,* 155–162.

Bennett, G. K., Seashore, A. C., and Wesman, A. G. (1973). *The differential aptitude test* (forms S, T.). New York: The Psychological Corporation.

Bleier, R., Houston, L., and Byne, W. (1986). Can the corpus callosum predict gender, age, handedness, or cognitive differences? *Trends in Neuroscience, 9,* 391–394.

Block, J., and Block, J. (1982). *Cognitive development from childhood to adolescence.* NIMH research grant MH16080. Manuscript.

Bock, R. D., Wainer, H., Petersen, A. C., Thissen, D., Murray, J.S., and Roche, A., (1973). A parametrization of human growth curves. *Human Biology, 45,* 63–80.

Brooks-Gunn, J., and Petersen, A. C. (Eds.), (1983). *Girls at puberty: Biological and psychosocial perspectives.* New York: Plenum.

Brooks-Gunn, J., and Reiter, E. O. (1990). The role of pubertal processes in the early adolescent transition. In S. Feldman and G. Elliot (Eds.) *At the threshold: The developing adolescent,* (pp. 16–33). Cambridge, MA: Harvard University Press.

Brooks-Gunn, J., Petersen, A. C., and Eichorn, D. (1985). The study of maturational timing effects in adolescence. *Journal of Youth and Adolescence, 14,* 149–161.

Carey, S., and Diamond, R. (1980). Maturational determination of the developmental course of face encoding. In D. Caplan (Ed.), *Biological studies of mental processes* (pp. 60–73). Cambridge, MA: MIT Press.

Carey, S., Diamond, R., and Woods, B. (1980). Development of face recognition— maturational component? *Developmental Psychology, 16,* 257–269.

Chugani, H. T., Phelps, M. E., and Mazziotta, J. C. (1988). Metabolic brain changes in adolescence—one aspect of a global reorganization. *Annals of Neurology, 24,* 465.

Connor, J. M., and Serbin, L. A. (1977). Behaviorally based masculine- and feminine-activity-preference scales for preschoolers: Correlates with other classroom behaviors and cognitive tests. *Child Development, 48,* 1411–1416.

Connor, J. M., Schackman, M., and Serbin, L. A. (1978). Sex-related differences in response to practice on a visual-spatial test and generalization to a related test. *Child Development, 49,* 24–29.

Crockett, L. J. and Petersen, A. C. (1987). Pubertal status and psychosocial development: Findings from the Early Adolescence Study. In R. M. Lerner and T. T. Foch (Eds.), *Biological-psychosocial interactions in early adolescence* (pp. 173–188) Hillsdale, NJ: Erlbaum.

Dubas, J. S., Crockett, L. J., and Petersen, A. C. (1990). *Cognition during early adolescence.* Submitted.

Duke, P., Carlsmith, J., Gross, R., Martin, J. and Dornbusch, S. (1982). Educational correlates at early and late sexual maturation during adolescence. *Journal of Pediatrics, 100,* 633–637.

Dulit, E. (1972), Adolescent thinking a la Piaget: The formal stage. *Journal of Youth and Adolescence, 1,* 281–301.

Eichorn, D. H. (1975). Asynchronizations in adolescent development. In J. E. Dragastin and G. H. Elder, Jr. (Eds.) *Adolescence in the life cycle: Psychological change and social context* (pp. 81–96). Washington, D.C.: Hemisphere.

Eichorn, D. H., and Bayley, N. (1962). Growth in head circumference from birth through young adulthood. *Child Development, 33,* 257–271.

Epstein, H. T. (1978). Growth spurts during brain development: Implications for educational policy and practice. In J. S. Chall and A. F. Mirsky (Eds.), *Education and the brain* (pp. 345–370). Chicago: Society for the Study of Education.

Fagot, B. I. (1985). Changes in thinking about early sex role development. *Developmental Review, 5,* 85–93.

Feinberg, J. (1987). Adolescence and mental illness [Letter]. *Science, 236,* 507–508.

Flin, R. H. (1980). Age effects in children's memory for unfamiliar faces. *Developmental Psychology, 16,* 373–374.

Goldstein, P., and Chance, J. (1965). Effects of practice on sex-related differences in performance on embedded figures. *Psychonomic Science, 3,* 361–362.

Goy, R. W. and McEwen, B. S. (1980). *Sexual differentiation of the brain.* Cambridge, MA: MIT Press.

Greenough, W. T., Black, J. E. and Wallace, C. S. (1987). Experience in brain development. *Child Development, 58,* 539–559.

Hahn, W. K. (1987). Cerebral lateralization of function: From infancy through childhood. *Psychological Bulletin, 101,* 376–392.

Harris, L. J. (1978). Sex differences in spatial ability; possible environmental, genetic, and neurological factors. In M. Kinsbourne (Ed.), *Asymetrical function of the brain.* (pp. 405–522). Cambridge: Cambridge University Press.

Herbst, L., and Petersen, A. C. (1980). Timing of maturation, brain lateralization and cognitive performance. Paper presented at the meeting of the American Psychological Association, Montreal, September.

Hill, J. P., and Lynch, M. E. (1983). The intensification of gender-related role expectations during early adolescence. In J. Brooks-Gunn and A. C. Petersen (Eds.) *Girls at puberty: Biological and psychosocial perspectives,* (pp. 201–228). New York: Plenum.

Hubel, D., and Wiesel, T. (1970). The period of susceptibility to the physiological effects of unilateral eye closure in kittens. *Journal of Physiology, 206,* 419–436.

Huston, A. C. (1983). Sex-typing. In E. M. Hetherington (Eds.), *Handbook of child psychology,* Vol. IV. New York: Wiley.

Huston, A. C. (1985). The development of sex-typing: Themes from recent research. *Developmental Review, 5,* 1–17.

Huttenlocher, P. R. (1979). Synaptic density in human frontal cortex—developmental changes and effects of aging. *Brain Research, 163,* 195–205.

Inhelder, B., and Piaget, J. (1958). *The growth of logical thinking from childhood to adolescence.* New York: Basic Books.

Kato, N. (1965). A fundamental study of rod-frame test. *Japanese Psychological Research, 7,* 61–68.

Kestenberg, J. (1968). Phase of adolescence with suggestions for correlation of psychic and hormonal organizations. Part III. *Journal of the American Academy of Child Psychiatry, 6,* 577–614.

LaCoste-Utamsing, C. de, and Holloway, R. L. (1982). Sexual dimorphism in the human corpus callosum. *Science, 216,* 1431–1432.

Lewis, D. A., Campbell, M. J., Foote, S. L., and Morrison, J. H. (1986). The monoaminergic enervation of the primate neo-cortex. *Human Neurobiology, 5,* 181–188.

Linn, M. C. and Petersen, A. C. (1985). Emergence and characterization of sex differences in spatial ability: A meta-analysis. *Child Development, 56,* 1479–1498.

Linn, M. C. and Petersen, A. C. (1986). A meta-analysis of gender differences in spatial ability: Implications for Mathematics and Science achievement. In J. S. Hyde and M. C. Linn (Eds.), *The psychology of gender* (pp. 67–101). Baltimore: Johns Hopkins University Press.

Linn, M. C., and Swiney, J. (1981). Individual differences in formal thought: Role of expectations and aptitudes. *Journal of Educational Psychology, 73,* 274–286.

Maccoby, E. E., and Jacklin, C. N. (1974). *The psychology of sex differences.* Stanford, CA: Stanford University Press.

Marshall, W. A., and Tanner, J. M. (1969). Variations in the pattern of pubertal changes in girls. *Archives of Disease in Childhood., 44,* 291–303.

Marshall, W. A., and Tanner, J. M. (1970). Variation in the pattern of pubertal changes in boys. *Archives of Disease in Childhood, 45,* 13–23.

McCall, R. B., Eichorn, D. H., and Hogarty, P. S. (1977). Transitions in early mental development. *Monographs of the Society for Research in Child Development, 42* (3, Serial No. 171).

Merola, J. L., and Liederman, J. (1985). Developmental changes in hemispheric independence. *Child Development, 56,* 1184–1194.

Meyer-Bahlburg, H. F. L., Bruder, G. E., Feldman, J. F., Ehrhardt, A. A., Healey, J. M., and Bell, J. (1985). Cognitive abilities and hemispheric lateralization in females following idiopathic precocious puberty. *Developmental Psychology, 21,* 878–887.

Newcombe, N. (1982). Sex-related differences in spatial ability: Problems and gaps in current approaches. In M. Potegal (Ed.), *Spatial abilities: Development and physiological foundations* (pp. 223–250). New York: Academic Press.

Newcombe, N., and Bandura, M. M. (1983). Effect of age at puberty on spatial ability in girls: A question of mechanism. *Developmental Psychology, 19,* 215–224.

Newcombe, N., and Dubas, J. S. (1987). Individual differences in cognitive ability: Are they related to timing of puberty? In R. M. Lerner and T. T. Foch (Eds.), *Biological-psychosocial interactions in early adolescence* (pp. 249–302). Hillsdale, NJ: Erlbaum.

Newcombe, N., Bandura, M. M. and Taylor, D. G. (1983). Sex differences in spatial ability and spatial activities. *Sex Roles, 9,* 377–386.

Petersen, A. C. (1976). Physical androgyny and cognitive functioning in adolescence. *Developmental Psychology, 12,* 524–533.

Petersen, A. C. (1979). Differential cognitive functioning in adolescent girls. In M. Sugar (Ed.) *Female Adolescent Development* (pp. 47–59). New York; Brunner/Mazel.

Petersen, A. C. (1980). Biopsychosocial processes in the development of sex-related differences. In J. E. Parsons (Ed.), *The psychobiology of sex differences and sex roles* (pp. 31–55). Washington, D.C.: Hemisphere.

Petersen, A. C. (1981). Sex differences in performance on spatial tasks. Biopsychosocial influences. In A. Ansara, N. Geschwind, A. Galaburda, M. Albert, and N. Gartrell (Eds.), *Sex Differences in Dyslexia* (pp. 41–54). Towson, MD: The Orton Dyslexia Society.

Petersen, A. C. (1984). The early adolescence study: An overview. *Journal of Early adolescence, 4,* 103–106.

Petersen, A. C. (1987). The nature of biological-psychosocial interactions: The sample case of early adolescence. In R. M. Lerner and T. T. Foch (Eds.), *Biological psychosocial interactions in early adolescence* (pp. 35–61). Hillsdale, NJ: Erlbaum.

Petersen, A. C., and Crockett, L. J. (1985). Pubertal timing and grade effects on adjustment. *Journal of Youth and Adolescence, 14,* 191–206.

Petersen, A. C., and Gitelson, I. B. Toward understanding sex-related differences in cognitive performance. Unpublished data.

Petersen, A. C., and Wittig, M. A. (1979). Sex-related differences in cognitive function-
    ing: An overview. In M. A. Wittig and A. C. Petersen (Eds.), *Sex-related differ-
    ences in cognitive functioning* (pp. 1–17). New York: Academic Press.
Petersen, A. C., Crockett, L., Richard, M. H., and Boxer, A. M. (1988). A self-report
    measure of pubertal status: Reliability, validity, and initial norms. *Journal of Youth
    and Adolescence, 17,* 117–113.
Piaget, J. (1972). Intellectual evolution from adolescence to adulthood. *Human Develop-
    ment, 15,* 1–12.
Reite, M. (1987). Commentary - some additional influences shaping the development of
    behavior. *Child Development, 58,* 596–600.
Richards, M. H. (1980). The relation of athletic activity to spatial ability in early
    adolescence. In A. Petersen (Chair), *Early adolescence: Biopyschosocial perspec-
    tives.* Symposium conducted at the annual meeting of the American Educational
    Research Association, Boston, April.
Rovet, J. (1983). Cognitive and neuropsychological test performance of persons with
    abnormalities of adolescent development: A test of Waber's hypothesis. *Child
    Development, 54,* 941–950.
Serbin, L. A., and Connor, J. M. (1979). Sex-typing of children's play preferences and
    patterns of cognitive performance. *Journal of Genetic Psychology, 134,* 315–316.
Swaab, D. F., and Fliers, E. (1985). A sexually dimorphic nucleus in the human brain.
    Science, 228, 1112–1115.
Thatcher, R. W., Walker, R. A., and Guidice, S. (1987). Human cerebral hemispheres
    develop at different rates and ages. *Science, 236,* 1110–1113.
Thurstone, L. L., and Thurstone, T. G. (1941). *The primary mental abilities tests.*
    Chicago: Science Research Associates.
Tobin-Richards, M., and Petersen, A. C. (1981). *Spatial and sex-appropriate activities.*
    Presented at the annual meeting of the American Psychological Association, Los
    Angeles, August.
Toepfer, C. F. (1976). The process of the middle school. Paper presented at the annual
    conference of the National Middle School Association in St. Louis, November.
Toepfer, C. F. (1980). Brain growth periodization in young adolescents: Some education
    implications. Paper presented at the annual meeting of the American Education
    Research Association, Boston, April.
Tomlinson-Keasey, C. (1972). Formal operations in females from eleven to fifty-four
    years of age. *Developmental Psychology, 6,* 364.
Vandenberg, S. G. (1975). Sources of variance in performance of spatial tests. In J. Eliot
    and N. J. Salkind (Eds.), *Children's spatial development* (pp 57–62). Springfield,
    IL: Thomas.
Volkmar, F. R., and Greenough, W. T. (1972). Rearing complexity affects branching of
    dendrites in the visual cortex. *Science, 176,* 1445–1447.
Waber, D. P. (1976). Sex differences in cognition: A function of Maturation rate?
    Science, 192, 572–574.
Waber, D. P. (1977). Sex differences in mental abilities, hemisphere lateralization, and
    rate of physical growth at adolescence. *Developmental Psychology, 13,* 29–38.
Waber, D. P., Mann, M. B., Merola, J., and Moylan, P. M. (1985). Physical maturation
    rate and cognitive performance in early adolescence: A longitudinal examination.
    Developmental Psychology, 21, 666–681.

White, S. (1976). Some general outlines of the matrix of developmental changes between five and seven years. *Bulletin of the Orton Society, 20,* 41–57.

Witelson, S. F. (1985). The brain connection: The corpus collosum is larger in left-handers. *Science, 229,* 665–668.

Wittig, M. A., and Petersen, A. C. (1979). *Sex-related differences in cognitive functioning.* New York: Academic Press.

Yakovlev, P. I., and Lecours, A. R. (1967). The myelogenetic cycles of regional maturation in the brain. In A. Minkowski (Ed.), *Regional development of the brain in early life* (pp. 3–70). Oxford: Blackwell.

Young, W. C., Goy, R. W. and Phoenix, C. H. (1964). Hormones and sexual behavior. *Science, 143,* 212–218.

Chapter 11

Assessment of Brain Functioning in Individuals at Biosocial Risk: Examples from Alcoholic Families

Jeannette L. Johnson, Jon E. Rolf, and James L. Rebeta

Introduction

The study of biosocial risk is dominated by research and theory on the relationship between the brain and behavior. Some of the dimensions of this relationship include how the brain regulates behavior, the consequences of our actions after this regulation, physiological influences on behavior (such as hormonal level), or cortical changes associated with maturation. Complete knowledge of the complex biological and social patterns of brain–behavior developmental relationships is presently not possible. What is achievable, however, is an outline of some of these patterns and how brain–behavior relationships are assessed.

Studying individuals at biosocial risk allows us to address the transactional relationships between the brain and behavior. Biosocial risk, in this case, pertains to the influences in the environment, which may operate through biological processes in etiology or pathogenesis (e.g., prenatal stress, diet, obstetrical complications, or other factors such as alcohol abuse). Thus, children and adults at biosocial risk provide an important focus for assessing brain–behavior relationships because they are at risk due to both genetic and environmental factors.

Individuals whose family history is positive for alcoholism are well suited for study of biosocial risk, because an understanding of the etiology and transmission of alcoholism requires both biomedical and behavioral research approaches. Studies of alcoholics might also provide paradigms for understanding many other problems requiring a multidisciplinary approach (Hamburg and Nightingale, 1987).

Offspring of alcoholics can be considered at biosocial risk because both biological and social factors place them at risk for alcoholism and other problems. Studies of children of alcoholics support the contention that they are more likely to develop alcoholism themselves and/or a range of other serious behavior disorders when they are compared to the offspring of nonalcoholics (Beardslee et al., 1986; Knop et al., 1985).

Genetic hypotheses concerning alcoholism have been advanced based on adoption, twin, and familial studies. These have reported that some offspring of alcoholics are at a significantly increased risk for becoming alcoholic themselves (Goodwin, 1971). From an environmental perspective, however, children of alcoholics can also be considered at high risk for alcoholism because families share experiences as well as genes (Fuller and Thompson, 1967).

Alcoholism as a Model for Biosocial Risk

Prevalence and Impact. Alcoholism is a major social and medical problem affecting both individual alcoholics and their family members. Ten percent of the adult population in the United States is alcoholic or has alcohol-related problems (U.S. Dept. of HHS, 1981). Health problems, drinking-related traffic accidents, and family disruption are the more visible adverse consequences of alcohol abuse. In 1975, health costs for alcohol-related problems were in excess of 12% of total health expenditures, and the estimated cost of alcohol misuse and alcoholism was $43 billion. Along with a host of other medical problems, alcoholism is associated with two organic brain diseases, Korsakoff's psychosis and alcoholic dementia. The most consistently observed negative effects for the alcoholic, however, have been found to be the impairment of cognitive functioning, including attention, memory, and information processing (Parsons, 1983).

Risk for Alcoholism

Research on biologically related individuals supports a genetic theory of alcoholism transmission (Amark, 1951; Cotton, 1979; Kaij, 1960; Schuckit et al., 1972; Goodwin et al., 1973). Goodwin (1985) reports that the prevalence of alcoholism among both male (25%) and female (5–10%) relatives of alcoholics exceeds the estimated population prevalence for alcoholics, which is 3–5% for men and 0.1–1% for women. The high incidence of alcoholism among offspring of alcoholics has generated much research into underlying biological mechanisms of transmission.

Isolating biological mechanisms that may distinguish populations at high or low risk for alcoholism has involved a variety of techniques (Cloninger, et al., 1979; Deitrich and Spuhler, 1984; Schuckit et al., 1985). These studies include measures of EEG (Gabrielli et al., 1982), event-related potentials (Begleiter et al., 1984), enhanced antagonistic placebo response (Newlin, 1985), and endocrine deviations (Schuckit, et al., 1983). On the basis of the particular biological measure assessed, many of these studies report that children of alcoholics can be differentiated from children of nonalcoholics. To date, however, no single biological pattern has been identified that distinguishes children of alcoholics from children of nonalcoholics with significant accuracy.

In addition to biological risk, transmission of alcoholism can also be maximized by environmental factors. Children of alcoholics can be considered vulnerable to alcoholism for reasons such as psychopathological or alcoholic parental models. Many reviews of psychosocial research on children of alcoholics conclude that although these children demonstrate differences in particular psychosocial dimensions, no single psychosocial profile has been identified that distinguishes children of alcoholics from children of nonalcoholics with significant accuracy.

Assessing Biosocial Risk

Among the prime research questions relevant to brain–behavior relationships is the extent of structural and functional brain damage that might be attributable to alcohol abuse and the risk for alcoholism. Neuropsychological and structural brain damage has been well documented in alcoholics (Tarter and Edwards, 1985; Wilkinson, 1982). The main question in this research, however, concerns whether the damage is a result of the alcoholism, or whether some type of deficit existed prior to the alcoholism. It may be that certain brain–behavior relationships constitute a risk factor for alcoholism. For persons at high risk for alcoholism (perhaps due to genetic predispositions and/or to pathogenic rearing environments), the salient research question is how to identify and assess these risk factors before the risk is expressed.

This assessment requires that we have, if not an operational definition, at least some understanding of the limits of our measurement technique. Assessing brain functioning from a biosocial perspective is a multivariate problem that must integrate diverse theoretical models, empirical research strategies, and appropriate technologies, each with their own tradition and history. Moreover, the biosocial perspective compels the researcher interested in brain function to recognize that both biological and social processes involve structural and functional elements that are subject to quantitative and qualitative change over time. Unlike previous notions that viewed the brain–behavior relationship unilaterally, the growing consensus is that this relationship is interactive; not only does the brain affect behavior, but the reverse may also be true. Depending on the stage of development, this transactional relationship may have different outcomes. Therefore, to understand brain–behavior relationships in individuals who are at biosocial risk we must also address the notion that quantitative and qualitative changes differentially characterize the organism at all stages of development (Figure 1).

Assessing brain–behavior relationships over the course of development in at-risk populations impels us to address the role of developmental change in the expression of the risk itself. The developmental perspective views the individual as a dynamic organism, namely, one that changes in many different dimensions

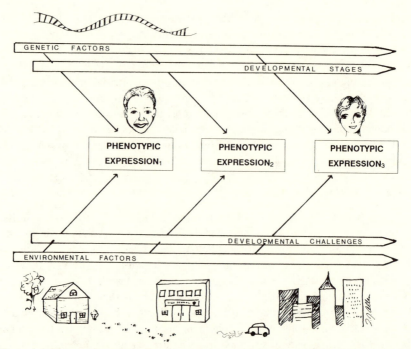

Figure 1. Phenotypic or behavioral expressions at early stages of development can be expected to influence later expressions, even though later experiences may be shaped by new developmental challenges or stages.

over time and circumstance. Because not all individuals who are at risk for alcoholism express the risk for alcoholism by abusive or dependent drinking, understanding the developmental contributions of brain and behavior relationships toward the suppression of this risk becomes an important research focus.

The purpose of this chapter is to selectively examine brain assessment techniques that have been used with individuals who are at risk for alcoholism. We also examine the influence of developmental processes on this assessment. Three techniques will be addressed: neuropsychology, event-related potentials, and *in vivo* assessments.

Developmental Issues Relevant to Brain Assessments

Development as Progression

Development, (defined as the progression from earlier to later stages of maturation) is an action characterized by constant change. The actions that accompany change are more than academic considerations, as the continuous change of development has important implications for brain–behavior relationships (Gottlieb, 1983), namely, brain–behavior relationships take different forms and states at different ages (Fig. 1). Even during periods of apparent passivity, especially during longer stages of development such as senescence, brain–behavior relationships are part of a continuous living and acting operational process attempting to maintain equilibrium or, conversely, manage disequilibration. This process becomes the driving force and the action of development.

Functional brain–behavior activity is seen in the changes that have been elaborately described by Piaget (1963) as a series of stages that are hierarchical and invariant in their order. Piaget's developmental model accounts for the changing and transformational character of how children and adults come to know the world in which they live. Piaget's (1970, 1971) genetic epistemological model views brain–behavior relationships as the expression of an intelligence which consists of a dual nature: it is both biological and logical. Intelligence, a system of living and acting operations providing the structural equilibrium of behavior, is the instrumental process for controlling the interactions between the person and the environment. The scope of these interactions goes beyond immediate and momentary contacts to achieve far-reaching and stable relationships between thoughts and actions. Thus, intelligence is viewed as a highly developed form of adaptation (Piaget, 1972).

Adaptation to the events, people, and objects in the environment enables a balance, or equilibrium, between oneself and the environment. For children to incorporate new experiences of the environment to already present cognitive structures, they must first be able to bring these experiences into the cognitive system. This is accomplished through assimilation. In the process of assimilating new experiences, however, existing cognitive structures must be adjusted to new elements. This is done through the second adaptive function, accommodation. Assimilation and accommodation occur automatically and often without the conscious awareness of the individual. Through these biologically determined processes, development is characterized by constantly changing structures which absorb (assimilate) more and different knowledge of the environment. Thus, development is seen as a self-generated or self-constructed cycle in which actions and thoughts feed back on their initial cognitive organization causing change in those structures that originally set the entire process into action.

Complications of Qualitative and Quantitative Interactions

The intricacies of maturational biological patterns require an understanding of how different stages of development may qualitatively, as well as quantitatively, influence behavior. Brain development, though elaborate, is generally believed to be an orderly, sequential process following principles of neural regulation and cerebral organization (Thatcher et al., 1987). Many elements of normal brain development have been well cataloged with regard to brain size, weight, and neural regulation (Gilles et al., 1983). What is not so well understood, however, is the relationship between the quantitative development of cortical organization and concurrent qualitative, behavioral changes. This relationship is further complicated by individual rates of change, which vary as a function of age.

Assessing the concurrence of brain and behavioral maturation in individuals at biosocial risk adds considerable complexity to the problem of understanding the brain–behavior relationship. How do we measure behavior and correlate it with the maturational processes of the brain at different developmental stages when an individual may be experiencing various degrees of risk (e.g., parents may drink during some periods but stop drinking during other periods of their child's development).

There exist many established links between cognitive abilities and brain functioning as a result of the recent ascendancy of cognitive science. The rise in research related to aging, the extension of neuropsychology to children, and the popularity of Piagetian theory have helped to direct the relevance of a developmental perspective with regard to brain functioning (A. Diamond, this volume; Gibson, 1977, 1981). With the availability of cross-sectional norms and developmental theory, it is possible to extend assessment questions to consider the more time-related questions of "How will present behaviors influence (and be influenced by) further brain development?"

Some recent evidence empirically addresses this question. Malerstein (1986) proposed a model for the interplay of brain development and cognitive functioning based on Piagetian principles. He discusses the role of the development of the visual cortex in the construction of the object concept and cogently argues that the maturation of relevant cortical areas parallels the unfolding of cognitive developmental structures described by Piaget (1963). Thus, as had previously been suggested (Gibson, 1977, 1981), behavior can be seen to co-occur simultaneously with biological maturation. Very recently, Thatcher and colleagues (1987) have provided some evidence regarding the development of the cerebral hemispheres. They suggest that the unfolding of specific corticocortical connections is genetically determined and occurs at specific postnatal ages, which are concurrent with Piagetian stages of cognitive development.

Acceptance of the relevance of developmental processes and stages to brain functioning leads to a number of challenging questions in biosocial research. Taking a life-span view, one important research question is to define how current cognitive functioning is a risk for or a protective factor against some future deficit syndrome. Studies of alcoholics and those at risk for alcoholism provide some clear examples, and it is to these we turn to extend this discussion.

Assessments of Brain Functioning

Understanding the relationship between the brain and behavior has been governed by changes in paradigmatic orientations, modifications in statistical approaches, and, more recently, technical advances in computer modeling capabilities. Answers to questions about how the brain regulates behavior, the consequences of behavioral actions on cortical regulation, or physiological influences on behavior depend on the assessment technique by which the data have been generated. As techniques have evolved, our understanding of brain–behavior relationships has changed. Conversely, as our knowledge changes and alternative theories are developed, auxiliary technology is designed to test new hypotheses.

Past Assessments of Brain Functioning

Older methods for studying the structure and function of the brain have included both direct and indirect approaches. Structural studies of the brain have involved direct surgical methods (e.g., biopsy and autopsy) and less direct radiological methods that can create two-dimensional models for visual analyses (e.g., X-ray angiograms and pneumoencephalograms). Knowledge of normative correlations between structural localization of function, obtained mostly through clinical studies of brain-injured persons, permits reasonable inferences about current brain function, given data on brain structure. Similarly, some functional inferences can be gained through study of body fluids such as blood, urine, and cerebro-spinal fluid.

There are some obvious limitations to these older clinical assessment methodologies. For example, body fluids, although valuable indicators of neuropharmacological activity, are removed in time and place from their functional relationship. Biopsy studies, while valuable for diagnosis, are seldom available for basic research because they can traumatize the brain. In any case, small scale biopsy studies cannot provide the range of data that reflects the enormous chemical and functional heterogeneity of brain areas, especially during development. Similarly, autopsy studies, while of great scientific interest for post-mortem confirmatory diagnoses, cannot provide useful diagnostic tests for the living. Isolated from behavior, these well-established assessments render static views of the brain. Static concepts and assessment techniques cannot reflect the enormous excitatory and inhibitory changes involved in neural regulatory mechanisms as they function over time. Therefore, our understanding of the relationship between the brain and behavior becomes inferential rather than observational. What is required to reflect these relationships are measures of brain activity that are reasonably concurrent with behavior. Can we see what happens in the brain while the person is thinking and acting at different stages of development?

More Recent Methods

There are a variety of more dynamic approaches to the assessment of brain function. These concern (1) metabolism (such as the release of heat in infrared scans or the uptake of radioactive trace elements in positron emission tomography), (2) presence of neurotransmitters in fluids or within the neural tissues of the brain that can be assessed through biochemical trace element binding site studies, (3) detection of electrical activity (e.g., event-related potentials and electroencephalography), and (4) intactness of sensorimotor and cognitive psychological functioning through neuropsychological examinations. More invasive techniques, such as the techniques involving implemented electrodes and canulae for direct electrical or chemical stimulation, are available; they are generally avoided, however, even in nonhumans because of their risks for permanent damage to the organism and discomfort to the subjects.

Brain Assessments in Alcoholics and Their Offspring

For both adult alcoholics and their children, brain assessments have generally involved neuropsychological or event-related potential techniques. *In vivo* techniques have been used primarily in adult alcoholics. The following selective reviews demonstrate some of the findings associated with these three assessment strategies.

Neuropsychological Assessment

Background. Neuropsychological assessment typically identifies brain damage in individuals and assesses the extent and nature of brain dysfunction. Research in human neuropsychology has been largely dependent on the evaluation of behavior in adults with documented lesions of the central nervous system (CNS) (Boll, 1985). Knowing the type, size, and age at which the injury is sustained, and the anatomical specificity (focal or diffuse) of the brain lesion has helped document the nature and severity of many behavioral disorders of motor, attentional, and visual systems (O'Leary et al., 1983). After brain damage has already occurred, determining the manner in which diseased brain tissue previously interacted with broader neural systems is difficult; thus, most of our information about neuropsychological processes in humans has been derived from individuals who suffer from some type of brain damage.

Neuropsychological assessment techniques are dominated by two test batteries, the Halstead–Reitan (Halstead, 1947) and the Luria–Nebraska (Golden, et al., 1985). Although each battery is composed of relatively simple test items, their administration and interpretation are complicated by the length of time it takes to complete the test and the number of items necessary to administer it. As an example, the Luria Nebraska Neuropsychological Battery (LNNB) is composed of 279 test items designed to assess a very broad range of neuropsychological functions. The LNNB typically takes 2–3 hours to complete, unlike the Halstead–Reitan, which can take up to 8 hours. The LNNB battery actually consists of 700 discrete tasks that, when scored, yield clinical, summary, localization, and factor scales. Each scale has a uniquely descriptive purpose. For example, the clinical scale measures 12 different functions such as motor, tactile, visual, receptive and expressive speech, memory, and intellectual processes. The summary scale describes five different types of summary scores:

pathognomonic, left and right hemisphere, profile elevation, and impairment. the localization scale describes left and right frontal, sensorimotor, parietal–occipital, and temporal brain areas.

Much neuropsychological research is concerned with the localization of brain dysfunction (Filscov and Boll, 1981). Localizing brain function by dividing the brain into localized, specific functions is complicated by the considerable interdependence of the systems (Figure 2). Nevertheless, neuropsychological assessment procedures have resulted in considerable progress in identifying functional

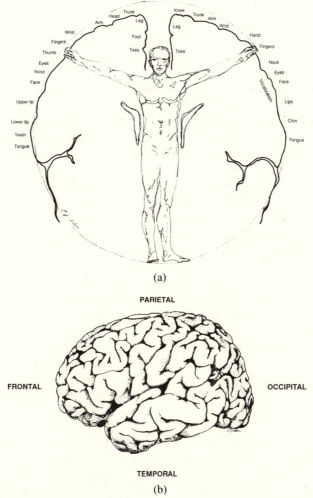

(a)

PARIETAL

FRONTAL   OCCIPITAL

TEMPORAL

(b)

Figure 2.   Due to the overlap of primary and secondary association areas in the cortex, localization of brain function has been difficult.

specificity in brain lateralization and asymmetry as well as in sensory and motor systems in adults. Neuroanatomic investigations have focused primarily on the frontal lobes and subcortical structures and their relationship to psychological capacities (Boll, 1985). Advances have suggested that higher order cognitive skills and brain systems, while interrelated to some extent, are differentiable and dissociable (Fisk and Rourke, 1983).

Studies of concurrent brain–behavorial relationships in normal children undergoing various stages of development are rare (Rourke et al., 1983). Much of what we understand about early stages of neuropsychological function in humans is either extrapolated down from adult studies, or obtained from studies of children with known brain disease (Telzrow, 1983). For example, neuropsychological functioning has been studied in childhood disorders such as Gilles de la Tourette (Incagnoli and Kane, 1983), schizophrenia (Krynicki and Nahas, 1979), learning disabilities (Rourke, 1985), and seriously delinquent adolescents (Brickman et al., 1984). Understanding the normal progression of neuropsychological functioning at various stages of development is therefore difficult from these sources of information.

Through the increasing sophistication in the documentation of the neurocognitive consequences and their associated neuropsychological disorders, Boll (1985) has suggested that the field of neuropsychology is just now maturing. Coincidental with this is the emergence of developmental neuropsychology, the application of neuropsychological techniques to the examination of brain–behavior relationships in children (Rourke et al., 1983).

Until recently, neuropsychology has been concerned primarily with the localization of brain function in the mature adult brain, which is viewed as having a consistent functional geography (Spreen et al., 1984). Plasticity of the developing brain and its capacity for recovery of function has introduced the notion that knowledge gained from the study of brain impairment in adults is not directly generalizable to children. The existence of both critical periods (which demonstrate rigidity) and neural plasticity (which demonstrates flexibility) implies that the organism may be differentially receptive or vulnerable to environmental influences, depending on developmental stage. Evidence for this has been reported in the work of Teuber and Rudel (1962) who demonstrated both task- and age-specific effects of brain damage. They concluded in their study of brain injury in children and adults that whereas some behaviors are impaired by brain injury at all ages, other behaviors can show immediate impairment that will disappear with development. Moreover, other behaviors show effects that do not appear immediately, but only with delay. Emphasizing the importance of developmental differences, Rourke et al. (1983) pose two questions relevant to this issue. First, what are the effects of brain defect on mental functions at different ages? Second, to what degree do preadaptive structures transform in immature brains and respond to training? Rourke and his colleagues (1983) suggest that a chart of the intrinsic regulations of cerebral growth is required to answer these questions.

The primary obstacle to charting this course is methodological. First, assessment measures have not been designed with the developing child in mind, but rather adult measures have been extended downward (Telzrow, 1983) according to the performance patterns of normal adult control groups. This is inappropriate for many reasons, especially since the CNS of the child is quite different from that of the adult in physiological characteristics and functional capacities. Second, studying a maturing nervous systems, which is in a state of rapid change, requires that the assessment tests account for the heterogeneous behavorial responses of childhood. Much variability characterizes the behavior of normal children; understanding what is abnormal behavior requires that we first understand the parameters of what is normal.

Neuropsychological assessment in alcoholics. Extensive research has documented the neuropsychological deficits associated with alcohol usage (Kleinknecht and Goldstein, 1972; Miller and Saucedo, 1983; Parsons and Farr, 1981). Neuropsychological deficits associated with alcohol usage have involved difficulties in complex problem solving and abstract reasoning processes, speed-dependent visual scanning, organization of eye–hand coordination responses, perception of spatial relations, motor control involving the integration of spatial elements, and short-term memory (Lishman, 1981; Parsons and Farr, 1981; Tarter, 1973).

The association between neuropsychological deficits and drinking history is quite complex. Aspects of alcohol use such as chronicity, quantity, or length of abstinence at the time when tested may offer a significant, but partial, explanation for the deficits or degree of dysfunction observed (Jones and Parsons, 1971). Although selective deficits associated with different combinations of recent and chronic drinking patterns have been found (Eckardt et al., 1978), the degree to which the severity of deficits correlates with some measure of alcohol use remains unclear (Golden, 1981). Researchers consistently observe that even after extended sobriety, neuropsychological functioning is incomplete and that differential recovery of neuropsychological functioning may be indicative of permanent residual impairment secondary to alcohol abuse (Tarter and Edwards, 1985). This has led some to suggest that impaired cognitive capacities may antedate the onset of alcohol abuse (Hegedus et al., 1984; Tarter and Edwards, 1985; De Obaldia and Parsons, 1984). Perhaps even before they start to drink, alcoholics begin with differential neuropsychological functioning.

Neuropsychological assessment in the offspring of alcoholics. Neuropsychological investigations of offspring of alcoholics represent only a segment of the considerable research into the hypothesized genetic predisposition to alcoholism (Schuckit, 1985). Broadly, such efforts have tried to define those at risk by identifying the biological mechanisms possibly contributing to this vulnerability, examining neurobehavioral evidence in those at risk, and determining whether there are neuropsychological concomitants that would perhaps predispose to, but certainly predate, adult alcoholism (Donovan, 1986; Grove and Cadoret, 1983; Peele, 1986; Schuckit, 1985).

From adult children of alcoholics, neuropsychological research provides suggestive, but inconclusive, support for cognitive dysfunction among those adults who are at risk for alcoholism through biologic parental alcoholism (Hesselbrock, 1983). Schaeffer and colleagues (1984) seem to have reported the strongest evidence. In their sample of 130 adults (age range 24–60 years), alcoholics performed predictably worse than did nonalcoholic controls on tasks of abstracting, problem solving, learning, and memory. Alcoholics with a parent, brother, or sister who were also alcoholic tended to perform more poorly than did alcoholics without an alcoholic first-degree relative. More importantly, however, familial history also distinguished the performance of nonalcoholic subjects. On tests of abstracting, problem solving, and perceptual-motor function, non-alcoholic males with a family history positive for alcoholism performed more poorly than did nonalcoholic males with a negative family history. Alcoholism and family history effects were also found to be independent, as well as additive, in relation to neuropsychological test performance deficits.

Although selective deficits might antedate the onset of adult alcoholism, few studies have actually evaluated adolescent or younger offspring of alcoholics. Recent studies have begun to compare the differences in cognitive performance between children of alcoholics and children of nonalcoholics. Ervin and her colleagues (1984) found the presence of an alcoholic father to be related to lower (but within normal range) intelligence and achievement scores in their study of 108 children ranging in age from less than 3 to more than 15 years. In a smaller and younger male sample, Noll and Zucker (1983) found that sons of alcoholics obtained significantly lower scores than did control children on Yale Developmental Inventory measures of fine motor and adaptive skills, and on language and personal/social development. Thus, support for selective neuropsychological inefficiency or deficits in prealcoholic children of alcoholics has been mild, but inconclusive (Alterman, et al., 1986).

Among studies of school aged children of alcoholics (Ervin et al., 1984; Gabrielli and Mednick, 1983; Hennecke, 1984), Tarter and his colleagues (1984) reported that sons of alcoholics performed more poorly on tests measuring attention, memory, perceptual-motor coordination, motor speed, spatial sequencing, and language capacity than did sons of nonalcoholic fathers. These deficits were also related to poorer performance on a standardized test of educational achievement, the Peabody Individual Achievement Test (Hegedus, et al., 1984). Tarter et al. (1984), however, did not control for confounding family history variables such as the prevalence of physical abuse from the father or psychiatric illness in the mother. With a well-controlled and homogeneous sample, however, these differences are reported to disappear (Rebeta, 1987).

Likewise, Drejer and colleagues (1985) evaluated the neuropsychological functioning of 204 males aged 18–19 years, that is, 134 sons of alcoholic fathers and 70 matched controls. The high-risk group evidenced a significantly poorer Wechsler Adult Intelligence Scale Vocabulary score and a higher error rate on both Category and Porteus Maze tests than did controls. Drejer and colleagues (1985) characterized the particular deficits in their high-risk group as reduced capacity for sustaining goal-directed activity, that is, diminished ability to maintain a cognitive set together with a rigid, inflexible approach to problem solving. The impulsiveness observed on the Porteus Mazes has also been reported by probands' teachers who described the high-risk group as being significantly more impulsive and less verbally proficient than the matched controls (Knop et al., 1985).

To evaluate learning and memory skills among adolescents with and without familial histories of alcoholism, Rebeta (1987) employed verbal and visual memory tests with combinations of immediate recall, post interference recall, and delayed-recall conditions. The sons of alcoholics included only those whose biological mother had no history of alcohol abuse or dependence, especially at the time of the child's conception, during pregnancy, or during the child's nursing period. Parents and adolescents were extensively interviewed to obtain detailed demographic and substance use information.

After adolescent eligibility was determined, memory and learning, both verbal and visual, were assessed with four tasks: (1) Rey Auditory–Verbal Learning Test (AVLT) with 30 min delayed recall; (2) Digit Span subtest from the WISC-R or WAIS; (3) Recurring Figures Test (RFT), which involves the recognition of geometric and nonsense designs; and (4) Complex Figure Test (CFT) with immediate and 30-min delayed recall, which requires the subject to reproduce from memory a design he has just copied.

Nonparametric statistical methods were used due to the nonnormal distributions and unequal group variances. Wilcoxon two-sample tests revealed no significant group differences on any of the selected measures of learning and memory, verbal or visual (Table 1). The FHP subjects, however, tended to do worse ($p = .066$) on the 30-min delayed recall portion of the CFT, a test of visual memory requiring a motor response. The AVLT (trials 1–5 recall, post-interference recall, word recognition, and delayed recall trials), Digit Span, RFT, and CFT (immediate and delayed recall) performances did not differ between groups.

Neither test of visual memory, the Recurring Figures Test or the Complex Figure Test, nor the test of immediate auditory memory (Digit Span), differentiated the FHP (family history positive for alcoholism) and FHN (family history not positive for alcoholism) groups. Verbal learning as evidenced by total number of words recalled over trials 1–5 on the Rey Auditory-Verbal Learning Test, by recognition trial performance, by free recall of the first word list after administration of an interference list, and by delayed recall performance, was comparable to normative samples (Taylor, 1959) and did not differentiate the FHP–FHN groups.

Table 1.   Mean Scores on Learning and Memory Test Variables

	FHP	FHN
Digit Span	11.33 (3.05)[a]	11.17 (3.66)
Auditory–Verbal Learning Test[b]		
Trials 1–5	55.53 (8.41)	56.93 (7.63)
Postinterference	11.33 (2.54)	11.63 (2.46)
Recognition	13.93 (1.70)	14.00 (1.11)
Delayed recall	11.50 (2.50)	11.53 (2.57)
Complex Figure Test		
Copy	29.37 (3.72)	30.50 (3.14)
Immediate recall	19.92 (5.87)	22.38 (5.26)
Delayed recall	18.58 (6.37)	21.57 (5.29)
Recurring Figures Test[c]		
Geometric designs	26.07 (2.45)	25.47 (3.03)
Nonsense designs	11.13 (7.55)	11.87 (8.14)
Total designs	37.20 (8.43)	37.33 (9.90)

[a] Standard deviation.
[b] Number of correct recalled.
[c] Number recognized, corrected for false positives. From Rebeta, 1987

On the CFT-immediate recall, however, mean scores placed the FHP subjects at the 25th percentile, and the FHN subjects at the 50th percentile of the 15-year-old cohort of Osterrieth's standardization sample (Taylor, 1959). Any FHP–FHN difference on this test is suggestive at best. FHP adolescents tended to do worse on only one of the CFT measures, namely, 30-min delayed recall ($p = .066$). Nevertheless, the possibility that adolescents who are at risk for alcoholism might perform worse on a test of visual and visuopractic memory as task difficulty increases is consistent with Ryan and Butters' findings (1980, 1983). They demonstrated that subclinical memory inefficiencies or deficits in subgroups of adult alcoholics emerge only as test demands increase. For offspring of alcoholics, the evidence presented here exemplified that phenomenon.

Rebeta (1987) concluded that learning and memory differences based on family history were not found in their study because of the possible presence of influential environmental factors. First, this study population represented a relatively affluent segment of suburban Washington, D.C. families. On a scale of 1 to 5, 1 being the most affluent, Hollingshead SES social stratum classification averaged 1.8 (SD = .66) for the FHP group, and 1.6 (SD = .56) for the FHN group. These demographic characteristics differed markedly from those of Tarter et al. (1984). In their study, 16-year-old juvenile delinquents averaged an SES classification of 4.8 (SD = .6) for FHP males and 4.9 (SD = 1.7) for FHN males. Tarter et al. (1984) also reported that their FHP subjects were more likely to have had perinatal complications, come from a broken home, suffer a head injury, have been physically abused, and evidence identifiable psychiatric illness. Their biological mothers were also more likely to have sought psychiatric treatment.

Learning and memory differences in children of alcoholics may derive more from the unknown influence of environmental characteristics than from the independent influence of family history (Beardslee et al., 1986). Rebeta's (1987) sample consisted of healthy, nondelinquent males; these environmental influences may serve as protective factors for learning and memory deficits in the offspring of alcoholics. The neuropsychological deficits in the offspring of alcoholics reported in previous studies may originate more from sample heterogeneity than from familial history. These differing outcomes may also emphasize the multifactorial, polygenic nature of vulnerability to alcoholism, and, by extension, to particular neuropsychological deficits with which alcohol abuse has been associated.

Summary. In summary, available research supports the following two conclusions. First, adult chronic alcoholics have evidence of selective neuropsychological performance deficits, especially in abstract problem solving, learning and memory, and perceptuomotor skills. This research has not determined premorbid functioning, which would be necessary to clarify whether these deficits predated the alcoholic behavior, or rather were a consequence of it. Second, although individuals from families with a history positive for alcoholism defines a population at risk, neuropsychological research has been limited and only suggests selective neuropsychological difficulties. Few studies have replicated the abstracting, problem-solving, and perceptuomotor inefficiencies observed by Schaeffer and colleagues (1984).

Event-Related Potentials

Background. Measurements of cortical electrical activity are accomplished by examining the electroencephalograph (EEG), a trace of the electrical fluctuations of the central nervous system. These fluctuations vary according to frequency and amplitude and measure generalized electrical states of cortical activity. Unlike generalized EEG, cortical activity associated with a specific cognitive task or perceptual event can be assessed with the event-related potential (ERP). Event-related potentials are cortical electrical response patterns to sensory input recorded from the scalp. ERPs provide more information than the EEG, which is ongoing electrical activity in the brain (Cobb and Morocutti, 1967; Lehmann and Callaway, 1979). Although the background EEG activity can vary and bear no fixed relationship to the stimulus, the ERP identifies the specific potential changes related to discrete external events or stimuli. Since an ERP always follows a sensory stimulus, it provides an opportunity to measure the specific neural activity responding to external stimuli or events that have occurred at a specific point in time. Detailed summaries of the ERP can be found in several sources (Cobb and Morocutti, 1967; Harmony, 1984; Regan, 1972).

Typically, ERPs are used to assess neurophysiological changes produced by auditory, visual, or somatosensory stimulation, or to assess the neurophysiological changes in psychological states or processes (Ford and Pfefferbaum, 1981). Experimental variations have described two groups of ERPs labeled exogenous ERPs and endogenous ERPs. Exogenous ERPs are stimulus dependent and occur within the first 50 msec of the waveform. On the other hand, endogenous ERPs are associated with perceptual, cognitive, and motor processes of the brain and are independent of external stimuli. Endogenous ERPs occur after the first 50 msec of the waveform and can be obtained from subjects stimulated by any event, (such as light flashes, clicks, tones, words, or geometric figures), which has a fast enough onset to produce synchrony of neural response and similarity from trial to trial.

There are five commonly used indicators for identifying the individual components found within the ERP waveform (Goff, et al., 1978; John, et al., 1978). A specific ERP component is typically referred to in either spatial or temporal dimensions. Spatial reference designates the first negative deflection of the ERP waveform as "N1" while a component labeled "P2" refers to the second positive inflection. Temporal reference, on the other hand, designates a negative wave occurring at 100 msec after stimulus onset as "N100," while a component labeled "P300" refers to a positive inflection of the waveform occurring at 300 msec after stimulus onset.

The primary value in recording the ERP stems from the noninvasive study of the nervous system (Donchin, 1979). The effectiveness of the ERP technique lies in the fact that as a time locked, stimulus-dependent measure, the ERP can assess levels of brain functioning and permit simultaneous investigation of cognition by recording responses from totally passive subjects from whom no overt task is required (Ford and Pfefferbaum, 1981), thus making it an ideal tool for children or patient populations. Coupled with recent technological advances in computer science, the ERP is an especially promising measure of the development of human neurophysiology.

ERPs in normal samples. The ERPs of normal school-aged children have been studied using a variety of experimental paradigms such as auditory (Callaway et al., 1970; Squires et al., 1973), cognitive (Courschesne, 1977, 1978), and somatosensory stimulation (Shagass and Schwartz, 1966). ERP studies of the maturing visual system have also been extensively investigated (Cohn, 1964; Dustman and Beck, 1969; Ellingson, 1960; Straumanis et al., 1965). Examples of developmental changes in the visual system will be briefly discussed to demonstrate how ERPs have been used to measure changes across age.

The amplitudes of ERPs to visual stimulation have been shown to change from infancy to adulthood in response to either light flashes or visual pattern presentation (Dustman et al., 1981; Moskowitz and Sokol, 1983). Both latency and amplitudes of the ERP have been reported to decrease with age (Ellingson et al., 1973; Horst et al., 1982; Lodge et al., 1969). Generally, during the first years of life, amplitudes increase rapidly but, after infancy, the major age-related changes of the visual ERP are primarily restricted to a decrement in responses from the occipital region (Schenkenberg, 1970).

Figure 3 illustrates a topographic technique that displays ERP responses to diffuse flash stimulation. Data were collected from 38 male and 40 female normal control children between the ages of 5 and 19; they were divided into four age groups (5 to 8, 9 to 12, 13 to 16, and 17 to 19) to compare age-related differences in ERP responses (Johnson, 1984). A placement of 12 reference locations on the left hemisphere and midline between the hemispheres was used based on the standardized International 10–20 Electrode Placement System (Jasper, 1958). In addition to these standard locations, four additional placements were used [PO (parietal–occipital), CP (central–parietal), TCP (temporal–central–parietal), and FTC (frontal–temporal–central)]. Gold–capped electrodes were attached to the scalp with calcium chloride-free electrode paste with impedance below 5 ω. After electrode placement, the child was seated in a quiet, darkened room for ERP data collection, which consisted of 4 min of diffuse flash stimulation presented randomly at four intensities (2, 30, 80, and 240 foot lamberts). The interstimulus interval between flashes was 500 msec.

Changes across age (because there were no sex differences, males and females were combined in one group) for all intensities of stimulation were significant, as illustrated in the visual displays of topographical distributions of cortical activity

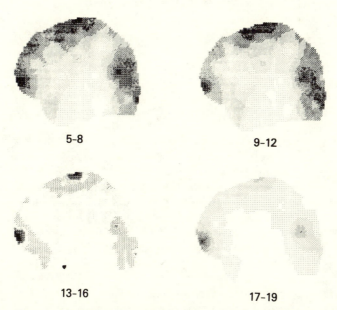

5–8   9–12

13–16   17–19

Figure 3. Topographic distributions of the N1 component of the ERP response to diffuse flash stimulation; subjects are separated by age group.

(Figure 3). The ERP component measured was N1, the first negative peak of the waveform. Across age, the decrease from darker to lighter density changes in the frontal, parietal, and occipital areas in the topographical maps suggests that as age increased, the N1 component of the ERP waveform decreased. Temporal cortical areas were rarely activated, as would be expected in a visual task. Primarily midline electrode sites (Fz, Cz, Pz, and Oz) (Figure 4) significantly discriminated between the four age groups.

These data demonstrate one aspect of cortical activity that may be relevant to the brain–behavior relationship in the maturing organism; however, the parameters of this relationship are unclear because the experimental paradigm merely asked whether ERP responses to visual stimulation changed across age. To better understand brain–behavior relationships, an ERP paradigm needs to assess specific aspects of behavioral development, which can then be tied to specific aspects of brain development. Such is the case with cognitive ERP paradigms, many of which have been used in studies of alcoholism.

ERP studies in alcoholics and their offspring. Evidence derived from EEG studies of alcoholics indicates that the spontaneous EEG associated with chronic alcohol abuse shows an increase of beta activity with small amplitudes and

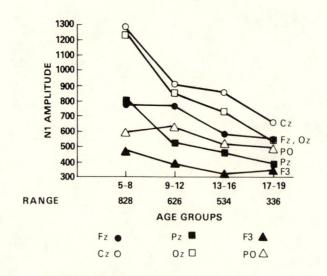

Figure 4.

appears to be lacking in alpha (Begleiter and Platz, 1972; Greenblatt et al., 1944; Spehr and Stemmler, 1985). ERPs have been reported to be the only technique that is differentially sensitive to the various phases of alcohol-related dysfunction such as acute and chronic alcoholization, tolerance, withdrawal, and long-term brain dysfunction (Porjesz and Begleiter, 1981). From these initial results, ERP studies have been conducted that examined specific brain responses as potential risk markers for alcoholism.

Because both adult alcoholics and their offspring frequently show cognitive deficits (Jones, 1971), recent ERP studies examined the P3 component (a positive peak occurring around 300 msec) of the ERP, which has been established as an endogenous index of cognitive processing (Brandeis and Lehmann, 1986). P3 amplitude during auditory ERP tasks has been shown to differ between those offspring with a positive family history and those without (Begleiter et al., 1986; Elmasian et al., 1982), although these findings have not been consistently reported (Baribeau et al., 1986). One landmark study (Begleiter et al., 1984) using a visual rotation paradigm reported decreased P3 amplitudes in 7- to 13-year-old sons of alcoholic fathers. Nevertheless, while the P3 component in children of alcoholics may be different than the P3 component in children of nonalcoholics, the meaning of this difference and its subsequent relationship to later problems remain unclear without further research into understanding the behavorial implications of this difference.

In Vivo Assessments

Background. Several *in vivo* assessment techniques are available for the purposes of diagnosis and research that offer challenging, exciting, and dynamic opportunities to study the brain. With imaging techniques such as positron emission tomography (PET), for example, it is possible to discern which parts of the brain are activated when cognitive information is processed or which parts have become dysfunctional as the result of a disease such as alcoholism. Tomographic or autoradiographic images provide numerical determinations of various processes (e.g., glucose utilization, blood flow, or protein synthesis in discrete brain regions). Brain images are then generated by highly computerized scanning procedures that have reconstructed slices of the brain, according to complicated algorithms, into a large matrix of picture elements (pixels). Each picture element, or pixel, quantitatively represents the physiological process or anatomy being measured by the particular scanning device. This quantitative representation can then be color coded using a computer algorithm that assigns various colors to each pixel value. This color-coded representation appears as a picture (brain image) with shades between black and white, or any color in between (Figure 5).

There are many types of brain imaging techniques currently in use. Cerebral blood flow reflects subtle changes in activity by estimating local cerebral metabolic activity by tracing radioactive xenon washout after carotid injection or gas

UNPROCESSED IMAGE

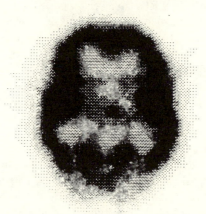

Figure 5.   Example of a positron emission tomographic scan. The unprocessed image is
a large matrix of numbers which is numerically determined by glucose uptake in the
brain. Each picture element of the matrix has been coded with a different shade of
gray which indicates activity in that specific brain region; the darker the shade, the
more glucose has been taken up, and, hence, the more activity in that area of the
brain.

inhalation. Nuclear magnetic resonance (NMR) images of water distribution
have even higher resolution of gray/white matter boundaries, allowing volumetric and densitometric studies of internal structure that may provide the key
to major neurotransmitter mechanisms, without the hazard of X-radiation
(Pykett, 1982; Radda and Seeley, 1979). While NMR is a relatively new
technique that is primarily used for anatomic visualization, it holds promise for
yielding images of molecules, such as phosphorus, which could also map energy
use (Marx, 1980). We will discuss below two techniques that are currently being
utilized in studies of alcoholism.

Computerized axial tomography.   Computerized axial tomography (CT) is
used primarily as a diagnostic tool on individuals with suspected brain lesion and
has consistently shown disease related diminutions, including the study of
diseases due to exogenous agents, such as alcohol (Cala and Mastiglia, 1981;
Carlen et al., 1978). CT scans of alcoholics have consistently revealed that
chronic abuse is associated with enlarged ventricles (Fox et al., 1976; Epstein et
al., 1977; Carlen et al., 1976) reflecting gross morphological abnormalities of
the brain, predominantly frontoparietal cerebral atrophy (Wilkinson, 1982). To
date, CT studies of either minor or adult offspring of alcoholics have not been
reported.

Although CT scanning has provided reliable and meaningful information
about structural abnormalities, our understanding about the exact pathogenesis of
cerebral damage associated with chronic alcohol abuse remains limited for two
reasons. First, because of technical limitations of the scanning process, quantita-

tive information obtained from CT is more reliable for cortical, than for subcortical (i.e., brainstem) regions. Thus, prognostic information regarding the neuropathology in the hippocampal complex and dorsomedial thalamus, which has been demonstrated in postmortem studies, cannot be obtained (Courville, 1966; Dreyfus, 1974). Second, CT provides a picture of gross brain morphology but fails to provide information regarding functional measurements of cerebral metabolism. However, when CT is used in conjunction with positron emission tomography (PET), as will be discussed below, the information derived from the combined methods increases our understanding of the relationship between cerebral structure and function. PET measures of physiological process can become anchored to a structural referent used in combination with CT.

Positron emission tomography. PET is a nuclear medicine research and diagnostic technique that generates a series of maps of the distribution of an administered radionuclide. Currently administered radionuclides are ^{18}F, ^{15}O, or ^{13}N. Depending on the biological function of the labeled substance, different physiological processes may be investigated. The primary value of PET is that it allows physiological processes in the living brain to be studied. Because PET is essentially a measure of brain function, it complements neuroanatomical or histological measures of structure, such as CT. For this reason, PET offers a number of important research and clinical possibilities to examine the brains of humans while they are in various states, be it resting or cognitive performance.

PET scanners measure the emission of positrons. Positrons are short lived and when they annihilate they simultaneously emit two equal gamma rays in diametrically opposite directions. At the time of annihilation, computerized detectors can pinpoint where the positron decayed. Most PET studies have measured localized glucose metabolism using a glucose analogue, ^{18}F-labeled 2-fluoro-2-deoxy-D-glucose (FDG), as the radioactive tracer based on the models developed by Sokoloff et al. (1977) and Reivich et al. 1979. With positron-labeled glucose circulating, energy demands of different areas of the brain are reflected in the precise quantification and localization in space of positron emitting isotopes. Very simply, glucose, the main energy source of the brain, is labeled with a positron emitting isotope. When these positrons bump into each other, they annihilate and emit a γ-ray that can be detected by a positron emission tomographic scanner, a computer designed to measure this annihilation. The more annihilation, the higher the presence of positron-labeled glucose. We also assume that the higher presence of glucose in the brain indicates more energy use in that area.

The measurement of the local tissue concentrations of the injected radioactive tracer produces three-dimensional mathematical reconstructions of the rates of uptake in specific brain regions (Phelps et al., 1982). Since glucose is the primary energy source for the brain, resulting PET scan images quantify regional brain metabolism with nonmetabolized FDG. With radioactive glucose, for example, the resulting images reflect glucose accumulation and regional brain activity, and local alterations in activity brought about by organism and environmental variables can be measured. When the scanning (radiation detection) device is used to take a series of scans of successive planes of the brain, the images are topographically analogous to CAT scans but reflect regional rates of glucose metabolism rather than anatomical detail (Figure 5).

A few studies of alcoholics with chronic organic brain syndrome utilized PET to investigate the pathophysiological damage related to alcohol abuse. Studies with this method in patients with nonalcoholic dementia have demonstrated a close relationship between functional activity and energy metabolism in the CNS (Sokoloff, 1981). In a preliminary study (Kessler et al., 1984), mean cerebral glucose metabolic rates in long-term abstinent alcohol amnestic patients were 22% lower than in age-matched normal controls. Significant decreases of regional metabolism were seen in medial prefrontal and medial temporal cortical areas in the thalamus and basal ganglia. With future studies, PET may also help distinguish pathophysiology related to Korsakoff psychosis and alcoholic dementia (Johnson et al., 1986) as it has in other studies of dementia (Farkas et al., 1982). To date, however, PET studies attempting to differentiate subtypes of alcoholism-related organic brain syndromes have not been reported.

Studies of the offspring at risk for alcoholism have not been done. This may be due, in part, to the invasiveness of the technique. Individuals participating in PET studies must receive a small dose of radiation, and while each protocol must be individually approved by radiation safety committees, to date, studies of children of alcoholics have not been reported. Clearly, a need exists.

Conclusions

The previous selective overview of three different types of brain assessments represented but a small portion of the research that is currently taking place in the field of alcoholism. This overview, however, was presented only to demonstrate the complexity of the brain–behavior relationship in some individuals at biosocial risk and to present some methods that have been used to assess this relationship. It is important to remember that although the extent and severity of alcohol abuse can be documented in many cases, to date, no single method has been successful in illuminating answers to questions that address etiology or transmission of alcoholism.

Among the questions surrounding brain and behavioral relationships in individuals at biosocial risk is a common, thematic problem. Namely, how do we measure brain and behavorial relationships in maturing, changing organisms at different stages of development so that we can describe the trajectory of the expression or nonexpression of the risk? The answer, of course, is that right now we cannot. Methodological limitations of the studies intrude on our ability to completely rely on some of the findings, especially when replication is not forthcoming. Although many studies have described differences between groups of individuals, important methodological issues should be considered in interpreting the results of these studies. First, most studies are not solidly based on a theoretical model with respect to the developmental sequence of the transmission of alcoholism. Although brain or behavorial deficits may be revealed among alcoholics and their children, such findings do not necessarily confirm or disconfirm a theory of etiology for alcoholism. Second, behavior is frequently determined by multiple factors, but many studies are univariate in their approach and do not take into account multiple measures of behavior. Studying one behavior may lead to oversimplified causal reasoning.

One other important reason for our inability to definitely identify risk or protective factors in brain–behavior relationships in the transmission of alcoholism is related to our knowledge about normally developing children and adults. It is imperfect. For example, we do not know, as Rourke (1985) has pointed out, how normal, neuropsychological functioning proceeds. The field of child neuropsychology has only recently been recognized.

Moreover, without a longitudinal perspective, it is difficult to know whether any of these childhood differences will show continuity with time and have an impact on development in adulthood. Very few longitudinal studies have examined differences in children of alcoholics. Werner (1986), however, recently reported on the results of a longitudinal study in which a subgroup of children of alcoholics with and without problems (defined as repeated or serious delinquencies or mental health problems requiring treatment) were followed from birth to age 18. Those 18-year-old children of alcoholics evidencing problems were primarily males who scored significantly lower than the children of alcoholics without problems on verbal and quantitative cognitive measures. These findings suggest that cognitive deficits may not characterize children of alcoholics as a group, but might characterize primarily male children of alcoholics who express maladaptive behavior at a later age.

Currently, we are experiencing an increase in the availability of highly computerized brain assessment techniques, such as positron emission tomography. With the availability of highly technical measurements of physiological and functional brain capacities, we are able to test more advanced theories of brain–behavior relationships. In turn, alternative theories of the brain are advanced with the contributions provided by new information. Although a few techniques have successfully articulated complicated interactions in brain and behavior relationships, others show great promise for advancing our theories about this relationship. Theories of the brain, which try to account for the complexities of human brain and behavorial development, can be strengthened or diminished according to how we understand the techniques we use.

Although these techniques are not without criticism (Johnson, 1987), combined multiple methods of assessment enhance the value of the measurements so that some limitations that apply to individual techniques become diminished in importance. For example, recent studies correlating EEG activity and PET suggest that neurophysiological activity parallels local cerebral glucose use (Buchsbaum et al., 1981). Thus, the noninvasive EEG recording may become a necessary supplement to PET studies. Similarly, morphological assessments of cerebral damage combined with assessments of cortical and subcortical metabolism may provide a powerful tool in the diagnosis and differentiation of different subtypes of alcoholism.

Questions about brain–behavior relationships in individuals at biosocial risk are complicated, at best, and, at worst, are impossible. No single method can describe brain–behavior relationships in a multifaceted phenomena, whether it is alcoholism or schizophrenia because different measures of CNS structure and function provide different types of information. Mechanisms underlying maturation and behavior are complex, and it may prove necessary to address more than one pathophysiologic mechanism in individuals; specifically, there may be simultaneous abnormalities requiring different techniques for assessment.

References

Alterman, A.I., Bridges, K.R., and Tarter, R.E. (1986). The influence of both drinking and familial risk statuses on cognitive functioning of social drinkers. *Alcoholism: Clinical and Experimental Research 10*, 448–451.

Amark, C. (1951). A study in alcoholism. *Acta Psychiatrica et Neurologica Scandinavia,* Suppl. *70*, 1–283.

Baribeau, J., Braun, C., Bartolini, G., and Ethier, M. (1986) Event-related potentials and selective attention in young males in relation to two risk factors for alcoholism: Family history and drinking behavior. Paper presented at the Eighth International Conference on Event Related Potentials of the Brain, Stanford, CA.

Beardslee, W.R., Son, L., and Vaillant, G.E. (1986). Exposure to parental alcoholism during childhood and outcome in adulthood: A prospective longitudinal study. *British Journal of Psychiatry, 149*, 584–591.

Begleiter, H., and Platz, A. (1972). The effects of alcohol on the CNS in humans. In B. Kissin and H. Begleiter (Eds.), *The biology of alcoholism* (Vol 2. pp. 293-343). New York: Plenum.

Begleiter, H., Porjesz, B., Bihari, B., and Kissin, B. (1984). Event related brain potentials in boys at risk for alcoholism. *Science, 225*, 1493–1496.

Begleiter, H., Porjesz, B., Rawlings, R., and Eckardt, M. (1986). Auditory recovery function and P3 in boys at high risk for alcoholism. Paper presented at the Eighth International Conference on Event Related Potentials of the Brain, Stanford, CA.

Boll, T.J. (1985). Developing issues in clinical neuropsychology. *Journal of Clinical and Experimental Neuropsychology, 7* (5), 473–485.

Brickman, A.S., McManus, M., Grapentine, W.L., and Alessi, N. (1984). Neuropsychological assessment of seriously delinquent adolescents. *Journal of the American Academy of Child Psychiatry, 23*(4), 453–457.

Brandeis, D., and Lehmann, P. (1986). Event-related potentials of the brain and cognitive processes: Approaches and applications. *Neuropsychologia, 24*(1), 151–168.

Buchsbaum, M.S., Coppola, R., and Cappeletti, J. (1981). Positron emission tomography, EEG and evoked potential topography: New approaches to local function in pharmacoelectroencephalography.

In E. Hermann (ed.), *EEG in drug research* (pp. 193–207). Stuttgart: Gustav Fischer, pp. 193–207.

Cala, LA., and Mastaglia, F.L. (1981). Computerized tomography in chronic alcoholics. *Alcoholism: Clinical and Experimental Research, 5,* 283–294.

Callaway, E., Jones, R., and Donchin, E. (1970). Auditory evoked potential variability in schizophrenia. *Electroencephalography and Clinical Neurophysiology, 29,* 421–428.

Carlen, P.L., Wilkinson, D.A., and Kiraly, L.T. (1976). Dementia in alcoholics: A longitudinal study including some reversible aspects. *Neurology, 26,* 355–360.

Carlen, P.L., Wortzman, G., Holgate, R., Wilkinson, D.A., and Rankin, J. G. (1978). Reversible cerebral atrophy in recently abstinent chronic alcoholics measured by computed tomography signs. *Science, 200,* 1076–1078.

Cloninger, C.R., Reich, T., and Wetzel, R. (1979). Alcoholism and affective disorders: Familial associations and genetic models. In D. W. Goodwin and C.K. Erickson (Eds.), *Alcoholism and affective disorders: Clinical, genetic, and biochemical studies.* New York: SP Medical and Scientific Books, pp. 57–86.

Cobb, W., and Morocutti, C. (Eds.) (1968). *The evoked potentials. (Electroencephalography and Clinical Neurophysiology)* Supplement 26. Amsterdam; Elsevier.

Cohn, R. (1964). Rhythmic after-activity in visual evoked responses. *Annals of the New York Academy of Sciences, 112,* 281–291.

Cotton, N.S. (1979). The familial incidence of alcoholism: A review. *Journal of Studies on Alcohol, 40,* 89–116.

Courschesne, E. (1977). Event-related brain potentials: Comparison between children and adults. *Science, 197,* 589–592.

Courchesne, E. (1978). Neurophysiological correlates of cognitive development: Changes in long-latency event-related potentials from childhood to adulthood. *Electroencephalography and Clinical Neurophysiology, 45,* 468–482.

Courville, C. B. (1966). *Effects of alcohol on the nervous system of man.* Los Angeles: San Lucas Press.

Deitrich, R.A., and Spuhler, K. (1984). Genetics of alcoholism and alcohol actions. In R. G. Smart, H.D. Cappell, F.B. Glaser, Y. Israel, H. Kalant, R.E. Popham, W. Schmidt, and E.M. Sellers (Eds.), *Research advances in alcohol and drug problems* (Vol. 8, pp. 47–98). New York: Plenum.

De Obaldia, R., and Parsons, O.A. (1984). Relationship of neuropsychological performance to primary alcoholism and self-reported symptoms of childhood minimal brain dysfunction. *Journal of Studies on Alcohol, 45,* 386–392.

Donchin, E. (1979). Event-related brain potentials: A tool in the study of human information processing. In H. Begleiter (Ed.), *Evoked brain potentials and behavior,* (Vol. 2, pp. 65–88). Downstate series of research in psychiatry and psychology. New York: Plenum.

Donovan, J.M. (1986). An etiologic model of alcoholism. *The American Journal of Psychiatry, 143,* 1–11.

Drejer, K., Theilgaard, A., Teasdale, T.W., Schulsinger, F., and Goodwin, D.W. (1985). A prospective study of young men at high risk for alcoholism: Neuropsychological assessment. *Alcoholism: Clinical and Experimental Research, 9* (6), 498–502.

Dreyfus, P.M. (1974). Disease of the nervous system in chronic alcoholics. In B. Kissin and H. Begleiter (Eds.), *The biology of alcoholism* (Vol. 3, Pp. 265–290), New York: Plenum.

Dustman, R., and Beck, E. (1969). The effects of maturation and aging on the wave form of visually evoked potentials. *Electroencephalography and Clinical Neurophysiology, 26,* 2–11.

Dustman, R., Snyder, E., and Schlehuber, C. (1981). Life span alterations in visually evoked potentials and inhibitory function. *Neurobiology of Aging, 2,* 187–192.

Eckardt, M.J., Parker, E.S., Noble, E.P., Feldman, D.J., and Gottschalk, L.A. (1978). Relationship between neuropsychological performance and alcohol consumption in alcoholics. *Biological Psychiatry, 13,* 551–565.

Ellingson, R.J. (1960). Cortical electrical responses to visual stimulation in the human infant. *Electroencephalography and Clinical Neurophysiology, 12,* 663–677.

Ellingson, R.J., Lathrop, G.H., Danahy, T., and Nelson, B. (1973). Variability of visual evoked potentials in human infants and adults. *Electroencephalography and Clinical Neurophysiology, 34,* 113–124.

Elmasian, R., Neville, H., Woods, D., Schuckit, M., and Bloom, F. (1982). Event-related brain potentials are different in individuals at high and low risk for developing alcoholism. *Proceedings of the National Academy of Sciences of the United States of America, 79,* 7900–7903.

Ervin, C.S., Little, R.E., Streissguth, A.P., and Beck, D.E. (1984). Alcoholic fathering and its relation to child's intellectual development: A pilot investigation. *Alcoholism: Clinical and Experimental Research, 8,* 362–365.

Epstein, P., Pisani, V., and Fawcett, J. (1977). Alcoholism and cerebral atrophy. *Alcoholism: Clinical and Experimental Research, 1,* 61–65.

Farkas, T., Ferris, S.H., Wolf, A.P., DeLeon, M.J., Christman, D.R., Reisberg, B., Alavi, A., Fowler, J.S., George, A.E., and Reivich, M. (1982). 18F-2-Deoxy-2-fluoro-D-glucose as a tracer in the positron emission tomographic study of senile dementia. *American Journal of Psychiatry, 139* (3), 352–353.

Filskov, S.B., and Boll, T.J. (1981). *Handbook of clinical neuropsychology.* New York: Wiley.

Fisk, J.L., and Rourke, B.P. (1983). Neuropsychological subtyping of learning-disabled children: History, methods, implications. *Journal of Learning Disabilities, 16* (9), 529–531.

Ford, J., and Pfefferbaum, A. (1981). The utility of brain potentials in determining age-related changes in central nervous system and cognitive functioning. In L.W. Poon (Ed.), *Aging in the 1980's: Psychological issues.* Washington, D.C.: American Psychological Association, (pp. 115-123).

Fox, J.H., Ramsey, R.G., Auckman, M.S., Proske, A.E. (1976). Cerebral ventricular enlargement: Chronic alcoholics examined by computerized tomography. *Journal of the American Medical Association, 236,* 365–368.

Fuller, J.L., and Thompson, W.R. (1967). *Behavior genetics.* New York: Wiley.

Gabrielli, W.F., and Mednick, S.A. (1983). Intellectual performance in children of alcoholics. *The Journal of Nervous and Mental Disease, 171,* 444–447.

Gabrielli, W.F., Mednick, S.A., Volavka, J., Pollock, V.E., Schulsinger, F., and Itil, T.M. (1982). Electroencephalograms in children of alcoholic fathers. *Psychophysiology, 19,* 404–407.

Gibson, K.R. (1977). Brain structure and intelligence in macaques and human infants from a Piagetian perspective. In S. Chevalier-Skolnikoff and F.E. Poirer (Eds.), *Primate biosocial development* (pp. 113-115). New York: Garland.

Gibson, K.R. (1981). Comparative neuroontogeny: Its implications for the development of human intelligence in early hominids. In G. Butterworth (Ed.), *Infancy and epistemology,* (pp. 52-82). Brighton, England: Harvester Press.

Gilles, F.H., Leviton, A., and Dooling, E.C. (1983). *The developing human brain: Growth and epidemiologic neuropathology,* Boston: John Wright.

Goff, W.R., Allison, T., and Vaughn, H.G. (1978). The functional neuroanatomy of event related potentials. In E. Callaway, P. Tueting, and S. Koslow (Eds.), *Event related brain potentials in man* (pp. 1-90). New York: Academic Press.

Golden, C.J. (1981). *Diagnosis and rehabilitation in clinical neuropsychology,* 2nd ed. Springfield, IL: Charles C Thomas.

Golden, C.J., Purisch, A.D., Hammeke, T.A. (1985). *Luria-Nebraska Neuropsychological Battery: Forms I and II.* Los Angeles, CA: Western Psychological Services.

Goodwin, D.W. (1971). Is alcoholism hereditary? A review and critique. *Archives of General Psychiatry, 25,* 545–549.

Goodwin, D.W. (1976). *Is alcoholism hereditary?* New York: Oxford University Press.

Goodwin, D.W. (1985). Alcoholism and genetics: The sins of the fathers. *Archives of General Psychiatry, 28,* 238–243.

Goodwin, D.W., Schulsinger, F., Hermansen, L., Guze, S.B., and Winokur, G. (1973). Alcohol problems in adoptees raised apart from alcoholic biological parents. *Archives of General Psychiatry, 28,* 238–243.

Gottlieb, G. (1983). The psychobiological approach to developmental issues. In P.H. Mussen (Ed.), *Handbook of child psychology,* (Vol. II, pp. 1-26). New York: Wiley.

Greenblatt, M., Levin, S., and DiCori, F. (1944). The electroencephalogram associated with chronic alcoholism, alcoholic psychosis, and alcoholic convulsions. *Archives of Neurologic Psychiatry, 52,* 290–295.

Grove, W.M., and Cadoret, R.J. (1983). Genetic factors in alcoholism. In B. Kissin and H. Begleiter (Eds.), *The biology of alcoholism: Vol. 7. The pathogenesis of alcoholism: Biological factors* (pp. 31-56). New York: Plenum.

Halstead, W.C. (1947). *Brain and intelligence: A quantitative study of the frontal lobes.* Chicago: University of Chicago Press.

Hamburg, D.A., and Nightingale, E.O. (1987). Conjunction of biomedical and behavorial sciences: Can research on alcoholism show the way? *Alcoholism: Clinical and Experimental Research, 11* (3), 229–233.

Harmony, T. (1984). *Functional neuroscience, Vol. III, Neurometric assessment of brain dysfunction in neurological patients.* Hillsdale: NJ: Erlbaum.

Hegedus, A.M., Alterman, A.I., and Tarter, R.E. (1984). Learning achievement in sons of alcoholics. *Alcoholism: Clinical and Experimental Research, 8* (3), 330–333.

Hennecke, L. (1984). Stimulus augmenting and field dependence in children of alcoholic fathers. *Journal of Studies on Alcohol, 45,* 486–492.

Hesselbrock, V. (1983). Neuropsychological test performance in offspring of an alcoholic parent and controls. Paper presented at the annual meeting of the National Council on Alcoholism, Houston, TX.

Horst, R.L., Thatcher, R.W., Lester, M.L., and McAlaster, P. (1982). Differential effects of age on sensory evoked potentials in children. In A. Rothenberger (Ed.),

Event related potentials in children (pp. 71-78). Amsterdam: Elsevier Biomedical Press.

Incagnoli, T., and Kane, R. (1983). Developmental perspective of the Gilles de la Tourette syndrome. *Perceptual and Motor Skills, 57* (3 PT 2), 1271–1281.

Jasper, H.H. (1958). The ten-twenty electrode system of the International Federation. *Electroencephalography and Clinical Neurophysiology, 10,* 371–375.

John, E., Ruchkin, D., and Vidal, J. (1978). Measurement of event related potentials. In E. Callaway, P. Tueting, and S. Koslow (Eds.), *Event related brain potentials in man* (pp. 93-138). New York: Academic Press.

Johnson, J.L. (1984). Developmental changes in the cortical topography of the event related potential in normal children. Unpublished doctoral dissertation, University of Vermont, Burlington, VT.

Johnson, J.L. (1987). Issues in brain imaging. *British Journal of Addiction, 82,* 1177–1179.

Johnson, J.L., Adinoff, B., Bisserbe, J.C., Martin, P.R., Rio, D., Rohrbaugh, J.W., Zubovic, E., and Eckhardt, M.J. (1986). Assessment of alcoholism-related organic brain syndromes with Positron Emission tomography. *Alcoholism: Clinical and Experimental Research, (1971). 10* (3), 237–240.

Jones, B.M. (1971). Verbal and spatial intelligence in short-term and long-term alcoholics. *Journal of Nervous and Mental Disease, 41,* 129–139.

Jones, B.J., and Parsons, O.A. (1971). Specific vs. generalized deficits of abstracting ability in chronic alcoholics. *Archives of General Psychiatry, 26,* 380–384.

Kaij, L. (1960). *Alcoholism in twins: Studies on the etiology and sequels of abuse of alcohol.* Stockholm: Almqvist and Wiksell.

Kessler, R.M., Parker, E.S., Clark, C.M., Martin, P.R., George, D.T., Weingartner, H., Sokoloff, L., Ebert, M.H., and Mishkein, M. (1984). Regional cerebral glucose metabolism in patients with alcoholic Korsakoffs syndrome. *Society of Neurosciences Abstracts, 10,* 541.

Kleinknecht, R.A., and Goldstein, S.G. (1972). Neuropsychological deficits associated with alcoholism: A review and discussion. *Quarterly Journal of Studies on Alcohol, 33,* 999–1019.

Knop, J., Teasdale, T.W., Schulsinger, F., and Goodwin, D.W. (1985). A prospective study of young men at high risk for alcoholism: School behavior and achievement. *Journal of Studies on Alcohol, 46,* 273–278.

Krynicki, V.E., and Nahas, A.D. (1979). Differing lateralized perceptual-motor patterns in schizophrenic and non-psychotic children. *Perceptual and Motor Skills, 49* (2), 603–610.

Lehmann, D., and Callaway, E. (1979). *Human evoked potentials: Applications and problems.* New York: Plenum.

Lishman, W.A. (1981). Cerebral disorder in alcoholism: Syndromes of impairment. *Brain, 104,* 1–20.

Lodge, A., Armigton, J.C., Barnet, A.B., Shanks, B.L., Newcomb, C.N. (1969). Newborn infants electroretinograms and evoked electroencephalographic response to orange and white light. *Child Development, 40* (1), 267–293.

Malerstein, A.J. (1986). *The conscious mind.* New York: Human Sciences Press.

Marx, J.L. (1980). NMR opens a new window into the body. *Science, 210* (17), 302–306.

Miller, W.R., and Saucedo, C.F. (1983). Assessment of neuropsychological impairment and brain damage in problem drinkers. In C.J. Golden, J.A. Moses, J.A. Coffman, W.R. Miller, and F.D. Strider (Eds.), *Clinical neuropsychology: Interface with neurologic and psychiatric disorders* (pp. 141–271). New York: Grune & Stratton.

Moskowitz, A., and Sokol, S. (1983). Developmental changes in the human visual system as reflections of latency of the pattern reversal VEP. *Electroencephalography and Clinical Neurophysiology, 56,* 1–15.

Newlin, D.B. (1985). Offspring of alcoholics have enhanced antagonistic placebo response. *Journal of Studies on Alcohol, 46,* 490–494.

Noll, R.B., and Zucker, R.A. (1983). Developmental findings from an alcoholic vulnerability study: The preschool years. Paper presented at the Annual Meeting of the American Psychological Association, Anaheim, CA.

O'Leary, D.S., Lovell, M.R., Sackellares, J.C., Berent, S., Giordani, B., Seidenberg, M., Boll, T.J. (1983). Effects of age of onset of partial and generalized seizures on neuropsychological performance in children. *The Journal of Nervous and Mental Disease, 171* (10), 624–629.

Parsons, O.A. (1983). Cognitive dysfunction and recovery in alcoholics. *Substance and Alcohol Actions/Misuse, 4,* 175–190.

Parsons, OA., and Farr, S.P. (1981). The neuropsychology of alcohol and drug use. In S.B. Filskov and T.J. Boll (Eds.), *Handbook of clinical neuropsychology* (pp. 320-365). New York: Wiley.

Peele, S. (1986). The implications and limitations of genetic models of alcoholism and other addictions. *Journal of Studies on Alcohol, 47,* 63–73.

Phelps, M., Mazziotta, J., and Huang, S. (1982). Study of cerebral function with positron computed tomography. *Journal of Cerebral Blood Flow and Metabolism, 2* (2), 113–162.

Piaget, J. (1963). *The origins of intelligence in children.* New York: Norton.

Piaget, J. (1970). *Genetic epistemology.* New York: Norton.

Piaget, J. (1971). *Biology and knowledge: An essay on the relations between organic regulations and cognitive processes.* Chicago: University of Chicago Press.

Piaget, J. (1972). Problems of equilibration. In C.F. Nodine, J. McGallagher, and R.H. Humphreys (Eds.), *Piaget and Inhelder: On equilibration* (pp. 1-20). Philadelphia: The Jean Piaget Society.

Porjesz, B., and Begleiter, H. (1981). Human evoked brain potentials and alcohol. *Alcoholism: Clinical and Experimental Research, 5,* (2), 304–317.

Pykett, I.L. (1982). NMR imaging in medicine. *Scientific American, 246*(5), 78–88.

Radda, G.K., and Seeley, P.J. (1979). Recent studies on cellular metabolism by nuclear magnetic resonance. *Annals of the Review of Physiology, 4,* 749–769.

Rebeta, J.L. (1987). Selective neuropsychological dysfunction in adolescent sons of alcoholic fathers. Unpublished doctoral dissertation, American University.

Regan, D. (1972). *Evoked potentials in psychology, sensory physiology, and clinical medicine.* London: Chapman and Hall.

Reivich, M., Alair, A., Greenberg, J., Fowler, J., Christman, D., Wolf, A., Rosenquist, A., and Hand, P. (1979). Metabolic mapping of functional cerebral activity in man using 18F-2-fluoro-2-deoxyglucose technique. *Journal of Computer Assisted Tomography, 2,* 656–665.

Rourke, B.P. (1985). Brain-behavior relationships in children with learning disabilities. *American Psychologist*, Sept., 911–920.

Rourke, B.P., Bakker, D.J., Fisk, J.L., and Strang, J.D. (1983). *Child neuropsychology: An introduction to theory, research and clinical practice*. New York: Guilford.

Ryan. C., & Butters, N. (1980). Further evidence for a continuum-of-impairment encompassing male alcoholic Korsakoff patients and chronic alcoholic men. *Alcoholism: Clinical and Experimental Research, 4*, 190–198.

Ryan, C., & Butters, N. (1983). Cognitive deficits in alcoholics. In B. Kissin and H. Begleiter (Eds.), *The pathogenesis of alcoholism: Vol. 7. Biological factors* (pp. 485-538). New York: Plenum.

Schaeffer, K.W., Parsons, O.A., and Yohman, J.R. (1984). Neuropsychological differences between male familial and nonfamilial alcoholics and nonalcoholics. *Alcoholism: Clinical and Experimental Research, 8*, 347–351.

Schenkenberg, T. (1970). Visual, auditory, and somatosensory evoked responses of normal subjects from childhood to senescense. Unpublished doctoral dissertation, University of Utah.

Schukit, M.A. (1985). Genetics and the risk for alcoholism *The Journal of the American Medical Association, 254*, 2614–2617.

Schuckit, M.A., Goodwin, D.A., and Winokur, G. (1972). A study of alcoholism in half siblings. *American Journal of Psychiatry, 128*, 1132–1136.

Schuckit, M.A., Parker, D.C., and Rossman, L.R. (1983). Ethanol-related prolactin responses and risk for alcoholism. *Biological Psychiatry, 18*, 1153–1159.

Schuckit, M.A., Li, T.-K., Cloninger, C.R., and Deitrich, R.A. (1985). Genetics of alcoholism. *Alcoholism: Clinical and Experimental Research, 9*, 475–492.

Shagass, C., and Schwartz, M. (1966). Age, personality, and somatosensory evoked responses. *Science, 148*, 1359–1360.

Sokoloff, L. (1981). Localization of functional activity in the central nervous system by measurement of glucose utilization with radioactive deoxyglucose. *Journal of Cerebral Blood Flow Metabolism, 1*, 7–36.

Sokoloff, L., Reivich, M., Kennedy, C., Des Rosiers, M.H., Patlak, C.S., Pettigrew, K.D., Sakurada, O., and Shinohara, M. (1977). The [14C]deoxyglucose method for the measurement of local cerebral glucose utilization: Theory, procedure, and normal values in the conscious and anesthetized albino rat. *Journal of Neurochemistry, 28*, 897–916.

Spehr, W., and Stemmler, G. (1985). Postalcoholic diseases: Diagnostic relevance of computerized EEG. *Electroencephalography and Clinical Neurophysiology, 60*, 106–114.

Spreen, O., Tupper, D., Risser, A., Tuokko, H., and Edgell, D. (1984). *Human developmental neuropsychology*. New York: University Press.

Squires, K.C., Hillyard, S.A., and Lindsay, P.L. (1973). Cortical potentials evoked by confirming and disconfirming feedback following an auditory discrimination. *Perception and Psychophysics, 13*, 25–31.

Straumanis, J., Shagass, C., and Schwartz, M. (1965). Visually evoked cerebral response changes associated with chronic brain syndrome and aging. *Journal of Gerontology, 20*, 498–506.

Tarter, R.E. (1973). Psychological deficit in chronic alcoholics: A review. *The Journal of Nervous and Mental Disease, 1557*, 138–147.

Tarter, R.E., and Edwards, K.L. (1985). Neuropsychology of alcoholism. In R.E. Tarter and D.H. Van Thiel (Eds.), *Alcohol and the brain: Chronic effects* (pp. 217-242). New York: Plenum.

Tarter, R.E., Hegedus, A.M., Goldstein, G., Shelly, C., and Alterman, A.I. (1984). Adolescent sons of alcoholics: Neuropsychological and personality characteristics. *Alcoholism: Clinical and Experimental Research, 8,* 216–222.

Taylor, E.M. (1959). *Psychological appraisal of children with cerebral defects.* Cambridge, MA: Harvard University Press.

Telzrow, C.F. (1983). Making child neuropsychological appraisal appropriate for children: Alternative to downward extension of adult batteries. *Clinical Neuropsychology, 5*(3), 136–141.

Teuber, H.L., and Rudel, R.G. (1962). Behavior after cerebral lesions in children and adults. *Developmental Medicine and Child Neurology, 4,* 3–20.

Thatcher, R.W., Walker, R.A., and Giudice, S. (1987). Human cerebral hemispheres develop at different rates and ages. *Science, 236,* 1110–1113.

U.S. Department of Health and Human Services. (1981). *First Statistical Compendium on Alcohol and Health.* DHHS Publication No. (ADM) 81–1115.

Wilkinson, D.A. (1982). Examination of alcoholics by Computed Tomographic (CT) scans: A critical review. *Alcoholism: Clinical and Experimental Research, 6*(1), 31–45.

PART IV

BIOSOCIAL SCIENCES AND THE NEUROLOGY OF LANGUAGE

Chapter 12

Levels of Structure in a Communication System Developed without a Language Model

Susan Goldin-Meadow and Carolyn Mylander

The Resilience of Language Development

Language is a robust phenomenon mastered by children experiencing a wide range of environments (cf. Wimsatt, 1981). Despite great variability in patterns of child–caretaker communications (e.g. Miller, 1982; Ochs, 1982; Pye, 1986; Schieffelin, 1979), virtually all children in all cultures master the language to which they are exposed. However, there do appear to be limits on the robustness of language development in children. If, for example, a child is not raised by humans (e.g., Lane, 1977) or is raised by humans under inhumane conditions (e.g., Curtiss, 1977), severe breakdowns in language development will occur.

Moreover, not all properties of language appear to be equally robust in the face of variations in environmental conditions. Certain properties of language have been found to develop in environments that deviate dramatically from typical language-learning environments, while other properties of language have not. For example, Sachs and her colleagues (Sachs et al., 1981; Sachs and Johnson, 1976) studied the language development of a hearing child who was exposed to an impoverished model of English by his deaf parents and found that this child developed some of the properties of English but failed to develop others. Thus, the child's dearth of linguistic input appeared to have had differential effects on his language development.

By observing the effects of variations in the linguistic environment on the development of language in children, we can hope to determine which properties of language will develop in child language across a wide range of linguistic environments, and which properties of language will develop in only a relatively narrow range of environments.

In our work, we focus on isolating those properties of language whose development can withstand wide variations in learning conditions—the "resilient'' properties of language. In an attempt to determine which properties of language can be developed by a child under one set of degraded input conditions, we observe children who have not been exposed to any conventional linguistic input. The children we study are deaf with hearing losses so severe that they cannot naturally acquire oral language. In addition, these children are born to hearing parents who have chosen not to expose them to a manual sign language. We have found that these deaf children, despite their impoverished language learning conditions, develop a gestural communication system that is structured in many ways like the communication systems of young children learning language in ordinary linguistic environments (Feldman et al., 1978; Goldin-Meadow, 1979, 1982; Goldin-Meadow and Mylander 1983, 1984).

In our previous work we demonstrated that the gesture systems our deaf subjects develop are structured at the sentence level of analysis; specifically, order and deletion patterns are identifiable *across* gestures in a sentence. However, natural languages, both signed and spoken, are known to be structured not only at the sentence level but also at the word or sign level. If a hierarchy of structured levels is common to all natural languages, it becomes important to ask whether the deaf children in our studies display such hierarchical structure in their gestural communication as well. In other words, we ask whether hierarchical structure is also a "resilient" property of language.

The primary objective of this study is to determine whether the deaf children's gesture systems are structured at this second level, the level of the word or sign. Thus, we ask whether structure exists *within* gestures as well as across them, and, if so, which aspects of structure at this level can be developed by a child without the benefit of a conventional language model.

Background

The sign languages of the deaf are autonomous languages that are not derivatives from the spoken languages of hearing cultures (Bellugi and Studdert-Kennedy, 1980; Klima and Bellugi, 1979; Lane and Grosjean, 1980). A sign language such as American Sign Language (ASL) is a primary linguistic system passed down from one generation of deaf people to the next and is a language in the full sense of the word. Like spoken languages, ASL is structured at syntactic (Fischer, 1975; Liddell, 1980), morphological (Fischer, 1973; Fischer and Gough, 1978; Klima and Bellugi, 1979; Newport, 1981; Supalla, 1982; Supalla and Newport, 1978), and "phonological" (Battison, 1974; Lane et al., 1976; Stokoe, 1960) levels of analysis.

Deaf children born to deaf parents and exposed from birth to a conventional sign language such as ASL have been found to acquire that language naturally; that is, these children progress through stages in acquiring sign language similar to those of hearing children acquiring a spoken language (Caselli, 1983; Hoffmeister, 1978; Hoffmeister and Wilbur, 1980; Kantor, 1982; Newport and Ashbrook, 1977). Thus, in an appropriate linguistic environment, in this case, a signing environment, deaf children are not handicapped with respect to language learning.

However, 90% of deaf children are not born to deaf parents who could provide early exposure to a conventional sign language. Rather, they are born to hearing parents who, quite naturally, tend to expose their children to speech (Hoffmeister and Wilbur, 1980). Unfortunately, it is extremely uncommon for deaf children with severe to profound hearing losses to acquire the spoken language of their hearing parents naturally, that is, without intensive and specialized instruction. Even with instruction, deaf children's acquisition of speech is markedly delayed when compared either to the acquisition of speech by hearing children of hearing parents or to the acquisition of sign by deaf children of deaf parents. By age 5 or 6, and despite intensive early training programs, the average profoundly deaf child has only a very reduced oral linguistic capacity (Conrad, 1979; Meadow, 1968; Mindel and Vernon, 1971).

In addition, unless hearing parents send their deaf children to a school in which sign language is used, these deaf children are not likely to be exposed to conventional sign input. Under such nonpropitious circumstances, these deaf children might be expected to fail to communicate at all, or perhaps to communicate only in nonsymbolic ways. This turns out not to be the case.

Previous studies of deaf children of hearing parents have shown that these children spontaneously use gestural symbols to communicate even if they are not exposed to a conventional sign language model (Fant, 1972; Lenneberg, 1964; Moores, 1974; Tervoort, 1961). These gestures are conventionally referred to as "home sign." Most of our work has focused particularly on the *structural* aspects of deaf children's home sign.

Syntactic Properties of Deaf Children's Home Sign Systems: Structure across Signs

The heuristic we have adopted in describing the deaf children's home sign systems has been to determine which of the properties of early child language can be found in the deaf children's gesture systems. We have observed the home sign of 10 deaf children of hearing parents and found that all 10 children developed gesture systems comparable in many respects to early child language (Feldman et al., 1978; Goldin-Meadow, 1979, 1982; Goldin-Meadow and Feldman, 1975, 1977; Goldin-Meadow and Mylander, 1984). In addition, we investigated the possibility that the deaf children might have learned their home sign systems from their hearing parents. In particular, we asked whether the parents, in an effort to communicate with their children, generated a structured gesture system that their children then imitated, or whether the parents shaped the structure of their children's gestures by patterning their responses to those gestures. We found no evidence supporting either of these hypotheses (Goldin-Meadow and Mylander, 1983, 1984).

The deaf children in our studies developed gestures that function as words do in the systems of hearing children learning conventional spoken languages, and as signs do in the systems of deaf children learning conventional signed languages (e.g., ASL). The children in our studies produced two types of gestures: (1) deictic signs used to refer to people, places, or things (e.g., a pointing sign at a snack), and (2) characterizing signs used to refer to actions or attributes (e.g., a fist held at the mouth accompanied by chewing [EAT]).[1] In addition, the deaf children combined their signs into strings that function as do the sentences of early child language in two respects: (1) The deaf children's sign sentences express the semantic relations typically found in early child language, with characterizing signs representing the predicates and deictic signs representing the arguments of those semantic relations. (2) The deaf children's sign sentences are structured as are the sentences of early child language; specifically, there are order and deletion patterns identifiable across signs (or words) in a sentence (e.g., the sign for the patient[2] role [snack] is likely to precede the sign for the act predicate [eat]). Moreover, the children exhibited the property of recursion in their sign systems and generated novel, complex sentences (containing at least two propositions) from combinations of simple one-proposition sentences. For example, one child pointed at a tower, produced the HIT sign [fist swatting in air] and then the FALL sign [flat palm flops over in air] to comment on the fact that he had hit [act_1] the tower and that the tower had fallen [act_2]).

In sum, in our previous work we found that deaf children, even without the benefit of a conventional linguistic model, can develop gestural communication systems that display some of the structural properties of early child language—in particular, structural properties at the level of the sentence. Thus, it appears that the human child has strong biases to communicate using strings of lexical items and to structure those strings in language-like ways.

Structure at a Second Level?

As described above, our previous work focused on the structural regularities across signs in our deaf subjects' gesture sentences. For the purposes of this "syntactic" analysis, we treated each sign as the minimal meaning-bearing unit. However, in the process of examining the corpus of signs produced by each child, we began to notice certain subsign forms (e.g., handshape and motion) that seemed to be associated with consistent meanings and that, furthermore, seemed to recur in the composition of different signs. For example, one child used the same motion form (moving the hand to and fro) to mean "movement back and forth" in at least two different signs: once with a fist handshape (resembling a person's hand moving a knife back and forth) and a second time with a flat palm handshape held vertically (resembling the knife itself moving back and forth). In addition to suggesting that the child can focus either on a person acting on an object or on the object itself in generating a sign, this example also suggests that handshape and motion might be separable forms associated with distinct meanings that combine to form signs in the child's gesture system; that is, the example suggests that handshape and motion function as morphemes in the deaf child's gesture system.

Examples of this sort do not by themselves provide evidence of a *system* of handshape and motion morphemes; selected examples may not be representative of the way in which the child constructs his entire lexicon. In order to argue that the deaf child's signs are consistently divisible into handshape and motion morphemes, we must review the entire corpus of characterizing signs and ask whether the set of signs meets the following criteria for structure at the level of the sign:

1. Is there a limited set of discrete handshape and motion forms in the child's corpus of signs? i.e., are the forms categorical rather than continuous?
2. Is a particular handshape or motion form consistently associated with a particular meaning (or set of meanings) throughout the corpus of signs? i.e., is each handshape and motion form meaningful?
3. Does a particular handshape or motion form/meaning pairing appear in more than one sign? i.e., is a particular form/meaning pairing an independent morpheme that can combine with other morphemes in the system—is the system combinatorial.

The present chapter focuses on structure across components (morphemes) within a sign; that is, we focus on structure at the "morphological" level. Our search for morphological structure in the deaf children's gesture systems is guided particularly by recent research on morphology in ASL. We begin by reviewing the findings of this literature that are relevant to our analyses.

Morphological Properties of the Deaf Child's Home Sign System: Structure within the Sign

Early research in ASL suggested that verbs in ASL, unlike verbs in spoken languages, appeared to be continuously varying forms constructed on the basis of analog representations of real-world events (DeMatteo, 1977). In other words, ASL verbs were thought not to be divisible into component parts, but rather were considered unanalyzable lexical items that mapped, as wholes, onto events in the world. Subsequently, verbs in ASL (particularly, the mimetic verbs of motion) have been more accurately described as combinations of a limited set of discrete morphemes (McDonald, 1982; Newport, 1981; Supalla, 1982). For example, to describe a drunk's weaving walk down a path, an ASL signer would *not* represent the idiosyncrasies of the drunk's particular meanderings, but would instead use a conventional morpheme representing random movement (i.e., a side-to-side motion) in conjunction with a conventional morpheme representing change of location. Mimetic verbs in ASL have been shown to be constructed from discrete sets of morphemes and to include, at a minimum, a motion morpheme combined with a handshape morpheme (McDonald, 1982; Newport, 1981; Supalla, 1982).

Morphemes in ASL (as in spoken languages) have been organized into frameworks or matrices of oppositions, referred to as "paradigms" (cf. Matthews, 1974). For example, the motion form "linear path" (representing change of location along a straight path) can be combined with any number of hand forms representing agents or actors (e.g., inverted V = human; a bent inverted V = an animate nonhuman; thumb + two fingers held sideways = a vehicle). These combinations create a set of signs whose meanings are predictable from the meanings of the individual motion and handshape elements (i.e., a human moves along a straight path, an animate nonhuman moves along a straight path, a vehicle moves along a straight path). In another example, a different motion form (e.g., "arc path," representing change of location along an arced path such as a jump forward) can be combined with any of these same handshape morphemes to create a set of signs whose meanings are also systematic combinations of the component parts of each sign (e.g., a human jumps forward, an animate nonhuman jumps forward, a vehicle jumps forward). Thus, many of the verbs of ASL can be described in terms of a combination of handshape and motion morphemes that together form complete paradigmatic sets.

To determine whether our deaf subjects' gestures can also be characterized by systematic combinations of meaningful forms, we selected one of our original subjects (David) and analyzed the characterizing signs (i.e., the mimetic signs) he produced during naturalistic play sessions videotaped in his home when he was 2;10, 2;11, 3;0, 3;3, 3;5, 3;11, and 4;10.[3] These ages span the age range during which both deaf (Supalla, 1982) and hearing (MacWhinney, 1976) children learning conventional languages have typically already begun to acquire certain morphemic distinctions.

The videotapes of David were coded initially at the sign level according to a system described in detail in Goldin-Meadow (1979) and Goldin-Meadow and Mylander (1984). We then coded each characterizing sign produced during these sessions in terms of its handshape and motion. Reliability between two independent coders ranged from 85 to 95% agreement for handshape and from 83 to 93% agreement for motion.

We begin by analyzing, first, the forms and meanings of the handshapes David used in his signs and, then, the forms and meanings of the motions in those signs. We next describe the combinations of handshapes and motions that occurred in the corpus of David's signs. Finally, we describe how motions combined with other motions in David's signs.

Handshape Morphemes

Handshape Forms. Following Supalla (1982) and McDonald (1982), we coded each handshape according to four dimensions: the shape of the palm, the distance between the fingers and the thumb, the number of fingers extended, and the presence or absence of spread between the fingers. At first, we coded handshapes continuously along each dimension without establishing a priori either discrete categories or boundaries. Thus, for example, we wrote down the exact distance (in inches) between the fingers and thumb of a particular hand-shape and did not try to force that handshape into a limited set of thumb–finger distances. We found, however, that David used only a restricted number of values on each of the four dimensions. Table 1 displays the five most frequent handshapes David used on these tapes described in terms of the relevant dimen-sions. These five handshapes accounted for 98% of all of the handshapes David produced ($N = 472$).

The remaining 2% of David's handshapes not represented in Table 1 were V (two fingers spread apart and extended), L (thumb and forefinger extended at right angles to each other), Thumb (thumb extended), F (thumb and finger touching with the other three fingers extended in the "okay" sign), and W (three fingers spread apart and extended). Each of these infrequently produced hand-shapes was used to represent only one object throughout the tapes (e.g., the V was used to represent scissors, the L was used to represent a gun). We saw no evidence that these handshapes participated in a generative way in David's sign system and, as a result, we eliminated them from further analyses.

Handshape Form/Meaning Mapping. We next determined whether David's handshapes mapped in any systematic way onto categories of meanings. We found that David used his handshapes in two ways: (1) to represent a HAND as it manipulates an object, or (2) to represent the OBJECT itself. For example (as described above), to describe a picture of a knife, David produced a Fist handshape (with a back and forth movement) that mirrors a cutter's hand manipulating a knife, and thus is an instance of a HAND handshape. In contrast, to again describe the knife, David produced in a separate sentence a Palm handshape held perpendicular to the table (with the same back and forth move-ment), mirroring the flat shape of the knife itself, and, therefore, meeting the criterion for an OBJECT handshape. The same hand/finger configuration could be used to represent either a HAND or an OBJECT morpheme in David's

Table 1. Description of Handshape Forms

Handshape Form	Description
Fist	Fingers and thumb curled into palm
O	Index finger or four fingers bent toward thumb with ½ inch or less between the thumb and finger(s)[a]
C	Index finger or four fingers bent toward thumb with 3 inches between the thumb and finger(s)[a]
Palm	Four fingers extended
Point	Index finger extended

[a] If only the index finger was bent toward the thumb in the O and C handshapes, the other three fingers were either curled into the palm or held sloppily in an untensed manner.

system. On one occasion, David used a C handshape to represent handling a cup—where the handshape mirrored the handgrip around the cup [HAND]. At another time, he used the same C handshape to represent the shape of a cowboy's curved legs as the cowboy sits astride a horse [OBJECT]. Orientation of the hand with respect to the motion was crucial in determining whether the hand represented a HAND handshape or an OBJECT handshape. In the above cowboy example where the C was used as an OBJECT handshape, the fingers and palm of the C handshape point downward as the motion descends, mirroring the shape of the cowboy's legs as they go around the horse. If, however, the C were perpendicular to the motion (oriented as a person's hand would be if it were placing the cowboy on the horse), the handshape would have been considered a HAND handshape rather than an OBJECT handshape.

To determine the meaning of each handshape form, we first listed all of the objects represented by each handshape form used with either a HAND or OBJECT meaning in the one-motion signs (signs that contained only a single motion) David produced during one session, the session at age 3;11. We then determined whether the set of objects associated with a particular handshape form could be said to share a common attribute or set of attributes. If so, we took that common core to be the meaning of the particular handshape form. We then used these form/meaning pairings to code the videotapes of the six remaining sessions.

Table 2 describes the meanings found to be associated with the HAND and OBJECT handshape forms in the session at age 3;11, as well as examples of the objects represented by each handshape form/meaning pairing. Table 2 also presents the total number of different types of objects represented by each form/meaning pairing and, in parentheses, the total number of times each form/meaning pairing was used throughout the seven videotaped sessions.[4] We found that 367 (95%) of the 386 handshapes David produced in his one-motion signs during the seven videotaped sessions could be classified into the form/meaning categories listed in Table 2. In addition, 68 (91%) of the 75 handshapes in David's two-motions signs (signs that contained two motions concatenated without a break so that both appeared to be within the same sign) were also found to conform to the form/meaning categories established on the basis of the one-motion signs produced during the 3;11 session. Note that the Palm and Point handshapes were each used to represent more than one class of objects (e.g., the OBJECT Palm was used to represent (1) flat, wide objects, (2) many small particles, and (3) vehicles and animate objects); each of these classes is considered to be a distinct morpheme. Exceptions to Table 2 consisted of form/meaning mismatches, such as a Fist form used to represent handling a small, *short* (rather than a long) object (e.g., a knob on a toy), or a Palm form used to represent a round inanimate object (e.g., a ball moving forward).

It is important to note that David's HAND morphemes were not always accurate representations of the way a hand grasps a particular object in the real

Table 2. Meanings of Handshape Forms[a]

Form	HAND Morphemes Meaning	Types (Tokens)	OBJECT Morphemes Meaning	Types (Tokens)
Fist	Handle small, long object (e.g., spoon, drumstick, balloon string, handlebar)[b]	19 (70)	Bulky object (hammer head)	1 (2)
O	Handle small object (e.g., crank, shoe lace)[b]	31 (102)	Round compact object (e.g., round hat, tree ball, bubble)	6 (17)
C	Handle large object (e.g., cup, horn, guitar neck)[b]	11 (20)	Curved object (e.g., cowboy's legs around a horse, turtle)	5 (7)
Palm	Handle flat surface (e.g., sides of toy bag, chair back)	12 (30)	Flat wide object (e.g., flag, bird wings)	9 (43)
	Handle many small surfaces (xylophone keys)	1 (3)	Many small particles (e.g., snow)	6 (9)
			Vehicle or animate object (e.g., car, sister, Santa, plane)	13 (26)
Point	Handle small surface (trigger)	1 (2)	Thin straight object (e.g., straw, bubble wand, pinwheel)	6 (12)
			Object of any shape (e.g., bear, penny, Susan)	13 (24)

[a]The table contains the handshapes found in David's one-motion signs during the seven videotaped sessions. The first number represents the number of different types of objects represented by the handshape, and the number in parentheses represents the total number of times the handshape was used for that meaning.
[b]Small = ≤2 inches in diameter; large = >2 inches in diameter; long = >5 inches in length.

world, nor were his OBJECT morphemes precise mimetic reconstructions of real world objects. For example, the same HAND form (the Fist) was used to represent grasping a balloon string, a drumstick, and handlebars—grasping actions that require considerable variety in diameter in the real world. David therefore appeared not to distinguish objects of varying diameters within the Fist category. However, he did use his handshapes to distinguish objects with small diameters *as a set* from objects with large diameters (e.g., a cup, a guitar neck, the length of a straw) that were represented by a C hand.

As another example, David used the same OBJECT form (the O) to represent a round hat, a Christmas tree ball, and a bubble—objects that vary in size in the real world. David did not appear to distinguish objects of varying sizes within the

O category, but rather appeared to categorize them all as round objects. However, David did distinguish these round objects *as a set* from curved objects (e.g., a turtle's back, a cowboy's legs around a horse) that were represented by a C hand. Overall, David thus appeared to consign handshapes to discrete categories, rather than utilize analog representations of "real world" objects.

Motion Morphemes

Motion Forms. We found that David used eight different types of motions, as well as a no-motion form, in his signs (Table 3). The motions were defined in terms of the type of trajectory traced by the hand (linear path, arced path, circle) or the motions of the hand in place (revolve, open/close, bend, wiggle). In addition, arcs were distinguished in terms of length of path (< 7 inches v. > 7 inches) and directionality (unidirectional vs. bidirectional). These motion forms account for 100% of the signs David produced during these sessions ($N = 514$).

Motion Form/Meaning Mapping. To determine whether each of David's nine motion forms was associated with a particular class of meanings, we began by listing all of the actions David represented with each of the nine motion forms in the one-motion signs he produced during the session at age 3;11. We then determined whether the actions associated with a particular motion form shared certain common attributes. If so, we took that common core to be the meaning of the particular motion form, and used the resulting set of form/meaning pairings to code the videotapes from the remaining six sessions.

Table 4 presents the meanings of the motion forms David produced in his one-motion signs during the session at age 3;11. The numbers in the table represent the total number of different types of actions represented by each form/meaning pairing, and (in parentheses) the total number of times each motion form/meaning pairing was used over the course of the seven videotaped sessions.

We found that David used his motion forms to represent four different types of change in the state of an object: change of location, change of position, change of

Table 3.   Description of Motion Forms

Form	Type of Motion
Linear	Hand moves in a straight path
Long arc	Hand moves in an arced path >7 inches in length unidirectionally
Short arc	Hand moves in an arced path <7 inches in length unidirectionally
Arc to and fro	Hand moves in an arced path of any length bidirectionally
Circular	Hand moves in circle, wrist or fingers revolve
Open/close	Hand or fingers open and/or close
Bend	Hand or fingers bend
Wiggle	Fingers wiggle
No motion	Hand held in place

Table 4. Meanings of Motion Forms[a]

Type of Motion	Form	Meaning	Types (Tokens)
Change of location	Linear	Change of location by moving along a path	16 (34)
	Long arc	Change of location by moving along a path, typically to or from a particular endpoint	19 (24)
Change of position	Arc to and fro	Reposition by moving back and forth	29 (114)
	Circular	Reposition by moving in a circle or rotating around an axis	15 (37)
	Short arc	Reposition (or reorient) in place; reposition in order to affect another object; or reposition with respect to another object or place	33 (71)
Change of shape	Open/close	Open/close, expand/contract, or flicker on/off	9 (16)
	Bend	Bend at a joint	2 (5)
	Wiggle	Wiggle back and forth	2 (3)
No change	No motion	Hold in place or exist	29 (91)

[a]The table contains the motions fround in David's one-motion signs during the seven videotaped sessions. The first number represents the number of different types of actions represented by the motion, and the number in parentheses represents the total number of times the motion was used for that meaning.

shape, and no change. He used the Linear and Long Arc forms to represent *change of location* along a path, either of an object (or person) moving on its own (that is, an intransitive motion, e.g., bubble go up, we go down), or an object being moved by a person (a transitive motion, e.g., move coat, scoop spoon). Although both forms were used to represent change of location, the Long Arc was typically used to represent a change of location bounded by a particular endpoint (e.g., penny arc forward [to a bank]), while the path represented by the Linear form could either be open-ended (e.g., bubble go upward) or bounded by an endpoint (e.g., we go down [to the bottom of the stair]).

David used the Arc To and Fro, Circular, and Short Arc forms to represent the *change of position* either of an object (or person) repositioning itself (that is, an intransitive motion, e.g., wheel tip-over), or an object being repositioned by a person (a transitive motion, e.g., turn-over clay). A change of position involved bidirectional repositioning around a center-point (the Arc To and Fro form, e.g., wings flap, jiggle handlebars side-to-side), unidirectional repositioning around an axis or center-point (the Circular form, e.g., wheel rotate, turn crank), or unidirectional repositioning having no center-point (the Short Arc form). There were three types of meanings conveyed by the Short Arc form: repositioning in the same spot (e.g., wheel tip-over), repositioning an object to affect another object (e.g., swing hammer [to knock tower], shake envelope [to release contents]), or repositioning an object with respect to another object or a place, either to remove the object (e.g., pick-up bubble jar [off table]) or to place the object (e.g., hook treelights [onto Christmas tree], push-down box lid [onto bottom of box]).

David used the Open/Close, Bend, and Wiggle forms to represent the *change of shape* either of an object altering its own form (an intransitive motion, e.g., bubble expands, fish bends [to swim]), or a hand altering its shape on an object (a transitive motion, e.g., hand closes around toy bulb, fingers wiggle to strike keys). The Open/Close form was used to represent an object (or hand) opening or closing (e.g., claw closes, hand closes [around toy]), expanding or contracting (e.g., bubble expands), or flicking on and off (e.g., treelights flicker). The Bend form was used to represent an object bending at a joint (e.g., fish bends). The Wiggle form was used to represent an object (or hand) wiggling (e.g., snow flutters, fingers wiggle [to strike piano keys]).

Finally, David used the No-Motion form to represent *no change* in an object as it is held in place (e.g., hold bubble-wand [at mouth]) or as it exists (e.g., puzzleboard exists, bubble exists).

We found that 395 (90%) of the 439 motions in the one-motion signs David produced during the seven videotaped sessions could be classified according to the form/meaning pairings listed in Table 4. In addition, 69 (92%) of the 75 motions in David's two-motion signs conformed to the form/meaning pairings established on the basis of the one-motion signs produced during the session at age 3;11. Exceptions to Table 4 consisted of form/meaning mismatches, such as a Short Arc form used to represent the path of a change of location (e.g., a turtle moving forward along a path), or a Long Arc form used to represent an object being repositioned (e.g., swinging a hammer).

Handshape and Motion Combinations

We have shown that David's signs can be described in terms of handshape morphemes (i.e., handshape form/meaning pairings) and motion morphemes (i.e., motion form/meaning pairings). We now attempt to demonstrate that the signs themselves were in fact composites of handshape and motion morphemes rather than one unanalyzed whole, i.e., that handshape and motion are separable units. Since signs are composed of hands moving in space, it is not possible to find handshapes that are actually separated from their motions. Nevertheless, if we find a handshape that is not uniquely associated with one sign but rather is combined with several different motions in different signs, we then have evidence that the handshape may be an independent unit in David's system. Similarly, if a motion is combined with different handshapes in different signs, we infer evidence for the separability of that motion. We will consider first David's HAND handshape morphemes in combination with motion morphemes and then David's OBJECT handshape morphemes in combination with motion morphemes.

HAND Handshape Morphemes Combined with Motion Morphemes.   Table 5 displays examples of the HAND handshape morphemes combined with each of the nine motion morphemes. Empty cells in Table 5 represent handshape/motion combinations that David did not use at all during these sessions. Two HAND morphemes—the Palm (Many Surfaces) and the Point—are not shown at all in Table 5 because the Palm (Many Surfaces) occurred with only two motion morphemes and the Point did not occur with any well-formed motion morphemes. The numbers in Table 5 represent the number of types of events represented by each pairing of a HAND handshape with one of the nine motions; the numbers in parentheses represent the total number of times a particular handshape occurred with a particular motion. The table contains David's one-motion signs, excluding those that were exceptions to either Table 2 (handshape form/meaning pairings) or Table 4 (motion form/meaning pairings). In Table 5 the handshapes represent an actor's hand shaped on or around a patient, and the motions represent events in which an actor manipulates a patient (i.e., transitive events).

Note that most of David's HAND handshape morphemes could be found in combination with more than one motion morpheme, and vice versa. As a result, David's signs can be said to conform to a framework or system of contrasts. As an example of how the meanings of David's signs systematically contrasted with

Table 5.   HAND Handshapes Used in Combination with Motions[a]

	Fist	O	C	Palm
Change of location Linear	—	—	—	Change the location of an object with a large flat surface 1(1), e.g., push toys away
Long arc	Change the location of a small long object 1(1),[b] e.g., scoop utensil	Change the location of a small object of any length 1(1), e.g., scoop spoon	—	Change the location of an object with a large flat surface 1(2), e.g., push chair (to wall)

(cont.)

Table 5. HAND Handshapes Used in Combination with Motions[a] *(cont.)*

	Fist	*O*	*C*	*Palm*
Change of position				
Short arc	Reposition a small long object 6(12), e.g., pull out newspaper	Reposition a small object of any length 10(20), e.g., take out bubble wand	Reposition a large object of any length 2(2), e.g., pick up bubble jar	Reposition an object with a large flat surface 2(5), e.g., lift up large toy bag
Arc to and fro	Move a small long object to and fro 7(28), e.g., wave balloon string back and forth	Move a small object of any length to and fro 7(42), e.g., move crayon back and forth (to draw)	Move a large object of any length to and fro 1(1), e.g., shake salt shaker up and down	Move an object with a large flat surface to and fro 5(8), e.g., swing child back and forth holding his rear-end
Circular	Move a small long object in a circle 1(1), e.g., wave flag pole in circle	Move a small object of any length in a circle 5(8), e.g., turn crank	Move a large object of any length in a circle 4(10), e.g., twist jar lid	—
Change of shape				
Open/ close	Grasp or release a small long object 1(1), e.g., grasp mower han- dle	Grasp or release a small object of any length 2(2), e.g., squeeze bulb toy	—	—
Bend	—	—	—	—
Wiggle	—	—	—	—
No change				
No motion	Hold a small long object 6(16), e.g., hold handle- bars	Hold a small object of any length 9(24), e.g., hold bubble wand	Hold a large object of any length 3(6), e.g., hold horn	—

[a] Two HAND handshapes, Palm (many surfaces) and Point, are omitted from the table because they occurred infrequently. Palm (many surfaces) occurred with two motions (Arc to and Fro and No Motion), and Point occurred only with motions that were not well formed.

[b] The first number represents the number of different types of events represented by the handshape/ motion combination. The number in parentheses represents the total number of tokens. Only one-motion signs are included in the table.

one another, the C handshape was used in combination with the Short Arc motion to mean "change the position of large object by hand" (e.g., pick-up bubble jar). The same Short Arc motion when used in combination with a different handshape (the Fist) meant "change the position of a small, long object by hand" (e.g., pull-out newspaper). In contrast, the same Fist handshape when combined with a different motion (the Arc To and Fro) meant "move a small, long object to and fro by hand" (e.g., wave balloon string back and forth).

Whereas change-of-position and no-change motion morphemes each formed a relatively complete matrix or paradigm with the HAND morphemes, certain of the other handshape/motion combinations were produced only infrequently. For example, the Linear motion morpheme occurred with only one HAND morpheme despite the fact that the Long Arc motion (which is comparable in meaning to the Linear motion) occurred with three of the four HAND morphemes. In addition, change-of-shape motions were found in only 2 of the 12 possible handshape/motion combinations shown in Table 5.

OBJECT Handshape Morphemes Combined with Motion Morphemes. David used OBJECT handshapes in three different types of signs: (1) signs describing an intransitive event in which an actor (animate or inanimate) propels itself and does not affect a patient, where the handshape represents a characteristic of the actor, e.g., a C handshape used with a Linear motion to describe a turtle moving forward; (2) signs describing a transitive event in which an actor affects a patient, where the handshape represents a characteristic of the patient, e.g., a C handshape used with a Short Arc motion to describe the curved shape of a cowboy's legs as someone places the cowboy on a horse; and (3) signs describing a static object, e.g., a C handshape used with a No-motion form to describe the arced shape of a block. David produced 72 (56%) signs of type 1 (OBJECT handshapes with motions representing intransitive events), 26 (20%) signs of type 2 (OBJECT handshapes with motions representing transitive events), and 31 (24%) signs of type 3 (OBJECT handshapes with the no-motion morpheme representing attributes of objects). We describe each of these types of signs with OBJECT handshapes in turn.

Intransitive meanings. Table 6 presents examples of the OBJECT morphemes combined with the nine motion morphemes when those motions were used to represent events in which an actor or mover propels itself and does not affect a patient, i.e., intransitive events. As in Table 5, empty cells in Table 6 represent handshape/motion combinations that David did not use at all during these sessions. Two OBJECT morphemes—the Fist and the O—are not included in Table 6 because they did not occur with motions describing intransitive events. The numbers in Table 6 represent the number of types of intransitive events represented by each pairing of an OBJECT handshape with one of the nine motions; the numbers in parentheses represent the total number of times a particular handshape occurred with a particular motion. The table contains David's one-motion signs, again excluding the exceptions to Tables 2 and 4.

Table 6. OBJECT Handshapes Used in Combination with Motions[a]

	C	PALM (flat and wide)	PALM (animal/vehicle)	PALM (particles)	POINT (thin-straight)	POINT (neutral)
Change of location						
Linear	Curved object changes location 2(2),[b] e.g., turtle go	Flat wide object changes location 1(1), e.g., skate glide	Animal or vechicle changes location 10(13), e.g., Santa goes down	—	Thin-straight object changes location 1(2), e.g., penny flies through air	Object of any shape changes location 3(7), e.g., cookie goes down
Long arc	Curved object changes location 1(1), e.g., turtle go	Flat wide object changes location 1(1), e.g., skate glide	Animal or vehicle changes location 4(4) e.g., plane goes up	Particles change location 1(1), e.g., snow falls down	Thin-straight object changes location 1(1), e.g., penny goes (to bottle bank)	Object of any shape changes location 2(4), e.g., Susan moves to couch
Change of position						
Short arc	—	Flat wide object repositions itself 1(1), e.g., butterfly wings come together	Animal or vehicle repositions itself 2(2), e.g., sister sits	Particled object repositions itself 1(1), e.g., wheel tips over	—	—
Arc to and fro	—	Flat wide object moves to and fro 4(17), e.g., birdwings flap	—	—	—	—
Circular	—	—	—	—	—	—
Change of shape						
Open/close	Curved object opens and/or closes 1(1), e.g., bubble expands	Flat wide object opens and/or closes 1(1), e.g., flat claws curl	—	Particles open and/or close 2(4), e.g., treelights flicker	—	—
Bend	—	Flat wide object bends 1(2), e.g., birdwings bend	Animal or vehicle bends 1(3), e.g., fish bends (to swim)	—	—	—
Wiggle	—	—	—	Particles go up and down 1(1), e.g., snow flutters	—	—
No change No motion	—	—	—	—	—	—

[a] Two OBJECT handshapes, Flat and O, are omitted from the table because they did not occur with motion morphemes representing intransitive events.

[b] The first number represents the number of different types of events represented by the handshape/motion combination. The number in parentheses represents the total number of tokens. Only one-motion signs are included in the table.

Most of David's OBJECT morphemes could be found in combination with more than one motion morpheme, and vice versa. Thus, David's signs composed of OBJECT handshapes and motions also appeared to fit into a framework or system of contrasts. As an example of how the meanings of these signs contrasted systematically with one another, the C handshape was combined with the Linear motion to mean "a curved object changes location" (e.g., a turtle moves forward). This same Linear motion when combined with a different handshape, Palm (Vehicle/Animate), meant "a vehicle or animate being changes location" (e.g., Santa goes down; car goes forward). In contrast, the same Palm handshape when combined with a different motion (the Short Arc) meant "a vehicle or animate being repositions itself" (e.g., a sister sits). The OBJECT morphemes in David's signs thus formed a relatively complex matrix or paradigm with the motion morphemes in the corpus of signs.

Note that the matrices in Tables 5 and 6 were roughly in complementary distribution. The motions that appeared infrequently in Table 5 (i.e., the Linear motion and the change-of-shape motions) were more likely to appear in Table 6 combined with OBJECT morphemes to describe intransitive events. Conversely, the motions that formed relatively complete matrices in Table 5 (the change-of-position motions and the no-change motions) were less frequently used with OBJECT handshapes to describe intransitive events in Table 6. Only the Long Arc motion seemed to be used both transitively with HAND morphemes (Table 5) and intransitively with OBJECT morphemes (Table 6). Apparently, David tended to use certain motion forms to represent transitive events and other motion forms to represent intransitive events.

Transitive meanings. As indicated above, OBJECT handshapes were combined not only with motions representing intransitive events but also with motions representing transitive events, i.e., events performed on a patient by an actor.[5] Table 7 presents examples of the OBJECT morphemes, including the Fist and the O, used in combination with the Short Arc motion. Note that in these signs, the handshape represents a characteristic of the patient and not of the actor. Thus, in contrast to the HAND morphemes used with transitive motions where attention is focused on the actor's manipulation of the patient, the OBJECT morphemes used with transitive motions focus attention on the patient alone. These combinations thus serve as a device to refocus attention.

As an example of the way David altered the form of his signs to refocus attention, David generated two distinct descriptions of the same event—a cowboy sipping on a straw. First, David held a O handshape (representing handling a small object, the straw) to his mouth,[6] a HAND morpheme that focused attention on the cowboy's hand actively manipulating the straw, as if to indicate "he holds the straw at mouth." In another representation of the same situation, David held a Point handshape (representing a thin, straight object, the straw) to his mouth, an OBJECT morpheme that brought attention to the straw alone, as if to indicate "the straw is held at mouth."

Table 7. Examples of OBJECT Handshapes Used in Combination with Transitive Repositioning Motions

	Fist	*O*	*C*	*Palm (animal or vehicle)*	*Point (Neutral)*
Short arc	Reposition a bulky object 2(3),[a] e.g., swing hammer head	Reposition a round compact object 2(3), e.g., put on hat	Reposition a curved object 1(2), e.g., place cowboy legs on horse	Reposition an animal or vehicle 2(2), e.g., put in bear	Reposition an object of any shape 3(3), e.g., turn over can of clay

[a]The first number represents the number of different types of events represented by the handshape/motion combination. The number in parentheses represents the total number of tokens. Only one-motion signs are included in the table.

David used OBJECT handshapes with five of the nine motion morphemes to represent transitive events. Table 8 presents the number of OBJECT morphemes used to represent the patient of a transitive action for each of the nine motions.[7] Note that the distribution of OBJECT morphemes with transitive motions (Table 8) appears very similar to the distribution of HAND morphemes with transitive motions (Table 5). In particular, there are no OBJECT morphemes combined with either Linear motions or change-of-shape motions. Thus, there appear to be

Table 8. Number of OBJECT Handshapes Used in Combination with Motions Representing Transitive Events[a]

	Number of Types (Tokens)[b]
Change of location	
Linear	—
Long arc	4(4)
Change of position	
Short arc	10(13)
Arc to and fro	1(1)
Circular	2(3)
Change of shape	
Open/close	—
Bend	—
Wiggle	—
No change	
No motion	3(5)

[a]Of the 26 signs in the table, 15 contained a Neutral Point handshape, thus focusing attention on the action itself rather than on the actor or patient.
[b]Only one-motion signs are included on the table.

restrictions on the types of motion forms David used to describe transitive events, independent of type of handshape (HAND or OBJECT). These restrictions may have been due to accidental discourse factors, e.g., David may not have had the opportunity to describe events in which an actor changed the shape of a patient or the shape of his hand on a patient. However, at least one of these restrictions (the absence of a transitive Linear motion) does not appear to be based on David's failure to describe a particular set of events. Note that David did describe events in which a change of location was performed transitively (i.e., events in which an actor acted on a patient to transfer it). However, when David described these events he tended to use the Long Arc motion (with either a HAND or an OBJECT handshape) and not the Linear motion. Thus, the restriction on a Linear motion form representing a transitive event may reflect a formal constraint within David's system.

Attribute meanings. David used four different OBJECT morphemes to represent attributes of static objects: the O (representing a round, compact object), the C (representing a curved object), the Palm (representing a flat, wide object), and the Palm (representing many particles). All of these OBJECT morphemes were used in combination with the No-motion morpheme. For example, the O morpheme was combined with the No-motion morpheme to describe a Christmas tree ball and a soap bubble; the C morpheme combined with the No-motion morpheme described an arced block; the Palm (Flat/Wide) morpheme combined with the No-motion morpheme described a flat puzzle-board; and the Palm (Many Particles) morpheme combined with the No-motion morpheme described a piece of train track with many spokes.

In sum, we found that the signs David produced during these sessions can be described in terms of frameworks or matrices of handshape and motion oppositions, i.e., handshape/motion paradigms. The meaning of each sign in the system thus appears to be based on a combination of the meanings of its parts—the handshape and motion morphemes.

Motions in Combination with Other Motions

Approximately 10% of David's signs contained two or more motions. All of the nine motion forms were produced in combination with other motions. In 32% (12/37) of these two-motion signs, the motions were produced sequentially (but without a break between the motions so that both appeared to be part of the same sign); in the other 68% (25/37), the two motions were produced simultaneously in a conflated motion.

The sequential two-motion signs typically described actions that occurred in sequence (12 signs). For example, David produced a Palm handshape (representing an animate object) combined first with a Long Arc motion (movement downward to an endpoint), then combined with a Short Arc motion (repositioning in place), and finally combined with a Linear motion (movement forward) to describe a penguin diving into the water, turning, and then going forward.

The simultaneous or conflated two-motion signs were used in three different ways: (1) The second motion represented the manner in which the first motion (always a change of location motion) was performed (10 signs). For example, David produced a Point handshape (representing a thin, straight object) combined simultaneously with a Wiggle motion (a quick to and fro movement) and a Linear motion (movement forward) to represent the way a straight and skinny dog nodded its head as it moved forward. (2) The second motion (always an open or close motion) represented the way an object was picked up before being moved (or released after being moved) (seven signs). For example, David produced a Fist handshape (representing handling a thin long object) with a Close motion (grasp) and a Short Arc motion (repositioning at the beginning of a change of location) to represent the way a long thin toybag was grasped in order that it be repositioned. Note that in signs of this type, the Close motion is performed simultaneously with the Short Arc motion—despite the fact that when the action is actually performed, the grasp motion precedes the repositioning motion. (3) The second motion (always a no change motion performed with the second hand) was used to establish the object on which the first motion was performed (eight signs). For example, one of David's hands formed a C (representing handling a large object) in combination with No Motion (hold) to represent holding a large, wind-up toy, while the other hand formed an O (representing handling a small object) in combination with a Circular motion (rotate) to represent rotating the knob of the wind-up toy.

Thus, just as the meaning of a simple one-motion sign in David's system can be described as the sum of the meanings of its hand and motion parts, so can the meaning of a complex two-motion sign in the system.

Summary of David's Morphological System

We have found that the corpus of signs David produced can be characterized as a system of handshape and motion morphemes; in particular, David's signs were composed of a limited and discrete set of five hand and nine motion forms each of which was consistently associated with a distinct meaning and recurred across different signs. Thus, David's signs appeared to be decomposable into smaller morpheme-like components, suggesting that his gesture system was indeed structured at the sign level.

David's signs did not always reflect referents in the real world as transparently as they might have. The signs were often more abstract and symbolic than a pantomime of a real world object or action would require and, as such, were not constrained by a tight fit between a sign and the object or action it represented. For example, despite the fact that in the manual modality one can, in principle, represent shapes and movements along a continuous dimension, David used discrete (not continuous) forms to represent objects and actions in his signs (e.g., he used the same handshape to represent holding a thin balloon string and a thicker steering wheel). When representing handling an object, David appeared to choose among the limited number of handshapes available in his system, rather than shaping his hand to match precisely his actual handgrip on the object. At some level, David seemed to be sacrificing the fit between a sign and its referent to achieve categorical representation (e.g., David used a Fist handshape to represent holding a banana despite the fact that bananas require a wider handgrip). Thus, like ASL, David's gesture system does not take advantage of the possibility of continuous and transparent representation afforded by the manual modality and instead appears to be based on categorical representation, as are all conventional languages.

In addition, to be able to manipulate the focus of attention in a sentence, David would, at times, use a less transparent, less pantomimic representation than he possibly could have used. For example, when describing how one could put a cowboy on a horse, David could (and did) shape his hand as though he were holding the cowboy and placing it on the horse (i.e., a HAND handshape used with a transitive motion). However, at times, to describe the same event, David shaped his hand as though he were representing the cowboy's legs as they were placed around the horse (i.e., an OBJECT handshape used with the same transitive motion). This second sign is less like a pantomime than the first and serves to focus attention on the patient alone rather than on the actor and patient.

Comparisons between the Home Sign System and ASL Morphology

We have found that the corpus of signs David produced can be characterized as a system of handshape and motion morphemes, comparable in broad outline to the handshape and motion system that underlies ASL. Not surprisingly, however, the system of subsign components developed by David is not as complex as the morphological system underlying ASL, a conventional language with a rich linguistic history and shared by a wide community of signers.

Handshape Morphemes

The five predominant handshapes in David's system represent the unmarked handshapes of adult ASL systems (cf. Klima and Bellugi, 1979), and are the same handshapes produced by young deaf children learning ASL from their deaf parents during their initial states of acquisition (McIntire, 1977). Since David used only the unmarked and none of the marked handshapes of ASL, he used fewer handshapes overall than are found in ASL, even in the ASL produced by young children. Nevertheless, David's use of handshapes to represent objects parallels closely the way handshapes are used in ASL.

David's handshapes represented objects in three ways. First, a set of David's OBJECT handshapes represented the visual–geometric characteristics of an object: First (bulky object), O (round, compact object), C (curved object), Palm (flat, wide object), Palm (many small particles), and Point (thin, straight object).

In ASL, handshapes (called size and shape specifiers, cf. Supalla, 1982) are also used to represent the visual–geometric properties of an object, but the set of handshapes available in ASL is much larger than David's set. Moreover, the visual–geometric handshapes in ASL consist themselves a group of simultaneous hand-part morphemes rather than a single handshape morpheme (Supalla, 1982). For example, the number of fingers extended represents the width or depth of an object (one finger = thin or flat, two fingers = narrow or shallow, four fingers = wide or deep) while the curvature of the palm represents the shape of an object (palm straight = straight object, palm curved = round object). These components are combined within a sign in ASL to represent the width/ depth *and* shape of an object, e.g., one straight finger = thin and straight object and one curved finger = flat and round object. At present, we have no evidence to suggest that David's handshapes themselves consisted of a number of simultaneous morphemes rather than one single morpheme.

Second, David used one of his OBJECT handshapes to represent a semantic subcategory of objects: Palm (vehicle or animate object), i.e., a self-propelling object. In ASL, this same category is represented but with many more distinctions. For example, ASL has separate handshapes to represent a human vs. a small animal, and separate handshapes to represent a wheeled vehicle vs. an airplane vs. a boat (Supalla, 1982).

Finally, David's HAND handshapes represented an object indirectly by reflecting the handgrip used to manipulate the object: First (handle a small, long object), O (handle a small object), C (handle a large object), Palm (handle a large, flat surface), Palm (handle many small surfaces). Again, ASL has a set of handshapes that is used in comparable ways but with many more distinctions (e.g., thumb and finger touching, with the other three fingers extended and spread = handle a small or flatish object; flat palm with the thumb spread = handle a wide flattish bottomed object; flat palm with the fingers spread = handle a flat plane; McDonald, 1982).

Interestingly, when deaf children acquire ASL from their deaf parents, they tend at the earliest stages to use some handshapes comparable in form and meaning to David's. Supalla (1982) studied the development of size and shape and semantic classifiers in verbs of motion and location in three deaf children of deaf parents (ranging in age from 3;6 to 5;11). He found that all three of the children used what Supalla called "primitive" handshapes, the Palm and the Point. Two of the children used the Point for any category (as David did with his OBJECT Point = any object) while the third used the Point for wide, flat, and cylindrical objects. All three of the children used the Palm for animals, wheeled vehicles, and airplanes (as did David), and one used the Palm for wide, flat, and cylindrical objects as well. Thus, even when provided with a conventional language model, children tend to use the same simple forms for the same general categories as did David. However, it is important to point out that, even by age 3;6, the children in Supalla's study were correctly producing the more specified handshapes for humans, animals, wheeled vehicles, and airplanes on a substantial number of the stimuli—handshapes and distinctions not seen in David's signs.

In sum, David's system of handshape morphemes resembles ASL in that handshapes are used to represent discrete classes of objects. Moreover, David's handshapes represent objects by capturing the same kinds of properties (size and shape, semantic category, handgrip) as are captured in the handshapes of ASL. Nevertheless, the structure of David's system of handshape morphemes is far less complex or intricate than the structure of handshape morphemes in ASL.

Motion Morphemes

David used nine motion forms in his signs, a set that is reminiscent of the set isolated by Newport (1981) and Supalla (1982) in their descriptions of motion in ASL. Moreover, the meanings of David's nine motion forms fall into the same four broad categories as do the motion meanings attributed to the signs of ASL, although the details of the motion meanings differ.

First, David used two forms (Linear and Long Arc) to represent change of location along *any* path. In ASL, the type of path is specified within the change of location morpheme: linear path means move along a straight path, arc path means move in an arc or jump (Supalla, 1982). Thus, the change of location morphemes in ASL are more specified than the comparable morphemes in David's system.

Second, David represented change of position with three forms, Short Arc (repositioning an object), Arc To and Fro (change position by moving back and forth), and Circular (move in a circular path or rotate). In ASL, two forms represent change of position or orientation: end-pivot means swing and mid-pivot means rotate (Supalla, 1982). A third ASL form, circular path, which means move in a circle, overlaps partially in meaning with David's Circular form but is listed as a change of location and not a change of orientation by Supalla.

Third, David used three forms to represent change of shape (Open/Close, Bend, and Wiggle). ASL has four forms that differ in detail from David's: spread, bend-flat, bend-round, and change-diameter, each of which reflects a change in the attributes of an object (Supalla, 1982).

Finally, David used his No-motion form to represent the existence of an object or holding an object in place. In ASL, a distinction is made between the existence and location of an object, and that distinction is conveyed through motion: a hold movement means existence and a minimal contacting movement means location (Supalla, 1982).

In addition, David's morphemic system resembles ASL in that it is combinatorial, i.e., motions can be combined with other motions. In both ASL (see Supalla, 1982) and David's system, motions combine with each other simultaneously or sequentially, and in either instance the meaning of a two-motion sign is the sum of the meanings of its motion parts.

The Role of the Child and His Environment in the Acquisition of Two Levels of Structure

Generating a Morphological System without a Conventional Language Model

Our analyses suggest that David developed a sign system that had morphological structure. In other words, when David generated a sign to refer to a particular object or action, the form of that sign was determined not only by the properties of the referent object or action, but also by how that sign fit with the other signs in David's lexicon. Thus, David's signs appeared to be created to fit into a framework, a system of contrasts. For example, David's motion form Long Arc, meaning change of location, contrasted with his motion form Short Arc, which meant change of position. Moreover, when the Long Arc was combined with a Fist (representing handling a small, long object), the meaning of the composite sign could be derived from the meanings of the individual motion and handshape forms (i.e., change the location of a small, long object) and differed systematically from the meaning of a Short Arc + Fist combination (which meant change the position of a small, long object).

The fact that David developed a morphological system without exposure to a conventional language model suggests that he might have been predisposed to develop a system of contrasts at the subsign level. David appeared to develop his lexicon by recruiting gestures from the actions of people and objects around him. We hypothesize that David first developed his lexical items by focusing only on the relationship between the form of the sign and the object or action it represented. Later (perhaps when he had accumulated a sufficient number of signs in his lexicon), David may have considered the form of one sign in relation to the form of other signs and may have regimented any regularities in his lexicon. For example, small, long objects tend to be held by a fist—not always, but perhaps often enough so that the Fist handshape might have predominated in the signs David created to represent handling small, long objects. David might then have made use of this trend in his lexicon and organized his system of contrasts around it.

If this hypothesis is correct, we would predict that David's lexicon ought to have changed over developmental time, simply because his early signs should have been created to conform only to sign–object constraints (i.e., the fit between the sign and the object or action it represents), while his later signs should have been created to conform to sign–sign constraints (the fit between a sign and the rest of the signs in the lexicon) as well as sign–object constraints. We would therefore expect it to be more difficult to describe David's early signs than his later signs in terms of a morphological system (i.e., there should be more "exceptions" in his early signs than his later signs, and perhaps different types of exceptions in his early signs than his later signs). Alternatively, we might expect "mismatches" between the signs David used and the objects and actions he represented with those signs in his later corpus after he had constructed a morphological system. Our future work will explore this prediction by analyzing the development of David's lexicon over time (Mylander and Goldin-Meadow, 1990).

In addition, this hypothesis implies that the details of David's morphological system depended not only on his propensity to impose an organization on his lexical items but also on the types of lexical items he created. We would therefore predict that if other deaf children inventing gesture systems without a conventional language model were to generate lexicons that differed substantially from David's lexicon in content and/or form, they might also generate morphological systems that differed from David's. In other words, the children might differ from David in the particular morphemes that comprised their systems but would not differ from him in having a morphological level. Our future work will explore this prediction by analyzing the lexicons of nine other deaf children who have invented gesture systems without exposure to a conventional language model.

The Resilience of Morphological Analysis

We have found that, even without the benefit of a conventional language model, a child can develop a communication system that has structure at the level of the word or sign, i.e., morphological structure. Thus, morphological structure appears to be a resilient property of language—a property that can be developed by a child despite a very impoverished language-learning environment. These findings support the hypothesis that children bring to language learning a predisposition for morphological analysis of a lexicon—either the conventional lexicon they are traditionally exposed to, or the lexicon they create on their own (see also Goldin-Meadow and Mylander, 1990a).

Evidence from other studies of language learning also argues for the resilience of morphological analysis in children. Children exposed to a spoken model of a conventional language that contains no morphology nevertheless tend to develop a morphological system in their own speech. For example, children who are exposed to pidgin languages that tend not to have morphology (i.e., structure within the world) have been found to creolize the language and in the process develop a system that has morphological structure (Kay and Sankoff, 1974; Sankoff and Laberge, 1973).

A second example of the resilience of morphological analysis comes from sign language. Deaf children are often born to deaf parents who learned ASL late in life, and some of these late-learning adults develop language systems that lack much of the morphological complexity of ASL (Newport, 1984). Nevertheless, the deaf children learning ASL from parents with incomplete morphological systems go on to develop sign systems with a complex morphological structure indistinguishable from the morphological systems developed by deaf children learning ASL from parents with complete systems (Newport, 1984).

These observations from ASL, taken in conjunction with the data we report here, suggest that although some aspects of morphology will develop in the absence of any linguistic model, the type of linguistic input a child receives from his environment exerts significant influence on the *complexity* of the morphological system the child develops. The deaf child in our study lacked entirely the lexicon of conventional sign language, and constructed a system with far less complexity than the morphological system of ASL. Apparently, a child not exposed to a conventional language model is able to take only small steps toward developing a morphological system. In contrast, the literature shows that deaf children exposed to a model of ASL, even one with incomplete morphological structure, are able to develop the richly elaborated morphological system of ASL in all of its complexity (Newport, 1984).

The linguistic environment to which a child is exposed thus appears to play a role in the complexity of the morphological system the child induces. Nevertheless, the fact that David could fashion a morphological system—albeit a simple one—even without any conventional linguistic input suggests that some aspects of linguistic analysis are strongly guided by internal factors. At the very least, these data suggest that, with or without a language model, children seek structure at the morphological level as well as at the sentence level when developing a communication system (see also Goldin-Meadow and Mylander, 1990b).

In sum, our data support the notion that a child may be predisposed to impose structure at the word level, whatever input he receives. If a child is exposed to a conventional language model, he quite naturally learns the morphological structure in that model. However, even if a child is not exposed to a conventional language model, or is exposed to a conventional language model that lacks complete or extensive morphological analysis, the child still seems to impose morphological structure on the units that serve as words in his system.

We have found in our previous work that, even without the benefit of a conventional language model, a child can develop a communication system that has structure at the syntactic level, i.e., at the level of sentence-like units. We find here that this same communication system is also structured at the morphological level, at the level of word-like units. We suggest that hierarchical structure (or at least two hierarchical levels) appears to be a resilient property of language—a property whose development can withstand a dramatic alternation of the learning conditions children typically experience when acquiring language. Moreover, the fact that a deaf child can develop a hierarchically structured communication system even when he has no explicit model for such a system suggests that the human brain is strongly canalized to produce linguistic systems with hierarchical organization. In this respect, the human brain differs greatly from the brains of great apes who, even when reared under similar conditions, do not spontaneously invent organized linguistic systems.

Notes

1. Characterizing signs are represented in capitalized letters, e.g., "EAT" represents a jabbing motion toward the mouth.

2. The term "patient" refers to objects that are affected by the actions of an actor (i.e., the object of a transitive event).

3. Two of the types of characterizing signs David produced during these videotapes are omitted from the analyses presented here and will be described in a forthcoming report: (1) 243 signs which were conventional in that they occur in the spontaneous gestures accompanying the speech of hearing adults and children in our culture (e.g., a flat hand extended palm-up to mean "give," or two fists held together and then rotated away from each other to mean "broken"), and (2) 68 signs in which the motion of the sign traces the extent or outline of an object.

4. Numbers reported for handshape (Table 2) reflect signs in which handshape was codable regardless of whether the corresponding motion could be seen and coded. Similarly, numbers reported for motion (Table 4) reflect signs in which motion was codable, again independent of whether the corresponding handshape could be coded. Numbers reported for handshape and motion combinations (Tables 5 and 6) reflect signs in which both handshape and motion were codable and neither handshape nor motion was an exception (i.e., could not be classified according to the form/meaning pairings described in Tables 2 and 4).

5. We use the term "actor" to refer to the doer in a transitive event rather than the term "agent" traditionally used in linguistic descriptions.

6. In addition to handshape and motion, we also coded information relevant to a possible third morpheme—place of articulation (i.e., the location where each sign was produced). These data are not analyzed here and will be described in a forthcoming report.

7. Of the 26 signs listed in Table 8, 15 contained a Neutral Point handshape. The Neutral Point does not actually capture characteristics of either the actor or the patient. Thus, for these signs, the focus of attention may have been on the action itself.

Acknowledgments

This research was supported by Grant BNS 8407041 from the National Science Foundation. We thank Ruth Berman, Julie Gerhardt, John Lucy, Rachel Mayberry, and William Meadow for their thoughtful comments on earlier drafts of this manuscript.

References

Battison, R. (1974). Phonological deletion in American Sign Language. *Sign Language Studies, 5,* 1–19.

Bellugi, U. and Studdert-Kennedy, M. (Eds.) (1980). *Signed and spoken language: Biological constraints on linguistic form.* Deerfield Beach, FL: Verlag Chemie.

Caselli, M. C. (1983). Communication to language: Deaf children's and hearing children's development compared. *Sign Language Studies, 39,* 113–144.

Conrad, R. (1979). *The deaf child.* London: Harper & Row.

Curtiss, S. (1977). *Genie: A psycholinguistic study of a modern "Wild-Child."* New York: Academic Press.

DeMatteo, A. (1977). Visual imagery and visual analogues in American Sign Language. In L. Friedman (Ed.), *On the other hand: New perspectives on American Sign Language* (pp. 109–136). New York: Academic Press.

Fant, L. J. (1972). *Ameslan: An introduction to American Sign Language.* Silver Springs, MD: National Association of the Deaf.

Feldman, H., Goldin-Meadow, S., and Gleitman, L. (1978). Beyond Herodotus: The creation of language by linguistically deprived deaf children. In A. Lock (Ed.), *Action, symbol, and gesture: The emergence of language* (pp. 351–413). New York: Academic Press.

Fischer, S. (1973). Two processes of reduplication in American Sign Language. *Foundations of Language, 9,* 469–480.

Fischer, S. (1975). Influences on word order change in ASL. In C. Li (Ed.), *Word order and word order change* (pp. 1–25). Austin: University of Texas Press.

Fischer, S., and Gough, B. (1978). Verbs in American Sign Language. *Sign Language Studies, 18,* 17–48.

Goldin-Meadow, S. (1979). Structure in a manual communication system developed without a conventional language model: Language without a helping hand. In H. Whitaker and H. A. Whitaker (Eds.), *Studies in neurolinguistics,* (Vol. 4, pp. 125–209). New York: Academic Press.

Goldin-Meadows, S. (1982). The resilience of recursion: A study of a communication system developed without a conventional language model. In L. R. Gleitman and E. Wanner (Eds.), *Language acquisition: The state of the art* (pp. 51–77). New York: Cambridge University Press.

Goldin-Meadows, S., and Feldman, H. (1975). The creation of a communication system. A study of deaf children of hearing parents. *Sign Language Studies, 8,* 225–234.

Goldin-Meadow, S., and Feldman, H. (1977). The development of language-like communication without a language model. *Science, 197,* 401–403.

Goldin-Meadow, S., and Mylander, C. (1983). Gestural communication in deaf children: The non-effects of parental input on language development. *Science, 221,* 372–374.

Goldin-Meadow, S., and Mylander, C. (1984). Gestural communication in deaf children: The effects and noneffects of parental input on early language development. *Monographs of the Society for Research in Child Development, 49,* 1–121.

Goldin-Meadow, S., and Mylander, C. (1990a). The role of parental input in the development of a morphological system. *Journal of Child Language.* In press.

Goldin-Meadow, S., and Mylander, C. (1990b). Beyond the input given: The child's role in the acquisition of language. *Language.* 66 (2) In press.

Hoffmeister, R. (1978). The development of demonstrative pronouns, locatives and personal pronouns in the acquisition of American Sign Language by deaf children of deaf parents. Unpublished doctoral dissertation, University of Minnesota.

Hoffmeister, R., and Wilbur, R. (1980). Developmental: The acquisition of sign language. In H. Lane and F. Grosjean (Eds.), *Recent perspectives on American Sign Language* (pp. 61–68). Hillsdale, NJ: Erlbaum Associates.

Kantor, R. (1982). Communicative interaction: Mother modification and child acquisition of American Sign Language. *Sign Language Studies, 36,* 233–282.

Kay, P., and Sankoff, G. (1974). A language-universals approach to pidgins and creoles. In D. DeCamp and I. Hancock (Eds.), *Pidgins and creoles: Current trends and prospects* (pp. 61–72). Washington, D.C.: Georgetown University Press.

Klima, E., and Bellugi, U. (1979). *The signs of language.* Cambridge, MA: Harvard University Press.

Lane, H. (1977). *Wild boy of Averyron.* New York: Bantam Books.

Lane, H., and Grosjean, F. (Eds.). (1980). *Recent perspectives on American Sign Language.* Hillsdale, NJ: Erlbaum Associates.

Lane, H., Boyes-Braem, P., and Bellugi, U. (1976). Preliminaries to a distinctive feature analysis of handshapes in American Sign Language. *Cognitive Psychology, 8,* 263–289.

Lenneberg, E. H. (1964). Capacity for language acquisition. In J. A. Fodor and J. J. Katz (Eds.), *The structure of language: Readings in the philosophy of language* (pp. 579–603). Englewood Cliffs, NJ: Prentice-Hall.

Liddell, S. (1980) *American Sign Language syntax.* The Hague: Mouton.

MacWhinney, B. (1976). Hungarian research on the acquisition of morphology and syntax. *Journal of Child Language, 3,* 397–410.

Matthews, P. H. (1974). *Morphology: An introduction to the theory of word structure.* Cambridge: Cambridge University Press.

McDonald, B. (1982). Aspects of the American Sign Language predicate system. Unpublished doctoral dissertation, University of Buffalo.

McIntire, M. L. (1977). The acquisition of American Sign Language hand configurations. *Sign Language Studies, 16,* 247–266.

Meadow, K. (1968). Early manual communication in relation to the deaf child's intellectual, social, and communicative functioning. *American Annals of the Deaf, 113,* 29–41.

Miller, P. (1982). *Amy, Wendy and Beth: Learning language in South Baltimore.* Austin: University of Texas Press.

Mindel, E. D., and Vernon, Mc C. (1971). *They grow in silence: The deaf child and his family.* Silver Spring, MD: National Association for the Deaf.

Moores, D. F. (1974). Nonvocal systems of verbal behavior. In R. L. Schiefelbusch and L. L. Lloyd (Eds.), *Language perspectives: Acquisition, retardation, and intervention* (pp. 377–418). Baltimore: University Park Press.

Mylander, C., and Goldin-Meadow, S. (1990). Home sign systems in deaf children: The development of morphology without a conventional language model. In P. Siple and S. Fischer (Eds.), *Theoretical issues in sign language research,* Vol 2: *Acquisition.* Chicago: University of Chicago Press. In press.

Newport, E. L. (1981). Constraints on structure: Evidence from American Sign Language and language learning. In W. A. Collins (Ed.), *Minnesota Symposium on Child Psychology* (Vol. 14, pp. 93–124). Hillsdale, NJ: Erlbaum Associates.

Newport, E. L. (1984). Constraints on learning: Studies in the acquisition of American Sign Language. *Papers and Reports on Child Language Development, 23,* 1–22.

Newport, E. L., and Ashbrook, E. F. (1977). The emergence of semantic relations in American Sign Language. *Papers and Reports on Child Language Development, 13,* 16–21.

Ochs, E. (1982). Talking to children in Western Samoa. *Language in Society, 11,* 77–104.

Pye, C. (1986). Quiche Mayan speech to children. *Journal of Child Language, 13,* 85–100.

Sachs, J., and Johnson, M. L. (1976). Language development in a hearing child of deaf parents. In W. von Raffler-Engel and Y. Lebrun (Eds.), *Baby talk and infant speech* (pp. 246–252). Lisse, Netherlands: Swets and Zeitlinger.

Sachs, J., Bard, C., and Johnson, M.L. (1981). Language learning with restricted input: Case studies of two hearing children of deaf parents. *Applied Psycholinguistics, 2*(1), 33–54.

Sankoff, G., and Laberge, S. (1973). On the acquisition of native speakers by a language. *Kivung, 6,* 32–47.

Schieffelin, B. B. (1979). Getting it together: An ethnographic approach to the study of the development of communicative competence. In E. Ochs and B. B. Schieffelin (Eds.), *Developmental Pragmatics.* New York: Academic Press.

Stokoe, W. C. (1960). Sign language structure: An outline of the visual communications systems. *Studies in linguistics, Occasional papers 8.*

Supalla, T. (1982). Structure and acquisition of verbs of motion and location in American Sign Language. Unpublished doctoral dissertation, University of California at San Diego.

Supalla, T., and Newport, E. L. (1978). How many seats in a chair? The derivation of nouns and verbs in American Sign Language. In P. Siple (Ed.), *Understanding language through sign language research* (pp. 91–132). New York: Academic Press.

Tervoort, B. T. (1961). Esoteric symbolism in the communication behavior of young deaf children. *American Annals of the Deaf, 106,* 436–480.

Wimsatt, W. C. (1981). Robustness, reliability, and overdetermination. In M. B. Brewer and B. E. Collins (Eds.), *Scientific inquiry and the social sciences* (pp. 124–163). San Francisco: Josey-Bass.

Chapter 13

Some Structural and Developmental Correlates of Human Speech

Arnold B. Scheibel

Introduction

The development of speech in the human infant represents a powerful convergence of neurological and psychological mechanisms, some of which are already
in operation long before the birth of the child. The embryological development of
the cerebral cortex has been well documented by a number of workers and
involves a host of distinct yet overlapping processes that include neuronal
replications, migration, and progressive maturation. The maturative process
involves an enormous extension and elaboration of the neuronal surface into a
dendrite system and a projective axon that establishes connections with other
neural elements (Ramon y Cajal 1911). Along with this gathering complexity of
neuronal circuitry, there is a coincident pruning back and destruction of redun-
dant elements as the particular, phenotypic brain approaches as closely as
possible the expression of the genetic plan. Possibly before birth and certainly
after it, the specific experiences of the infant become a second shaping force in
the subsequent elaborations of central nervous system structure. In fact, it is now
clear that without the latter, brain structure cannot mature and will in fact
regress, so that the forces of "nature" and "nurture" are, as always, closely
intermingled.

It has been known for well over one hundred years that speech is functionally
localized in the dominant (usually the left) hemisphere (Broca, 1865) and that
such asymmetry also gains expression at the gross structural level, especially on
the superior surface of the superior temporal lobe (planum temporale) (Geschwind and Levitsky, 1968), which is involved in the receptive and interpretative
components of speech. The anterior speech zone (Broca's area on the dominant
side) is concerned with the motor elements of speech and may also show some
degree of morphologic asymmetry, although no unequivocal data have yet been

345

produced. Of particular interest is the apparent functional equivalence of the two sides during the first few years of life and the progressive lateralization of function that occurs during the first 6 to 10 years (Krashen, 1973; Lenneberg, 1967). On the basis of this time scale, note that at least some degree of functional symmetry may exist for several years after a high order of speech facility is attained. Thereafter, the nondominant side becomes increasingly "wordless," serving eventually as the master, only, of speech prosody and a few affectually laden expletives.

The Problem

The following report summarizes some of our initial attempts to find evidence for histologic correlates of this functional asymmetry. The anterior (motor) speech area of Broca (pars orbitalis and triangularis of the inferior frontal convolution) and its homologous area on the nondominant side were selected for the study because of their relatively restricted area and apparently greater degree of gross symmetry bilaterally when compared with the parietotemporal areas subserving the sensory aspects of speech. Tissue specimens from the *motor speech* area of the frontal lobe, and from the somatic *motor strip* area just behind, were obtained at autopsy within 5–28 hours after death in eight adult male patients without known neurological disease. Their ages ranged from 58 to 77 years (mean age 65.9, SD 6.4). The tissue was stained by a modification of the chrome-silver impregnation method of Golgi to reveal neurons, dendrites, and axonal structures.

We limited our study to those neurons found in a zone between 400 and 1300 μm beneath the pial surface. These supragranular layers (laminae 2 and 3) consist almost entirely of small- and medium-sized pyramidal cells and are believed to be among the last to migrate into the cortical plate. Their rather consistently pyramidal structure provides enough structural regularity to allow quantitative comparisons bilaterally while their more "recent" embryological appearance has been tentatively correlated with a high degree of plasticity.

Two methods of analysis of basilar dendrite patterns were used. In the first, following a method originally described by the English mathematician–neurobiologist Donald Sholl (1956), a series of concentric rings etched into the microscope eyepiece at regular intervals were centered over the image of the nerve cell body. The number of dendritic intersections with each successive ring then provided a surprisingly adequate first order quantitative description of the dendritic arbor. In the second, the sampled cells were carefully traced by means of a camera lucida onto a digitizing tablet connected to a TRS-80 microcomputer, and the data were then transferred to a main frame computer for analysis.

The study was based on three a priori hypotheses: (1) differences in dendritic architecture and dimensions should somehow reflect unique functional capacities of each cortical area; (2) the presumably more complex role of the left (dominant) motor speech area should result in neuronal dendritic trees that are more extensive and complex than those in the right homologous area; and (3) formulation of speech strategies in the dominant motor speech area should result in dendrite arbors that are more complex than those of the adjacent precentral motor zones concerned exclusively with the control of the orofacial muscles used in speech articulation. Results of this study indicate that our presuppositions were correct in principle but incorrect in detail (Scheibel et al., 1985).

The Data

Concentric Ring Analyses

The graphs in Figure 1 illustrate the kind of data made available by the ring analysis of dendritic patterns. Brains 1, 2, and 4 resemble each other in the greater number of dendrite intersections (and therefore, the richness of branching patterns) for cells in the left opercular (Broca's) area compared to all other areas. The most obvious differences occur between rings 6 and 14 reaching levels of significance at and beyond 160 μm from the cell body. This represents, roughly, the zone of transition between third and fourth order dendrite branches. We were surprised by the results in case 5, where values for the right opercular area (right Broca!) exceeded those of the left. This result became more reasonable when we learned at the conclusion of the study that this patient was one of two non-right-handers in our series.

Quantitative Analysis of Dendritic Length and Branching Patterns

This portion of the study, based on computer-aided analysis of the dendrite systems, provided a considerable amount of information about the length and number of dendrite branches of various orders. As with the Sholl-type analysis already mentioned, the data were treated without reference to handedness patterns of the individuals. When all of the data had been accumulated and processed, information about handedness was sought, and it is a tribute to the persistence of one of our colleagues, Dr. A. Wechsler, that such information finally became available. Once such behavioral data were at hand, the subjects were divided into two groups; the right-handers and the non-right-handers, since it appears that language dominance is either less clearly evident or is in some cases reversed for this second smaller group. In our subject group, it turned out that six had been life-long right-handers and two were non-right-handers.

Three measures of dendritic structure were of particular interest: (1) the total dendritic length (tdl) of the basilar dendrite tree serving as an index of total dendrite membrane area for presynaptic terminal input and information process-

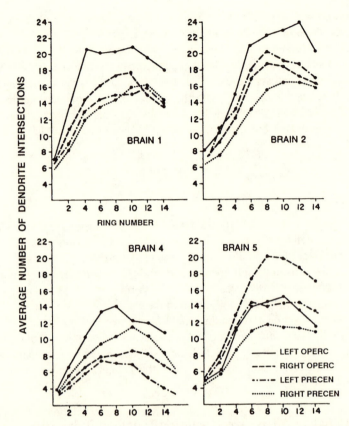

Figure 1. Graphic representation of the number of dendrite crossings of every second concentric circle in a Sholl type measuring array as explained in the text. Abbreviations: left opercular, left operc.; right opercular, right operc.; left precentral, left precen.; right precentral, right precen.

ing operations; (2) average segment length (asl), providing an index of the length achieved by dendrite segments of a certain order; and (3) the average number of dendrite segments (asn) of a certain order, providing an index of the degree of complexity or branchedness achieved by the dendrite tree at that segment level.

Among the findings of note, we list the following as being of potential correlative interest to verbal behavior.

1. The total dendritic length (tdl) of opercular (Broca) neurons exceeded that of precentral (orofacial motor) cells by at least 10%, a difference that we found to be significant ($p < 0.05$) only in the left hemisphere. We attribute this difference to the more extensive information processing needs of cells in the speech *strategy* (opercular) as compared to speech tactics (precentral) area. In this case, by strategy, we mean the choice and

formulation of discrete words, i.e., the development of the lexical component of speech. Tactics, on the other hand, consists of the innumerable
separate commands to muscles of the oropharynx, tongue, and lips, and
the respiratory and laryngeal systems, all of which are involved in the
production of words.

2. To our surprise, there was no significant differences between the tdl of
    basilar dendrite systems of the right and left sides (i.e., left opercular,
    2714.5 μm vs. right opercular, 2540.8 μm, nonsignificant; and left
    precentral, 2208.3 μm vs. right precentral, 2499.9 μm, nonsignificant).
    According to our a priori hypotheses, we would have expected tdl of
    opercular neurons on the dominant side to have been significantly greater
    due to the presumably enhanced processing load engendered by speech
    strategy operations.

3. Segment-by-segment analysis, however, revealed significant differences
    in the internal organization of dendrite arbors on left and right sides
    (Figure 2). In essence, a larger fraction of the dendrite arbor on the right
    (nondominant) side was made up of lower order (1, 2, 3) branches,
    whereas on the left (dominant) side, a larger fraction of the arbor was
    accounted for by the higher order (4, 5, 6) dendrite branches. The actual
    expression of these differences was also interesting. Lower order

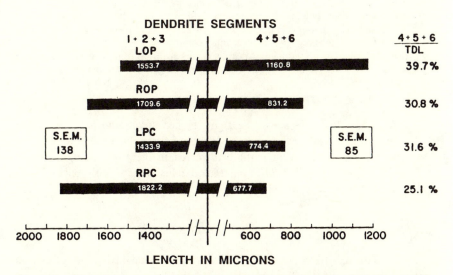

Figure 2. Bar graph comparing dendrite length and proportion of the dendritic ensemble
composed of lower order (first, second, and third) and higher order (fourth, fifth, and
sixth) dendritic segments in left opercular, LOP; right opercular, ROP; left precentral, LPC; and right precentral,, RPC, regions. Boxed figures represent standard
error of the mean, SEM. The column of figures on the far right shows the percentage
of total dendritic length, TDL, occupied by higher order dendrites in each region.

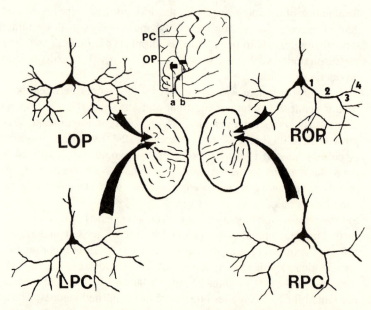

Figure 3. Somewhat schematized drawing of typical dendrite ensembles from cells of the four regions studied. Note the increased number of higher order dendrite segments in the left opercular region, LOP, compared with all other regions, and the somewhat greater lengths of second and third order branches in right operculum, ROP, and the right precentral, RPC, region. The left precentral region shows somewhat enhanced higher order branching compared to the right side but much less than the LOP. The inset drawing above indicates positions from which Broca, a, and motor, b, tissue specimens were obtained in the opercular, op, and precentral, pc, gyri.

branches were longer on the right: higher order branches were more numerous on the left (Figure 3). It was of particular interest to discover that these values were partially reversed in the two non-right-handed individuals, thereby indicating that the histological differences might indeed be related to behavior.

Discussion

These data may be considered in both an anatomical–physiological and an ontogenetic setting. Both provide valid contextual frames, and both are likely to contribute to the picture that we have sketched. Within the former frame, variations in dendritic structure may subtly yet powerfully affect processing operations of the neurons. For example, first-order dendrites are usually the largest in diameter, have the lowest internal resistance values, and bear the fewest dendrite spines (Marin-Padilla, 1967; Krasen, 1973). Related to the sparsity of spines is a proportionately larger group of synaptic terminals of type II variety that are usually considered to be inhibitory in function (Uchizono, 1965). Dendrite branches of successively higher order are characterized by progressively smaller shaft diameter, higher internal resistance values, and greater spine density, although spine number tends to decrease as the outermost branch systems are approached (Marin-Padilla, 1967; Krashen, 1973). Coincidental with the increased numbers of dendrite spines are greater numbers of type I, probably facilitatory synapses (Colonnier, 1967). Additionally, the number and order of dendritic bifurcations are of differential significance. Each branch point is also a decision point for the patterns of local activity that are constantly waxing, summating, and waning along the dendritic membrane. In the broadest sense, the greater the branchedness, the higher the degree of freedom and complexity in information processing.

Viewed within the context of ontogeny, the dendrite configuration may be thought of as reflecting the developmental history of the neuron since there is an approximately time-linked progression in the development of successive dendrite systems (Conel, 1939–67). We might liken the successive orders of dendrite segments to the rings in the trunk of a felled tree. Since it seems clear that each ring represents 1 year of growth, it follows that a thicker ring suggests a better or longer growing year with enhanced periods of sunlight, more rain, etc. Similarly, longer individual dendrites, or more of a certain dendrite segment order may indicate enhanced dendrite building activity during a certain developmental period. In the neocortex, there is a rather *wide range of species-specific maturational timetables,* but, in general, in the human fetus early order dendrite segments begin to develop in the early or mid-portion of the third intrauterine trimester, so that at birth most cortical neurons bear first and usually second order dendrite branches, while third- and fourth-order branches begin to develop almost immediately afterward. Between 6 months and 1 year of age, higher order dendritic growth becomes very active, and by the second or third year of age the cerebral cortex begins to approach, to qualitative visual inspection at least, the dendritic complexity of the mature brain (Conel, 1939–67), and Scheibel, unpublished data). If we are justified in viewing these dendritic patterns as a "fossilized history" of early dendritic growth, even with the well-known capacity of dendrite systems to progressively prune and reshape themselves to varying input patterns (Diamond et al., 1983), then we may attempt to interpret these data. Initially, longer, lower order dendrite segments on the nondominant side (compared to the side that will ultimately achieve dominance) suggest greater activity here during the late prenatal and early postnatal (nonverbal) periods of life—the sensorimotor period of Piaget (1954). The marked increase in numbers of higher order branches on the left side relative to the right suggests enhanced dendritic growth activity at a time when the beginnings of internalization and conceptualization mark the onset of language competence in the child. It is certainly of more than passing interest that an apparent preponderance of dendritic tissue on the nondominant side is gradually lost as speech function commences.

Although these data provide interesting correlations, it is not possible to decide from them alone whether the development of greater complexity in dendrite systems on the dominant side represents a genetically determined preparation for the increased functional load of speech processing, or whether it is a response to the enhanced neural processing activity accompanying speech behavior. The first would certainly suggest an enlarged role for "nature," the second for "nurture," as causal factors in the functional maturation of speech cortex.

In an attempt to answer this question, we have recently pursued a companion study in an attempt to characterize quantitatively the development dendrite systems in anterior speech and orofacial motor areas of 17 age-graded infant brains ranging from birth to 6 years of age (Simonds and Scheibel, 1988). These data have just been collected and are not yet fully analyzed. However, initial evaluation suggests that the nondominant cortex "leads" the other in terms of dendrite length (tdl) for only 3–6 months, after which the dendrite systems on the soon-to-be-dominant side overtake the other. This represents an earlier crossover of dendrite growth patterns than we had expected, coming as it does appreciably before the onset of language behavior. It is conceivable that this represents a primarily genetic effect. These data also suggest a second burst of dendrite building activity at 12 to 18 months, differing in both site of origin on the nerve cell body and in hierarchical order in the dendrite segment sequence. We wonder whether this might represent a response to the demands of early language learning and utilization and therefore more of an environmentally triggered reaction. It would certainly not be surprising if both endogenous and exogenous (nature and nurture) factors were involved in the maturation of the language-involved portions of the brain. A successful analysis of the component mechanisms should prove of considerable interest at conceptual, diagnostic, and therapeutic levels.

References

Broca, P. (1865). De siège de la faculté du langage articulé. *Bulletin Mémoire Société d'Anthropologie Paris, 6*, 377–393.

Colonnier, M. (1967). The fine structural arrangement of the cortex. *Archives of Neurology (Chicago), 16*, 651–657.

Conel, J. (1939–67). *The postnatal development of the human cortex*, Vols. 1–6. Cambridge, MA: Harvard University Press.

Diamond, M. C., Johnson, R. E., Young, D., and Singh, S. S. (1983). Age related morphologic differences in the rat cerebral cortex and hippocampus: male-female, right-left. *Experimental Neurology, 81*, 1–13.

Geschwind, N., and Levitsky, W. (1968). Left-right asymmetries in temporal speech area. *Science, 161,* 186–187.

Krashen, S. (1973). Lateralization, language learning, and the critical period. Some new evidence. *Language Learning, 23,* 63–74.

Lenneberg, E. H. (1967). *Biological foundation of language.* New York: Wiley.

Marin-Padilla, M. (1967). Number and distribution of the apical dendritic spines of the layer V pyramidal cells in man. *Journal of Comparative Neurology, 131,* 475–489.

Piaget, J. (1954). *The construction of reality in the child.* New York: Basic Books.

Rall, W. (1967). Distinguishing theoretical synaptic potentials compiled for different somadendrite distributions of synaptic input. *Journal of Neurophysiology, 30,* 1138–1168.

Ramon y Cajal, S. (1911). *Histologie du Systeme Nerveux de l'Homme et des Vertebres.* Paris: A. Maloine.

Scheibel, A. B., Paul, L. A., Fried, I., Forsythe, A., Tomiyasu, U., and Slotnick, J. (1985). Dendritic organization of the anterior speech area. *Experimental Neurology, 87,* 109–117.

Simonds, R. and Scheibel, A. B. (1988). The postnatal development of the motor speech area. A preliminary study. *Brain and Language, 37,* 42–58.

Sholl, D. A. (1956). *The organization of the cerebral cortex.* London: Methmen.

Uchizono, K. (1965). Characteristics of excitatory and inhibitory synapses in the central nervous system of the cat. *Nature (London), 207,* 642–643.

Chapter 14

Neurobiology of Cognitive and Language Processing: Effects of Early Experience

Helen J. Neville

Introduction

Philosophers have discussed the contribution of experience to normal neural and behavioral development over the last several hundred years, at least since the time of Descartes. This is currently a key issue in the neurosciences, both because this information is critical to an understanding of how functional neural systems are formed in normal development, and also because knowledge about the extent of neural plasticity in response to environmental stimulation will have important clinical implications in cases of abnormal neural development. In spite of the long-standing interest in this issue, systematic research on the effects of experience on neural development began only about 20 years ago. Most of this work has been performed on the visual system of cats and monkeys, and includes the work of Wiesel and Hubel, which showed that following deprivation of visual input to one eye, most cells in primary visual cortex respond only to stimulation of the experienced eye (Wiesel and Hubel, 1963). These results by themselves were not necessarily strong evidence for the role of experience in the development of visual cortex. It could be, for example, that a genetically determined program that specifies visual development requires a trigger in the form of visual input to run its maturational course. By this view, however, total (i.e., binocular) visual deprivation should lead to even more abnormalities in visual cortex than monocular deprivation. However, it has been shown that neurons in primary visual cortex are in fact more normal following total visual deprivation than after monocular deprivation (e.g., after total visual deprivation there are more binocularly driven neurons, with more normal receptive fields and they can even display ocular dominance columns, i.e., whereby each eye innervates different neurons; Wiesel and Hubel, 1965). These results documented an important role for visual experience in the development of striate cortex, and further they led to the proposal that one important mechanism underlying neural organization in striate cortex is competition between the different inputs from the two eyes for cortical synaptic sites.

Competition in Development

More generally these results imply that active neural systems compete for and take over cortical synaptic sites that do not receive input from other sources. Additionally, and more relevant to the data presented in this chapter, there is evidence that this type of competition between inputs within both the visual system and the somatosensory system (Merzenich and Kaas, 1982) may also occur between different sensory modalities. For example, there is evidence that in polymodal brain regions (including superior colliculus and parietal cortex), when input from one modality is missing, the number of neurons responsive to remaining modalities is increased. In early blinded animals in the superior colliculus, in extrastriate cortex, and in parietal cortex there is both a marked reduction in the number of visually responsive neurons and a corresponding increase in the number of neurons responsive to somatosensory stimulation (Cynader, 1979; Hyvarinen, 1982). It is conceivable that these specific neurophysiological changes could account for the behavioral consequences of visual deprivation that have been well described in humans. The reduction of visually responsive neurons in these areas could account for the marked deficits in visual functioning that occur following even limited periods of early visual deprivation, and the increase in neurons responsive to somatosensory input could account for the reports of superior somatosensory skills in blind individuals. However, typically in research on animals, the physiological consequences of altered sensory experience have not been linked to behavior, and, conversely, in humans while the behavioral consequences of sensory deprivation have been extensively studied, little is known about the changes in neural organization that underlie these behavioral consequences.

Neural Development in Humans

It seems likely that early experience could significantly impact neural development in humans. The postnatal development of the human brain is very protracted and, according to most parameters studied, including the size of neurons, the extent of dendritic branching, myelinization, and number of synapses, these parameters do not reach mature values until at least 15 years after birth (Conel, 1939–1963; Schade, 1961; Huttenlocher, 1979). For example, the number of synapses in human frontal and occipital cortex displays a prolonged developmental course that does not stabilize until 20 years of age (Huttenlocher, 1979; Huttenlocher et al., 1982). Moreover, the developmental course is similar to that observed in other animals. During an early period (in humans from birth to 2 years of age), there is a rapid rise or transient exuberance in the number of synapses followed, from 2–15 years of age, by substantial elimination of synapses. In at least some animal neural systems, one important factor in determining which synapses are stabilized and which are eliminated is the pattern of activity of cortical inputs (e.g., as occurs in the formation of ocular dominance columns; Wiesel and Hubel, 1965). It is our working hypothesis that a similar situation exists in humans. Clinical studies of humans have shown that during the time from birth to puberty, structural damage to the brain can produce very marked changes in cerebral organization. Moreover, these changes are often associated with relatively preserved behavior (Smith, 1981; Dennis and Whitaker, 1977). For example, even if one entire cerebral hemisphere is removed during this time period, an individual can develop relatively normal cognitive and language skills. Thus, during this time there must be a substantial degree of redundancy and/or plasticity of cerebral connections. Further, it is conceivable that as in other animals, experience (i.e., functional activity) acts to reduce the redundancy and increase the specificity of neural connections during this period.

Epigenesis

One conception of how this might work, based on research on animals, has been presented by Changeux (1985) in his theory of epigenesis by selective stabilization of synapses. The idea is that there is an initial period of growth of neurons, axons, and dendrites, much of which occurs prenatally, and that this growth is determined genetically—or as Changeux puts it, occurs within a genetic envelope of possibilities. This would include, for example, the formation of ocular dominance columns that can occur, as mentioned above, in the absence of visual input. We also know that these initial biases are not immutable, as they can be substantially altered by visual experience (e.g., monocular deprivation). Following the period of initial growth there is a transient period of redundancy or exuberance of connections that has been documented in several species, in several brain regions both in humans (Huttenlocher, 1979; Huttenlocher, 1982) and animals (Cowan et al., 1984). This transient redundancy may underlie the ability of inputs from an experienced eye to take over neurons that would normally receive input from an unexperienced eye as occurs following monocular deprivation. It has also been shown that there are early, transient connections between different sensory modalities, for example, from the retina to the ventrobasal (somatosensory) nucleus of the thalamus (Frost, 1984); and there are cortical connections between auditory and visual cortex that are present in the neonatal kitten but that are eliminated around 3 months of age (Innocenti and Clark, 1984). Additionally, there is an early period when the callosal fibers that join the two hemispheres are considerably more numerous than in the mature animal (Innocenti, 1981). So, during this time, which is probably different for different brain regions, there is maximal diversity of connections. The subsequent pruning of these diverse connections occurs in a few well-documented cases as a direct consequence of activity that selectively stabilizes certain connections, while others that do not receive input are eliminated or suppressed. It is further hypothesized that in addition to competition between inputs the temporal patterning between inputs is an important variable in setting up neuronal systems or groups; that is, neurons that are active together tend to aggregate. A major question in our research program has been to determine in humans both what is innately biased (i.e., which aspects of cerebral organization are similar following different types of early experience), and what aspects of cerebral organization can be altered by specific experiences.

Electrophysiological Method

Our approach to the study of cerebral organization in humans is to obtain behavioral data employing standard measures of signal detection and reaction time and to simultaneously record, from electrodes placed over different regions of the scalp, the electrical signals that are time locked to discrete sensory or cognitive events such as the presentation of a flash of light, or the correct recognition of a word. Averages of epochs of electrophysiological activity associated with similar stimuli or responses are termed event-related brain potentials or ERPs. Over the past two decades this approach has proven to be valuable in assessing the integrity of neural systems and in elucidating the time course and subprocesses of several cognitive functions (see Hillyard and Kutas, 1983; Kutas and Hillyard, 1984, for review).

Subjects

We have employed the combined behavioral–electrophysiological approach in the study of individuals who have had a very extreme and highly specific form of altered experience. These are deaf individuals who have sustained total auditory deprivation since birth. All of our deaf subjects were born bilaterally and profoundly deaf, and they were born to deaf parents. Thus, their deafness is genetic, in which case the cochlea does not differentiate normally. The central nervous system (CNS) is not directly affected by the disease, and our subjects are otherwise neurologically normal and tend to be college students as are our normally hearing control subjects.

In humans, and probably in other animals as well, the impact of unimodal deprivation extends well beyond the development of sensory functions. Thus, our deaf subjects, as a consequence of their auditory deprivation, have also had markedly abnormal language experience. None of them has acquired speech, nor any auditory language comprehension. Instead they learned, from their deaf parents, at the normal age for language acquisition, American Sign Language (ASL). The perception of ASL relies heavily on peripheral vision since in sign discourse the eyes are typically focused on the eyes and face of the signer, so that

Table 1. Abbreviations used in this chapter.

ERPs	event-related brain potentials
CNS	central nervous system
ASL	American Sign Language
HD subjects	hearing subjects born to deaf parents
HD Ss or HD	
Ss	subjects
lvf	left visual field
rvf	right visual field
S	subject
(N = 17)	number of subjects is 17
msec	millisecond

much of the signed information falls outside the foveal region. The vocabulary and grammar of ASL make extensive use of visual space and of modulations of hand movements. For example, the same handshape presented at different locations, or with different motions, can convey different semantic or grammatical information (Klima and Bellugi, 1979).

In several studies we compared cerebral organization in deaf and hearing subjects during different sensory, cognitive, and language tasks. To dissociate the influences of auditory deprivation and the acquisition of a visual language on the differences between deaf and hearing subjects we compare these results with a third group of subjects: these are normal hearing subjects, who were born to deaf parents and so have acquired ASL as a first language like the deaf subjects, but have not experienced any auditory deprivation (hearing subjects born to deaf parents or HD subjects).

Visual Sensory Processing

In one study we tested the hypothesis that the visual system might be organized differently following auditory deprivation, in view of the evidence for competition between inputs from different modalities (Neville et al., 1983). Briefly, we recorded the evoked response to a small square of light presented in the periphery of the left or right visual fields, or in the foveal region. A major result was that over classical auditory brain regions, i.e., over temporal cortex, hearing and deaf subjects displayed similar evoked responses to the foveal stimuli, but the peripheral stimuli elicited responses that were two to three times larger in the deaf than in the hearing subjects. To assess the possibility that the acquisition of sign language contributed to this group difference we tested the HD subjects on this paradigm as well (see Neville and Lawson, 1987b). As seen in Figure 1, the HD subjects, like the hearing subjects, displayed considerably smaller ERPs over these brain regions than did the deaf subjects, suggesting the

VEP RECOVERY CYCLE
Peripheral Stimuli

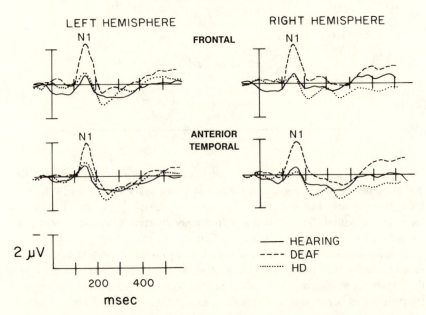

Figure 1. ERPs to peripheral visual stimuli in the paradigm described in Neville et al. ERPs from hearing, deaf, and HD Ss recorded over frontal and anterior temporal regions of the left and right hemispheres. From H. J. Neville and D. Lawson, attention to central and peripheral visual space in a movement detection task. III. Separate effects of auditory deprivation and acquisition of a visual language. *Brain Research, 405,* 284–294. Copyright © 1987. Reprinted with permission of Elsevier Science Publishers.

effect was due to auditory deprivation, not to acquisition of ASL. This pattern of group differences was similar over both hemispheres and was obtained only for the peripheral stimuli.

These results suggest that the visual system may be organized differently after auditory deprivation, and moreover that the systems involved in processing peripheral visual information may undergo more compensatory changes than do the systems that mediate the processing of foveal visual information. This could arise because, whereas normal hearing subjects rely on audition to detect important events in the periphery, deaf subjects must rely on peripheral vision. A related possibility is that the structures of the peripheral visual system may be more modifiable than are the structures of the primary visual system. In agreement with this hypothesis, it has been reported that the Y cells in the retina, which are more abundant in the peripheral retina, develop later and are more altered by visual experience than are the X cells, which are clustered in the foveal region (Sherman, 1985). The increased response amplitude in the deaf may be the result of early, normally transient, visual afferents to auditory and/or superior temporal polysensory cortex that become stabilized when auditory input to these areas is absent.

Visual Attention

To further explore the hypothesis that the systems that subserve the processing of foveal and peripheral visual information are differentially affected by auditory deprivation since birth, we compared processes associated with attention to peripheral and central visual space. We first had to determine whether attention to peripheral and central space would be associated with different ERPs in normal hearing adults, and then determine whether ERPs associated with attention to the peripheral and foveal regions would be differentially altered in the deaf subjects (Ss). To tax the secondary visual system we designed a difficult task that required the perception of direction of motion.

Methods

The stimuli were presented on a darkened video screen. In the center of the screen was a small black dot that subjects fixated during recording blocks. The standard stimuli were small, 1/2° white squares presented 18° in the left and right visual field and in the center of the field. Stimuli were presented for 33 msec in these three positions randomly with variable interstimulus interval of 280–480 msec. On different blocks of trials Ss were asked to attend without moving their eyes to the stimuli in the left or right visual field, or to the center, in order to detect occasional (20% probable) apparent movements of these stimuli in the attended field only. The movement actually consisted of the illumination for another 33 msec of the adjacent 1/2° square. This resulted in an impression of smooth motion of about 1/2°, which occurred randomly along the vertical, horizontal or diagonal axes. Ss pressed one of eight different keys as accurately and quickly as possible to indicate the direction of motion in the attended visual field.

ERPs were recorded from electrodes placed over frontal, anterior temporal, temporal, parietal, and occipital brain regions of each hemisphere. All electrodes were referenced to the linked mastoids (bandpass .01–100% Hz). Blinks and vertical eye movements were monitored from an electrode beneath the left eye, and horizontal eye movements were monitored via bipolar recordings from the external canthi. As seen in Figure 2, the ERPs to these stimuli displayed two early positivities around 130 and 230 msec (P1 and P2) separated by a prominent negative peak around 160 msec (N1). Following these peaks there occurred broad shifts in amplitude whose polarity depended on the direction of attention.

The peak and area voltages of each of the components were measured by computer and the values were subjected to analyses of variance with repeated measures (see Neville and Lawson, 1987a,b,c for complete details).

Hearing Subjects

Hearing subjects were more accurate at detecting the direction of motion when it occurred in the left (lvf) rather than the right (rvf) visual field. In Figure 2 (left panel) are superimposed ERPs to stimuli in the lvf when Ss were attending the lvf and to the same stimuli when they were attending the rvf. Since the stimulus and task are identical in the two conditions, differences in the ERPs reflect the effects of focused attention.

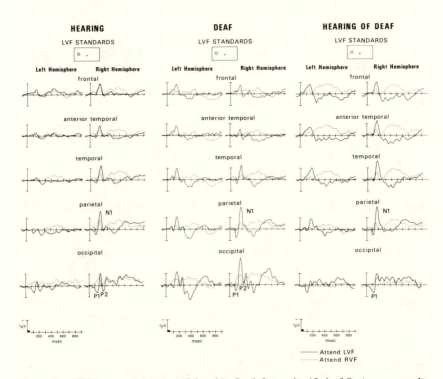

Figure 2. ERPs averaged across 12 hearing Ss (left panel), 12 deaf Ss (center panel), and 12 HD Ss (right panel) to standard stimuli presented to the left visual field (lvf) when attended (attend lvf) and when inattended (attend rvf). Recordings from left and right frontal, anterior temporal, temporal, parietal, and occipital cortex. From H. L. Neville, "Cerebal organization for spatial attention: Effects of early sensory and language experience." In J. Stiles-Davis, U. Bellugi and M. Kritchevsky (Eds.), *Special Cognition: Brain Bases and Development.* Copyright © 1988. Reprinted by permission of Elsevier Science Publishers.

A prominent effect of attention was to increase the amplitude of N1. For peripheral stimuli this effect was most prominent over the parietal and temporal regions of the hemisphere contralateral to the attended visual field (see Figure 2 and 3 left, bottom). By contrast, with attention to the central field the major increase occurred over the occipital regions where it was bilaterally symmetric (Figure 3 left, top). Later attention-related changes, where the ERP was negative to inattended stimuli but slightly positive to attended stimuli, were largest over temporoparietal regions. These effects were symmetrical with attention to the center, but were larger from the right than the left hemisphere with attention to both the lvf and rvf.

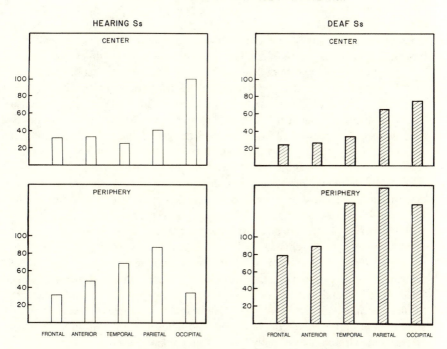

Figure 3. Percentage by which N1 amplitude was increased from inattend to attend conditions for hearing and deaf subjects. Top: center standards, mean of left and right frontal, anterior temporal, temporal, parietal, and occipital sites. Bottom: peripheral standards, mean of contralateral frontal, anterior temporal, temporal, parietal, and occipital sites. From H. J. Neville and D. Lawson. "Attention to central and peripheral visual space in a movement detection task: An event-related potential and behavioral study. II. Congenitally deaf adults. *Brain Research, 405,* 268–283. Copyright © 1987. Reprinted with permission of Elsevier Science Publishers.

These results suggest that in normal hearing Ss attention to peripheral and central regions of visual space are mediated by different neural systems. Moreover, the distributions of these effects are in agreement with considerable data from nonhuman animals showing that information presented to the fovea is processed by the retinogeniculostriate pathway, while processing of and attention to peripheral visual information is associated with increased activity in parietal cortex. They further suggest, in agreement with clinical studies, a greater role for the right hemisphere in visuospatial attention, especially to the periphery.

Deaf Subjects

With attention to the center, deaf Ss' behavior and the attention-related changes in the ERPs were similar to those of the hearing Ss (see Figure 3 right, top). However, deaf Ss responded more quickly than hearing Ss to motion in the periphery and, in contrast to the hearing Ss, they detected the direction of motion more accurately when it occurred in the rvf than the lvf. In addition, the attention-related changes in the ERPs were considerably larger in deaf than hearing Ss under conditions of attending the periphery (see Figure 3 bottom). As seen in Figure 2, whereas both deaf and hearing Ss displayed attention increases in N1 amplitude over the parietal and temporal regions of the hemisphere contralateral to the attended periphery, the deaf Ss, unlike the hearing Ss, also displayed attention-related increases in N1 and in the 300–600 msec positivity over the occipital regions of both hemispheres. In addition, deaf Ss displayed considerably larger attention-related increases over the left temporal and parietal regions than did the hearing Ss. Both of the group differences, the increased occipital ERPs and the increased amplitudes over the left hemisphere in deaf Ss, occurred independently of whether attention was focused on the lvf or rvf.

The specific pattern of group differences can be considered with respect to anatomical and physiological evidence from experimental animals that shows that two major types of changes can occur following unimodal sensory deprivation since birth. First there is evidence for increased growth and activity of remaining sensory systems or "compensatory hypertrophy" (Burnstine et al., 1984). The bilateral increase of attention-related changes in occipital regions in the deaf Ss may represent this type of change and may be due to increased visual activity in posterior polymodal brain regions and/or to the stabilization of visual afferents on what would normally be auditorily responsive cells in these regions. Second, there is evidence that brain systems that would normally subserve functions that are lost—in the case of the deaf Ss these are audition, speech, and auditory language skills—may maintain rather than eliminate early, exuberant input from the remaining modality (Burnstine et al., 1984). These results suggest that areas within the left hemisphere that would normally subserve speech and auditory language comprehension are active in attention to and perception of movement in the peripheral visual fields in deaf Ss.

It may be that since these regions of the left hemisphere are not used for the production and comprehension of speech, they instead come to process this type of visual material through the stabilization of visual afferents in these areas. Alternatively, it could be that the observed increase in left hemisphere activity in the deaf Ss in this task was not a consequence of auditory deprivation but rather arose in conjunction with the acquisition of a visual, sign language. If the acquisition of sign language is mediated by the left hemisphere, as is the case in the acquisition of speech, perhaps nonlanguage information that is temporally coincident with and critical to the production and perception of sign language— such as attention to space and perception of motion—is also mediated by the left hemisphere, by virtue of their temporal correlation. This would be analogous to the situation in hearing Ss where the perception of temporal order of rapidly presented nonlanguage material is mediated by the left hemisphere, perhaps because the perception of temporal order is critical in the production and perception of speech (Albert, 1972; Efron, 1963).

Hearing Subjects Born to Deaf Parents

We dissociated the possibly separate effects of the deaf Ss' auditory deprivation from the effects of acquiring a visual language whose grammar relies on the perception of motion on this pattern of group differences by testing the hearing Ss who were born to deaf parents (HD Ss). If the enhanced attention effects over the bilateral occipital regions seen in the deaf Ss were a consequence of auditory deprivation, the HD Ss should not display these results. On the other hand, if the increased attention effects over the left temporoparietal regions are attributable to acquisition of ASL, the HD Ss should display results similar to those of the deaf subjects.

As seen in Figure 4, the HD Ss, like the hearing Ss, were significantly slower than those of the deaf Ss in responding to peripheral motion. Likewise, over the occipital regions bilaterally, the attention effects in the ERPs were considerably smaller in the hearing and HD Ss than in the deaf Ss (see Figure 2, right panel). These results are in agreement with the hypothesis that the faster reaction times and increased occipital attention effects are a consequence of auditory deprivation since birth, and are not due to the acquisition of a visual language.

In contrast to these results, over temporal and parietal regions of the left hemisphere, hearing Ss display small attention effects on N1, but both deaf and HD Ss displayed large, and equivalent attention effects. Additionally, whereas hearing Ss detected the direction of motion more accurately when it occurred in the lvf, both deaf and HD Ss displayed the opposite pattern (Figure 5).

Thus, these results suggest that the increased attention effects over the left temporoparietal regions in the deaf and HD Ss in this task may be attributable to the acquisition of a language that relies critically on the perception of motion. If the left hemisphere plays the greater role in acquisition of ASL, as in the

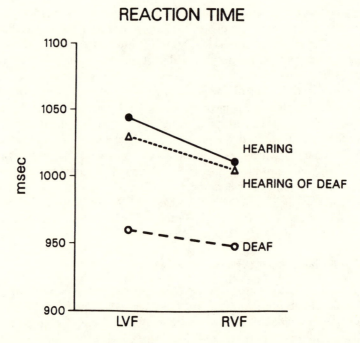

Figure 4. Reaction times (in msec) to detect the direction of motion of target stimuli in the left (LVF) and right (RVF) visual fields. Data from hearing Ss, deaf Ss, and hearing Ss born to deaf parents.

acquisition of speech, then perhaps it also mediates the perception of motion even in a nonlanguage task like this one.

Taken together, these results suggest that aspects of the anterior–posterior organization of the visual system within both hemispheres are significantly affected by early auditory deprivation. This reorganization of the visual system may include both an anterior expansion, into areas normally used for auditory processing (as seen in the first experiment described, as well as increased activity of the posterior visual cortical areas. Both of these effects could be accounted for by early exuberant visual afferents that are stabilized when competing input from the auditory modality is absent. Additionally, the results suggest that aspects of the different cerebral specializations of the two hemispheres may be determined by the nature and modality of language acquisition. Since part of our interpretation of these results rests on the assumption that the left hemisphere is specialized for both signed and spoken languages, we conducted research, described below, in which we tested this hypothesis and further explored the effects of language experience on the different functional specializations of the hemispheres in these subjects.

DETECTION OF
DIRECTION OF MOTION

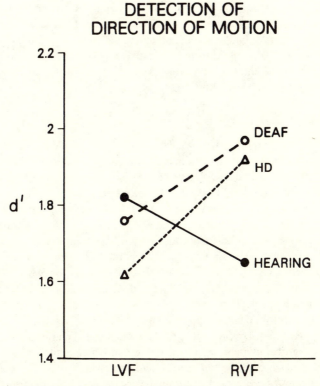

Figure 5. Detection (d') of moving targets in the left and right visual fields (LVF and RVF) for hearing, deaf, and HD Ss. From H. J. Neville and D. Lawson. (1987b) "Attention to central and peripheral visual space in a movement detection task. III. Separate effects of auditory deprivation and acquisition of a visual language." *Brain Research, 405*, 284–294. Copyright © 1987b. Reprinted with permission of Elsevier Science Publishers.

Language Processing

Considerable controversy still surrounds the nature of the special role of the left hemisphere in language processing, the degree to which it may be determined at birth, and the role that experience might play in its development. As mentioned above, clinical studies of hemispherectomized patients show that early in development each hemisphere has similar, if not identical, capabilities to sustain language and other cognitive skills. However, little is known about the role of language experience in reducing the redundancy and increasing the specificity of hemispheric function in adults. If language experience does impact cerebral development, then aspects of cerebral specialization ought to be different in deaf and hearing Ss when they read English. Hearing people learn English first through the auditory modality and they utilize this information in learning to read. According to several studies, when hearing Ss read they translate the visual word to an auditory sound (so-called phonological decoding). On the other hand, deaf Ss apparently do not perform this visual–auditory phonological conversion (Conrad, 1977). Would these different experiences result in different patterns of cerebral activity during reading?

Hemifield Studies

English.   To study this issue we developed a paradigm that produced reliable evidence of cerebral specialization during reading in normal adults, and then compared results from deaf Ss. Briefly (see Neville et al., 1982a), words were projected to the left or right visual fields or bilaterally for 100 msec and, 2 sec following word onset, Ss wrote the word. Every hearing S reported the words more accurately after they were presented to the rvf, i.e., to the left hemisphere, thus providing behavioral evidence that the left hemisphere was more active than the right in this task. The simultaneously recorded ERPs to each word presentation displayed a different pattern of activity depending on where, within and between the hemispheres, they were recorded. ERPs from over left and right occipital regions reflected the anatomy of the visual system, i.e., the N1 component was larger from the hemisphere contralateral to the visual field in which the word was presented. By contrast, ERPs recorded over anterior temporal regions were asymmetrical in the same way regardless of where in the visual field a word appeared. In each case the left hemisphere response displayed a negative (410 msec)–positive (560 msec) shift that was absent or smaller than in ERPs from over the right hemisphere (see Figure 6). This asymmetry, like the behavioral asymmetry, was evident in each of the hearing Ss, and appeared to index some aspect of the left hemisphere's greater role in this reading task.

The results from the congenitally deaf adults (all were bilaterally and profoundly deaf, had acquired ASL as a first language, and had not acquired speech) were markedly different from those of the hearing Ss (see Neville et al., 1982b). Neither the behavioral data nor the ERPs displayed evidence of left hemisphere specialization in this task. The deaf subjects reported the words as accurately as the hearing Ss, but they were equally accurate when words were presented to the lvf and rvf. In addition, whereas over the left anterior temporal region hearing Ss displayed a prominent negative–positive shift, deaf Ss did not (see Figure 6). However, deaf Ss displayed a negative potential in right temporal region that was much less prominent in hearing Ss ERPs.

There are several possible reasons why deaf Ss did not display the pattern of left hemisphere specialization observed in the hearing Ss. It could be, as has been proposed, that the left hemisphere is specifically specialized for the phonological decoding that characterizes reading by hearing but not deaf Ss. On the other hand, it has also been proposed that the special role of the left hemisphere for language arises in conjunction with the acquisition of the grammatical or propo-

HEMIFIELD WORDS

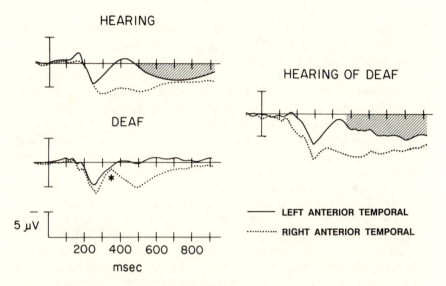

Figure 6. ERPs recorded to English words presented to the right visual field. Recordings from over left and right anterior temporal regions. Grand mean ERPs from 10 hearing, 8 congenitally deaf, and 10 hearing Ss born to deaf parents.

sitional coding strategies that characterize hearing subjects' language use (Liberman, 1974). Since deaf Ss typically do not acquire full grammatical competence in English, this may be the reason they do not display left hemisphere specialization during reading. Alternatively, a third possibility is that the acquisition of two languages by the deaf Ss (i.e., ASL and English) would account for these results. One way we investigated this third possibility was to test the hearing Ss born to deaf parents (HD) on this task. If the acquisition of two languages was an important variable in determining this pattern of results their data should parallel those of the deaf Ss. On the other hand, if the left greater than right asymmetry is a manifestation of phonological decoding or grammatical encoding of English then the HD Ss should display results similar to those of the hearing Ss, even though in the perception of motion task they displayed lateral asymmetries opposite in direction to those of the hearing Ss.

The HD Ss, like the hearing Ss, reported the words more accurately after presentation to the rvf than to the lvf, suggesting left hemisphere specialization. The ERPs from this group (see Figure 6) over the anterior temporal region displayed an asymmetry similar to that observed in the hearing Ss. This pattern occurred independently of the visual field to which words were presented. These results suggest that the absence of this negative component in the deaf subjects was not attributable to the acquisition of ASL as a first language, but may instead index the activity of processes involved in either phonological or grammatical decoding.

American Sign Language. To assess the roles of phonological processing versus acquisition of grammatical competence in producing left hemisphere specialization for English (observed in the hearing but not the deaf subjects), we performed a version of this experiment with ASL. Since ASL is not phonological (i.e., not sound based), but is highly grammatical (Klima and Bellugi, 1979), if grammatical recoding is an important variable and if phonological decoding is not essential in the development of left hemisphere specialization for a language, deaf Ss should display left hemisphere specialization in processing ASL. We digitized filmed sequences of a person signing (6 frames per sign, 180 msec) and presented each sign once to the left and once to the right visual field as we had presented the English words. Two seconds after sign onset, Ss made the sign just presented. Every deaf subject reported the signs more accurately after they were presented to the rvf, suggesting a greater role for the left hemisphere. This is what was observed when hearing Ss read English, and contrasts with the results for deaf subjects reading English. Moreover, these signs—which are physically very dissimilar from printed words—elicited ERPs from over anterior temporal regions that displayed a similar pattern of results to that seen in hearing Ss reading English. That is, they were characterized by a negative–positive shift that was larger from the left than the right hemisphere (see Figure 7). Moreover, this asymmetry occurred independently of where in the visual field a sign appeared, as we had observed in ERPs from hearing Ss reading English words. We also recorded ERPs from normally hearing subjects to the ASL stimuli. These Ss did not know ASL, but were asked to mimic the signs as best they could. ERPs from these subjects did not display the asymmetrical negativity characteristic of the deaf Ss but instead displayed a prolonged positive shift that was symmetrical from the two hemispheres (see Figure 8).

These data suggest that (1) similar neural systems within the left hemisphere mediate the processing of formal (i.e., grammatical) languages that have evolved through different modalities, (2) phonological processing is not necessary for the development of left hemisphere specialization for language, and (3) the special role of the left hemisphere in language processing may develop along with the acquisition of competence in the grammar of language.

Sentence Processing. We have further tested this hypothesis in studies of the processing of English sentences where we have compared and contrasted cerebral organization during aspects of grammatical and semantic processing. Briefly (more fully reported in Neville et al., 1990), we presented sentences, one word (duration 200 msec) at a time, to the central 2° of vision. ERPs to the words in the middle of the sentences were coded according to whether they were content or "open class" words (nouns, verbs, and adjectives, i.e., words that make reference to specific objects and events) or whether they were function or

**DEAF SUBJECTS
HEMI-FIELD SIGNS**

RIGHT VISUAL FIELD

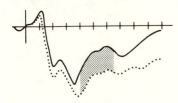

BILATERAL

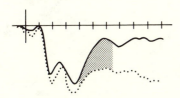

LEFT VISUAL FIELD

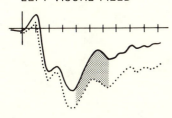

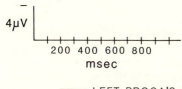

4µV

200 400 600 800
msec

——— LEFT BROCA'S
········ RIGHT BROCA'S

Figure 7. ERPs from 9 congenitally deaf Ss recorded over left and right frontal regions (over Broca's area) to signs presented in the right or left visual field or to two different signs in each visual field.

"closed class" words (e.g., pronouns, prepositions, articles, conjunctions, i.e., the small, "closed" set of words that specifies the relations between content words). The closed class words are viewed as providing much of the syntactic structure to sentences, while the open class words carry semantic information. Clinical data documenting the effects of lesions suggest that nonidentical neural systems mediate these two aspects of language processing. For example, lesions

**HEARING SUBJECTS
HEMI-FIELD SIGNS**

RIGHT VISUAL FIELD

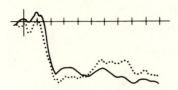

BILATERAL

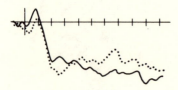

LEFT VISUAL FIELD

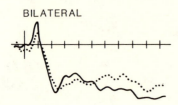

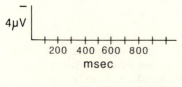

4μV

200 400 600 800
msec

——— LEFT BROCA'S
········ RIGHT BROCA'S

Figure 8. ERPs from 10 normally hearing Ss recorded over left and right frontal regions (over Broca's area) to signs presented in the right or left visual field or to two different signs in each visual field.

to the anterior regions of the left hemisphere disrupt the use and comprehension of the closed class vocabulary, while lesions to posterior regions of the left hemisphere disrupt the use of open class words. Additionally, lesions to posterior areas of the right hemisphere diminish some aspects of semantic functioning (Wapner et al., 1981). ERPs from hearing Ss ($N = 17$) also provide evidence that different systems are active in processing these different types of words. As seen in figure 9, ERPs to closed class words display a negative peak around 280 msec (N280) that was most evident over the left hemisphere. This peak was evident from anterior brain regions but not over parietal cortex. By contrast, ERPs to open class words did not display a prominent N280 in ERPs from the anterior areas, but (from over parietal) regions they displayed a negative component around 350 msec (N350) that was evident in ERPs from both hemispheres. We determined that the different morphologies and distributions of ERPs to these different classes of words were not attributable to the frequencies of the words in the language, their lengths, or their imagability scores. Thus, the ERP differences likely index different functions in language processing.

To further explore the hypothesis that incomplete acquisition of the grammar of English by deaf Ss may have been an important variable in their lack of left hemisphere specialization for English (as was observed in the studies reported above), we recorded ERPs to these same sentences from 10 congenitally deaf adults. As seen in Figure 10, ERPs to the closed class words, in contrast to those of the hearing Ss, did not display the N280 component, nor any asymmetries in

ENGLISH SENTENCES
17 HEARING SUBJECTS

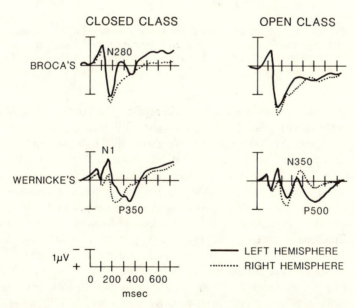

Figure 9. ERPs to open and closed class words within English sentences, from normal hearing Ss, recorded anterior temporal (near Broca's area) and parietal (over Wernicke's area) sites of the left hemisphere and homologous positions over the right hemisphere.

ENGLISH SENTENCES
10 DEAF SUBJECTS

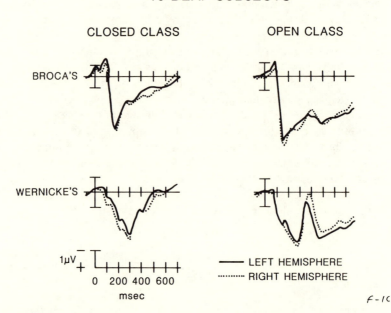

Figure 10. ERPs to open and closed class words within English sentences, from congenitally deaf Ss, recorded over anterior temporal (near Broca's area) and parietal (over Wernicke's area) sites of the left hemisphere and homologous positions over the right hemisphere.

amplitude, from anterior or posterior brain regions. Each of these deaf Ss scored significantly lower (mean 75% correct) on tests of English grammar than did our hearing Ss (range 95–100% correct). We also studied four congenitally deaf Ss who scored perfectly on the tests of English grammar (Figure 11). Theses Ss, like the other deaf Ss, were congenitally, bilaterally, and profoundly deaf, had not acquired speech, and used ASL as their major form of communication. Nonetheless they did display a pattern of hemispheric specialization similar to that observed in the hearing Ss. Thus these data are compatible with the idea that grammatical competence in a language is an important factor in the development or stabilization of left hemisphere specialization for that language.

In contrast to these results for the closed class words, deaf and hearing Ss displayed ERPs more similar to the open class words. In each group ERPs to these words displayed a prominent negative peak between 350 and 400 msec over left and right parietal regions. To the extent that this component reflects aspects of semantic processing, these results suggest that there are strong similarities in this aspect of processing, the different early language experience of

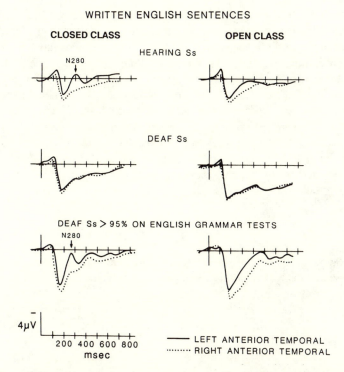

WRITTEN ENGLISH SENTENCES

CLOSED CLASS   OPEN CLASS

HEARING Ss

DEAF Ss

DEAF Ss > 95% ON ENGLISH GRAMMAR TESTS

4μV

200 400 600 800
msec

——— LEFT ANTERIOR TEMPORAL
········· RIGHT ANTERIOR TEMPORAL

Figure 11. ERPs to open and closed class words recorded over left and right anterior temporal regions. Recordings from normal hearing Ss and from congenitally deaf Ss who scored poorly (middle) and well (bottom) on tests of English grammar.

the deaf Ss notwithstanding. Further studies of semantic priming in deaf and hearing Ss are consistent with this view (Neville, 1985; Kutas et al., 1987).

In summary, these data suggest that the systems that mediate the acquisition of aspects of syntactic processing appear to be more vulnerable to and dependent on specific aspects of early language experience, but that aspects of semantic processing develop in a very similar fashion under widely varying conditions of early language experience. This may be because there are strong biological constraints on the development of the systems that are used to process semantic information, or it may be that they are more dependent on more general cognitive experience that is more similar in deaf and hearing Ss than is language experience per se.

These results are of interest in view of studies of language development that show earlier acquisition of the open than the closed class elements of language. Of additional interest are reports that variations in maternal speech have virtually no effect on the time of acquisition of open class elements of the language, but that they do affect the rate of acquisition of closed class items (Newport et al.,

1977). Moreover, it is of interest that deaf children who have not been formally exposed to a sign language and have not acquired speech invent signs for objects and events in the world (open class items) and that the age of acquisition of these language milestones occurs as in normal children. In contrast, these children display little evidence of acquiring any grammar, i.e., they do not invent closed class items (Goldin-Meadow, 1979; Goldin-Meadow and Mylander, this volume). Thus it appears that whereas the acquisition of lexical semantics is not dependent on language input, some grammatical input is necessary for the systems that mediate the acquisition of grammar to unfold. It will be important for future research to determine whether there are critical or sensitive periods when particular types of language input are necessary for language acquisition to proceed normally.

Summary and Conclusions

The results presented in this chapter concerning effects of sensory and language experience on neural development can be summarized within the framework discussed initially, which is outlined in Figure 12. The left-hand column of Figure 12 is taken (and modified) from *Neuronal man,* by Changeux (1985). According to this view, there is an initial period of growth that is genetically influenced. In the visual system this includes, for example, the growth of retinal afferents to primary visual cortex, where they form ocular dominance columns. Following this time there is transient, exuberant growth of connections that includes extensive multisensory innervation (e.g., visual afferents into auditory and polysensory cortex). Our data on visual processing in congenitally deaf Ss are compatible with the idea that in the absence of auditory input to these regions, visual afferents are stabilized and in some cases their activity is increased. This would account for our observations of increased visual ERP amplitudes over temporal cortex and over posterior brain regions of both hemispheres.

The studies of the functional specializations of the two hemispheres, which show a greater role for the left hemisphere in the processing of both spoken and signed languages (by competent users of the language), indicate a strong initial bias for the left hemisphere to mediate language. This bias may also underlie the anatomical asymmetry in the planum temporal, observed by Geschwind and colleagues, where the left side is larger than the right, by 28 weeks gestation (Geschwind and Levitsky, 1968). Later on, in postnatal development at least until 10 years of age, as shown by clinical data on hemispherectomy cases, there is considerable redundancy such that each hemisphere can support many aspects of both language and visuospatial processing. This redundancy may be supported by extensive callosal fibers, which, at least in other species, are more abundant in the immature than the mature animal (Innocenti, 1981).

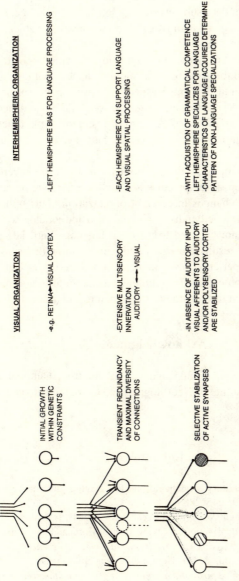

Figure 12. Summary of results presented within the framework of Changeux's (1985) conception of the epigenesis of functional neural systems. From *Neuronal Man: The Biology of Mind* by Jean-Pierre Changeux, translated by Dr. Lawrence Gray. Translation Copyright © 1985 by Random House, Inc. Reprinted by permission of Pantheon Books, a division of Random House, Inc.

Our work suggests that one factor that is important in establishing or maintaining the specialization of the left hemisphere for language is the acquisition of competence in the grammar of language. This would account for the data showing hearing but not deaf subjects display left hemisphere specialization for English, and for the data showing deaf but not hearing subjects show left hemisphere specialization for ASL.

Finally, the data from the visual attention study showing opposite patterns of cerebral asymmetries in the perception of motion suggest that characteristics of the language first acquired determine aspects of hemispheric specialization for certain nonlanguage material. For example, the temporal coincidence of motion perception and of the grammar of ASL may result in these functions being organized together within the province of the language-specialized left hemisphere.

Future research will focus on the possibility that there are specific times or critical periods in human development when auditory deprivation and language experience can lead to changes in cerebral organization. This will include the study of postnatally deafened individuals and also individuals who, although deaf since birth, were not exposed to a formal language until late in development. In summary, the results presented here clearly show that sensory experience and language experience have marked and different effects on human neurobehavioral development. The combined behavioral–electrophysiological approach can be useful in further studies of the nature and timing of these effects.

Acknowledgments

Supported by Grants NS 14365 and NS 22343 from National Institute of Health and National Institute of Neurological and Communicative Disorders and Stroke.

References

Albert, M. L. (1972). Auditory sequencing and left cerebral dominance for language, *Neuropsychologia, 10,* 245–248.

Burnstine, T. H., Greenough, W. T., and Tees, R. C. (1984). Intermodal compensation following damage or deprivation: A review of behavioral and neural evidence. In C. R. Almli and S. Finger (Eds.), *Early brain damage, 1, Research orientation and clinical observations* (pp. 3–34). New York: Academic Press.

Conel, J. L. (1939–1963). *The postnatal development of the human cerebral cortex,* Vols. I–VI. Cambridge, MA: Harvard University Press.

Changeux, J. P. (1985). *Neuronal man.* New York: Pantheon Books.

Conrad, R. (1977). The reading ability of deaf school-leavers. *British Journal of Educational Psychology, 47,* 138–148.

Cowan, W. M., Fawcett, J. W., O'Leary, D. D. M., and Stanfield, B. B. (1984). Regressive events in neurogenesis, *Science, 225,* 1258–1265.

Cynader, M. (1979). Competitive interactions in the development of the kitten's visual system. In R. D. Freeman (Ed.), *Developmental neurobiology of vision.* New York: Plenum Press.

Dennis, M. D., and Whitaker, H. A. (1977). Hemispheric equipotentiality and language acquisition. In S. J. Segalowitz and F. A. Gruber (Eds.), *Language development and neurological theory* (pp. 93–106). New York: Academic Press.

Efron, E. (1963). Temporal perception, aphasia, and deja vu. *Brain, 86,* 403–424.

Frost, D. O. (1984). Axonal growth and target selection during development: Retinal projections to the ventrobasal complex and other 'nonvisual' structures in neonatal Syrian Hamsters. *Journal of Comparative Neurology, 230,* 576–592.

Geschwind, N., and Levitsky, W. (1968). Left-right asymmetry in temporal speech region. *Science, 161,* 186–187.

Goldin-Meadow, S. (1979). Structure in a manual communication system developed without a conventional language model: Language without a helping hand. In H. Whitaker and H. A. Whitaker, (Eds.), *Studies in neurolinguistics* (Vol. 4, pp. 125–209). New York: Academic Press.

Hillyard, S. A., and Kutas, M. (1983). Electrophysiology of cognitive processing. *Annual Review of Psychology, 34,* 33–61.

Huttenlocher, P. R. (1979). Synaptic density in human frontal cortex-developmental changes and effects of aging. *Brain Research, 163,* 195–205.

Huttenlobher, P. R., Courten, C., Garey, L., and Van Der Loos, D. (1982). Synaptogenesis in human visual cortex-evidence for synapse elimination during normal development, *Neuroscience Letters, 33,* 247–252.

Hyvarinen, J. (1982). *The parietal cortex of monkey and man.* New York: Springer-Verlag.

Innocenti, G. M. (1981). Growth and reshaping of axons in the establishment of visual callosal connections. *Science, 212,* 824–827.

Innocenti, G. M., and Clark, S. (1984). Bilateral transitory projection to visual areas from auditory cortex in kittens. *Developmental Brain Research, 14,* 143–148.

Klima, E. S., and Bellugi, U. (1979). *The signs of language.* Cambridge, MA: Harvard University Press.

Kutas, M., and Hillyard, S. A. (184). Event-related potentials in cognitive science. In M. S. Gazzaniga (Ed.), *Handbook of cognitive neuroscience* (pp. 387–409). Chap. 19. New York: Plenum Press.

Kutas, M., Neville, H., and Holcomb, P. (1987). A preliminary comparison of the N400 response to semantic anomalies during reading, listening and signing. *EEG Supplement, 39,* 325–330.

Liberman, A. M. (1974). The specialization of the language hemisphere, In F. O. Schmitt and F. G. Worden (Eds.), *The neurosciences third study program* (pp. 43–56). Cambridge, MA: MIT Press.

Merzenich, M. M., and Kaas, J. H. (1982). Reorganization of mammalian somatosensory cortex following peripheral nerve injury. *Trends in Neurosciences, 5,* 434–436.

Neville, H. J., Kutas, M., and Schmidt, A. (1982a). Event-related potential studies of cerebral specialization during reading: I. Studies of normal adults, *Brain and Language, 16,* 300–315.

Neville, H. J., Kutas, M., and Schmidt, A. (1982b). Event-related potential studies of cerebral specialization during reading: II. Studies of congenitally deaf adults, *Brain and Language, 16,* 300–315.

Neville, H. (1985). Biological constraints on semantic processing: A comparison of spoken and signed languages. *Psychophysiology, 22*(5), 576.

Neville, H. J. (1988). Cerebral organization for spatial attention: Effects of early sensory and language experience. In J. Stiles-Davis, U. Bellugi, and M. Kritchevsky (Eds.), *Spatial cognition: Brain bases and development* (pp. 327–341). Hillsdale, NJ: Erlbaum Associates.

Neville, H. J., and Lawson, D. (1987a). Attention to central and peripheral visual space in a movement detection task: An event-related potential and behavioral study. II. Congenitally deaf adults. *Brain Research, 405,* 268–283.

Neville, H. J., and Lawson, D. (1987b). Attention to central and peripheral visual space in a movement detection task: III. Separate effects of auditory deprivation and acquisition of a visual language. *Brain Research, 405,* 284–294.

Neville, H. J., and Lawson, D. (1988). Attention to central and peripheral visual space in a movement detection task: An event-related potential and behavioral study. I. Normal hearing adults. *Brain Research, 405,* 253–267.

Neville, H. J., Schmidt, A., and Kutas, M. (1983) Altered visual-evoked potentials in congenitally deaf adults. *Brain research, 266,* 127–132.

Newport, E. L., Gleitman, H., and Gleitman, L. R. (1977). Mother I'd rather do it myself: Some effects and noneffects of maternal speech style. In C. E. Snow and C. A. Ferguson (Eds.), *Talking to children: Language imput and acquisition* (pp. 109–149). Cambridge, MA: Cambridge University Press.

Schade, J. P., and Van Groenigen, W. B. (1961). Structural organization of the human cerebral cortex. *Acta Anatomica, 47,* 74–111.

Sherman, S. M. (1985). Development of retinal projections to the cat's lateral geniculate nucleus. *Trends in Neuroscience, 86,* 350–355.

Smith, A. (1981). Principles underlying human brain functions in neuropsychological sequelae of different neuropathological processes. In S. Filskov and T. Ball (Eds.) *Handbook of clinical neuropsychology* (Vol. 6). New York: Wiley Press.

Wapner, W., Hamby, S., and Gardner, H. (1981). The role of the right hemisphere in the apprehension of complex linguistic materials, *Brain and Language, 14,* 15–33.

Wiesel, T. N., and Hubel, D. H. (1963). Effects of visual deprivation on morphology and physiology of cells in the cat's lateral geniculate body. *Journal of Neurophysiology, 26,* 978–993.

Wiesel, T. N., and Hubel, D. H. (1965). Comparison of the effects of unilateral and bilateral eye closure on cortical unit responses in kittens. *Journal of Neurophysiology, 28,* 1029–1040.

Index